Applied Mass Communication Theory

Applied Mass Communication Theory

A Guide for Media Practitioners

Jack Rosenberry
St. John Fisher College

Lauren A. Vicker
St. John Fisher College

Boston   New York   San Francisco
Mexico City   Montreal   Toronto   London   Madrid   Munich   Paris
Hong Kong   Singapore   Tokyo   Cape Town   Sydney

Acquisitions Editor: *Jeanne Zalesky*
Editorial Assistant: *Brian Mickelson*
Marketing Manager: *Susan Czajkowski*
Production Supervisor: *Patty Bergin*
Editorial Production Service: *Nesbitt Graphics, Inc.*
Composition Buyer: *Linda Cox*
Manufacturing Buyer: *JoAnne Sweeney*
Electronic Composition: *Nesbitt Graphics, Inc.*
Cover Administrator: *Elena Sidorova*

For related titles and support materials, visit our online catalog at www.ablongman.com.

Between the time Web site information is gathered and then published, it is not unusual for some sites to have closed. Also, the transcription of URLs can result in typographical errors. The publisher would appreciate notification where these errors occur so that they may be corrected in subsequent editions.

Library of Congress Cataloging-in-Publication Data

Rosenberry, John.
  Applied mass communication theory : a guide for media practitioners /
John Rosenberry, Lauren A. Vicker.
      p. cm.
  Includes bibliographical references and index.
  ISBN-13: 978–0–205–54873–6 (pbk.)
  ISBN-10: 0–205–54873–3 (pbk.)
  1.   Mass media—Research. 2.   Mass media--Philosophy. I. Vicker,
Lauren A. II. Title.
  P91.3.R67 2009
  302.2307'2—dc22
                                                                          2007039583
Printed in the United States.

10   9   8   7   6   5   4   3   2   1   12   11   10   09   08

Credits appear on page 291, which constitutes an extension of the copyright page.

Dedication

To our students, from whom we have learned so much about teaching research and theory.

BRIEF CONTENTS

CONTENTS

INTRODUCTION

The Value of Theory

The reaction of many communications students to a college course on theory is something like the reaction children have to a plate of broccoli: "Ew-w-w-w! Do I have to eat this (learn this)? Can't I just have my ice cream instead?"

In this analogy, the ice cream is the skills material that most communication students enjoy studying because they find the coursework interesting and even fun. It is easy for students to see the relevance and practical value (i.e., how they connect to "the real world") of courses on how to write a newspaper or magazine article, craft a public relations plan, design an advertisement, or edit a video production. Those connections, and that relevance, are not as obvious in theory-based courses but are no less relevant to the media practitioner's work.

To illustrate this, consider a theory that is on the minds of many people because of attention from the media: the theory of global warming, or global climate change, as it is sometimes called. As Chapter 1 discusses in more detail, theories are statements that seek to describe how certain things are related to one another in ways that will predict or explain the nature of the relationship. The theory of global climate change says that changes in the composition of the Earth's atmosphere are causing the planet to retain more heat from the sun, a way of *explaining* rising temperatures of the atmosphere and oceans. The theory in turn *predicts* that these changes will affect global weather patterns. The main culprits in atmospheric change, according to the theory, are greater amounts of so-called greenhouse gases, such as carbon dioxide and water vapor, that trap the sun's heat. So, the theory offers the further explanation that human activity—notably burning fossil fuels such as gasoline in vehicles and coal in power plants—contributes to the situation.

It is important to remember that the theory of global climate change is controversial. Not everyone accepts with certainty that global temperatures will change enough to cause the catastrophic results some predict are coming over the next several decades. And not everyone agrees that human activity is the leading cause of the changes. This lack of certainty is what makes global climate change a *theory*. It is a *possible* explanation for how the observed phenomena are related, and a prediction of what will happen over future decades. Instead of proof, we have suggestions (more formally called *hypotheses*) and evidence about the effects of temperature changes over recent years, predictions about the consequences of such rising temperatures, and proposals for changing human activity to reduce the volume of greenhouse gases that is being produced.

Even though global climate change is "just a theory," it is used by a wide variety of people to better understand the world around them, and it has an effect on the decisions that they make regarding that world. Scientists conduct research seeking objective evidence that informs the debate. Environmentalists use the theory's predictions and explanations to encourage people to change their behavior to reduce greenhouse emissions. Government policy makers take into account the theory when deciding about matters such as fuel-efficiency standards for autos and pollution controls for factories and power plants. Insurance executives consider how the predictions of increased coastal flooding and more hurricanes packing greater destructive power will influence the policies they issue in places that could be affected by such activity. Importantly, none of these people dismiss the potential effects of global climate change because it is "just a theory" or disregard its relevance for that reason either. Indeed, all of these examples illustrate how the theory of global climate change can be used as a valuable tool to better understand the real world and guide decisions made within it.

Similarly, learning about theories of mass communication can help students gain knowledge about their work in the media and its implications. It is one thing to be able to write an effective news release or design a clever advertisement. It is another to comprehend the effect that such communication likely has, and *how* it makes that effect, through theories of persuasion and attitude change. One of the authors of this book worked for more than 20 years at daily newspapers, and in all that time, never heard the phrase "agenda setting" used in the newsroom. But when journalists talk about writing an important story because "the public needs to know," they are talking about the same process: using the media to focus public awareness on an issue in ways that are explained by the formal theory known as agenda setting.

To return to the original example, certainly most college students today are familiar with (or at least have heard about) the theory of global warming/global climate change. Many of them, particularly those with environmentalist sympathies, may even use the theory to guide their own behaviors by conserving energy where they can, encouraging friends and family members to do the same, and looking at fuel-efficient car models when it is time to buy a new car.

Similarly, those students will find that knowledge about formal theories of mass communication helps them understand the implications of their work as media practitioners. In fact, the theory of agenda setting partially explains why global climate change is a topic of so much discussion today. News coverage of the controversy—especially accounts of the scientific and political activity surrounding the theory and its controversial aspects—has made the public more aware of the theory of global climate change.

Like the child who grows up and figures out somewhere along the way that not only is broccoli good for you, but that it also can be a tasty side dish, the college student who learns about theory will find out that it can lead to a deeper understanding of media practices, which will make him or her a more effective professional.

Not Your Parents' Theory Textbook

Readers who carefully noted the dedication page may have been surprised that this book was dedicated to the authors' students—after all, what do students know about theory? Quite a lot, actually. That dedication is a clue that this textbook is designed specifically to appeal to students who don't know why they should have to study theory and what it has to do with their professional goals of working in the mass media.

Three discrete sections or units provide a perspective on theory as the bridge to the real world that students often want and need. Unit 1 lays the groundwork to define and describe theory and research. In Unit 2, the reader learns about the variety of theories in mass communication, always with an eye to their practical application. Unit 3 provides an overview of some practical applications for the toolkit of every media practitioner. The book concludes by applying specific mass media theories to the real world. While the book is ideally read sequentially, students (or instructors) who skip around will find all the chapters cross-referenced.

- *Unit 1 Mass Communication Theory and Research.* Many upper-level college courses, especially those at or near the end of a course of study, require students to complete an original research project. The four chapters in this unit review theory-based research, provide an overview of research methodologies, and build a framework for constructing an undergraduate research project. The book begins with this section to give you time to adequately plan and execute your own project during the semester.
- *Unit 2 Mass Communication Theories.* The four chapters in this section walk you through a chronological progression of the development of theory in mass communication. This chronology includes an historical overview, a look at how individuals interact with media (the psychological perspective on media effects), a review of how large groups up to and including the whole society interact with media (the sociological perspective on media effects), and finally critical and cultural theories of media and society. Some of these theories may be a review from earlier courses, some may be new. What makes this unit useful is the integration of the theories into a model that shows how they relate to each other. Real-life, practical examples are provided along the way, so you may see the value of putting theory into practice.
- *Unit 3 Bridge to the Real World.* The five chapters in this unit provide information that will be important as you begin your first job in your career as a media practitioner—a role that you have been planning for these past four years of college. The chapters concern media law, media ethics, media economics, careers in the mass media, and the role of theory and research in everyday life and work in the media.

We welcome your comments and questions on this book and the material we present. Please e-mail us at any time, and we will respond promptly to your concerns. We also encourage your suggestions for how we might improve the information presented in this book; tell us what worked well for you and also what could be improved upon for future editions.

Jack Rosenberry   Lauren A. Vicker
jrosenberry@sjfc.edu   lvicker@sjfc.edu
June, 2007

ACKNOWLEDGMENTS

We wrote this book in response to our own need to find a textbook that worked for our students and our curriculum, but we had help from many individuals along the way.

We thank Dr. Jean Maley of the economics department at St. John Fisher College. Her work with us on the initial survey of all the mass communication programs in AEJMC helped us verify the need for the book and determine the content.

We thank John Lowe from Allyn & Bacon/Longman. John is an extraordinary sales representative whose enthusiasm for this project went a long way toward getting the attention of the editors there, especially Karon Bowers, who helped to launch the project, and Jeanne Zalesky, who provided support and perspective throughout the process.

We express our appreciation and gratitude to the following academic colleagues who reviewed this new textbook and made many suggestions that we have incorporated into the final product. Thank-you: Craig Allen, Arizona State University; Monica Brasted, State University of New York—Brockport; Donald Diefenback, University of North Carolina—Asheville; Dr. Tamara L. Gillis, Elizabethtown College; Linda Mann, Point Park University; W. Bradford Mello, Trinity Washington University; and Robert O'Gara, Point Park University.

We are especially grateful to Dr. David Pate, St. John Fisher College's dean of arts and sciences, whose office awarded us a faculty development grant to enable us to work on the first draft of the book.

We thank our colleagues in St. John Fisher College's communication/journalism department for their support and feedback, particularly Dr. Dougie Bicket for his careful editing of the early draft and for his advice on content in several key chapters and Professor Mary Loporcaro for the additional feedback she gained from conversations with alumni and students.

And finally, we thank our families for their patience and support during the drafting and editing, and re-drafting and re-editing processes.

J. R.
L. V.

UNIT ONE

Theory and Research

1 Theory and the Study of Communication

The starship Enterprise, *answering a distress call from another vessel, finds itself in danger from a rogue energy field that has already destroyed one ship as the* Enterprise *crew watched, and is now coming perilously close to the* Enterprise *itself:*

Chief Engineer Scott: *There's just no way to disrupt a gravimetric field of this magnitude. . . .*

Ensign Damora Sulu *(interrupting): Hull integrity failing.*

Scott: *. . . But I do have a theory.*

Captain Kirk: *I thought you might.*

—From the opening scene of *Star Trek: Generations*
(Berman, Moore, and Braga, 1994)

THIS CHAPTER WILL:

- Describe how theory contributes to the development of knowledge.
- Introduce different types of theory, emphasizing the social scientific approach but also discussing alternative ways of theorizing about communication.
- Describe some of the common goals and functions for theory, as well as the criteria that can be used to evaluate a theory.

"Whaddya know?" Or, as we say today, "What's up?"

But what *do* you know, really, and how do you know it? In a way, that is what the first section of this book is about. Or, to put the question less personally and more generally, how do people come to acquire knowledge?

Such a question lies at the heart of a book about theory and research. This is because knowledge, theory, and research are interrelated; theory coupled with research can create new insights and extend knowledge in virtually any field. The general process of developing theories and using research to explore and validate them is the same in any discipline from medicine to physics to psychology to anthropology. The field of particular concern here, of course, is mass communication and mass media. Theory and research form the basis of the communication field of study, as they do with many other academic disciplines. The Introduction to this book gives the example of using the theory of global climate change as a tool for gaining knowledge about changes in the environment, quite literally. But what is a theory, and in general terms, how can it be applied for a better understanding of the world around us?

Theory, Research, and Knowledge

Theory is a common word, and most people have at some point in their lives learned about some theories, especially in the natural sciences. For instance, almost everyone has at least heard of the big bang theory in astronomy, Darwin's theory of natural selection (or evolution) in biology, or Einstein's theory of relativity in physics. One thing that all of these theories have in common is that they are attempts to explain something about the world around us by answering a question. How did the universe come into being? The big bang theory supplies one possible explanation. How did various species of plants and animals arise? Charles Darwin offers an answer. Albert Einstein's famous equation of $e = mc^2$ seeks to explain how energy (e) and matter (m) are related to one another. In the realm of mass communication, theories seek to explain what happens when, for example, some topics get more coverage in the news than others, or what happens when audiences are exposed to graphic violence or sexuality on television, in movies, or in music recordings.

Finding a single, formal definition for theory is not easy because many such definitions exist. They range from very simple ones to very complex ones, depending on the source and the author. But whatever the approach, definitions of theory generally incorporate two common themes:

- Theories seek to answer questions about how certain things are related to one another.
- Answering these questions offers explanations or predictions about how some aspect of the world works.

As researchers Kerlinger and Lee put it, "The basic aim of science is to explain natural phenomena. Such explanations are called theories" (2000, p. 11).

So, does Scotty have a theory that will save the *Enterprise*? Not really. What he has is a hypothesis—an idea that he thinks might work and wants to test. (His hypothesis, as it plays out in the movie, is that a release of antimatter can disrupt the dangerous energy field and save the ship, a strategy that

Definition
Theory: A statement that predicts or explains how certain phenomena are related to one another.

mostly works. The ship is damaged but survives, but so does the energy field.)

But using the definition that a theory is something that predicts and explains how certain phenomena are related to one another means Scotty's idea can't be called a theory. The distinctions between theories and hypotheses, and also how they are related to each other, are discussed in Chapter 2.

Types of Knowledge

Theory and research are associated with what is called scientific knowledge, which is a specific way of knowing things about the world around us. The important words in that description are *way of knowing*, which goes back to the question asked in the first part of this chapter, *what do you know?*

Everyone *knows* many things, with this knowledge coming from a wide variety of sources. People know things such as their Social Security and student ID numbers, their home addresses, and their friends' phone numbers. They know things they have read in books and have been taught in classrooms. Most people know how to ride a bicycle, and many college students know which location is the most popular place to hang out on the weekend and which pizza restaurants near campus offer the most reliable delivery service.

This short list illustrates two important ways of knowing, namely *experience* and *authority*. Experience is learning something by directly participating in it, while authority is learning something by taking someone's word for it. People know who is the president of the United States, but not because they counted all the ballots personally. Instead, the knowledge comes from authoritative sources: election officials who tallied the votes and news media that reported the results. Much of what students learn in school has the same basis, coming from books and teachers that are, presumably, authorities on the topics.

Ways of Knowing
Experience: Learning something by participating in it.
Authority: Learning something by taking someone else's word for it.
Scientific knowledge: Learning through systematic and accurate observation of evidence in such a way that it can be verified independently and objectively.

Leaning to ride a bike, on the other hand, is purely experiential. Learning by doing is the only way to acquire that knowledge. Learning to drive a car or play a sport also comes mostly through experience (called practice), although this knowledge also may come in part from the authority of a classroom teacher in a driver's education course or from a coach who helps the athlete learn particular techniques.

As useful and valuable as these ways of knowing are, a third way of gaining knowledge is the most important for our purposes here. This is *scientific knowledge*, which is defined as learning through systematic, accurate observation of evidence in such a way that it can be verified independently and objectively. This is the type of knowledge embodied in the *scientific method*: defining a problem or question to be answered, investigating it by collecting evidence, and evaluating the evidence to determine the answer to the question. This approach is taught to most students in elementary school or high school, often accompanied by application of the principles with simple experiments in classes such as earth science, biology, or chemistry.

Theory Genres

The most prevalent way of studying communication practices, known as *communication science*, has its roots in the scientific method, as just described. This style of developing knowledge draws heavily on observation of the parts of communicative processes that can be objectively measured using some of the tools that are discussed in Chapter 3. But because communication processes and effects happen in many ways that cannot be discretely measured, communication science is not the only way scholars pursue this task. Other common perspectives in the field include interpretive theory, critical theory, and normative theory. (See Figure 1.1.)

Communication Science.   When most people hear the word "science," they think about the natural sciences, which are disciplines that seek to explain the physical world around us. But science encompasses more than biology, chemistry, and physics. Communication theory belongs to a different set of disciplines called *social* sciences, or fields of study that seek to explain how people behave within societies by applying the scientific method to studying social phenomena. The social sciences include economics, political science, psychology and sociology, to name just a few.

In fact, the dominant way of theorizing about and studying communication as a human activity has become what two eminent scholars in the field refer to as "communication science," which they define as a discipline that "seeks to understand the production, processing and effects of symbol and signal systems by developing testable theories that explain phenomena associated with production, processing and effects" (Chaffee & Berger, 1987, p. 17). In other words, this means theory and research can be used to develop scientific knowledge (knowledge obtained through observation and verification of empirical evidence) about the processes and effects of communication at various levels including interpersonal, group/organizational, and mass-mediated communication. Many of the original theories of mass communication as described in Chapter 5 are rooted in this style of research, as are most of the theories of the effects tradition described in Chapters 6 and 7. This style of investigating communication has its roots in other social sciences, notably sociology and psychology, which use many of the same research techniques and tools.

Definition
Social sciences: Fields of study that seek to explain how people operate within societies by using the scientific method to study social phenomena.

Interpretive Theory.   The other major way of learning more about communication and its processes and effects focuses on interpretation of texts and human actions. Rather than gaining knowledge or developing meaning from the scientific method, in this research tradition meaning is arrived at subjectively from the words or other symbols themselves, as well as the symbols'

FIGURE 1.1   Communication Theory Genres

Communication science: Testable theories that explain social phenomena associated with production, processing, and effects of symbols and symbol systems used to communicate (Chaffee & Berger, 1987).

Interpretative theory: Subjective interpretation of meaning from words or symbols themselves as well as their context, combined with the scholar's own interpretations of similar and different texts and contexts.

Critical theory: Analysis that seeks to reform media systems that contribute to the influence of a dominant social class by promoting that group's ideas ahead of others, which makes media organizations part of the society's power establishment and defenders of the status quo.

Normative theory: An attempt to describe not how things are, but how they should be according to some ideal standard of social values.

context and the scholar's own understandings of similar and different texts and contexts. A great deal of interpretive research is built upon rhetorical theory, or how people construct and use texts to do things such as informing or persuading other people. (It should be noted that while the word "text" is used as part of defining interpretive and rhetorical theory, it can mean more than just words on paper; a "text" could be an ancient culture's picture drawings or a modern culture's films or advertisements.)

Scholars from the interpretive tradition tend to reject communication-science-styled theory as too simplistic. In their view, the use of quantitative data and scientific method to investigate how people communicate limits the researcher to only measuring certain aspects of behavior. But these scholars are interested in broader understanding, and they think that just measuring something cannot help them understand why or how that behavior occurred or what its implications are. This is because the measurements, no matter how accurate or precise they are, usually lack context. And for the interpretive researcher, context is crucial to understanding, as well as taking into account the points of view of those who are doing the communication. Interpretive theory is discussed in greater detail in Chapter 8.

Critical Theory.   Critical theory similarly rejects the idea that merely offering explanations or predictions—as communication science seeks to do—is either sufficient or worthwhile in the practice of studying communication. But instead of *interpreting* social reality, this body of theory seeks to *reform* social reality. To scholars in this tradition, what a theory says and proposes is not an academic exercise; rather, it should be meaningful and focused on making society better for its members. The critical school emphasizes the social structures in which communication takes place, such as educational institutions that impart knowledge and mass media organizations that supply news and entertainment, and explores the issue of who controls these communication systems.

Critical theory starts from the viewpoint that the effects of the media on society are not always helpful or even benign. It is largely based on the ideas of the German political philosopher, Karl Marx, best known for his radical theories on economics and government. Marx was a "critical theorist" who sought reform through his criticism of the established powers in nineteenth-century European society. He argued that this ruling class, whom he called by the French word *bourgeoisie*, dominated and oppressed the working class, or proletariat. Marx created a theory of politics and economics, called communism, which was designed to end these abuses and release the workers from their oppression.

Extending these ideas to critical studies of communication results in a perspective that media are part of the power establishment and support the status quo by giving voice to and furthering the influence of a dominant class that unfairly oppresses many members of society. Partly because of its European roots, this viewpoint-based form of theorizing is particularly popular outside of the United States. But many American scholars work in this tradition as well, and this book explores these ideas in more depth in Chapter 8.

Normative Theory.   Finally, one body of theory does not seek to explain, interpret, or reform what is theorized about. This is normative theory, which attempts to describe not how things *are*, but how they *should be*. It has similarities to critical theory, because it does not accept the status quo as the best possible way to do things. But normative theories seek to establish ideal standards for the way society should operate. The term *normative* comes from the word *norms,* which are values and guidelines for the operation of a social system. It is important, however, to recognize that social norms may differ from culture to culture. American social norms, for example, emphasize personal liberty. When these norms are extended to mass media, the result is freedom of expression as embodied in the U.S. Constitution's First Amendment. But other societies may not have the same values, and may view the importance of free speech or a free press differently. This is why the well-known set of normative theories called the "Four Theories of the Press" identify not only the free-speech or libertarian ideal, but other models that allow more government control of the media. Normative theory is also discussed in greater detail in Chapter 8.

Purposes and Evaluation of Theory

Theory has several purposes, and several accompanying ways of assessing whether it is productive. The main purpose or goal of theory is to pose questions that provide explanations about phenomena, but there are other, more specific uses for it as well. Littlejohn lists nine general functions for theory, whether in mass communication or other social contexts (1999, pp. 30–31). According to this perspective, theory should:

- Organize and summarize knowledge.
- Focus attention on certain relationships.

- Define what to observe and how to observe it.
- Clarify observations.
- Make predictions.
- Generate new theories and research ideas.
- Communicate researchers' thoughts to one another.
- Generate ideas for change (a purpose of critical theory, especially).
- Provide ideas for controlling activities (a purpose of normative theory).

And according to two other well-known researchers (Severin & Tankard, 2001, p. 12), theory as specifically applied to mass communication can be used to:

- Explain the effects of mass communication on those who are exposed to it.
- Describe the ways people use mass media, and why they use it.
- Show how people learn from mass media.
- Interpret the role of the media in shaping values of those exposed to it.

Pretty much anything that seeks to offer an explanation could be called a theory, and anyone can theorize about any topic whether or not they are qualified to do so. But not all theories are created equal, and some are better than others. The following criteria (Littlejohn, 1999, pp. 35–37) are often used to evaluate the worth of a theory:

- **Scope:** how generally or widely the theory can be applied. For example, a theory that seeks to predict or explain the way advertisements of *one* particular company communicate their message or the effects of *one* specific television show would not be very valuable because of its narrow focus, compared to a theory that could be applied to *any* advertisement or *any* television program.
- **Appropriateness:** logical consistency of the theory to the assumptions behind it and what it is theorizing about. For example, both of this book's authors live in houses with only two numbers in the street address; both also are college professors who hold doctorate degrees. So, one could theorize that people with advanced college education tend to live in low-numbered houses. But the theory would have little appropriateness since there is nothing that should logically connect a person's street address with their educational achievement.
- **Heuristic value:** the ability to generate new ways of thinking and new research ideas about the subject to which the theory pertains. The more "generative" a theory is, the more valuable it is as a tool for understanding how things work
- **Validity:** the degree to which a theory is able to predict and explain the events as the theorist proposes that it will. A theory that supposedly was able to provide such explanations, but in practice could not, would not be a valuable theory.
- **Parsimony (or simplicity):** In general, simpler theories are thought to be superior to overly complicated ones.
- **Openness:** adaptability to new conditions and, especially in communication, to new technologies.

Other criteria cited by scholars to evaluate the worth of a theory include:

- **Practicality:** theories that fail to address real-world phenomena in a practical or useful way are not very valuable (Baran & Davis, 2006, p. 35).
- **Testability:** sometimes referred to as whether the theory can be "falsified."

Sparks defines *falsification* as the ability to say, in advance, what sort of data could be observed that would demonstrate that the theory did not work as intended (2002, p. 9). For example, the theory of gravity says that large bodies such as stars and planets are attracted to each other. It also explains why smaller objects are attracted to the surface of a planet rather than float away from it. But it is possible to specify the conditions under which gravitational attraction and motion of a body cancel each other out, leading to the weightlessness that space travelers experience. Being able to falsify the theory in this way helps give it more credibility. The logic of falsification is that if something cannot be proved to be wrong, it cannot be proved to be right, either. Something that cannot be proved to be either true or false is either a statement of faith (such as belief in the existence of an afterlife) or an opinion ("I don't think green is a good color for a house"). But it is not a theory.

Common Theories in Mass Communication

Every scholarly discipline has an active body of theories, which researchers in that discipline use as a basis for their work. For example, in addition to the big bang theory that seeks to explain the origin of the universe, the discipline of astronomy has numerous other theories related to the composition of the universe, formation of galaxies, existence of planets orbiting stars that are distant from the Earth's solar system, and so on. The field of mass communication is no different. It has an active body of theories that mostly fit under the umbrella described by Chaffee and Berger relative to "production, processing and effects of symbol and signal systems" (1987, p. 17). This has become the dominant approach in U.S. communication research, according to renowned theorist Denis McQuail (2005, p. 65).

In 2004, two scholars sought to identify the most frequently-used theories in the field by examining the number of times that specific theories were mentioned in articles in three of the top scholarly journals in the field. They examined more than 1,800 articles in the journals over a 44-year period (1956 to 2000) and identified 26 theories that were used in 10 or more pieces of research over that time (Bryant & Miron, 2004). Topping the list were agenda-setting theory, and uses and gratifications theory, tied for first with 61 mentions each. Other frequently-used theories were cultivation, social learning, Marxist theory (critical theory), and diffusion of innovations. (All of these theories and others are described in detail in Chapters 6 through 8.)

A similar study by two different researchers at around the same time (Kamhawi & Weaver, 2003) looked at 889 articles from different journals over a different time span and measured the popularity of theory in a different way, using proportions rather than a raw count. Not every article had a theory mentioned, but among the articles that were based on theory some of the more popular ones were information processing, uses and gratification, media construction of social reality, hegemony (also a critical theory), cultivation, agenda setting, and diffusion of innovations.

Note that while the lists have some differences, four theories do stand out because they were high on both lists: agenda setting, uses and gratifications, cultivation, and diffusion of innovations. These similarities support the argument that there is a well-defined body of knowledge and way of thinking about mass communication in the scholarly community today embodying the communication-science perspective. Notably, however, two different forms of critical theory were found to be popular by both studies as well. This is an increasingly popular way of looking at mass communication, with a focus that goes beyond measuring the effects of messages to considering mass communication as a process with broad implications for society.

QUESTIONS FOR DISCUSSION/ APPLICATION EXERCISES

1. Take a theory you know something about, such as one in natural science or social science that you have learned about in another class, and apply the criteria set forth by Littlejohn, Baran and Davis, and Sparks to evaluate whether it is a good one. As a reminder those criteria are: scope (breadth of application), appropriateness (logical consistency), heuristic value, validity, parsimony (simplicity), openness (adaptability), practicality, and testability. The more "yes" answers you get (e.g., yes, it can be applied broadly; yes, it is simple; yes, it has practical value), the stronger a theory it is. Be sure to describe which characteristics of the theory make it generalizable, simple, practical, and so on.

REFERENCES

Baran, S., & Davis, D. (2006). *Mass communication theory: Foundations, ferment and future* (4th ed.). Belmont, CA: Wadsworth.

Berman, R., Moore, R., & Braga, B. *Star Trek: Generations* screenplay final draft (March 16, 1994). Retrieved May 29, 2006, from: http://www.imsdb.com/scripts/Star-Trek-Generations.html.

Bryant, J., & Miron, D. (2004, December). Theory and research in mass communication. *Journal of Communication* 54(4), 662–704.

Chaffee, S. H., & Berger, C. R. (1987). The study of communication as a science. In C. R. Berger & S. H. Chaffee (Eds.), *Handbook of communication science* (pp. 15–19). Newbury Park, CA: Sage Publications Ltd.

Kamhawi, R., & Weaver, D. (2003, Spring). Mass communication research trends from 1980 to 1999. *Journalism & Mass Communication Quarterly* 80(1), 7–27.

Kerlinger, F., & Lee, H. (2000). *Foundations of behavioral research* (4th ed.). Fort Worth, TX: Harcourt.

Littlejohn, S. (1999). *Theories of human communication*. Belmont, CA: Wadsworth.

McQuail, D. (2005). *McQuail's mass communication theory* (5th ed.). London: Sage Publications Ltd.

Severin, W., & Tankard, J. (2001). *Communication theories: Origins, methods and uses in the mass media* (5th ed.). New York: Addison Wesley Longman.

Sparks, G. (2002). *Media effects research: A basic overview*. Belmont, CA: Wadsworth.

Research Principles and Practices

THIS CHAPTER WILL:

■ Provide an overview of the research process and design of theory-based research.

Theory and research work together to develop new insights about human activity. This happens through the systematic process of:

1. defining a problem;
2. constructing an explanation, better known as a *theory*; and
3. making inquiries (doing the actual research) that seek to validate or illustrate how that theory or explanation works.

Connecting Theory to the Research Process

Research inquiries can take different forms, depending on the style of theory involved. Communication science-styled research consists of "a set of procedures for the systematic and objective collection, processing, analysis and reporting of information" (Poindexter & McCombs, 2000, p. 5) to obtain what are called empirical data. This is also known as the *positivist method*, a term coined by mathematician and philosopher Auguste Comte in the early 1800s. "Positivism," as Comte defined it, adapts the scientific method and numerical measurements as used in the natural sciences to reach conclusions about human behavior.

Definition
Positivism: Using investigative methods of the physical sciences, such as experiments and objective measurement of specified criteria, to address and understand social phenomena.

Critical and cultural studies researchers, however, rely on qualitative methods rather than quantitative ones. They use ideas and evidence drawn from sources such as interviews and written texts that are augmented by the researchers' own ideas and logic. Positivist researchers seek to generalize and explain phenomena across a variety of settings; interpretive scholars prefer to provide unique explanations about specific situations to

Research styles
Qualitative research: Ideas and evidence drawn from personal observations, interviews, or texts (other published work) that is augmented by the researcher's own ideas and logic.
Quantitative (empirical) research: Research based on numerically stated values of observed data.

develop deeper understandings of those situations. As Wimmer and Dominick put it, "whereas positivist researchers strive for breadth, interpretive researchers strive for depth" (2000, p. 104).

The positivist approach is the oldest and most widely used method of inquiry in communication research. The theories that are most popular among communication researchers are best validated through positivist methods, such as content analyses and surveys (Kamhawi & Weaver, 2003). But the interpretive paradigm has become an important part of the discipline as well, starting in the 1950s and gaining in recognition throughout the 1970s, 1980s, and 1990s (Wimmer & Dominick, 2000, p. 104). This chapter starts with a review of how theory and research work in tandem in the communication science tradition, then turns to a review of the interpretive paradigm.

Theory and Research in the Communication Science Tradition

The hallmark of the communication-science tradition is that research is done in ways that emulate the "hard" sciences, such as chemistry and physics. This starts with development of a question the researcher wants to explore and continues through systematic observation and collection of data to help answer the question.

Research Questions and Hypotheses

All theory-research inquiries start with defining the problem. In quantitative or positivist social science research, this generally consists of stating either a research question or a hypothesis. A research question is just what the word says it is: a question that can be answered with some type of research such as, "what happens when people view violent movies and television?" or "do people get a greater awareness about political issues from reading newspapers or from viewing the television news?"

Some research questions are open-ended and explorative. But a hypothesis is a particular type of research question, with the difference being that it states the question in a particular way. A hypothesis makes a prediction that can be tested by observing and analyzing some type of evidence. As Sparks defines it, a hypothesis should be "a specific prediction about what will happen under a certain set of well-specified conditions" (2002, p. 9). Turning the research question above about newspapers versus television news into a hypothesis, then, requires rewording it to make it into a testable proposition: "People who rely on newspapers as a news source will have a greater awareness of political issues than those who rely on television as a news source."

FIGURE 2.1   Theory-to-Research Example

Paradigm	Moderate effects (communication science basis)
Theory	Agenda setting
Hypothesis	People who rely on newspapers as their primary news source have greater awareness of political issues than those who rely on television news.
Variables	Independent Variable = news source (newspaper, television) Dependent Variable = awareness
Hypothesis restated with variables included	Newspaper used more than television = higher issue awareness Newspaper used less than television = lower issue awareness
Measurement (Operationalization)	Independent Variable: Number times/week reading paper Number times/week watching news Dependent Variable: Questionnaire with 1–5 scale of awareness of 20 top issues in the news

Definition
Hypothesis: A prediction about how certain things are related that can be tested by observing and analyzing evidence that will illustrate whether or not the prediction is correct.

The fact that it can be *tested* is what makes a hypothesis a valuable and powerful research tool. And the thing that makes it testable is that it makes a prediction about how things are related. As Kerlinger and Lee point out, facts cannot be tested but relationships can (2000, p. 27). In the research question just described, the hypothesis seeks to relate "news source" and "awareness of political issues" to each other; the strength of this relationship can then be observed so that the prediction can be shown to be either correct or incorrect. (Figure 2.1 follows the progression of this research design.)

Scope of the Research

Like theories from which they are often derived, good hypotheses are neither too narrow nor too broad. If a problem is too general or too vague, the researcher will have great difficulty gathering and evaluating the evidence needed to reach a conclusion about it. An example of an overly vague research question might be: "What impact does the Internet have on college students?" Today's college students have literally grown up with the Internet and it affects many aspects of their lives. So, where would such an investigation start, and what could it hope to conclude? On the other hand, if the research topic is too narrow or specific, the research will end up being inconsequential because the answers it produces just will not matter to enough people. An example of that might be: "What are the major patterns of Internet use among the students in the Senior Seminar Course at State University?" Note that the research question does not say that the class is being used to represent any other students; in fact the wording of the research question specifically says the results do not apply to any students other than the ones in that class. The results might be interesting to the class members, but probably not to anyone else.

A more effective research scope might entail investigating a specific aspect of students' use of the Internet and how it changes a particular aspect of their lives, but in a way that could predict or explain the impacts on many students rather than on just a narrow group. For example, a researcher with an interest in social networks such as MySpace or Facebook could develop a hypothesis that explores the relationship of student interaction on those Web sites with their friendships or social networks in the "real world." The researcher might then try to answer the question: "Are students with large virtual networks in MySpace or Facebook also likely to join in more student clubs or activities? Or are they less likely to be real-world 'joiners' because their online friendships substitute for real-world ones?" This question is small enough in scope that the researcher can answer it effectively, but important enough to be interesting to many people.

Establishing "Proof" and Causality

A further connection between theories and hypotheses is that testing the hypothesis can help to validate or "prove" a theory. ("Prove" is in quotes because social scientists generally think that theories can never be proved beyond all doubt; more commonly they say that theories are either *supported* or *challenged* by investigations into them.) This support for a theory often comes from a hypothesis about a causal relationship; that is, when one condition can reasonably be said to *cause* another. The MySpace/Facebook example is not stated as a causal relationship, but the news media example from earlier is stated that way because greater readership of the newspaper might be seen as causing greater issue-awareness on the part of readers.

Establishing a causal relationship requires that three specific conditions be met, however. First, the effect that is being observed and the condition that is thought to be causing the effect must have some sort of connection, such as both increase or both decrease in a coordinated fashion. Finding evidence of such coordination is a major part of many research projects. The second condition is that the cause must happen before the effect. And the third is that other potential causes must be ruled out. This is often a key consideration in the research design as well. In trying to say that paying greater attention to newspapers causes people to be more aware of political issues, the researcher would have to be sure that other factors, such as being active within an organization that had some sort of political agenda, were not the real reason a respondent was more aware.

To briefly recap, theories are *general* statements that seek to predict or explain how certain phenomena are related to one another. Hypotheses are *specific* predictions that can be tested by collecting and analyzing observations to illustrate whether or not the prediction is correct. When the general ideas of the theory are used to create the specific predictions represented in the hypothesis, then proving the hypothesis is a way of validating—showing support for—the theory.

Definitions
Construct: An abstract concept defined in such a way that it has a specific purpose for a research hypothesis.
Operationalization: Process of establishing the rules for how a construct will be observed and measured.
Variable: The operational definition of a construct, with the rules of measurement and observation defined in such a way that it can take on different numerical values to be used in the analysis.

Constructs, Variables, and Measurements

Questions or topics that are theorized or hypothesized about are variously called *concepts*, *constructs*, and *variables*, three terms that are related but not interchangeable. Kerlinger and Lee (2000) draw the distinction between them by saying that a *concept* is an abstract idea that the researcher is interested in, such as "political awareness" in the example described earlier. A *construct* is a concept that is more precisely defined in connection with a research hypothesis. Continuing the news media/issue awareness example, the concept of "awareness" could mean almost anything, from simply knowing something—anything—about a war, taxes, or economic conditions (general awareness); to having a keen understanding of differences among various ideas that government officials and political parties are proposing to address those concerns (detailed awareness). So, turning "awareness" from a concept into a construct means that the researcher has to describe and define exactly what it means to be aware.

Operationalizing a Construct

Doing that describing and defining is called making an *operational definition* of the construct, or *operationalizing* it. The word seems complicated, but it simply means setting up the rules for how the construct is going to be observed and measured. For example, suppose a researcher wanted to operationalize "class participation" for a particular course. What set of guidelines could be used for deciding whether students were participating, or measuring how much they were participating? A researcher could just look at attendance statistics; showing up for class is one way students participate. She could observe the class and count the number of times each student raises his or her hand to ask a question or offer a comment as another way of defining participation. She could give a quiz at the conclusion of every class designed to measure what the students recall from the class, since paying attention is also a component of participation. The point is that any of these *could* be used to measure participation. It would be up to the researcher to decide which way was best for the specific research project being conducted, and then to specify exactly how the measurement would be made or operationalized.

Once the operational definitions have been made and the rules for measurement have been decided, the construct then can be measured as a *variable*. Continuing the politics-and-media example, the researcher may decide to operationalize "issue awareness" by having a questionnaire that measures what individuals know about national politics. This questionnaire could be constructed in such a way that a high score would indicate a highly aware person and a low score would represent someone with less awareness. In one study, this exact procedure was used, with a survey that asked questions about the respondents' understanding of U.S. Constitutional provisions, knowledge of which political party controlled Congress, and ability to identify political figures. The more they knew, the more "politically aware" the respondents were said to be (Koch, 1998).

Measurement and Human Behavior. Making such definitions and decisions about measurement can be challenging for communication science researchers, and other social science researchers as well. The problem occurs when trying to apply hard-science methods to activities involving people. Chemists and physicists have reliable and precise ways to measure properties of the things they study, such as the temperature of a reaction or the wavelengths of light. Such exactness can be difficult to obtain when studying human beings, however. A chemist can stick a thermometer in a beaker to take a reaction's temperature, but the social scientist does not have a comparable tool to precisely measure a characteristic such as "motivation," or "anxiety," or "political awareness." A communication researcher may want to study people who "regularly" view the television news, but what does "regularly" mean? Every day? A few times a week? Defining "regular viewing" does not have a firm standard the way that, say, the boiling point of water does. In practice, social science researchers must decide what measures will be used and explain why they are appropriate for the construct that is being studied. For example, in his studies of cultivation theory, George Gerbner defined a heavy television viewer as one who watched four or more hours of television per day.

The lack of ability to directly and precisely measure human behavior and attitudes is only part of the problem communication scientists face in trying to use positivist methods to evaluate human behavior. Collecting and evaluating such data also is complicated because people think about their actions and have decision-making ability. One beaker of water cannot "decide" that it wants to boil at a different temperature from the one next to it on the lab bench, or "learn" about boiling so that it boils faster next time. But humans can and do react differently even in very similar circumstances, and their responses to situations do change over time. These two characteristics make human behavior difficult to measure with the kind of precision social scientists would like to have. Baran and Davis note that some other characteristics with the same impact are that human behavior is abstract and complicated, and also that causes are hard to attribute because so many things can lead to a particular behavior. Measuring human behavior may also be complicated by the fact that people can behave in complex and abstract ways, and so many different things can cause a particular behavior (Baran & Davis, 2006, pp. 27–28). For example, a toddler may act out because he is angry about not getting the ice cream he wanted, or because he wants attention and his mother is on the phone with a friend, or maybe because he saw a child throwing a tantrum on television.

Using mass media and their messages as an area of study complicates things further. For example, would a researcher studying violent images in the media classify violent acts in an R-rated action movie or war movie, which could be quite graphic, the same as violence on broadcast television, which is more implied? What about cartoon violence, comedic violence, or depiction of the victims of violence on the television news? Using the media and their messages as variables makes mass media research even more complex than other types of human behavior or social science research, such as psychological studies.

Dependent versus Independent Variables.   In spite of the problems inherent in measuring human behavior detailed in the previous section, quantitative social science research relies on such measurements, and a key part of any research project is carefully defining the constructs and setting up the measurement rules that apply to them. This includes selecting and operationalizing the variables on both sides of the hypothesis, referred to as the independent and dependent variables. As described above, the point of many research studies is to determine whether one construct can plausibly be said to cause changes in the other. The characteristic that appears to be causing the changes under observation is called the *independent variable*; the one that is being affected is called the *dependent variable*. A good way to remember this is that what happens to the dependent variable *depends* on changes in the other one. Continuing the news/awareness example described earlier in this chapter, news sources (newspaper readership and television news viewing) are the independent variables and level of political awareness is the dependent variable. According to the hypothesis, the level of awareness is caused by (or depends on) the amount and type of media exposure to the news sources.

Definitions
Independent variable: The construct that appears to be causing the changes under observation.
Dependent variable: The construct that is being affected by the independent variable (i.e., whose characteristics depend on the other variable).

Levels of Measurement

Operationalizing a construct, or establishing guidelines for assigning values to it, can be challenging in social science research not only because of the variability of human behavior but also because of the inability to directly observe a construct, such as "awareness." This means values assigned to the construct often must be inferred indirectly from observations of other characteristics. In the example described above, subjects' knowledge of things such as control of Congress and information about the Constitution were used as indirect indicators of their level of political awareness.

Quantitative social science data can be measured in one of four ways, and the measurement rules must specify which of these four levels should be used for each variable. The four levels form a hierarchy from the broadest or least specific up to the most specific. They are:

■ **Nominal measurement or categorization.** This is commonly used because researchers frequently want to examine similarities or differences between groups of people who differ in some respect. Such categories often are used to define the independent variables in a research study, such as those who read newspapers and those who do not. Nominal measurement also is used for demographic classification; for example, categorizing research subjects by gender, age, or race.

■ **Ordinal measurement.** In this scale, the values of the variable are put in some sort of ranked order (*ordinal* is derived from the word *order*). Think of a list of newspapers in order of circulation size, for example, or a list of most-watched television shows or most popular songs. An important, and limiting, characteristic of this level of measurement is that it does not have a common space or "distance" between the values. Picture 10 items in rank order, such as 10 people arranged by height. Would number 10 (the tallest) be twice as tall as number 5? He might be if he were a 6-foot tall adult and the fifth person in line was a 3-foot-tall kindergartner. But the same would not hold true for a lineup of 10 average adults. Rank order thus cannot be used to distinguish differences of magnitude in the lists. In an ordinal ranking of popular songs, the number 1 hit CD album on the charts might have sold 10 million copies to earn its place at the top, compared to 4 million for the second-place CD, 2 million for the third-place entry, and only 1 million for fourth. In this case the distances between 1 and 2 and 3 and 4 are clearly unequal; in fact the second-ranked seller is closer to number 4 than it is to number 1. (See Figure 2.2.)

■ **Interval measurement.** As with an ordinal scale, interval measurement takes place when variables are evaluated as greater or lesser than one another,

FIGURE 2.2 Measurement Levels

Nominal:	Categorization
Ordinal:	Ranking
Interval:	Ranking with equal spacing between values
Ratio:	Interval scale with a meaningful zero point

Example: Note that the ratio scale gives the most information about each case relative to the others, and the nominal scale has the least relative information.

Ratio scale (raw number of CD albums sold)	**Ordinal scale** (rank in sales)	**Nominal scale** (2 categories: top of the charts, or not)
10 million sold	1st	Top-seller for week
9 million		
8 million		
7 million		
6 million		
5 million		
4 million	2nd	Non-top-seller
3 million		
2 million	3rd	Non-top-seller
1 million	4th	Non-top-seller

but has the added characteristic of equal steps in the interval: the distance between 1 and 2 is the same as the distance between 5 and 6, or any other two values. Interval measurement may seem like the typical way that things are measured, but it has an important limitation in that an interval scale has no true 0 point. The classic example of this is temperature measurement. The difference between 25 and 30 degrees Fahrenheit is the same as the difference between 55 and 60 degrees, so the interval is meaningful. But the zero on a temperature scale is purely arbitrary. Remember, 0 is different in the Fahrenheit, Celsius, and Kelvin scales; 0 Celsius is equal to 32 degrees Fahrenheit. And, for that matter, the scales have different intervals; a change of 45 degrees in the Fahrenheit system would be a movement of only 25 degrees Celsius. So it is not accurate to say that 60 degrees is twice as warm as 30 in either system.

■ **Ratio measurement** is similar to interval measurement but it has the additional characteristic of a meaningful 0 point, which allows numbers to be compared to each other as ratios. It may be impossible to describe today's temperature as twice as warm as yesterday's but it is possible to say a 160-pound parent weighs twice as much as his 80-pound child. Most of the routine measurements of life—distances, heights, weights, salaries, ages, and so forth—take place with ratio measurements. An important type of ratio measure used in much social science research is proportions (or percentages). So if 70 percent of 60-year-olds watch the network news but only 35 percent of 20-year-olds do, it can be said that young people's viewing rate is only half that of the older generation.

Why Understanding Measurement Scales Matters.   An important characteristic of these measurement systems is that they are hierarchical; higher-order systems can be used to derive lower-order measurements, but the process does not work in the other direction. In other words, data about a variable that is expressed in interval or ratio terms could be used to create an ordinal scale or a nominal classification. But it is not true the other way around.

One helpful way to think about this distinction is in terms of numerical, letter, and pass/fail grades. Numerical assessments follow a ratio scale, letter grades represent the ordinal scale, and pass/fail is a nominal measurement (the student is in one of two categories). If a teacher measured all assignments in a course pass/fail, at the end of the course she would have enough information to decide whether a student had passed or failed, but not enough to decide whether the student deserved an A or a D in the course. The categorical data cannot be used to create an ordinal listing of student performance because simply grading an assignment "pass" does not distinguish between outstanding work, mediocre work, and poor-but-still-passable work. On the other hand, if all assignments were given a letter grade, the teacher could derive whether each student deserved an A, B, C, and so on. But she also could tell whether a student should pass the course. This is an example of the interval scale (letter grades) being used to derive a nominal classification (pass or fail).

Now, take the example of a teacher who puts a numerical grade on every assignment and has a "curve" that specifies how many points translate into an A, a B, and so on. Such a scale would allow the teacher to give each student an ordinal value letter grade. But it also could determine that one B student actually performed better than another (say, an 88 average grade versus an 81). And ratio-level numerical grades could easily categorize the passing students from the failing ones by setting a cutoff point for passing or failing, for example, 60 points on the scale.

Understanding the types of measurement is valuable for students in doing their own research because the time will come in any research project when it is necessary to operationalize the constructs—to decide which data are necessary to actually test the hypothesis, and to establish the guidelines for collecting it and comparing it. For example, a student doing a survey might want to classify the survey respondents *nominally* (by gender, age, or some other demographic characteristic) but will collect the survey responses in *ordinal* form (on a 1 to 5 scale of agreement, perhaps). A student doing a content analysis of television shows, on the other hand, might employ ratio-level data, such as minutes of airtime for a particular character or number of times a product placement happens. Looking at the different ways that data can be measured will help students think more systematically about how to assign measurement rules for the variables in their projects. Understanding the ways data are measured also will help in understanding other research studies that employ quantitative data that students will have to read about in conducting a literature review for their own projects.

Reliability and Validity

No matter which level of measurement is used, the adequacy of a measurement rests on four criteria (Stamm, 2003, p. 131):

- **Reliability:** How well the rules for measurement will yield the same results if repeated.
- **Validity:** The extent to which the variable actually measures what it is supposed to measure.
- **Power:** How precisely the measurement can be made.
- **Efficiency:** The ease of application to data collection.

A reliable measurement is one that is both accurate and consistent. For example, consider three scales and a pile of weights such as the ones used in a weightlifting set that are accurately labeled:

- **Scale 1:** With this scale, when plates totaling a certain stated weight are piled on it, the scale reads out a total weight that matches the totals on the weight plates. Different stacks are always weighed at their stated value. And when a stack is taken off and then put back on, the scale gives the same reading. This scale is both accurate and consistent.

■ **Scale 2:** This scale tends to read out a weight about 10 pounds less than the labeled value of the plates. When a stack of weights is taken off and put back, the same weight is reported each time. But no matter how much the stack weighs, the scale's measurement is always 10 pounds less than the stated total value of the plates. This scale is consistent, but not accurate. It suffers from what is called *systematic error*, or bias.

■ **Scale 3:** This scale sometimes reads a stack of scales correctly, but at other times, reports it too heavy or too light. And this one, oddly, will take an identical stack that is placed on it three times in a row and report three different weights. It is neither accurate nor consistent, and suffers from what is called *random error*.

This concept of measurement error is especially important in quantitative social science research because of the abstract nature of what must be measured and how it is measured, as discussed earlier. As a practical matter, nearly any measurement is going to have some degree of error. Even scale number one, the most accurate and consistent scale in the example, will have some random variability in how it measures. But as long as the fluctuations are relatively small and truly random—sometimes high, sometimes low—the measurement is reliable. In the example, scale number one is reliable. The second scale, however, is not a reliable measurement tool because even though its random error seems small (it is consistent), it has a strong systematic error component or bias in that it measures 10 pounds too light. The third scale's large random error makes it unreliable as well.

Defining the rules for measurement in such a way that the measurements can be done as accurately and consistently as possible is at the core of both reliability and validity. For a measurement to be valid, it must first be reliable. But simply because a measurement is reliable does not necessarily make it valid. Validity has some other considerations as well.

The key consideration regarding validity is whether the way the variable is operationalized is truly capable of measuring the construct the way it is supposed to. The example was given earlier about operationalizing the variable known as "temperature" in a chemistry experiment, which is easily done because there are standard ways of evaluating it and precise tools to make the measurement. But to make a valid measurement the scientist would need to have the proper tool. A time-and-motion experiment in a physics class that needed precise measurements of time (down to, say, one-tenth of a second) could not be measured with a wall clock that only ticked away the minutes. Such a measurement would require a stopwatch with the proper calibration. Similarly, a scale cannot measure temperature (that requires a thermometer) and a thermometer cannot measure atmospheric pressure (a barometer is needed for that). Using the wrong tool for a purpose would clearly result in an invalid measurement, no matter how reliable, accurate, and consistent the device was.

Definitions

Reliability: The degree of accuracy and consistency in measurement, such that the measurements made according to the guidelines will end up with the same results if repeated or used by different researchers.

Validity: The degree to which the variable actually measures what it is supposed to measure (internal validity) and can be extended to cases outside the test set (external validity).

But this again is an example of how the social sciences are trickier than the natural sciences, where the correct measurement scale and correct tool to evaluate it usually are fairly obvious, such as a thermometer for temperature readings. It is harder to find the correct scales and tools for measuring human characteristics. For example, what constitutes a valid measure of "intelligence"? Could it be operationalized by shoe size—people with bigger feet are more intelligent? Obviously not; such a measurement would certainly be invalid. How about by a student's grade point average (GPA)? That is certainly more valid than shoe size; how smart people are and the grades they attain might be related. But many other factors influence a student's GPA, so it is not a valid measure of intelligence, either. How about a score from a standardized intelligence test? While some people even take issue with these instruments, they still can be seen as a more valid way of measuring the construct "intelligence" than either shoe size or GPA.

Ensuring that the measurement accurately represents the construct it is supposed to, such as using someone's shoe size to operationalize the size of his or her feet or a well-regarded standard test to measure intelligence, is called internal validity. Another issue, however, is external validity, which is whether the results of a measurement can be generalized beyond the subjects actually being measured. For an example, consider two classes (two sections of the same course, actually, with similar exams and assignments) taught by professors with dramatically different grading curves:

Prof. Tuff	*Prof. Softie*
A = 98–100	A = 70–100
B = 90–97	B = 60–69
C = 85–89	C = 50–59
D = 80–84	D = 30–49
F = 79 or lower	F = 29 or lower

Assuming the tests were graded fairly, a student would know that anything in the 70s would earn a particular score (an A from Softie, an F from Tuff). Thus, the scores could have perfect internal validity: the grade matches the numerical score exactly as the curve defines it and would be an accurate comparison of students *within* the course. But the F that appears on the transcripts of many students who were unfortunate enough to take Professor Tuff's class, and the As that go to Professor Softie's class do not have the same meaning as the As and Fs of other students in the school (or even of those same students' grades in other classes). Thus, the grades would be said to lack external validity: an A or an F should have similar meaning across the college regardless of the course, but grades from Professors Tuff and Softie have little to do with the students' actual performance compared to the performance of their classmates in other courses.

Unless a measurement is reliable (consistent and accurate) and valid (both internally and externally), it has little value in any type of research that involves quantitative measurement. The corollary of that statement also is true: research that is based on unreliable or invalid measures has little value, either. Creating good hypotheses, defining proper constructs, and making operationalizations that result in valid, reliable measurements are the heart of any effective communication-science-styled research project.

Theory and Research in the Interpretive Tradition

The value and effectiveness of positivist communication-science research largely depends on the quality of the measurement that is done, as explained in the last section, to test a stated hypothesis. But theory and research in the interpretive tradition have different purposes. Here, the main goal is to understand the meanings behind communication and the viewpoints of the actors in the situation rather than seeking evidence to test a hypothesis. The goal of the interpretive researcher is "to understand how people in everyday natural settings create meanings and interpret the events of the world" (Wimmer & Dominick, 2000, p. 103).

Often this involves interaction or involvement with the subject(s) of the research, which is something positivist researchers seek to avoid. But for those doing interpretive research, "one needs to see a social situation from the point of view of the actors in order to understand what is happening in that situation" (Lindlof, 1995, p. 30). Once this is done, the investigation is connected to theory through patterns or themes that allow for application to other similar situations. As with positivist research, theory provides a general perspective that helps to guide execution of the specific project.

But rather than being based on testable hypotheses, the interpretive approach to research design is based on developing "articulate, compelling and researchable questions" that are interesting and important both for the researcher and a wider audience (Lindlof, 1995, p. 64). The point of interpretive research is to see the possible understandings that might develop rather than trying to measure or refute the existence of certain data as specified ahead of time (the data that would "prove" or "disprove" the hypothesis).

Another distinction with qualitative research projects is that they often employ multiple methodologies in a combination that uniquely fits a particular project, rather than the more standardized, single-method approaches common to much quantitative research. And finally, the development of many interpretive, qualitative projects takes shape as the project progresses instead of having all the definitions and operationalizations established from the beginning. The purpose, goals, and often the research questions themselves frequently are adjusted along the way in a process known as *inductive* research (compared to the *deductive* approach of the scientific method). "Through induction, data slowly resolve into concepts and specific research propositions through the investigator's own increasing skill at understanding. It is only near the end of a project that one learns what it is all about" (Lindlof, 1995, p. 57).

Summary

Theory and research are two powerful tools for learning more about the way the world around us works, including important aspects of how people communicate in that world and what happens to them when they do. Theory- and research-based knowledge has particular value for students enrolled in mass communication for two reasons: first, many communication programs have capstone courses that require students to complete theory-based original research projects (Rosenberry & Vicker, 2006); second, and more importantly, students will find a clearer and deeper understanding of the mass media when they understand the way the media is studied and how theory can explain those findings. Such understanding can pay big dividends not only for students who attend graduate programs in mass communication, but for media practitioners who can apply their knowledge to media jobs in the real world.

Communication as an academic discipline can take various theoretical orientations, but the most common approach is communication science, or the study of communication activities with observable, empirical measurements similar to other social sciences, such as psychology. Social scientific research of this nature poses some challenges because of the difficulty in measuring intangible concepts of human behavior that cannot be directly observed, such as attitudes and personal characteristics.

Nevertheless, communication researchers in the positivist tradition frequently conduct their projects by formulating a hypothesis (making a testable prediction about the relationship of two variables), stating the rules for measurement and evaluation of the variables in the hypothesis, and trying to collect the data in the most systematic, reliable, and valid way possible. Alternatively, interpretive researchers craft research questions that get at a deeper understanding of the meaning of a situation. Some of the specific methods for engaging in both practices are described in Chapter 3.

QUESTIONS FOR DISCUSSION/ APPLICATION EXERCISES

1. This chapter cites some examples of authority and experience-based knowledge. Think about the content that was covered in your courses last semester. What did you learn that was authority-based and what did you learn that was experience-based? Develop some other examples of both of these ways of acquiring knowledge.

2. Figuring out how to measure abstract concepts is one of the most important—and most challenging—aspects of effective research. In this chapter, examples of this process were given for the concepts of *political awareness* and *class participation*. Take one or more of the concepts listed at the end of this question and define it as a construct, then operationalize it (state how it would be observed and measured). Here are some ideas for topics to conceptualize and operationalize: campus involvement, community service, alcohol abuse, sexually active behavior.

3. Vulgar song lyrics, demeaning images of women in music videos, and excessive or gratuitous use of sex and violence in movies and on television are popular topics of complaint about the media. Develop a research hypothesis that examines some aspect of how such content affects the behavior of those who are exposed to it. Remember, it is not a real hypothesis unless it states some sort of relationship that can be tested. Once you have the hypothesis, try to operationalize the constructs: just how would you observe and measure the items of interest that your hypothesis relates to each other?

R E F E R E N C E S

Baran, S., & Davis, D. (2006). *Mass communication theory: Foundations, ferment and future* (4th ed.). Belmont, CA: Wadsworth.

Kamhawi, R., & Weaver, D. (2003, Spring). Mass communication research trends from 1980 to 1999. *Journalism & Mass Communication Quarterly 80*(1), 7–27.

Kerlinger, F., & Lee, H. (2000). *Foundations of behavioral research* (4th ed.). Fort Worth, TX: Harcourt.

Koch, J. (1998, Summer). Political rhetoric and political persuasion: The changing structure of citizens' preferences on health insurance during policy debate. *Public Opinion Quarterly 62*(2), 209–230.

Lindlof, T. R. (1995). *Qualitative communication research methods*. Thousand Oaks, CA: Sage Publications.

Poindexter, P., & McCombs, M. (2000). *Research in mass communication: A practical guide*. Boston: Bedford/St. Martins.

Rosenberry, J., & Vicker, L. (2006, Autumn). Capstone courses in mass communication programs. *Journalism & Mass Communication Educator 61*(3), 267–284.

Sparks, G. (2002). *Media effects research: A basic overview*. Belmont, CA: Wadsworth.

Stamm, K. (2003). Measurement decisions. In G. Stempel, D. Weaver, & G. C. Wilhoit (Eds.), *Mass communication research and theory* (pp. 129–146). Boston: Allyn & Bacon.

Wimmer, R. D., & Dominick, J. R. (2000). *Mass media research: An introduction* (6th ed.). Belmont, CA: Wadsworth.

3 Research Methods

- Build on the general description of research from Chapter 2 to explain specific communication research methodologies:
  - Quantitative methods such as surveys, content analyses, and experiments.
  - Qualitative research procedures such as observation, interviews, and documentary analysis.
- Discuss the difference between quantitative and qualitative research, and the appropriate uses of each.

By now, the relationship of research and theory should be fairly clear. Research and theory are used together to develop knowledge. In the interpretive tradition, this knowledge comes about in the form of new understandings of the meanings of communication and its effect on society. In the communication-science tradition, it comes about through application of the scientific method.

This process starts with a hypothesis that can be used to test or validate theories; research then documents the evidence that illustrates whether the variables are really related to each other in the way that the hypothesis supposes. But this process of turning a research *idea* into a research *project* requires one final stage: selecting and implementing a set of methods to actually collect and evaluate the evidence. In communication-science research, this usually involves two steps:

1. Showing that the dependent and independent variables in the hypothesis are somehow related or connected. For example, the project might investigate whether they both increase or decrease at the same time, a characteristic called *correlation*, such as a correlation between a student's time spent studying and the grades achieved. Or the project might determine that different independent variables have different effects on a common dependent variable, such as a situation in which those who watch a lot of television have lower grades than those who watch less.

2. Showing that the changes in the dependent variable cannot be attributed to anything other than the changes in the independent variable. This is done by ruling out other potential causes, so that the only likely cause of variation in the independent variable is the effect on it by the dependent variable. For example, students who spend all of class time text-messaging their friends are likely to understand and retain less of the class content than those who actively pay attention to the professor. While there may be other factors that affect a student's classroom success, it is likely that the amount of time spent text-messaging during class (independent variable) will be a significant predictor of comprehension and retention of class material (dependent variable).

It is important that both of these points be demonstrated. Theories and hypotheses by definition are based on relationships of certain phenomena, so failing to show a relationship or connection between the variables obviously means there is no "proof" for the hypothesis. And showing that there is a relationship but failing to rule out other potential influences means it is not possible to claim that the independent variable really is causing the observed effects in the dependent variable. Thus, successful research requires careful selection of methods that will give the researcher the strongest tools to demonstrate these two characteristics.

Comparing Qualitative and Quantitative Methods

Research conducted in the manner described above is commonly referred to as *empirical* or *quantitative research* because it uses numerical measurements of the variables as evidence of the relationship at the center of the hypothesis, such as the percentage of heavy television watchers who behave in a certain way compared to the percentage of light television watchers who act similarly. This type of research often is contrasted with qualitative or nonnumeric research. Recall from the Chapter 1 discussion on theory genres that several types of theory, such as interpretive and critical theories, rely on texts and logic as evidence, rather than on numbers.

Within the mass communication field, however, the most common way of doing research is quantitatively, which Chaffee and Berger (1987) refer to as "communication science." In the same study cited in Chapter 1 that documented some of the most popular theories used in research, Kamhawi and Weaver (2003) also reported that 75 percent of the nearly 900 articles they surveyed used one of three quantitative methods, with the remaining 25 percent using a qualitative approach to analysis. Mixtures of the methods also are becoming more common. "Many researchers are now using a combination of the qualitative and quantitative approaches to understand fully the phenomenon they are studying" (Wimmer & Dominick, 2000, p. 104). In this chapter, quantitative methods will be introduced first and qualitative research will be discussed later.

Quantitative Research Methods

In documenting their evidence that quantitative methods were the most popular among researchers, Kamhawi and Weaver (2003) also found that three methods in particular were the most widely used (and explored in detail below):

- Surveys: 33 percent of the articles in their study.
- Content analysis: 30 percent.
- Experiments: 13 percent.

Survey Research

Surveys are not only the most common technique for researching mass communication, but also one of the most familiar methods for nearly any research purpose. Surveys are the basis of television and radio ratings. They collect the data used to report voters' preferences in an election and the popularity of officials once they are elected. Many readers of this book likely have participated in a survey, either by being called on the telephone, or by being the target of a survey conducted by a clipboard-wielding interviewer at the shopping mall (referred to as an *intercept* survey), or by filling out course evaluations at the end of a semester.

A survey is defined as a research technique for collecting information from people by asking them a structured series of questions. Breaking down the definition helps to identify the key issues in designing survey research:

- Collecting information: What questions will be asked? This is directly related to the researcher's hypothesis and what data are needed to evaluate it.
- From people: Who and how many people will be questioned? How will the researcher determine whom to include?
- In a structured way: How will questions be put to the respondents? This applies to both the format of the questions (e.g., Will they be multiple choice, or more open-ended?) and the circumstances under which they will be asked (e.g., Will interviews take place in person? Over the phone? Online? Some other way?). The structure of the survey with regard to both the style of the questions and the circumstances in which they are asked is closely related to its credibility, meaning its reliability, or consistency of measurement, and its validity, which is defined as measuring what the researcher actually intends to measure.

Fink and Kosecoff (1998, p. 3) list the following steps for designing surveys:

- Deciding on how the survey will be administered (by mail, phone, or face-to-face).
- Selecting the content and writing of the questions.
- Selecting the respondents.

- Administering the survey to collect the data.
- Processing, analyzing, and interpreting the results.
- Reporting the results.

Training the interviewees who will conduct the surveys is also an important part of the process, since improperly-asked questions can inject bias.

Fink and Kosecoff also recommend that the last of these steps—how the data will be used in the analysis and reporting of results—be the first thing the researcher considers, because design of the survey, construction of the questions, selection of the respondents, and actually conducting the survey all should be done with the end results in mind (1998, p. 5).

Survey Administration.   Surveys are a popular way of gathering information, but they also can be a resource-intensive way of collecting it. For a survey to be truly worthwhile, it must include a fairly large number of responses. Furthermore, each respondent must be contacted individually and the information collected and recorded from each individually. Because of the large number of respondents required, this process takes time; time frequently translates into money because people must be hired to conduct interviews and tabulate data.

How the survey is administered also affects the response rate among the pool of potential respondents and the amount of time it takes to collect the data. The most common ways to administer surveys have tradeoffs in how time-consuming or expensive the process is for the researcher compared to the response rate and the timeliness of data collection. These methods and their strengths and weakness are:

- **Mail surveys:** These are the least time-consuming surveys for the researcher because respondents complete them without assistance or intervention. But they are the slowest in terms of time it takes to gather all the data and also have the worst response rate because it is easy for potential respondents to ignore the letters. The low response rate can add to the overall cost due to the need to find a larger potential response pool, and to send out more contact letters, which adds to printing and postage expense.
- **Online surveys:** These are written and administered nearly the same way as mail surveys, the only difference being that respondents fill them in with a mouse and keyboard rather than a pencil or pen. Potential respondents are e-mailed the questions and use an e-mail reply function, or are e-mailed a link to a special Web site where the survey can be completed. If respondents act quickly on the call to participate, these surveys can collect data in a more timely way than waiting for land mail to go out and be returned. But online surveys suffer from the same drawback as regular mail surveys do: a low response rate because it is just as easy to ignore an e-mail as it is to ignore a letter. The solicitation also may not reach some of those to whom it is directed because of spam filtering.

- **Face-to-face interviewing:** This has a better response rate and more timely data collection than mail or e-mail surveys, but is the most time-consuming and expensive way of doing a survey because the researchers (or individuals paid to work with them) must locate and meet with each respondent, then take the time to do the interview and record the responses.
- **Phone interviews:** This has the same response rate and timeliness advantages as personal interviewing, and is nearly as time consuming because trained interviewers still must go through an interview with each individual respondent. But it is more efficient in that interviewers spend a greater portion of their time with the respondents. Making the next phone-interview contact takes only seconds compared to, for example, having to travel to a location and wait for someone to come to the door for a personal interview. In recent years, however, it has become more difficult to find a representative sample to respond to phone interviews. More people work outside the home, screen their calls with answering machines and caller identification, and elect not to have a landline in their home and instead use their cell phones.

In addition to the question of how to approach respondents, another decision to be made when designing a survey is what time frame it will cover. Surveys can be done either at a single point in time, known as a *cross-sectional* survey, or at different times, referred to as a *longitudinal* approach. Longitudinal data allow for comparisons of how the respondents' ideas, attitudes, or knowledge changed as time passed. They can take one of three forms:

- **Trend surveys:** These ask the same questions of a similar group at a different time, but not necessarily the same individuals. A good example of this type of survey is recurring polls of political popularity when the similar grouping consists of members of a particular political party, or people who identify themselves as likely voters.
- **Cohort surveys:** These also survey different individuals, but take into account the passage of time and control for it by "aging" the respondent pool accordingly. An example of a cohort study would be a survey of college freshmen about a particular topic that was followed up by a survey of seniors three years later to see whether their ideas on the subject had changed during their first three years in college.
- **Panel studies:** These take before and after measurements, but are different from cohorts because the surveys are given to the same individuals at both points in time.

Survey Instruments. The actual questionnaire or survey instrument must include both the questions themselves and the guidelines for administering it. These instructions may be addressed either to the respondent for a self-administered

survey or to the interviewer for a phone or face-to-face data collection. Poindexter and McCombs (2000, p. 58) note that a survey instrument should have the
following components:

- **Record keeping:** The name of the person who did the interview (and their
  comments, if any), the interview's circumstances (such as date and time) and
  location (for a personal interview), and the phone number called (for a phone
  interview).
- **Introduction:** A brief statement indicating the purpose and sponsor of the
  research, an estimate of how long it will take to complete the survey, a promise
  of confidentiality of the information provided, and possibly a screening
  question to determine whether the person being interviewed is qualified to
  respond. An example Poindexter and McCombs use is that for a survey about
  cable television, a screening question to make sure the potential respondent
  subscribed to or regularly watched cable should be included. They further point
  out that the introduction should assume the respondents are going to answer
  the survey and not give them a chance to decline, as this will depress the
  response rate.
- **Content/questions:** Format and wording of questions are discussed below.
- **Closing:** Notifies the respondents that the questioning is completed and thanks
  them for their participation.

Constructing Survey Questions.   The central feature of a survey, of course, is the
questions that are directed to the respondents. Exactly what questions are asked,
what form they take, and how many there are depend on the purpose of the
research—exactly what is the researcher trying to find out? A clear answer to
that question is vital for properly constructing the question set.

For example, this book's authors once did a survey about capstone courses
in communication programs. This research was not a hypothesis test, but rather a
piece of descriptive work designed to answer the research question: what characteristics are common in mass communication capstone courses?

The first thing the researchers wanted to know was how common such
courses were, so the initial question in the survey was: "Does your school or
department offer a capstone course?" (This also served as a filter question, which
will be described shortly.) From reading scholarly articles about capstone courses
done by other researchers, the authors knew that issues such as whether or not
the course is required, how many students are in a typical class, and how many
different faculty members teach the course can differ from college to college; so
they wanted to find out what the trends in each of these areas were in mass
communication departments. They decided the research would be most effective
if it could describe the purposes capstone courses were meant to serve, which
strategies instructors used to teach them and grade them, and which topics were
most commonly covered in them. They were curious about whether capstone
teachers were satisfied with the courses, or had ideas for changing them.

All of these different purposes of the research went into construction of the
survey instrument, which ultimately contained 18 questions to gather the data.

It was administered online, with e-mail solicitations to college faculty and administrators who might be involved with capstone courses.

Question Formats.   Questions themselves can take one of two primary forms:
closed-ended questions (sometimes called forced-choice questions) and open-
ended ones. In an open-ended question, the respondents can answer in any
way they choose. In the capstone-course survey, one of the open-ended questions was, "If you see a need for change in the capstone course, what would
be your top priority?" and respondents answered with a sentence or two
describing that.

In a closed-ended question, the researcher provides responses and an
instruction to the respondent about selecting them such as, "Check the most
appropriate response" or "Check all that apply." Closed-ended questions can take
a variety of common forms including, either/or (yes/no), checklists, and ranked
comparisons or range of agreement responses (Fink & Kosecoff, 1998, p. 9). The
authors' survey included single-check responses for questions such as, "Does
your school or department offer a capstone course? (1) Yes (2) No" and a range-
of-agreement response about course satisfaction in which respondents checked
one of five levels ranging from "very satisfied" to "very dissatisfied." An example
of a check-all-that-apply option was "Which of the following content areas
are included in your capstone course?" with respondents given a choice of nine
different course subjects including theory, research, ethics, law, and others.

Any sort of question with a check-only-one-response limitation must be
carefully worded to ensure that the answer choices are both *mutually exclusive*
(the respondent can logically pick only one) and *exhaustive* (a wide enough range
of choices that the respondent will be able to pick *something*). (See Figure 3.1.)
For example, take the following hypothetical survey question:

Which source do you use for news?

A. Television

B. Internet

C. Newspaper

This is not mutually exclusive, because some people might use two or even all
three news sources, so which one would they check? It is also not exhaustive,
because other news sources such as magazines and radio are not on the list.

A better way of wording the question would be:

Which of the following news sources do you use the most?

A. Newspaper

B. News magazine

C. Network broadcast news

D. Local affiliate broadcast news

   E. Cable news channels

   F. Radio

   G. Other (please specify) _____

This wording of the question, by asking for the respondents to pick their *most-used* source, makes the choices mutually exclusive. Even if people use more than one of the items on the list, only one can be used the *most*, and the question directs respondents to select that one. And the question also is exhaustive, by both providing a more complete set of common choices and by inclusion of the category, "other." Respondents who really do not get news from any of the A through F choices are free to fill in what they do use (such as *The Daily Show*).

A special type of question included in many surveys is the filter or screening question, which is used to determine whether a respondent meets qualifications that the researcher has in mind for answering a particular question. As mentioned earlier, a screen might be included in the introduction to qualify a respondent for the entire survey. For example, a survey about cable-television usage would have a filter question, such as "Does the respondent subscribe to cable or regularly watch it?" This question screens out individuals who watched only broadcast programming and therefore could not competently answer the survey questions. But as respondents work their way through the survey, such filters can be applied as well. They require an instruction about what to do next based on the answer to the filter question, such as, "If you answered 'yes' to question 12, go on to question 13; if you answered 'no,' skip questions 13 to 15 and go to question 16." These may be directed either at the respondent in a self-administered survey such as

FIGURE 3.1 Mutual Exclusivity and Exhaustiveness

Proper analysis of many survey questions requires that they be both mutually exclusive and exhaustive, which are defined as:

- **Mutually exclusive:** Respondents can reasonably select only one possible choice.
- **Exhaustive:** The range of choices is wide enough that all respondents can select something.

For example, suppose a survey of college students asked whether someone:

   Worked at a store
   Worked at a restaurant
   Worked at a factory
   Attended school

This would not be mutually exclusive, because many college students work at stores and restaurants (and some may even work in factories, at least during the summer). So it would be impossible for many people to make a single choice. It also is not exhaustive. People can work for the government, for nonprofit agencies, and for many other types of organizations not on the list. When survey questions (or content analysis categories) are not mutually exclusive or exhaustive, respondents can be confused and the data that are collected can be unreliable.

a mail questionnaire, or given as an instruction to the interviewer for a phone survey.

Wording of Survey Questions.   Students planning a career in mass communication must be good writers, and communication researchers need this skill as well, particularly when it comes to writing survey questions. Poorly-worded questions can undermine the survey and make its results less valuable because they could confuse respondents. Poindexter and McCombs (2000, pp. 49–51) provide a list of ideas for making sure survey questions are worded properly. According to these researchers, questions should be:

- Short, specific, and limited to a single idea to avoid confusion.
- Phrased clearly.
- Unbiased, meaning they avoid wording that might cause respondents to select a particular answer.

The responses that a survey offers for respondents to select should be:
- Uncomplicated.
- Appropriate to the question.
- Mutually exclusive and exhaustive if a single-choice response.

Furthermore, questions should avoid:
- Jargon and terms that would be unfamiliar to many respondents.
- Emotionally loaded words and phrases.
- Asking about multiple topics in one question.
- Using the word *not* or other formulations that state ideas in the negative. For example, the following negatively-worded question—"Is it ethically better for journalists not to practice deceptive news gathering?"—could be reworded as, "Should ethical journalists avoid deceptive news gathering?"

The quality of the survey instrument, including instructions, question-wording, and potential difficulty with responses, can be checked by testing it before it is used. Such a pre-test is absolutely necessary, according to experts in the craft, so that questions and responses can be rewritten if necessary to correct problems with them before actual data collection begins (Poindexter & McCombs, 2000, p. 74; Fink & Kosecoff, 1998, p. 33). Poindexter and McCombs suggest that if one-third or more of the respondents in the pre-test have difficulty with a particular question or instruction, then it should be revised. The pre-test also gives the researcher an idea of how long it will take to do the survey.

Survey Respondents.   This section of the chapter has so far addressed the first and third points of the original description of survey research, elaborating on "collection of information" and "in a structured way." But the middle part—"from people"—is another special concern in survey research. The researcher must decide how many people will be questioned, and who they will be.

FIGURE 3.2   **Typical Wording of Category Scales in Surveys**

Strongly approve
Approve
Neither approve nor disapprove
Disapprove
Strongly disapprove

Definitely agree
Probably agree
Neither agree nor disagree
Probably do not agree
Definitely do not agree

Frequently
Sometimes
Almost never

Very favorable
Favorable
Neither favorable nor unfavorable
Unfavorable
Very unfavorable

Source: Fink & Kosecoff (2000, p. 21)

One way to conduct a survey is to complete a census, which would question every member of a population. The U.S. government does this every 10 years to document the nation's demographics. It is an expensive, complicated process to collect information about more than 100 million households and more than 280 million individuals, which was the country's approximate population during the 2000 census. (The data, which are sometimes used in social science research, can be found at www.census.gov.) Usually a census survey is not realistic except for small, well-defined populations such as all the members of a school's graduating class or all the students in one class completing course evaluations at the end of the semester. So researchers frequently rely on a sample survey, administered to only part of the population.

Samples come in two varieties, *probability samples* (also known as random samples) and *non-probability samples*. Which type of sample is used greatly affects interpretation of the results.

Random (Probability) Sampling.   The basis of a random sample is that it assumes every element of the population has an equal probability of being included. When this is done, the principles of statistical probability allow the researcher to specify a sampling error and make valid inferences from the sample to the entire population. This is a common practice in political polling, for example, when the researcher will report results such as: "55 percent of people surveyed say they are likely to vote for candidate X, with a margin of error of plus or minus 3 percentage points at a confidence level of 95 percent." What this means is that even though not all of the potential voters were actually questioned, the researcher can say with some certainty (only a 5 percent chance of being incorrect) that the true proportion of the candidate's support within the larger population is between 52 and 58 percent (55 percent plus 3 points, and 55 percent minus 3 points).

Effective random or probability sampling requires a list of potential people to be surveyed, called a *sampling frame*. The frame should be as comprehensive and current as possible to represent the population and should include the information necessary to contact individuals within it, such as street addresses for a mail survey, e-mail addresses for an online survey, or phone numbers for a phone survey. Once the frame is in hand, the researcher then must select elements for the sample with a procedure that meets the assumption that every element of the population has an equal probability of being included. Some of the ways this can be accomplished include:

■ **Simple random sampling**, in which elements are literally drawn at random. For example, suppose the population of interest was a class of 60 students and the desired sample was 12 individuals. The frame is simply the class list. A simple random sampling procedure could be done by putting the 60 names on slips of paper in a box and drawing out 12. This works with such a small population and sample frame, but obviously would not be efficient in selecting, for example, several hundred names out of 100,000 voters in a particular district or 1,000 voters out of more than 1 million residents of a city. So other methods have been devised that can have the same probabilistic result.

■ **Systematic random sampling** is one of those alternative procedures, in which elements from the population or sample frame are methodically selected at a regular interval after starting at a random point. Using the class example above, the desired sample was one-fifth of the individuals. To make a systematic random sample, the names would be placed in a 60-item list, a starting point would be selected randomly, and every fifth person after that would be used in the sample; for example, starting with the fifth name on the list and continuing with the 10th, 15th, 20th, and so on. One of the authors once used this technique to select a sample of 60 newspapers from the listing of approximately 1,500 in a directory of every daily newspaper in the United States. The sample was about 1/25th of the entire population, so a random starting point was selected and every 25th paper was selected after that through the end of the list.

■ **Stratified random sampling** uses a random method such as one of the two described above. But before the random selection is applied, the population is divided into various strata or subdivisions to ensure some sort of equivalent representation of the divisions. For example, suppose instead of one class, the survey was meant to apply to the entire campus—but the campus has unequal gender balance (60 percent women and 40 percent men) and the researcher wants to know that men and women are fairly represented in the sample. Separate random selections would be done of women and men to select a final number of each such that the sample would preserve the 60-40 ratio, such as 30 women and 20 men in a 50-person sample.

■ **Cluster sampling** is another method of random sampling, which has some similarities to stratified sampling but involves administering the survey by clusters or groups of respondents selected at random. For example, in a campus-wide survey it would be easier to give questionnaires to entire rooms of students all at once rather than do a simple random sample that might pick a small number of students from each classroom to take the survey. So entire classes of students are selected to be surveyed, but on a random basis such as putting all the room numbers in a box and drawing out the required number of classes/clusters.

In all of the examples given so far, the population has been well defined and known for use as a sampling frame. This is sometimes the case in survey research. In the various school examples, enrollment data would provide names and contact information for all the students in the population. Or, a newspaper that wanted to survey its subscribers would have names, addresses, and other contact information about them. But many surveys use all the residents of a city, state, or other defined area as their population. Comprehensive lists of all the residents of such an area are harder to obtain, although sometimes sources such as voter registration records are used in political polling.

But in these cases, when the surveys are typically conducted by telephone, random telephone dialing is often used to reach potential respondents. This technique meets the test of being a probability sampling method by giving everyone in the area with a telephone an equal likelihood of being included. Why not simply use the telephone directory as a sampling frame? If the book were a comprehensive listing of all households, that would be feasible. But by definition it does not have unlisted numbers. So to make sure unlisted households are not excluded from the sample frame, telephone survey researchers have devised two different randomization techniques. One involves using the phone directory as a frame (say, by conducting a systematic random sample with random starting point and *nth* entry selection, as described above) to generate a list of initial numbers, then changing the last digit of the number by adding "1" to it (e.g., 234-5678 becomes 234-5679). This is called *plus-one random dialing*.

Another technique, called *random-digit dialing*, involves randomly generating four-digit values that are paired with the various prefixes or exchanges in an area. A drawback to both techniques is that they will generate some nonworking numbers. But that is less of a problem for the survey's validity than deliberately excluding a certain subset of the population (i.e., those with unlisted phone numbers).

Non-Probability Sampling. Any time the researcher wants to make mathematically valid inferences about the larger population based on the results of a sample, it is necessary to do a probability sample. But for various reasons ranging from simple convenience to the sheer impossibility of doing a true probability survey, many surveys rely on non-probability samples. These types of samples still can produce interesting and useful data, and give insight into the larger population from which they are drawn, even though they lack statistical "proof." Many researchers do not see this as a major problem because even probability samples are subject to random error and interpretation of what the numbers mean. So a well-constructed non-probability sample is often suitable for conducting a survey.

Two common types of non-probability sampling are *self-selection surveys* and convenience samples. Self-selection is just what the name implies: the researcher publicizes the survey and invites responses, and respondents decide whether to include themselves in the survey. Examples of this include mail-in surveys, such as clipping a form from a newspaper or magazine and returning it; online polls found on many Web sites; and the telephone and text-message surveys associated with some television shows in which viewers can vote for a particular outcome. The

Definitions
Probability (random) sampling: Every element of the sample frame has an equal likelihood of being selected. This is important if the researcher wants to use the sample to make inferences about a larger population, such as an opinion poll designed to represent public opinion in general.
Non-probability sampling: Elements for the sample are selected by the researcher according to convenience or for a specific purpose. These can still be useful samples, but cannot be used to infer information about a larger group.

definition of a convenience sample also is built into the name, because it means respondents are included primarily because the researcher has easy, convenient access to them. Many student research projects use exactly this type of sample when students survey friends, classmates, and people they contact in the student union or dining hall. On a more professional level, an example of a sample of convenience is the so-called intercept survey taken at shopping malls where people employed by a researcher ask any willing shopper who passes by to take the survey.

A third type of convenience sample is the quota sample, which has some similarities to stratified random sampling in its effort to make sure all groups from a population are represented according to a quota system in which the researcher specifies in advance how many respondents are needed from each classification. A quota sampling of students at a college might, for example, set the numbers of freshmen, sophomores, juniors, seniors, and graduate students according to their ratio in the overall school population. The difference is that after the quotas are set, the specific respondents are chosen by the convenience method rather than any random method directed toward equal likelihood of inclusion for all members of the population.

Sample Size.   The general rule on how many individuals should be included in the sample to ensure good results can be summarized as follows: the bigger the sample, the better—up to a point. In other words, researchers want enough respondents to give the results meaning but do not want to lose sight of the idea that the survey is coming from a sample, not a census.

For an idea of how important sample size can be, consider a survey about television viewing with a ridiculously small sample of three individuals. If all three of them report that they watch a particular show, would it be reasonable to assume that the show had 100 percent viewing among the general population? If none of them watch a show, does that mean it has zero ratings? Clearly the answer is "no" in both cases, and the reasons are pretty obvious: three people cannot adequately represent a television audience of tens of millions of viewers. But the same principle that prevents this unusually small sample from accurately representing the larger group applies to any sample of less-than-adequate size.

Sample size is especially important with probability samples because it is directly related to the size of the sampling error (the plus/minus figure that is used to adjust the sample mean from the survey). Larger samples mean smaller error intervals and more precise results.

Take the example from earlier in the chapter, in which a hypothetical political poll reported that one candidate had support from 55 percent of the voters, ±3 percentage points. This means the researcher could report with some confidence that the candidate's actual support among the whole voting population was somewhere in a range of 52 to 58 percent. But if the sample were smaller and the sampling error were larger, such as ±6 percentage points, then the range would expand to actual support being somewhere between 49 and 61 percent of the voters (55 percent, ±6 points). Since the same range applies to the other candidate who received 45 percent support in the poll, it means his "true" support is somewhere between 39 and 51 percent. So even though the poll shows one candidate 10 points ahead of the other, the sampling error makes the race too close to call because the intervals overlap. There is a reasonable possibility that the two candidates actually may be splitting the vote close to 50-50.

So what *is* a good sample size for a survey? With non-probability sampling it has to be large enough that the researcher can logically say that the results are meaningful. Clearly, that would not be possible with the three-person sample of television viewers used as an example earlier. But whether a sufficient number is 50, 100, or 1,500 respondents depends on the nature of the research, the logic of the researcher, and the size of the population from which it is drawn.

With probability sampling, the sample has to be large enough to minimize the sampling error to a reasonable level. As the political poll example illustrates, ±6 percentage points is not really sufficient for political polling data, and probably would not be sufficient for many other types of surveys, either. But bigger is better only up to a point, because every extra respondent adds time, effort, and cost to the collection process. So, after a while the additional precision that another 1,000, 500, or 100 responses would add to a project is not important enough to go to the trouble of obtaining them.

With large-scale surveys such as national political polls, the sweet spot or ideal number is around 1,500 respondents selected through probabilistic random methods, which would yield a sampling error of ±2.5 percentage points with 95 percent confidence of being within the stated interval. News stories about presidential popularity and other issues frequently report that the results were based on surveys with approximately this number of respondents and sampling error. (See Figure 3.3 for examples of newspaper reporting of error margins.)

But as the sample sizes decline from this typical level, the margins of error increase. A sample of 1,000 individuals would have a sampling error of ±3.0 percentage points, while a sample of 500 would have error of ±4.4 percentage points (both still at the 95 percent confidence level). Sampling 200 individuals would result in a sampling error of ±6.9 percentage points, and a sample of only 10 would have an error of ±30.1 percentage points. (Figures taken from Poindexter & McCombs [2000, p. 84] were adapted from Weaver & Wilhoit [1990].)

Another consideration in sampling, however, is the issue of subgroups about which the researcher may want to report. Suppose that a 1,000-response sample was about equally split between men and women, and the researcher wanted to investigate whether certain responses differed by gender. The overall error for 1,000 respondents is ±3 points. But because the inferences would be made from a set of only about 500 responses for each sex, the sampling error would be larger (±4.4 percentage points) for those subgroups. In general, the more subgroups a survey researcher wants to report about, the larger the overall sample needs to be so that each subgroup is large enough to make reporting on the results meaningful.

Analysis of Results. Reporting on the results of a survey again comes back to the issue of whether it was done with a probability or non-probability sample. With a convenience sample or other type of non-probability selection, results can be

FIGURE 3.3 Newspaper Reporting of Error Margins

Even newspapers report data-collection details and margins of error when reporting on surveys, as this article excerpt shows:

"With military commanders weighing possible troop reductions in Iraq, Americans are sharply divided along partisan lines over whether to set a deadline for withdrawing all U.S. forces there, according to a new Washington Post-ABC News poll. About half, 51 percent, oppose a deadline for getting out of Iraq, but the margin has dwindled as insurgents have continued to kill U.S. troops. . . .

"President Bush's approval rating rebounded from its lowest point a month ago and now stands at 38 percent. That is five points higher than it was in May, though still weak enough to cause Republicans to worry about their electoral chances in November. . . . A total of 1,000 randomly selected adults were interviewed June 22–25 for this survey. The margin of sampling error is plus or minus 3 percentage points for the overall results."

Source: Balz & Morin (2006)

reported *for the survey respondents only*. Strictly speaking, they cannot be used to imply that similar characteristics or relationships exist in the larger population; such extrapolation can be done only with probability samples. Nevertheless, non-probability samples are frequently used and can develop useful data that can be inferred to apply to larger groups using logic, sometimes in combination with other supporting data that help the researcher explain the significance of the results.

Fink and Kosecoff (1998, p. 5) list some of the common types of results drawn from surveys for a researcher's report:

- Proportions of the sample reporting each response; e.g., presidential approval ratings and other political poll results used as examples throughout this chapter.
- Comparison of groups; e.g., the number of men versus women watching reality television shows. This can be done either proportionally (55 percent of a show's audience is women, 45 percent are men) or with raw numbers (the show's viewers included 3.2 million women and 2.6 million men).
- Relationship of items surveyed about, again with either proportions or actual scores; e.g., the percentage of teens who say they are sexually active.
- Changes over time (for longitudinal surveys only); e.g., the percentage of foreign students in the United States a year after September 11, 2001, versus a year before.

Ultimately, what the researcher decides to report from the survey is directly related to the original research question or hypothesis. After all, the whole point of the survey construction, administration, and analysis is to document evidence that illustrates how the variables that interest the survey researcher are related to one another.

Content Analysis

Surveys are clearly a popular and powerful way for social science researchers to collect data about their interests. But Kamhawi and Weaver (2003) discovered that after surveying, content analysis was the second-most popular form of research published in major communication academic journals, used in approximately 30 percent of the articles they investigated.

The classic definition of content analysis is generally attributed to Bernard Berelson, who described it as "a research technique for objective, systematic and quantitative description of the manifest content of communication" (Berelson [1952], cited in Stempel [2003], p. 210). Generally, this has come to mean sorting messages into different categories according to some set of classification criteria. Content analysis can be applied to any form of communication, such as categorizing statements made in conversations as part of studying interpersonal communication. As applied to mass communication, it usually means evaluating and categorizing elements of media messages such as newspaper or magazine articles and advertisements, or television shows and commercials, for a particular research purpose. A major benefit of content analysis is its data-reduction capacity: the ability to take large amounts of material and organize it into fewer categories for more manageable analysis.

Stempel (2003, p. 210) deconstructs Berelson's definition of content analysis as follows:

- **Objective:** The classification criteria are defined in such a way that different people would classify the same messages in the same way.
- **Systematic:** All content is evaluated in the same way. In other words, categories are set up so that nothing is overlooked in the analysis, and the results are organized in ways that make them useful as research data.
- **Quantitative:** The end product of the analysis is numerical values used for the analysis. Usually, these are either frequencies (raw counts) or proportions of content in the various categories.
- **Manifest:** Analysis is objectively focused on the content as it appears, not on any interpretation the analyst reads into it.

Neuendorf (2002) says this systematic quantification makes content analysis different from other types of text interpretation such as rhetorical analysis, semiotics (analysis of symbols and their meanings), and critical analysis, all of which are described later in this chapter as methods of qualitative research. Nevertheless, those who are not familiar with the process sometimes confuse a qualitative descriptive content review for a quantitative content analysis. In other words, simply describing media messages in narrative terms, such as a student writing in a paper that "A content analysis of MTV's *Real World* illustrates that it contains frequent references to sexual activity by cast members in the show and frequent discussion and depiction of alcohol use," does not constitute actual content analysis. A student researcher seriously intending to do a content analysis of the show should create categories and count instances, then report in the research paper something such as: "In a content analysis of five episodes of MTV's *Real World*, there were an average of 9.4 references per episode to sexual activity by one of the cast members, 8.6 references to or discussions about alcohol abuse, and 4.7 instances per episode in which alcohol use was shown." Elsewhere in the paper the student would have to describe the procedures and definitions used to create the categories and do the measurements, specifying how it was decided that a particular comment was a "discussion about alcohol abuse" and then describing how the results related to the research question or hypothesis at the center of the project. This section of the chapter is intended to explain how this is done.

Neuendorf (2002, pp. 50–51) provides a nine-step process for developing an effective content analysis, which includes:

1. Developing the research question or hypothesis.
2. Defining the constructs (or what the analysis intends to measure), and describing how each of them relates to the hypothesis or research question.
3. Operationalizing the constructs, which means specifying the categories and the rules for assigning content to fit within them.
4. Writing a codebook that explains all of the operationalizations in detail.
5. Selecting the items to be analyzed, which often entails taking a sample of all available content. As with surveys, if the researcher wishes to make valid

statistical inferences that go beyond the sample, the selection must be done in ways that create a random or probability sample.

6. Training coders and doing reliability trials.

7. Doing the actual coding. For the best and most reliable results, any project should include multiple coders with some overlap of the coding work to provide a second reliability check.

8. Judging the final reliability.

9. Tabulating and reporting the results. Because content analysis by definition generates numerical results, this often involves statistical analysis.

Units of Analysis.   As with surveys and, indeed, all social science research, a content analysis project starts with a specific research question or hypothesis. But while surveys are designed to collect information from people, content analysis is designed to describe the attributes of messages based on what is in them. This is what Berelson meant by *manifest* content; Neuendorf calls this measuring the variables as they "reside within the message" (2002, p. 96).

Defining and operationalizing the constructs to be measured first requires selecting a *unit of analysis*, which, according to Neuendorf (2002, p. 71), is an identifiable component that:

- Helps to identify the population to be studied;
- Provides a way to measure the variables; and
- Can be used as the basis for reporting the analysis.

In the MTV *Real World* example above, the unit of analysis is one episode of the show; the researcher's goal is to measure the frequency of statements about sex, drugs, and alcohol made within the show.

The unit of analysis can be as general as the entire issue of a newspaper or the entire episode of a television show, or as detailed as individual words within a newspaper article or television script. Often, it is somewhere in between, such as individual articles within the newspaper or specific scenes within a show. The unit

FIGURE 3.4 Large-Scale Content Analysis

The Readership Institute, a newspaper research organization affiliated with the Media Management Institute at Northwestern University, used content analysis on a massive scale to find out more about which topics were most typically covered by U.S. daily newspapers.

This effort, called the Impact Study, categorized more than 47,000 articles from 100 daily newspapers by coverage topics. The study found sports, politics, and disasters/crime took up 56 percent of total story space, and that most papers devoted about 34 percent of space to local news, 16 percent to state and regional, 40 percent to national, and 10 percent to international.

Source: Nesbitt & Lynch (2002)

CHAPTER 3 / Research Methods

of analysis should be selected with regard for what needs to be examined to understand the message pool in the medium that is being studied (Neuendorf, 2002, p. 96). For example, if the goal of the content analysis is to seek out bias in news broadcasts, the entire show might be the effective unit of analysis if the researcher were trying to show that certain *networks* were biased in certain ways. But if the goal was to show biased word choices *within* the news pieces, the analytical frame would be the script of a news package.

Defining the unit of analysis provides a starting point for doing the measurement. For example, if the purpose of a content analysis is to determine characteristics of a newspaper's political coverage, such as conservative bias, then the number of articles that include certain characteristics that were defined as biased with a conservative slant might be counted to help determine that. Likewise, if the purpose of a television show's content analysis is to evaluate its portrayal of African-American or Hispanic characters, then counting the number of scenes in which characters with that description appear and comparing that to the total number of scenes would be one way to gather and evaluate data about that question.

Finely-grained content analyses might even reach to the paragraph or individual-word level, such as defining a list of words that are considered to be racist or sexist, and counting the number of times they appear in a magazine article or television script. Or an analysis might examine paragraphs of text in a newspaper or magazine to classify them as having positive, neutral, or negative implications about a person or group as a way of determining whether the coverage was balanced or slanted with regard to that person or group.

Sampling Content. As with surveys, content analyses may be done on either an entire population of message units or on some subset (or sample) of it. Which level the researcher chooses to analyze depends mostly on the size of the population.

If the point of the research is to draw implications about "prime time television," a census would be impossible; some sort of sample would have to be used instead, because there are hundreds of hours of such programming every month on the major networks alone, and thousands of hours if cable networks are included. But if the sole target of the study was a particular show, it might be possible to analyze the entire population—in other words, all the episodes of the show. The population of interest sometimes is defined by boundaries set by the researcher. For example, a project might seek to analyze all the stories on a particular topic in a particular newspaper during a set time frame, which might range from a few dozen to a few hundred. Or a television content analysis might focus on a specific show during a specific season of 20 or so episodes. With a population that small, every element could be subjected to analysis.

More frequently, content is sampled from a larger population. As with surveys, sampling for content analysis can be done in a fashion that is either probabilistic (random), or non-probabilistic (convenience). The same statistical principle described in the section of this chapter about surveys applies to content analyses:

If the researcher wishes to generalize to the larger population, the sample must be selected in such a way that each element of the population has the same like-lihood of being included in the sample. In the example given earlier about using systematic random sampling to select 60 newspapers from a list of approximately 1,500, the purpose was to obtain a representative, probability-based sample of the U.S. daily newspaper population for detailed content analysis. A second randomization was done to select the actual days to be analyzed.

But many content analyses are done on convenience samples; sometimes these are even based on which materials happen to be available and accessible to the researcher. One of the authors, for example, once conducted a trend study to see whether the way newspaper leads were written had changed over time, and wanted to look at this trend over a period of 30 years (1975–2005). The content selection was done by means of *purposive sampling*, which is selecting a convenience sample but choosing it in a deliberate way with a specific purpose in mind (hence, the name *purposive*). In this case, the four newspapers used in the study were selected partly because they were from similar markets (one purpose of selection). But these papers also were selected partly because the researcher had access to microfilm copies of them from the 1970s to the present (a convenience factor).

Categorizing Content. After deciding on a unit of analysis and determining whether to sample or analyze all of the units in the population, the researcher's next decision in designing a content analysis project is establishing the categories into which the content will be classified. Stempel (2003, p. 212) lists three crite-ria for a good classification system:

- Categories must be pertinent and closely related to the hypothesis or research question.
- Categories must be functional, meaning the data gathered about them ought to be useful in evaluating the hypothesis or research question.
- The overall system must be manageable.

A key feature of content analysis categories is that they must be *exhaustive* and *mutually exclusive*. In other words, a given content item logically can be placed in only one of the categories (which is mutually exclusive), and there is a wide enough range of choices that the coder should be able to choose someplace for every item to go (which is exhaustive). In surveys, some questions are mutually exclusive and exhaustive while others are written in a "check all that apply" manner or are open ended. But content analysis categorization cannot have "all that apply" classifications. The categories *must* use the principles of mutual exclu-sivity and exhaustiveness, or else the coders will be confused and the results inferred from the data that is collected will not be valid.

Sometimes, coding categories are set up to capture multiple dimensions at the same time. But these principles of exclusivity and exhaustiveness still apply. So, for example, a content analysis that sought to characterize the types of statements made by minority characters in a television drama might code both the race or ethnicity of the character as well as the emotional nature of the statement (friendly, angry, or neutral, for example). Within each dimension, however, every statement should have only one place in which it can logically be categorized.

Coding Reliability and Validity. Both reliability and validity are as important to content analysis as they are to surveys, and the same principles apply: a project's conclusions cannot be considered valid unless they are reliable. But even with reliability—consistency of results—other considerations come into play in determining whether results of a content analysis are valid, especially whether the constructs were selected in such a way that they actually measure what they are intended to measure. A word of caution that researchers often issue about validity is that content analysis cannot be used to infer meanings about the content under study, which is related to what Berelson meant by *manifest* content. Content analysis is most effectively and properly used to describe characteristics of messages or to identify relationships among them (Neuendorf, 2002, p. 53). A valid coding scheme should do this rather than trying to find latent or hidden meanings, or asking coders to "read between the lines" in assigning content to categories.

Reliability is largely related to how consistently the material is coded. Recall that one of the elements listed by Berelson in the classic definition of the process was objectivity, which Stempel further defined as establishing classification criteria in such a way that different people would classify the same messages in the same way (2003, p. 210). Common threats to this type of reliability, according to Neuendorf (2002, p. 145) are:

- Poorly designed coding schemes.
- Inadequate coder training.
- Coder fatigue.
- Coders who either cannot or will not act in a reliable fashion.

The best way to address the first two of these problems is to create a *codebook*, a detailed document that meticulously spells out the coding scheme, and includes all of the rules defining the units of measurement and guidelines for classifying each of them into one of the content categories. "The goal in creating codebooks and coding forms is to make the set so complete and unambiguous as to almost eliminate the individual differences among the coders" (Neuendorf, 2002, p. 132).

In the same way that survey instruments should be tested to discover and eliminate problem questions, coding rules should be tried to see whether any of them are confusing, incomplete, or in any way problematic. This is done by having coders undergo training in use of the codebook and categories. During this developmental phase, many things about the project will be in flux as the codebook is revised, and individuals who will be doing the coding learn more about the project and the process.

Intercoder Reliability. At some point in the process when the coding rules have been revised to a workable level and the coders seem to have a good grasp of their assignments, a trial run for reliability is typically conducted. This is done by having coders go through the procedure and then checking the results to see how closely they agree on categorization of the material. Usually this is conducted with material that is similar to—but not a part of—the actual data set. For example, if certain issues of a newspaper or certain episodes of a television show were going to be analyzed, the reliability trial would include different issues or episodes of the same material. If agreement among the coders seems sufficient at that stage, then coding of the actual data can begin. If agreement is insufficient, further coder training and/or codebook revision are needed until the researcher decides the team is ready for another trial. In addition to the reliability trial that is done before actual coding begins, on many projects some of the material will be coded by multiple coders and used for a second reliability test.

This intercoder reliability is usually reported as the percent of cases in which coders agree on an evaluation. For example, suppose two coders were categorizing a series of 10 newspaper articles as positive, neutral, or favorable to a certain position, and these were the results:

	Coder A	*Coder B*	*Agree*
Article 1	Positive	Positive	Yes
Article 2	Positive	Neutral	No
Article 3	Negative	Negative	Yes
Article 4	Positive	Positive	Yes
Article 5	Neutral	Positive	No
Article 6	Negative	Negative	Yes
Article 7	Positive	Positive	Yes
Article 8	Neutral	Neutral	Yes
Article 9	Positive	Neutral	No
Article 10	Positive	Positive	Yes

The intercoder agreement in this case is 70 percent, or .70 (they reached the same conclusion 7 out of 10 times). Is that sufficient? Some people might say so, although the answer is not clear-cut. According to Neuendorf, who summarized discussions from several content analysis guidebooks, there is no firm agreement among researchers about what constitutes sufficient intercoder agreement. But taking the general themes of what other scholars said, she concluded that "reliability coefficients of .90 or greater would be acceptable to all, .80 or greater would be acceptable in most cases and, below that, there exists great disagreement" (Neuendorf, 2002, p. 143).

Content analysts have developed a variety of statistical measures that modify simple percent agreement to take into account the likelihood of chance agreement. For instance, in the example above, suppose an unethical and lazy coder decided not to read all of the articles assigned to him and only marked "neutral" on the coding forms for every one. Then the results of the agreement test would look similar to this:

	Coder A	*Coder B*	*Agree*
Article 1	Neutral	Positive	No
Article 2	Neutral	Neutral	Yes
Article 3	Neutral	Negative	No
Article 4	Neutral	Positive	No
Article 5	Neutral	Positive	No
Article 6	Neutral	Negative	No
Article 7	Neutral	Positive	No
Article 8	Neutral	Neutral	Yes
Article 9	Neutral	Neutral	Yes
Article 10	Neutral	Positive	No

As the chart shows, the coders agree 30 percent of the time even when one of the coders is behaving in a fashion that should make him 100 percent unreliable. (As they say, even a stopped clock is correct twice a day.)

So any sort of intercoder reliability must take into account the possibilities that coders will put material in the same categories purely by accident. Even when coders are behaving carefully and conscientiously, there are times when this will happen because they are classifying content into a limited number of categories, and one or both of them makes an honest mistake in judgment. This happens more with a small number of categories, which increases the probability of chance agreement.

So an assortment of intercoder reliability statistics have been developed that content analysts frequently use in addition to (or sometimes instead of) simple percent agreement. These procedures, such as Scott's pi, Cohen's kappa, and Krippendorf's alpha—named after the researchers who developed them—generally take the raw percent agreement figure and lower it to adjust for the likelihood of chance agreement. Students should be familiar with these terms and know that they are measures of intercoder agreement because they will appear in journal articles that are part of the background research for a project. In a project done by one of the authors, he and a student assistant were both coding newspaper leads to categorize each of them with a value according to a four-point scale (1 through 4). Their simple percentage agreement was approximately .80, but Cohen's kappa and Scott's pi both were .70, indicating less agreement and possibly less reliability.

Statistics about intercoder reliability are usually reported as part of the research, in the same way that sampling error is reported in survey research. It is an admission of some margin for error, which means the results cannot be taken exactly as stated. But it also is an attempt to quantify how large that error might be, which adds credibility to the results that are reported.

Reporting Results.   The final stage of a content analysis, again analogous to survey research, is the tabulation and reporting of the results. Depending on the design of the research, the content measurements might be either the independent or the dependent variable, and the frequencies or percentages observed in the various categories are used to illustrate the relationship of those variables.

Taking two more examples from work by one of the authors, in the just-mentioned newspaper leads project, the result of the content analysis—the index measures of each lead—was the *dependent* variable. The project sought to document that the writing style (as operationalized by that index) had changed over time, so the year in which the leads were published was the *independent* variable (Rosenberry, 2005a). Another project categorized newspaper content by topic, such as how much of a paper's coverage was political news, how much was sports news, and so on. A statistical analysis was done to determine whether newspapers with different news mixes would have differences in circulation performance of the paper. Here, the content categories were used as the *independent* variables, while circulation performance was the *dependent* variable (Rosenberry, 2005b).

So exactly how the researcher uses the content analysis depends largely on which results the project is designed to show. Differences or similarities are often evaluated with statistical tests that allow the researcher to state at a certain confidence level that two measurements are essentially the same or significantly different. Extending the example, the newspaper leads project was evaluated with statistical tests to measure whether entries in different categories were different enough to say that the way they were categorized is likely to be the cause of the observed differences. Specifically, these tests were used to determine whether index values of the leads (the dependent variable) differed significantly according to year of publication (the independent variable), which they did. In the actual paper, tables and charts comparing the index numbers were used to illustrate the differences between the different years.

Experiments

The third most popular form of mass media research as documented in Kamhawi and Weaver's survey (2003) is a form that many students will be familiar with from classes in the natural sciences (at least in elementary and high school, if not in college). This is the experiment.

The key aspect of an experiment is the control under which it takes place. An experiment can be defined as a research technique in which the independent variable is intentionally manipulated by the researcher under controlled conditions so that effects on the dependent variable can be observed. Sparks (2002, p. 33) specifies three features that create this sense of control:

1. **Manipulation of a key variable**, one that the researcher thinks might be the cause of impacts on another variable. This manipulated variable often is called the experimental treatment.

2. **Random assignment of subjects** to groupings that will either (a) be manipulated or (b) not be manipulated. Random has the same meaning as random selection in a probability sample for a survey or content analysis: Each subject

CHAPTER 3 / Research Methods

in the experiment has an equal probability of being selected to face the experimental treatment or not face it. The subjects that do not face the treatment are called a *control group*.

3. **Identical treatment** of these different groupings except for the intentional manipulation.

Grabe and Westley (2005) assert that experiments are the strongest tool that researchers have for showing causality and making predictions. This is because experiments give the researcher the greatest control over alternative explanations (or alternative causes) of the changes observed in the dependent variable. This allows the researcher to more confidently predict that changes in the independent variable truly are causing those changes in the dependent variable. This means experiments have great internal validity, which is why they are often used in settings such as medical research. To get this internal validity, however, they make a trade-off in external validity, or the ability to generalize the results of the experiment to a larger population. Experiments are often conducted with relatively small numbers of individual subjects, and those subjects are rarely selected by a random or probability method that would allow the experimenter to say they represent the larger population.

In addition to small, nonrepresentative samples, Poindexter and McCombs (2000, p. 224) say that the conditions typical of experiments further reduce the ability to say that the results apply to a larger group. One of these characteristics is the pre-testing of subjects. Many experimental designs include some sort of evaluation of subjects before the treatment takes place. But anyone who has not participated in the experiment has not had this experience, so the results of the experiment may not apply to them. Also, experiments often happen under artificial conditions, which means the findings may not apply to people doing the same activities in more natural settings.

For example, much experimentation about news media has involved having subjects watch newscasts or read newspapers or online news Web sites that are altered in some way to reflect the experimental manipulation. Experimenters try to be careful and subtle about the manipulation and the questions that are asked about it so that it will not be obvious to the experimental subjects what they should be looking for. But watching a newscast or viewing a Web site at home is still different from watching it with a group of other people in a college classroom or computer lab, especially when the watchers know that they are involved in some sort of experiment and either know or suspect that they will be asked questions about what they have seen. One of the authors of this book was involved in a research project on what happens to people physically when they deliver presentations. She had to speak in front of a group of researchers while wearing electrodes over much of her body and a blood pressure cuff—which clearly are conditions most people do not face when giving a speech or presentation.

To counter this, experimenters sometimes conduct field experiments, in which subjects are observed in natural settings rather than in the artificial environment of a lab. This reduces the ability to put strict physical controls on the process but researchers often try to still maintain a sense of controlling the process through selection of the subjects, making sure some have experienced the conditions (or treatment) that the experimenter is interested in studying and others have not (for a control group). When consumer-goods manufacturers test new marketing procedures, they often conduct field experiments. In other words, rather than bringing people into a lab to evaluate the marketing message, they distribute that message in one or more actual markets and vary the conditions under which the marketing takes place. In a field experiment for the advertising and promotion of a new breakfast cereal, for example, one market might get heavy television advertising, another might receive extensive radio advertising, and another might experience print advertising with coupons for the cereal. In a fourth market, the cereal would be introduced with no advertising to serve as a control group. Note that what makes this an experiment is the deliberate manipulation of message exposure for the different groups. Results across the markets then can be compared to see what the most effective media-message strategy is.

Experimental Designs.   Experiments may be designed differently in terms of pre- and post-testing of subjects, delivery of treatments, and the number of experimental groupings. Some of the most common experimental designs are:

■ **Single-group:** A group of individuals is evaluated before experimental treatment, exposed to the treatment, and evaluated again to see if any changes can be detected. Although this is the simplest design, it also has the weakest internal validity because it does not control for the possibility of outside influences on the dependent variable.

■ **Single test with control group:** Two groups are created through random assignment, but only one is exposed to the experimental treatment. After that exposure, both are tested and the results are compared to see whether the treatment seems to have had an effect on those exposed to it.

■ **Pre- and post-test with control group:** In this format, two groups again are created through random assignment. But both are evaluated at the beginning *and* end of the experiment. Comparison of the pre-tests and post-tests should show whether there was a change in the experimental group that did not happen in the control group. Use of the control group in this fashion helps to control for exterior influences.

■ **Four-group design:** One concern in some experiments is that the pre-test may somehow influence the results by creating an awareness or sensitivity about the topic of the experiment among the subjects. The four-group design seeks to control for this by having control groups for both the pre-test and the experimental treatment itself, as follows:

- An experimental group undergoes pre-testing, treatment, and post-testing.
- A control group undergoes pre- and post-testing without treatment.
- A third group is not pre-tested but is given the experimental treatment and post-test.
- A fourth group is given the post-test only.

Notice that in the four-group design, the first two groups are identical to a standard two-group design, but adding the third and fourth groups helps the experimenter to control for the effect of the pre-test. Because neither of those groups undergoes pre-testing, their post-test responses help the researcher determine what effect, if any, the pre-test may have had on the first two groups.

A four-group design to test the impact of an advertisement might be organized as follows:

- **Group 1:** This group would receive a pre-test to evaluate their knowledge of the product being advertised, view the advertisement, and then undergo a post-test to determine whether they have additional knowledge or information gained from exposure to the ad. (So that it will not be obvious to the subjects exactly what the researcher is trying to find out, both the before and after questionnaires will contain a variety of questions, some related to the advertisement or product and some unrelated. The advertisement most likely would be shown with other advertisements, and maybe even shown in the context of a popular television show to make the viewing more realistic. This is another way to reduce testing effects and get more accurate results.)

- **Group 2:** This group would face a pre-test and post-test questionnaire—identical instruments to the ones given to Group 1—but would not be exposed to the advertisement. This is the traditional control group.

- **Group 3:** This group would not be pre-tested, but would view the advertisement and get the post-test to evaluate their knowledge about the product.

- **Group 4:** This group would get the post-test only. Their response to it would be compared to the response of Group 2 members (the traditional control group) to see whether Group 2 was affected in some way by undergoing the pre-test.

Evaluating Experiments.   How does the researcher determine whether or not the results of one group really are different from another? It often is done with the same types of statistical tests (described at the end of the content analysis section) that can be used to state, with some level of confidence, that measurements from one group are substantially different from the others (called a *statistically significant difference*). If the experimental group changes in a significant way and the control group does not, the researcher can reasonably conclude that the independent variable is influencing the dependent variable.

Qualitative Research Methods

The communication-science method is the dominant approach to communication research and was the first to emerge (Wimmer & Dominick, 2000) as sociologists and psychologists began to investigate the effects of mass communication in the early to mid-twentieth century. (This history is discussed in Chapter 5.) But a great deal of interesting and valuable research also is conducted with methods that do not involve communication science or quantitative analysis. Much of this work comes from what McQuail called the "alternative paradigm," a critical and ideological view of media in a cultural context that he contrasts with the dominant paradigm of studying a transmission model of effects with the tools of communication science (2005, p. 65).

This interpretive research tradition, which began to emerge in the 1950s, was promoted by researchers who viewed narrow, numerically based studies commonly done at that time as inadequate for answering broader questions about the role and effects of media in society. These researchers developed new ways of looking at communication, based on research methods that have come to be known as *qualitative measures* (in contrast to quantitative ones).

Qualitative Data

The fundamental difference between qualitative and quantitative research is what "counts" as evidence—a term that may be taken literally. The three empirical social science data-collection techniques described earlier in this chapter all have a common end result; namely, counting things to produce a set of numbers that represent or describe the variables under study. These results are usually evaluated with statistical tools that highlight similarities and differences among those sets of numbers. When the samples to be evaluated are selected in a random, probabilistic manner, these statistical tools can make valid inferences to the larger population from which the sample was drawn. And even non-probability samples can be used to obtain useful knowledge about mass media phenomena.

But qualitative research uses no such numerical representation and no such methods of mathematical inference. It rests instead on descriptions of situations, behaviors, or texts. According to a research roundtable sponsored by the National Science Foundation (NSF) that explored the topic, "Qualitative researchers often are interested in narrative data (e.g., autobiographies, literature, journals, diaries, firsthand accounts, newspapers) because narratives often provide important keys to both process (and thus mechanisms) and subjectivity. Further, qualitative researchers often seek to make sense of a case as a whole, and narratives offer an important way to gain a more holistic view, especially of actors often overlooked in 'official stories'" (Ragin, Nagel, & White, 2004, p. 14).

Reflecting the underlying contrast between communication science methods and narrative approaches, the participants in the NSF workshop further noted "A qualitative/quantitative divide permeates much of social science, but this should be seen as a continuum rather than a dichotomy" (Ragin, Nagel, &

White, 2004). The NSF workshop report listed some other characteristics of qualitative research as:

- Involving in-depth study of a relatively small number of cases, including the single case study. Within the public relations field, for example, case studies are a popular form of research, especially for crisis communication analyses that often examine how an organization responded to the crisis and what made their response effective or ineffective.
- Seeking detailed knowledge of those specific cases, focused on how and why things happen.
- Having a goal of making facts understandable, with less emphasis on deriving inferences or finding patterns (as many quantitative projects do).

A case study may be thought of as a version of the sampling done by quantitative researchers, with the purpose of systematically investigating a "sample" consisting of a single unit, and of gathering enough detail to answer questions of "why" or "how" the event, situation, or organization came to acquire certain characteristics. Gathering and examining a wide body of evidence about the specific situation allows the researcher to do this. A weakness of case studies is that they cannot be generalized, except through the logic of "if it happened here, it can happen elsewhere." This is not a guarantee or a prediction that characteristics observed in the case study definitely *do* exist elsewhere, but it is a way of documenting that they *could* or they *might*, which can be important conclusions in their own right. Case studies often employ one or more of the methodologies that will be described in this section, plus others, in the interest of developing this intensive understanding of a particular situation.

The lack of numerical or statistical analysis does not mean qualitative research is simpler, easier, or less rigorous than quantitative forms. But it does mean that the interpretation and analysis take on a different character and approach from the comparison of numbers with statistical tools, which is at the heart of communication science. Three types of data are commonly considered to be at the heart of qualitative research: observation, interviews, and written documents (Trochim, 2005). Berger (2000) describes a similar typology, saying that the three primary ways of getting information about people are by watching them (observation), by asking them things (interviews), and by examining the documents and artifacts they produce (documentary analysis).

Observation. Observing people in their natural settings is the most fundamental form of qualitative research. "All qualitative research in some ways follows the mode established by participant observation because the goal in each case is access to the 'insider' perspective" (Priest, 1996, p. 103). For example, a researcher investigating the workings of a media organization such as a newsroom or advertising agency might examine these questions (Priest, 1996):

- What are the work roles?
- How are the different roles seen and thought of within the organization?

■ How are decisions made?
■ How do members talk about their work?

When conducting observation, the researcher has to decide what level of involvement to take in two ways: whether to be overt (obvious to everyone who is being observed); or covert (less obvious, to at least some of the observed); and whether to be a participant in the environment under study or to be a more detached observer. Even with covert observation, research ethics dictate that the researcher gets permission to conduct the observations, and uses measures to protect the privacy of the research subjects even if not all of them are aware of the ongoing observation.

Participant observation is often associated with a research style known as *ethnography*, in which the goal is to understand the workings of a culture (Lindlof, 1995). The researcher literally becomes a part of the culture or environment, living and working among the subjects to gain a better understanding of them. This research style has its roots in anthropology, especially in documenting the workings of undeveloped and indigenous societies. But it also has been expanded to include investigating other forms of social interaction, such as organizations (e.g., a "corporate culture").

Detached (but still direct) observation is similar to ethnography, except the researcher seeks to remain apart from the group under study rather than becoming a part of it. A famous example of this kind of observation involving the mass media was done by Harvard Business School professor Chris Argyris, who wrote a book about the organizational culture of a major metropolitan newspaper (*Behind the Front Page*, 1974) after spending several months in the newsroom alongside the journalists. Note that this work also could be called a "case study," because it is the detailed observation of a single case (one newspaper).

An important aspect of observation as a research technique is that the researcher must have detailed, carefully constructed notes. As the note-taking is done, the researcher must be careful not to filter or edit because it is impossible to know as things are unfolding what will be important later on; to the degree that is possible, the researcher must seek to capture everything within the field of observation. Special attention should be paid to things that are confusing, surprising, or interesting to the researcher since such occurrences often turn out to be important (Priest, 1996, p. 105).

The strengths of observation as a research technique include its use of the natural setting and its ability to give the researcher that true insider's perspective. Some drawbacks to it are that the researcher's presence can change the behavior of the observed subjects and that studies of a unique situation seldom can be generalized beyond that specific case. The data collected also are affected by the observer's own perceptions, judgments, and preconceived ideas (Wimmer & Dominick, 2000, p. 113). But these weaknesses can be mitigated by using multiple observers and by "triangulating" the research results by comparing them to data collected by other means. Observation, in fact, is often the starting point for a research project that may later incorporate other methods such as qualitative interviews or documentary analysis, or even quantitative studies such as surveys or experiments.

Interviews and Focus Groups. Interviews are one of the most common data-gathering techniques for qualitative research, and are valuable because they enable researchers to obtain information that cannot be gathered through observation alone. "At its best, the qualitative interview creates an event in which one person (the interviewer) encourages another person to articulate interests or experiences freely. The interview's ability to access experiential or subjective realities has made it a pre-eminent method in communication and other social sciences" (Lindlof, 1995, p. 163).

Interviewing has some similarities to survey research, in that both are based on asking people questions and collecting their answers. But there are some important differences as well. "The key thing that distinguishes the depth interview from survey research is the researcher's flexibility to explore interesting things that come up. This is the direct opposite of the goal of survey questions, which is to ask each respondent exactly the same thing so that results are reliable and valid measures" (Priest, 1996, pp. 107–108).

Another difference is that researchers seldom seek any sort of probabilistic or random sample of interview subjects. In fact, the opposite is usually the case: rather than being chosen at random, respondents for in-depth interviews are deliberately selected because of their characteristics, background, or insights that the researcher wants to learn more about. Finally, while the goal of surveys is to develop quantitative measures (e.g., "What proportion of respondents answered 'yes' to Question X?"), the goal of interviews is exactly the opposite. "Numbers, percentages and statistics are avoided and the research expert discusses the results in terms of general impressions and themes" (Poindexter & McCombs, 2000, p. 270).

Researchers often distinguish among different types of interview techniques based on the amount of structure that is built into them. These strategies (Berger, 2000) include:

- **Informal interviews:** These consist of essentially general conversation with no set agenda, and often used to help the researcher and the subjects become familiar with each other.
- **Unstructured interviews:** The researcher has a focus or agenda but proceeds in an informal manner and exercises little control over the respondents' answers.
- **Semi-structured interviews:** The researcher starts with a detailed agenda or list of questions, but tries to maintain an informal approach and is free to explore avenues apart from the agenda if they seem interesting or worthwhile.
- **Structured interviews:** The interviewer has a detailed list of questions and follow-ups, all of which must be covered according to the way they were prepared in advance.

An important aspect of an in-depth interview, as with observation, is detailed and accurate recording of the respondent's answers. For this reason, interviews are frequently recorded with audio or video equipment for later review and analysis. Sometimes they also are observed (through a one-way mirror, for example) by researchers other than the interviewer. In addition to careful recording of the content of the answers, it is useful to make notes about the context of the interview such as the interviewee's attitude or apparent state of mind (did he or she seem relaxed, nervous, agitated, etc.) and the physical setting of the interview (was everyone comfortable, was it in a quiet place, was it in the respondent's natural setting such as home or office, were there distractions such as phone calls interrupting the questions or answers). Other aspects of an effective in-depth interview include the interviewer's ability to stay focused and on task, to ask clear questions, to prompt respondents for elaboration when necessary, to be nonjudgmental, and to ask questions in a way that does not "lead" the respondent or prompt any particular answer (Berger, 2000). "The main event of the interview is dialogue. Chance, surprise and persistence contribute at least as much to the happy results of an interview as advance planning" (Lindlof, 1995, p. 194).

Focus Groups.   In-depth interviewing of a small group of people rather than single individuals is often called a *focus-group study*. In this method, a trained moderator leads the group through a series of questions comparable to an unstructured or semi-structured interview. This methodology "uses open-ended, follow-up and probing questions to scratch below the surface of a small group of participants' attitudes, opinions and behaviors to understand motivations, feelings and reactions" (Poindexter & McCombs, 2000, p. 240). Much of the value of a focus group comes from the interaction among the group members as they elaborate on, question, or challenge each other's statements. The goal is to have that interaction "creating a richer set of data than can sometimes result from a single interviewer's interaction with a single respondent" (Priest, 1996, p. 109).

Focus groups usually have six to 12 participants and are conducted by a trained moderator over a period of one to two hours. Often the actual interview session is accompanied by having the subjects fill out survey-like questionnaires to gather background about them. The size of the group has an impact on its effectiveness. Experts recommend at least six but no more than 12 participants because the group needs to be large enough that participants react to each other's statements but not so large that it becomes unmanageable and some people do not get a chance to express their views. As with some individual interviews, the focus-group session may be recorded on video or audio tape for transcription and later analysis, and may be observed by researchers other than the moderator. The role of the moderator is pivotal in making sure that no one person excessively dominates the discussion or opinion in the group and to keep the group focused on the subject of the research.

In another similarity with one-on-one in-depth interviews, the researcher usually does not try for any sort of probabilistic or random sampling in selecting those included in the group; rather, they are chosen because of their background or knowledge about a subject. If, for example, the purpose of a group was to explore reactions to the advertisements that typically appear on soap operas or in televised professional sports, the researcher would want focus-group participants who were regular watchers of the soaps or the games, respectively. This makes focus groups easier to organize and administer than, for example, a large-scale probabilistic survey. These aspects of focus groups, combined with their flexibility in exploring topics in unstructured or semi-structured ways, make them especially useful for exploratory research (although they also are used for research in other stages of projects as well).

Documentary Analysis. Written documents, both personal (diaries, correspondence) and public (newspapers, magazines, research reports, and Web sites) are another source for much qualitative research. Unlike the numerical measurement done in objective content analysis, qualitative investigation of documents is focused on their meanings and contexts. Altheide defines document analysis as a process for "locating, identifying, retrieving and analyzing documents for their relevance, significance and meaning" (1996, p. 2). Specific types of document-based investigation include semiotic analysis, which examines symbols used within the text and their meanings; rhetorical analysis, which reviews how syntax and structure of the text creates its meanings; and qualitative content analysis, which evaluates and describes meanings within the text.

Semiotics. Semiotics is the study of signs and symbols, and how those symbols relate to concepts and objects that they signify. The basis of semiotics is that by studying these relationships a greater understanding can be gained of how meaning is created by a particular symbol or a collection of them (such as the words and images in a book, newspaper, movie, or television show). "Semiotics helps us understand how to decipher the messages we are sent and understand better the messages we send" (Berger, 2000, p. 43).

This technique for understanding the meanings of a text evolved from the discipline of linguistics, especially that of Swiss linguist Ferdinand de Saussure, who developed a form of semiotic analysis known as *structuralism.* Saussure defined a sign as being composed of a "signifier," which is the form that the sign takes, and the "signified," or the concept it represents.

Contemporary semioticians refer to the creation and interpretation of texts as "encoding" and "decoding" respectively. But decoding involves not simply basic recognition and comprehension of what a text says but also the interpretation and evaluation of its meaning. Semiotic researchers are especially concerned with the differences in denotations (literal meanings) and connotations (implied meanings) of words, and how that difference affects the meaning of communication.

For example, the letters C-A-T form a common English word that is a symbol for something else, namely a mammal of the feline genus. That is its denotation, or "signifier," to use Saussere's term. But different people who read or hear the word *cat* might have different reactions to it or understandings of it—different connotations. Cat owners might think of their own pets; someone who loved seeing the "big cats" at the zoo might think of a lion or tiger; and someone who is allergic to cats might think of the last case of hives they had when they came into contact with one. An avid reader of the newspaper comics might think of Garfield, Heathcliff, or the Catbert character in *Dilbert*. Which of these varying connotations did the author most likely have in mind in "encoding" the text and how can the potentially different "decodings" affect the meaning of the text for the reader? Semiotics would look at the symbol (the word *cat*) in its context (other words and images around it) to try to make that determination. In semiotics "the critical emphasis is on trying to unravel the author's assumptions, motives and consequences as revealed by analysis of the document" (Altheide, 1996, p. 7).

As semiotics has developed, the structuralist approach pioneered by Saussere has been augmented with social semiotics, which is how the meanings of texts (especially mass media messages) have an effect on society around them. "Signs do not just 'convey' meanings, but constitute a medium in which meanings are constructed. Semiotics helps us to realize that meaning is not passively absorbed but arises only in the active process of interpretation" (Chandler, 2002).

Often, these meanings and their effects on an audience member's life are not obvious to the individual consumer of the message; one goal of semiotic analysis is to reveal the deeper meanings. "Semiotics is important because it can help us not to take 'reality' for granted as something having a purely objective existence which is independent of human interpretation. It teaches us that reality is a system of signs. . . . It can help us to realize that . . . meaning is not 'transmitted' to us—we actively create it according to a complex interplay of codes or conventions of which we are normally unaware" (Chandler, 2002).

This is especially important because the reality most people experience is *not* from personal experience but from what they experience through signs and symbols—such as coming to understand people they do not know who live in another part of the country or the world. As Chandler further writes, "Although things may exist independently of signs we know them only through the mediation of signs. We see only what our sign systems allow us to see" (2002).

One area of mass media research in which semiotic analysis is widely used is investigation of the meanings of advertising texts. Examples of this include a project that examined the meanings found in advertising for antidepressant medications (Grow, Park, & Han, 2006), and one that explored how Nike ads were presented toward women (Grow, 2006).

Semiotics also plays a valuable role in understanding how encoding and decoding of mass media texts helps some ideas to become dominant in society and prevents other, nonmainstream ideas from becoming more widely known. This has been done through the research tradition known as cultural studies that is described further in Chapter 8.

Rhetorical Analysis. In addition to semiotics, another way of "unpacking" or deconstructing the meaning of texts is through rhetorical analysis. *Rhetoric* is classically defined as persuasive speech, with definitions that go back to ancient Greece and Rome, where philosophers such as Aristotle and Cicero developed public speaking techniques used to sway audiences. In a more contemporary way, Berger notes that "In media and communication research, rhetoric plays an important role because it gives us a large number of concepts that enable us to understand how a text generates meaning and helps shape people's emotions and their behavior" (2000, p. 68).

Much rhetorical analysis consists of the identification of what are known as rhetorical devices—such as allegory, comparison, definition, and irony—within a document and analysis of how these affect the text's ability to persuade the audience. The set of devices rhetorical analysts have available can be quite extensive; one rhetoric professor had more than 60 listed on a Web site devoted to the practice (Harris, 2005) and another had nearly 150 (Nordquist, 2006).

Analysis of the rhetorical/persuasive strategy of a particular author or document is done in a framework, such as Aristotle's classic formulation of ethos, pathos, and logos (Berger, 2000):

- **Ethos:** Speaker's personal characteristics, such as credibility.
- **Pathos:** Appeals made to the audience's emotions.
- **Logos:** Logical appeal of the argument being made.

But while classical conceptions of rhetoric entailed a single source seeking to persuade others, with all of the power supposedly in the hands of the person delivering the message, updated versions of rhetorical theory focus more on construction of meaning, similar to the way semiotics operates. Contemporary rhetorical analysis is "focused less on power and public persuasion than on meaning acquisition . . . in the New Rhetoric meanings are reconstituted rather than created" (Groenbeck, 1991, p. 8). One of those frameworks is provided by Kenneth Burke's theory of symbolic action, which examines the motivations for a particular discourse on five levels based on the metaphor of the theater, which has come to be known as Burke's pentad:

- **Act:** What is being done.
- **Scene:** Where it is being done.
- **Agent:** Who is doing it.
- **Agency:** How they are doing it.
- **Purpose:** Why they are doing it.

As with semiotics, the choice of words and the construction of a passage affect meanings to the point that, in Burke's view, "people's actions and thoughts begin to be swayed and even governed by the language we use to define our reality. With language as our symbolic action, all of our rhetorical motives become dependent upon that symbolic action" (Simmons, 2001).

Rhetorical analysis has wide applications outside of mass media, as it is often used in literary contexts, such as analysis of poetry, novels, or short stories. But it also can be used for analysis of material such as news reports. One study of the news coverage of a famous incident early in the Iraq War—the capture and rescue of Private Jessica Lynch in 2003—used rhetorical analysis of reports about the incident to conclude that the persuasive purpose behind how the military portrayed the situation was to reinforce typical male warrior hero roles (Howard & Prividera, 2004). When Lynch herself testified before Congress in 2007 about what had happened to her, she confirmed that the military public relations statements that tried to make her seem like "a little girl Rambo" (her description of herself) were not true because she was injured early in the attack and did not fight back at all before her capture.

Qualitative Content Analysis. A step up in scope from semiotic and rhetorical analysis of documents is a technique that Altheide refers to as *ethnographic content analysis*, sometimes referred to as *qualitative content analysis* (to distinguish it from the objective, quantitative content analysis described earlier in the chapter). In this technique, the researcher "interacts" with the documentary materials, much like a participant-observer doing an ethnographic study interacts with his environment, to analyze the documents and better understand their meanings in context. "Good qualitative content analysis requires an open-minded researcher, a specific research question and a systematic way of looking at whatever content is chosen" (Priest, 1996, p. 114).

Exactly which documents the researcher examines are selected "for conceptually or theoretically relevant reasons" (Altheide, 1996, p. 34). After that, the analysis starts with a protocol, or list of questions, ideas, or categories about which the investigator seeks to learn more from the documents. The emphasis is on capturing definitions, meanings, and themes of the narrative and descriptions in the text. The process involves "extensive reading, sorting and searching through materials, comparing within categories, coding and adding key words and concepts," then summarizing the results according to the research questions as identified in the original protocol (Altheide, 1996, p. 43).

Analysis of Qualitative Data

Qualitative research does not separate data collection and analysis as definitively as positivist quantitative social science research does. Rather, "Researchers analyze data as they collect them and often decide what data to collect next based on what they have learned. . . . In this respect, qualitative research is a lot like prospecting for precious stones or minerals. Where to look next often depends on what was just uncovered" (Ragin, Nagel, & White, 2004, p. 12). The National Science Foundation (NSF) workshop on qualitative research (from which this statement was taken) nevertheless developed some guidelines for approaching qualitative studies (Ragin, Nagel, & White, 2004, p. 12), including:

- Researchers should have substantial knowledge of the topic before starting, although this also creates a risk that the researcher will approach the project with preconceived notions.
- Researchers should be guided by theory, using it to aid selection of cases to be studied, and should formulate projects in such a way that they can extend or elaborate on existing theory.

- Researchers should not ignore competing explanations and interpretations, but should address them and evaluate them. Some of these may not be apparent beforehand and may emerge along the way in the research process.

Validity and Measurement.   Quantitative researchers have several well-defined techniques for assessing the validity of their data, starting with reliability of how it is collected. Recall from the earlier discussion about quantitative methodology that for a researcher using the scientific method, reliability is rooted in consistently assigning the values to variables; a content analysis is considered reliable, for instance, if the coding instructions are written such that different coders would assign the same content to the same categories. Numerical measurement and the tools of statistics add to the quantitative data's validity by providing a basis for specifying values such as sampling error, confidence levels, and intercoder agreement levels.

Qualitative research has no such set of tools. As the NSF report pointed out, "the procedures for analyzing such data are not codified nor are there established standards or conventions for judging the validity of the data or the credibility of the analysis" (Ragin, Nagel, & White, 2004, p. 13). The process is further complicated by the fact that qualitative data are seldom about what a set of facts *are*, but instead are about what a set of facts *mean* and the context in which they occur.

Authenticity.   So how are qualitative data evaluated for validity? One technique for enhancing validity is by enhancing authenticity. This is why observing and collecting data in their natural environments and proper contexts are important for qualitative research. A researcher wishing to observe newspaper reporters constructing their stories would want to see them doing it in the newsroom rather than bringing them on campus and observing them in a computer lab. If the goal was to observe how stories are written on deadline, the researcher would have to visit the newsroom around deadline rather than at a different time of day. "For qualitative researchers, the context in which the practice takes place has an important bearing upon that practice and research should be rooted accordingly" (McBride & Schostak, 2003). Two other authors on the topic add that, "Cultural analyses tend to favor natural, non-controlled settings. . . . If the data accurately reflect the natural circumstances, those data are valid and reliable even though not based on randomization, repeated and controlled observation, measurement and statistical inference" (Fortner & Christians, 2003, pp. 351–352).

Validity of data also depends on the methods and behavior of the individual researcher. "Observations must reflect genuine features of the situation under study, and not aberrations or hurried conclusions that merely represent observer opinion" (Fortner & Christians, 2003, p. 352). Systematic and unobtrusive collection of the data helps to reach this goal. As Fortner and Christians also state, "Culturalists consider it their highest priority to see the world as the actors themselves imagine or interpret it" (2003, p. 353).

Detail. The hallmark of qualitative research is its emphasis on drawing meaning out of the details that are gathered. "Whether you are working with participant observation notes, transcriptions of interview or focus-group data, or actual mass-media stories or programs, identifying recurrent themes and patterns is often the next goal" (Priest, 1996, p. 187). Indeed, using these themes or interconnections to create what is called *thick description* lies at the heart of effective qualitative investigations. Holliday (2002) defines "thick" description as that which goes beyond simply describing surface observations to interpret what they mean, such as how the body language or gestures of people whom the researcher is observing might indicate which individual has more power or control over the other in the relationship. Collecting enough of the right data is important, but so is using it to make these interpretations. "An important criterion for good data is the degree to which it provides the potential for thick description by revealing different, deeper aspects of the phenomenon being studied" (Holliday, 2002, p. 97).

Gathering data under authentic conditions, following systematic procedures so that no important details are missed, and trying to be cognizant of the potential for the researcher to affect the results (if he or she is not careful) are the primary ways that qualitative researchers seek to improve the validity of their work. "Good qualitative work proceeds from an open mind, takes all available data into account as systematically as possible, is guided by a carefully chosen research question rather than the impulses of the researcher and makes a contribution to theory. . . . In other words, qualitative work is as rigorous as quantitative work. Doing qualitative work is not the same as writing an opinion piece!" (Priest, 1996, p. 181).

The Value of Evidence

The primary goal of communication research, whether from a quantitative scientific-method perspective or from a more qualitative/interpretive perspective, is to provide the evidence that supports a researcher's claims, either stated through a formal hypothesis testable with empirical data, or through an analytical, qualitative framework in which discovery of meaning is the primary goal. In either case, the carefulness of the researcher and the methods used to collect, compile, and analyze the data are intricately related to the quality and outcome of the research project.

Neither quantitative nor qualitative methods have a monopoly on wisdom in the field. Both are used widely, and the proper method to be employed depends on the nature of the project and what the researcher hopes to demonstrate. Numerical analyses and hypothesis testing remain the most popular ways of conducting communication research, but not everything can or should be researched that way. One of the first things the researcher must do in designing a project is to think about exactly what he or she hopes to learn from it, and then to select the best methods for that purpose.

Effective research can combine methodologies as well. The landmark research that defined the agenda-setting theory (described in detail in Chapter 7) combined surveys and content analyses, for example. Surveys are thought of primarily as a quantitative instrument, and numerical tallies and statistical analysis of closed-ended responses are a common way of analyzing survey data. But many surveys also include open-ended responses, which are a form of qualitative study, and can augment and deepen the researcher's understanding about what the numerical report on the closed-ended questions really mean. Likewise, the content analysis of statements made by minority characters in a television show (using an example from earlier in this chapter) might be done to see whether evidence of stereotyping could be found. To do this, the study would seek to measure quantities or proportions of statements that reflect stereotypical views. But defining and operationalizing what constitutes a stereotype is a job for qualitative analysis. Thus, research that combines quantitative and qualitative methods can yield insights that neither approach can reveal on its own. (Ragin, Nagel, & White, 2004, p 18).

QUESTIONS FOR DISCUSSION/ APPLICATION EXERCISES

1. Search a database of news articles, such as LexisNexis, for stories about political poll results. Find three different articles and note the following about each, if it is reported:
   What size sample was the poll based on?
   How was the poll conducted (via mail, phone, or e-mail)?
   What was the time frame in which it was conducted?
   What sampling error do the poll results have?

2. Conduct a qualitative observation exercise by visiting a dining hall, student union, residence hall lounge, or some other place where people gather and interact. Spend about an hour observing and making detailed notes on your observations. Afterward, re-read your notes several times and try to identify some themes that would summarize the activity you observed.

3. Look through several editions of a scholarly journal that publishes research about media topics such as *Journalism and Mass Communication Quarterly* to find one example of each of the methods outlined in this chapter (survey, content analysis, experiment, and qualitative methodology). Then try to find articles that use a combination of methods, particularly ones that combine a quantitative approach with a qualitative one.

REFERENCES

Altheide, D. (1996). *Qualitative media analysis.* Thousand Oaks, CA: Sage Publications.
Balz, D., & Morin, R. (2006, June 27). Nation is divided on drawdown of troops; poll shows growth in support for Bush. *The Washington Post*, p. A1.
Berger, A. A. (2000). *Media and communication research methods.* Thousand Oaks, CA: Sage Publications.
Chaffee, S. H., & Berger, C. R. (1987). The study of communication as a science. In C. R. Berger & S. H. Chaffee (Eds.), *Handbook of communication science* (pp. 15–19). Newbury Park, CA: Sage Publications.

Chandler, D. (2002). *Semiotics: The basics*. London: Routledge. Online edition retrieved May 12, 2007 from: http://www.aber.ac.uk/media/Documents/S4B/semiotic.html.

Fink, A., & Kosecoff, J. (1998). *How to conduct surveys: A step-by-step guide* (2nd ed.). Thousand Oaks, CA: Sage Publications.

Fortner, R., & Christians, C. (2003). Separating wheat from chaff in qualitative studies. In G. Stempel, D. Weaver, & G. C. Wilhoit (Eds.), *Mass communication research and theory* (pp. 350–361). Boston: Allyn & Bacon.

Grabe, M. E., & Westley, B. (2003). The controlled experiment. In G. Stempel, D. Weaver, & G. C. Wilhoit (Eds.), *Mass communication research and theory* (pp. 267–298). Boston: Allyn & Bacon.

Groenbeck, B. E. (1991). The rhetorical studies tradition and Walter J. Ong: Oral literacy, theories of mediation, culture and consciousness. In B. E. Groenbeck, T. J. Farrell, & T. Soukup (Eds.), *Media, consciousness and culture* (pp. 5–24). Newbury Park, CA: Sage Publications.

Grow, J. M. (2006). Stories of community: The first ten years of Nike women's advertising. *The American Journal of Semiotics 22*(1–4), 167–198.

Grow, J. M., Park, J. S., & Han, X. (2006, April). Your life is waiting!: Symbolic meanings in direct-to-consumer antidepressant advertising. *The Journal of Communication Inquiry 30*(2), 163ff.

Harris, R. A. (2005). A handbook of rhetorical devices. Retrieved May 15, 2007, from: http://www.virtualsalt.com/rhetoric.htm.

Holliday, A. (2002). *Doing and writing qualitative research*. Thousand Oaks, CA: Sage Publications.

Howard, J. W. III, & Prividera, L. C. (2004, Fall). Rescuing patriarchy or saving Jessica Lynch: The rhetorical construction of the American woman soldier. *Women and Language 27*(2), 89–98.

Kamhawi, R., & Weaver, D. (2003, Spring). Mass communication research trends from 1980 to 1999. *Journalism & Mass Communication Quarterly 80*(1), 7–27.

Lindlof, T. R. (1995). *Qualitative communication research methods*. Thousand Oaks, CA: Sage Publications.

McBride, R., & Schostak, J. (2003). An introduction to qualitative research. Retrieved June 5, 2006, from: http://www.enquirylearning.net/ELU/Issues/Research/Res1Cont.html.

McQuail, D. (2005). *McQuail's mass communication theory* (5th ed.). London: Sage Publications Ltd.

Nesbitt, M., & Lynch, S. (2002). How to analyze your content and increase your readership. The Poynter Institute. Retrieved Aug. 17, 2006, from: http://www.poynter.org/content/content_print.asp?id=9644&custom=

Neuendorf, K. (2002). *The content analysis guidebook*. Thousand Oaks, CA: Sage Publications.

Nordquist, R. (2006). An illustrated glossary of rhetorical terms (9th ed.). Retrieved May 15, 2007, from: http://www.nt.armstrong.edu/terms.htm.

Poindexter, P., & McCombs, M. (2000). *Research in mass communication: A practical guide*. Boston: Bedford/St. Martins.

Priest, S. H. (1996). *Doing media research: An introduction*. Thousand Oaks, CA: Sage Publications.

Ragin, C., Nagel, J., & White, P (2004). Workshop on scientific foundations of qualitative research. Washington, D.C.: National Science Foundation. Retrieved June 5, 2006, from: http://www.nsf.gov/pubs/2004/nsf04219/.

Rosenberry, J. (2005a). Second servings: Online publication and its relationship to second-day leads in newspapers. Paper presented at national conference of Association for Education in Journalism and Mass Communication, San Antonio, Texas, August 2005.

Rosenberry, J. (2005b). The effect of content mix on circulation penetration for U.S. daily newspapers. *Journalism & Mass Communication Quarterly 82* (2), 377–397.

Simmons (2001). Kenneth Burke: Symbolic Action. Retrieved May 15, 2007, from: http://www.colostate.edu/Depts/Speech/rccs/theory58.htm.

Sparks, G. (2002). *Media effects research: A basic overview*. Belmont, CA: Wadsworth.

Stempel, G. (2003). Content analysis. In G. Stempel, D. Weaver, & G. C. Wilhoit (Eds.), *Mass communication research and theory* (pp. 209–219). Boston: Allyn & Bacon.

Trochim, W. (2005). The research methods knowledge base (2nd ed.). Retrieved June 6, 2006, from: http://www.socialresearchmethods.net/kb/qual.htm.

Wimmer, R. D., & Dominick, J. R. (2000). *Mass media research: An introduction* (6th ed.). Belmont, CA: Wadsworth.

4 The Research Project in a Theory-Based Course

THIS CHAPTER WILL:

- Describe the requirements for completing an original research project.
- Provide a systematic process to guide the researcher.
- Offer suggestions for conducting research using different designs.
- Describe the process for writing an original research project paper.
- Offer guidelines for presenting the research project to a group.

On the first day of class when the authors' students are asked what they have heard about their theory and research course, they invariably comment, "There is a really, really big paper." And they are right—the course does have a major research project as its largest assignment. This is frequently true on other campuses as well. Rosenberry and Vicker (2006) found that almost 64 percent of instructors in mass communication capstone courses cover research as a major topic area and 62 percent require students to complete a research paper. In some theory courses, instructors limit the assignment to the design of a research proposal, which includes an introduction, review of the literature, and plans for conducting the research but stops short of actual data collection and analysis. This chapter, however, will overview the entire process of planning, conducting, and reporting on an undergraduate research project. It may seem like a daunting challenge, but proceeding systematically through each step in the process will not only make it a manageable experience, but also an immensely satisfying one. Most students report they are proud of their completed projects and enjoy sharing their findings with others.

Getting the Research Project Started

The research project in the theory-based course is different from other papers that students have written in two key ways:

First, it has an original component. Rather than a paper that entails the student looking up articles and writing a report on a topic, the research project also includes some work that has never been done before, such as research on a timely topic, a redesigned or innovative look at a former topic, or a local application of a topic done by others. The research project is designed to be a somewhat scaled-down version of the professional research done by graduate students and professors for academic conferences and scholarly journals. Research at that level is supposed to advance the state of knowledge in the discipline, or create new knowledge that has not been demonstrated before. An undergraduate project might not reach that goal, but still should include a novel or original aspect that makes it unique.

Second, mass communication theory is used to explain the findings in the paper. The purpose of theory is to explain findings to aid the understanding of a specific phenomenon. The research project will be an example of the use of theory to explain a finding.

Choosing a Topic

It is easiest to begin the project with a topic in mind, which provides a reference to follow the steps involved in the project. When choosing a research project topic, it is helpful to pick an area of personal interest or passion; with so many mass media choices, it is easy to identify a general focus. One way is to begin broadly with a particular medium and its subcategories:

- Print: newspapers, magazines, online publications.
- Broadcasting: television, cable, radio, podcasts.
- Advertising: print, broadcast, Web, stealth/viral marketing.
- Public relations: agency, nonprofit, corporate, government.
- Internet: e-mail, instant messaging, Web pages, blogs.
- Film: drama, comedy, children, art, documentaries.

From this list, students can begin to narrow the focus. For example, an interest in television can be further narrowed to a focus on news, sports, advertising, children's programming, reality television, drama, comedy, interview shows, soap operas—the list is seemingly endless. Within the narrowed category, it is wise to refine the focus further. An interest in children's programming could include educational television, commercial networks, advertising, and product placement within children's programs, among others.

An alternative strategy for choosing a topic is to pick something very focused that is the subject of great passion or interest: for example, Facebook, ESPN's *Sports Center*, conservative bloggers, *Oprah*, the campus newspaper, or public access programming, to name just a few. From this focused area, reading extensively on the topic will help determine what types of research questions need to be answered—in other words, what is deserving of study and explanation? This will be the basis for the research, and the theory that will explain the findings.

Finally, most research articles published in scholarly journals conclude by pointing to a direction for future research, so current articles may be a rich source of topic ideas. Trade publications in the field also inspire projects on timely topics in mass media.

Still other students begin by choosing their personal preference from among these broad categories of research: historical research, which looks back at a media phenomenon from the past; descriptive research, which observes things as they occur in the real world; and experimental research, where some of the variables are manipulated under controlled conditions. These three may be done in either a quantitative or a qualitative study, as will be discussed later in this chapter, but this typology may also be a starting point for selecting a topic.

The list in Figure 4.1 provides examples of some of the recent topics that students at the college where the authors teach have used for their research topics.

Narrowing the Research Question

The biggest mistake undergraduate students make in trying to complete a research project is defining the topic too broadly, such as, "What are student patterns of Internet use?" At first, this may seem like an interesting topic, but within the concept of "Internet use," many things could be subjects for a research study: instant messaging, e-mail, research for school assignments, online social network Web sites such as Facebook and MySpace, shopping, and music downloads, just to name a few. Interest in this topic requires a much narrower focus in order to have a manageable topic that can be completed in one semester. "How do students use the Internet for classroom assignments?" is easier in terms of focus for a project, but still fairly broad because of the range of classes and assignments that might be involved.

The research question will eventually become the hypothesis for the study, but most likely not until the review of the literature is completed. It is, however, a starting point for the study and should be articulated as early as possible in the process.

Background Research

A researcher always works in the context of other work in the field. Even the most ground-breaking research is based on the work of others: Jonas Salk developed the polio vaccine using a new process for culturing tissue developed by a Harvard researcher; and those who developed the *oral* polio vaccine built on Salk's work. In any field, before beginning any research project, it is important to ascertain what has been done before, what has been found out, what works, and what does not work. This enables the person designing the study to profit from the errors and successes of those who have researched the topic before. And recall that this is how theory is developed, when research studies build upon one another. Thus, the first step after a topic has been selected is to study the work

FIGURE 4.1   Examples of Student Research Topics

Examples of student projects using content analysis

How does the content of the *NBC Nightly News* compare to *The Daily Show?*
How much foreign news is included in television news reports?
Have the content standards for film ratings changed over time?
Are broadcasters employed by a professional sports team biased in their comments during games involving that team?
How are Italian-Americans portrayed in entertainment programming?
Has the level of substance versus style in sports broadcasts changed over time?
Do reality dating television shows affect the attitudes college students bring to dating?
Are U.S. celebrities over-represented in Canadian and British magazine advertising?

Examples of student projects using survey research

Does use of Internet news sites affect perceptions of the Iraq war?
What are the newspaper readership tendencies among college students?
How aware are college-age women of digital manipulation of magazine photos and its impact on body-image?
Audience awareness of female sports broadcasters.
Audience receptivity to adoption of HDTV.
Is the popularity of televised poker related to playing the game in real life?
Audience perceptions of the war on terror and its effect on the 2004 presidential election.
What kind of image does the public relations profession have?
What characteristics make for an effective television commercial?
Does liquor advertising affect purchase decisions of college students?
Do the behavior and image of female pop stars influence the behavior of teenage girls?
How are views of the legal system influenced by crime-drama entertainment shows?
Do parents who seek stricter regulation of broadcast television expect the government to do the parenting for them?

Examples of student projects using case studies

Publicity techniques used by a community's nonprofit agencies.
Crisis public relations: reaction of a utility to an ice storm that left thousands without power.
Coverage of the Ukrainian "Orange Revolution" in local media.

Examples of student projects using experiments

Does the campus newspaper set the agenda for the campus?
Did viewing the movie *Fahrenheit 9/11* affect voters' perceptions of candidates in 2004?

Examples of student projects using multiple methods

Survey plus content analysis: readership patterns among young adults of free weeklies in the local market.
Content analysis plus focus group: what is the impact of images in fitness magazines on women's attitudes toward fitness and exercise?

that has been done before. In the actual research paper, this section is called the "review of the literature," and it is described in more detail later in this chapter. In the initial stage of the project, however, it is important to acquire a basic understanding of the research designs and findings of the past. Most research studies also end with suggestions for future research, and looking at such suggestions in published research articles might provide guidance for selecting or focusing a topic. At this early stage, the researcher can also take note of what theories might be connected to the chosen topic. Since the theory is the explanation for the findings in the research, this is a valuable tool to guide the researcher.

What is a good starting point for the background research? Students may be tempted to go online and type their topic into Google to see what pops up. While Internet search engines have their value (for example, if a student comes down with hives, information on potential cures can be found online), background for the research project should be based on information found in scholarly or refereed journals. These journals contain research done by scholars in a particular field, such as mass media.

The unique feature of a refereed journal is that the articles submitted undergo a peer-review process. This means that two or three reviewers, who are also experts in the field, review and comment on the article, and recommend to the journal editor whether it should be published. These reviews, which are done anonymously, also often include ideas about revising or improving the article that the editor passes along to the author. This vetting process ensures that the journals will publish research that is credible, heuristic (i.e., it will help to generate more research), and valuable for the field. So students should always start their project research with refereed journals. These can be accessed via a number of databases, including ProQuest, Academic Search Premier, ABI/INFORM, and Expanded Academic ASAP, which are available through most college libraries. College reference librarians are experts in these databases and can help students search on their topics. The easiest way to identify a refereed journal is by the presence of a significant number of in-text citations or footnotes in the article. At the end of the article, there usually will be a reference list or a set of numbered endnotes, depending on the journal editor's preference. An instructor or reference librarian can help if the student still cannot tell whether the source of the article is refereed or not. Figure 4.2 provides examples of some common refereed journals in the mass media field.

Not every topic a student wishes to study, however, will be available in a refereed journal. This is especially true if a timely topic is chosen, such as the latest reality television craze or the most recent political campaign. Refereed journals generally work on a schedule that keeps them months, in some cases years, behind public events. For example, a research paper based on a survey that the authors of this book did in the summer of 2005 was not published in a journal until more than a year later. When refereed journals cannot be found, students may use trade publications, such as *American Journalism Review, Broadcasting and Cable, Editor and Publisher, PR Week, Public Relations Quarterly,* and *Advertising Age.* These publications are generally more timely in their coverage of events than refereed journals and provide a starting point for background information. They

FIGURE 4.2   **Refereed Journals in Mass Communication**

Communication Arts
Communication Quarterly
Communication Research
Critical Studies in Mass Communication
Critical Studies in Media Communication
Discourse & Society
European Journal of Communication
Film Quarterly
Human Communication Research
Journal of Broadcasting & Electronic Media
Journal of Communication
Journal of Communication Inquiry
Journal of Mass Media Ethics
Journal of Media Economics
Journalism & Mass Communication Quarterly
Mass Communication & Society
Media, Culture & Society
New Media & Society
Newspaper Research Journal
Public Opinion Quarterly
Television & New Media
Television Quarterly

lack the peer review, however, that is so valuable in the scholarly field. Finally, if the topic is so new that it is unavailable in the trade publications, students may need to use more general sources such as the *New York Times*, the *Washington Post*, or a weekly news magazine. Note that trade and general publications will rarely include a theory related to explaining the topic. They also will lack any in-text citations or reference list. Trade and general publications may be included in a review of the literature, but they should not be the *only* sources included in it. This is discussed in more detail later in this chapter.

Reading about the topic should provide information about what has already been done in the field that the student wishes to investigate. These articles may also suggest avenues for further research, which in turn provide support for the topic the student wishes to study. This information may be valuable in further refining the research question, and for turning it into a hypothesis, where students predict the outcome of their study.

Research Designs

Chapter 3 describes some of the common methods of research that are used in media studies. This section reviews those methods with suggestions for how they might be applied to a student research project in a mass communication theory or capstone course.

Surveys

Surveys involve collecting information from people in a structured way. This is the most popular form of research, but it should not be chosen just because it is common, because it is easy, or because everyone else in the class is doing a survey. Rather, it should be selected if it is the *best* way to answer the research question. The main components of a survey include:

- **Topic:** The research question or the hypothesis based on the theory being investigated.

- **Sample:** Who will be asked to respond to the survey? How will they be located? Why are *these* people rather than others being selected as respondents? In a quantitative student research project, a minimum of 50 respondents is recommended. More can be used if the survey is short or if populations are easily contacted for participation.

- **Questionnaire:** A broad research topic is broken down into specific questions for the study (which are usually objective but sometimes open-ended). Pre-testing the survey is always wise to make sure that the questions can be understood and the survey is easy to administer. In a student research project, at least six questions beyond the demographic data should be part of the survey for a quantitative analysis.

- **Findings:** When survey answers are compiled, analysis should show relationships among variables as described in the hypothesis. While undergraduate students are not expected to use advanced statistical analyses, percentages should be computed and the numbers should be represented visually using a chart or graph.

The above steps refer to a survey that is done using quantitative methods. Not all surveys involve a large sample size with results that can be shown using statistics and graphs. Some surveys might be done in depth with a fairly small sample size, using the technique of in-depth interviewing as described in Chapter 3. For example, one student was interested in the impact that media deregulation was having on local television news. She conducted personal, in-depth interviews with the news directors of the five local news channels. Her findings were reported in text format, but she also summarized the findings in a chart so the reader could compare the responses from the different professionals.

Another qualitative method for gathering opinions is the use of *focus groups*. Focus groups are personal interviews that involve meeting with 6 to 12 people together, instead of interviewing individuals one at a time. The purpose of a focus group is to get in-depth opinions on a topic, and to also allow the focus group members to build on the ideas of each other. Skill is required on the part of the focus group leader to keep the group on topic, to be sure that all opinions are expressed, and to prevent any one or two members from dominating the group opinion. The authors are members of a communication department that once used focus groups of current students and alumni to determine the feasibility of adding a graduate program. Their college also used student focus groups in determining a new format for the campus newspaper. Findings from focus groups are generally reported in text form only, rather than in a quantitative form with charts, tables, or graphs. In an undergraduate research project, it is recommended that at least two focus groups be used for a topic, with a minimum of six participants in each. For example, one student whose project was about media portrayals of Italian-American women conducted two focus groups: one of working Italian-American mothers and another of stay-at-home Italian-American mothers, to gather their perceptions on the topic.

Content Analyses

Content analysis is the systematic collection and analysis of messages as they appear in media (newspapers, magazines, television shows, etc.), usually through category assignment. The most important features of content analysis are that it be both rigorous and systematic in nature. For example, consider a content analysis to detect bias in a newspaper's coverage of a political candidate. Would it be enough to look through issues of the newspaper and point out examples of biased coverage? No, because such a process does not tell the researcher anything about a pattern of bias, which is what content analysis seeks to establish. In order to detect bias, a researcher would need to set up the categories of bias that she was using, examine every article from the publication about the political candidate, and keep statistical data about the incidence of bias as identified by whatever measure she selected to operationalize the concept (such as a list of key words that reflect favorable or unfavorable opinion about the candidate). Even with such a measurement, finding five articles that contain bias might not be all that meaningful because it could turn out that if all of the articles were examined, only a very small percentage of them would be found to be biased.

In the event that there are too many articles to examine every instance, the researcher still must set up a systematic way to make the observations. For example, only Sunday issues of the newspaper may be used in the content analysis, or only front-page articles, or only those between particular dates. As long as researchers establish systematic and consistent parameters, they should feel confident in their data. One student who compared the news content of the *NBC Nightly News* with the news content of *The Daily Show* watched each show nightly for four weeks to get a sample. Another student who wanted to compare celebrity endorsements in magazine advertising from different countries reviewed all of the ads in different editions (the U.S. edition and two foreign editions) of *Elle* magazine for three monthly issues.

Components of quantitative content analysis include:

- **Topic:** What data will be collected? For what purpose? The research question should be the key to defining the topic and determining how the content analysis will answer the question.

- **Units of analysis:** At what level will data be collected? Content can be defined broadly or narrowly, so defining the topic at this level is important. For example, the content of television news can be defined in terms of full stories (many of which last 90 seconds or more), word choices (which last less than 1 second), number of stories (with or without regard to length), or images (which can be still, live, or recorded), among many others.

■ **Sample:** How will the number of units to be analyzed be determined? It is recommended that at least 6 to 10 units of analysis be used (6 television shows, 6 newspapers, 6 commercials), but this depends on the level of analysis. Scanning an episode of *The Simpsons* for current-event relevance takes less time than doing an interaction analysis for all the dialogue in *Desperate Housewives*. Similarly, a study of advertising clutter in women's fashion magazines can be time-consuming with a single issue often running well over 300 pages.

■ **Operationalization:** What categories will be created? What rules will determine which items go into which categories? This step is important to ensure consistency among those who will code your research (see coder reliability in Chapter 3), or to be sure that the researcher as the sole coder is consistent in categorizing each unit. Practicing with the coding system will reveal flaws and inconsistencies that must be corrected for the final results to make a meaningful statement. For example, one of the criticisms of George Gerbner's studies of television violence is that he classified all violence in the same way—there was no distinction among brutal violence, cartoon violence, or slapstick violence. While Gerbner was consistent in his use of these indices of violence, he had to answer his critics who maintained there was a difference in terms of effect.

■ **Analysis and findings:** How will the relationship among variables in the hypothesis be shown? As with a survey, it is expected that the findings would be described in the text of the paper but also shown in a graph and/or chart.

Experiments

When a researcher conducts an experiment, data are gathered under controlled conditions. There is an effort to control variables that may influence results in the real world. Key features of an experiment include:

■ **Random assignment to groups.** Subjects in an experiment are assigned either to a group that receives the experimental effect or to a control group, which does not receive the effect. This assignment must be done randomly. A familiar example is prescription-drug testing, where one group receives the new drug and another receives a placebo. In a media experiment, one group might watch a television program shown with particular commercials in order to help assess those commercials, while the control group would watch a show with different commercials unrelated to the topic under study.

■ **Manipulation of a key variable** for one (experimental) group versus no manipulation for a second (control) group. With the exception of the experimental effect, each group should be treated essentially the same way. In the random assignment example given above, the types of commercials are the manipulated variable. In another student project, the researcher was interested in finding out whether moviegoers were influenced by reviews done by movie critics. He had one group of students watch and evaluate movies after reading a review written by a movie critic. His control group saw and evaluated the same movies but did not read the critic's reviews.

■ **Surveys or focus-group style interviews in data collection** are a common way of recording the experiment's results. One student had one group read the city's daily newspaper every day for six weeks. A second group read the alternative weekly newspaper. At the end of the time period, he conducted focus group interviews with each group to see how the nature of the news they consumed affected their perceptions of an upcoming election.

■ **Presentation of findings and analysis** depends on the technique used. If quantitative data is generated, this is presented in the findings, similar to the approach used for surveys and content analysis. However, focus groups may yield more textual analysis.

Case Studies

A case study is a descriptive analysis of characteristics surrounding a particular case or situation. Severin and Tankard characterize a case study as trying to learn everything about a subject over a period of time (2001, p. 39). Case studies are most often associated with the qualitative or cultural theories perspective. For example, Sparks says case studies provide information about idiosyncratic cases rather than broad general patterns (2002, p. 12). Most familiar to mass media students are public relations case studies, such as those that examine how organizations handle crises. One student who worked for the local cable company in Rochester, New York, did a case study of how the company communicated with its customers during an ice storm that tore wires down and caused massive service disruptions. His access to the internal memos as well as the external communications allowed him to ascertain the company's effectiveness in reacting to a crisis.

Choosing a Theory

The theory as an explanation may be chosen at any point in the research process. Often a study is actually built around a theory. For example, a student interested in the use of the Web site www.Facebook.com by college students may go into the study knowing that uses and gratifications will be the theory applied to this topic. Other times the theory is revealed through the background research on the topic. If many studies of press coverage of an event use the theory of agenda setting, then this would be an appropriate choice. Some topics will suggest application to more than one theory, which is appropriate for complex topics for which there is more than one application

General Issues around Writing a Research Paper

The research paper in the mass communication theory course is a new writing experience for many students. Not only is there the need for an original component and the need to tie in a theory as explanation, but the outline and writing style are very prescribed. Social science research follows a specific format, which includes:

■ **Writing in the third person:** Occasionally this rule will be broken in scholarly journals and refereed conference papers, but by and large a research paper is written in the third person. Rather than saying, "My research is about . . . ," it would be phrased, "This research examines . . . ." If the writer needs to refer to himself in the paper, he is "the researcher" or "the author."

■ **Attention to references and citations:** Some students may believe that they only need to cite direct quotes, but this is not the case. Any information that is not the writer's own idea must be cited. General information that is widely known (e.g., "Instant messaging is popular among college students") does not need to be cited. However, specific facts and information ("There are 55 million registered users of AOL Instant Messenger") must have a citation. In addition, the general rule of thumb is that the citations must be provided in such a way that the reader can easily locate any of the sources.

■ **Citations in the research paper:** Students should include in-text citations as well as a reference list or bibliography at the end. There are several different styles for annotating a paper. Three of the most popular are style guides developed by the American Psychological Association (APA), Modern Language Association (MLA), and University of Chicago (Chicago style). Each style guide has its own rules for how to format in-text citations and also for the type of information and how it is presented (order, capitalization, punctuation, etc.) in footnotes, endnotes, or a reference list. Some disciplines actually specify a certain style; for example, psychology uses APA exclusively. Mass media often uses APA, but some publications use MLA or Chicago. Some professors specify a certain format for their students and others let students use the style with which they are most familiar. The key is that the writer must use one style throughout the paper, rather than combining elements of different styles within the same paper. Most college libraries have helpful guidelines for citing sources on their Web sites. A thorough description of APA and MLA styles can be found at Purdue University's Online Writing Lab or OWL at www.owl.english.purdue.edu/owl. (The references in this book are formatted according to APA, and readers are invited to look at them, especially at the ends of the chapters, as an example of the type of information needed in an effective reference as well as an example of APA style.)

■ **Avoiding plagiarism:** The use of online resources to complete assignments has increased the incidence of plagiarism. The authors' institution posts its academic honesty policy on the college intranet page, where it defines plagiarism as "handing in academic work in any format which is not the original work of the student and is not properly documented as the work of another (e.g., word-for-word copying, patching together various sections of others' work, or paraphrasing the work of another)" (www.sjfc.edu/PDFs/AcademicHonesty.pdf). The authors' experience has shown that some plagiarism is the result of misunderstanding by students as to what constitutes academic dishonesty, which is why it is important for students to understand their institutions' policies.

While plagiarism has increased, however, so has the ability of professors to detect and identify the sources of the plagiarized work. Search engines such as Google as well as software such as Turnitin.com have enabled professors to better ensure that the work students submit will be 100 percent their own. Anything else is plagiarism, which is a serious offense both academically and professionally. Communications professionals who plagiarize the work of others are fired from their jobs; students can expect severe repercussions as well. The authors and many of their colleagues assign a grade of "zero" on any assignment that the instructor discovers has been plagiarized, with no chance of extra credit or re-doing the assignment. At many institutions, plagiarism is also punishable by further sanctions, up to and including expulsion from school. The lessons are simple: do not plagiarize and, if in doubt, use a citation in the paper. As a final note, colleges that use www.Turnitin.com have a feature whereby a student may check the paper before submitting it to the instructor for evidence of plagiarism. Students who take advantage of this opportunity rarely get into trouble with plagiarism.

The Process of Writing a Research Paper

This section explains in detail each part of the research report as it should be written.

Introduction.   The introduction should answer the following questions:

■ Why is this project being done?
■ What interesting or important information will come out of it?
■ What is the "road map" (the scope and means of investigation) for the project?

In order to get the reader to begin thinking about the subject, the introduction should begin with a "hook" that relates to the topic. Beginning with a sentence such as, "This paper examines agenda setting in the case of the Shoe Bomber," does not do anything to grab the reader's attention. Just as a speech should not begin with the thesis, the research paper should be introduced in a way that draws the readers in and makes them want to care about reading further and learning more about the topic:

> On December 22, 2001, Richard Reid boarded an American Airlines flight in Paris headed for Miami. Midway through the flight, a fellow passenger screamed when she noticed that Reid was trying to light a fuse protruding from his shoes. Other passengers overpowered him and a doctor sedated him. It was found that his shoes were filled with explosives and that Reid intended to blow up the plane over the Atlantic Ocean (Elliott, 2001). Thus began the saga of the man who came to be known as the Shoe Bomber. As a follow-up to the September 11, 2001, attacks, it was a defining moment in agenda setting in the War on Terror.

The introduction should then go on to set the stage and clearly lay out the purpose and scope of the project, so the reader knows what to expect. Near the end of the introduction, the hypothesis (or testable proposition) should be clearly stated. In terms of length, the introduction will probably be two to three standard, double-spaced pages.

Theoretical Basis. The theory section should provide:

- The theory (or theories) that underlies (or underlie) this research.
- A brief description of specifics and background of theory, from a properly cited source.
- An explanation of why this particular theory is appropriate.
- A description of how the project will use theory to predict or explain how real-world phenomena *relate to each other* as stated in the hypothesis.

The theory may be mentioned in the introduction, but providing its own section will ensure that it is addressed in sufficient detail, usually about one or two standard pages.

Literature Review. The review of the literature is that point in the paper where the writer provides the background research on the topic. In this section, the writer should:

- Describe what other researchers have done on related topics.
- Use this research to justify why this project is being done: in what ways is it similar to but also distinctly different from what has been done before?

The review of the literature should be drawn mostly from scholarly sources from refereed publications. Trade journals or general literature may also be included but should not be the primary source of information in the review. Substandard material, including most Web-based information (such as information from Wikipedia), should *not* be used in the research paper.

In reviewing what others have done before, students do not have to give detailed descriptions of each study. Generally speaking, an overview of the study's purpose, subjects, and findings will suffice. Each study's review can usually be completed in a single paragraph. Here is an example of the review of one study from a student paper on the under-representation of female athletes in the media (Shaller, 2006):

> Studies have been done to prove these ideas [that women are portrayed differently from men] true. One study, found in Knight and Giuliano's article, "He's a Laker; She's a Looker: The Consequences of Gender-stereotypical Portrayals of Male and Female Athletes," demonstrates how attractive female athletes are perceived in the media. Knight and Giuliano presented participants in a survey with an image of a physically attractive female athlete and a list of her accomplishments. They were given a second image of another female athlete, not so attractive, but with similar athletic accomplishments. The students were also given the same two types of images for male athletes. They were asked to rate the athlete on various characteristics based on his or her appearance (Knight & Giuliano, 2001). The results were parallel to the authors' ideas. The female athlete depicted in terms of her attractiveness was seen as more attractive than the one depicted in terms of her athleticism only. The male athletes had no difference in their perception of being attractive. Also, those athletes whose coverage focused on their attractiveness were seen as less aggressive, less talented and less heroic (Knight & Giuliano, 2001).

A typical research project published in a scholarly journal will have a deep, thorough review of the literature, usually with several dozen citations drawn from 15, 20, or more previously published research articles. For undergraduate research, the bar is not quite as high, but even at that level a good review of the literature will contain a minimum of three to five studies from refereed publications. For some topics or some theories that have been extensively researched, it might be necessary to include even more to provide the proper context for the current study. This material from scholarly publications may be supplemented by trade or general publications where appropriate.

What should students do if there are no research studies in their particular topic area? This is frequently a problem when a student is doing a very current topic, such as an up-to-date controversy in the media or a new form of media such as a new reality show. In the event that, after searching databases and enlisting the help of a reference librarian, no research in refereed journals can be found, here are two suggestions:

■ Find research in an allied topic area. For example, when one of the authors was researching the use of role models in teaching public speaking, she found that no research had been done specifically in that field. However, there was research that examined using role models in teaching interviewing. Those studies formed the basis for her review of the literature. (And, by the way, they also provided the theoretical foundation, which was Bandura's social learning theory;

see Chapter 6.) So, research on a new television show might be based on research about another show in the same genre (e.g., other sitcoms, crime dramas, reality shows, or news magazines). One student who did an original research project on perception of crime in television shows obtained most of his background research from studies of crime movies.

■ Locate research studies that use the same theory. A review of the critical research using the theory that will be related to the project can often yield relevant research for a project.

If even one or two articles that are relevant to the student's research study can be found, the literature review can be expanded by harvesting the reference lists of those articles. In other words, by reviewing some of the same articles that those authors did in compiling their literature reviews, the researcher can get a more complete perspective on the topic being studied. The reference list should provide enough information about each source—author's name, and date and journal of publication—for it to be found in a database search. Note that this should not turn into plagiarism of the other article or a point-by-point repetition of its literature review. Rather, it should be seen as a way for the researcher to expand the pool of original sources that can be reviewed for information relevant to the new study that the researcher is completing. Looking at sources used by other scholars working on similar topics will provide extra insight for the researcher into whatever he or she is investigating. Finally, students can use trade journals and general sources, as well as expert opinions on the topic, to bolster the review. But refereed journal studies must be at the heart of the literature review to ensure the study's credibility.

Methodology. The methodology section (sometimes called "collection of data") should include:

■ The means used to collect/observe data.
■ The reason why this method was chosen, and what makes it the most appropriate method.
■ A restatement of the hypothesis, elaborating on it.
■ The choice of variables that were studied, and why.
■ How the variables were operationalized.
■ A description of the data collection (e.g., number of surveys, dates collected, who they were collected from, how the sample was drawn, etc.).
■ A survey or rating form if it was used to gather the information. (Often, this is included as an appendix to the paper with a notation in the "methodology" section for readers to examine it there.)

Findings. This section, sometimes called the "analysis of the data," should include:

■ A description of the research findings in the text of the paper.
■ A presentation of charts, tables, and/or graphs with data findings from the study.

In this part of the research paper, the author does not draw any conclusions or make any comments; the findings are presented in an objective and unbiased way. Here is an example of a paragraph from the text findings in Jessica Shaller's paper:

> The analysis showed that 266 out of the 281 (*Sports Illustrated*) issues' covers featured a male athlete. The remaining 15 featured women. Ninety-five percent of *Sports Illustrated* publications from January 2000 to November 2005 portrayed a man on the front of the magazine. Seventy percent of males pictured on the covers were depicted as actively participating in their respective sports. Only 40 percent of females were seen in action.

Discussion.   The discussion is the section where the researcher gets the opportunity to draw the entire project together. It generally includes a summary overview of the findings of the study. This is followed by an analysis or interpretation of the findings: Was the hypothesis supported? If so, what does that mean? If the hypothesis was not supported, what does that mean? Were any extraneous variables noted that might have had an effect on the study? For example, if the study analyzed educational programming and occurred during a public television station's fund drive, that would have an impact on the results of the research. Some students have found their research affected when there is a catastrophic news event, such as the September 11, 2001, attacks, which pre-empted other programming and news coverage for days. Similarly, doing research during a holiday season might affect programming and/or advertising in a way that might not occur during other times of the year.

The discussion section is also the key area where the researcher uses the theory as an explanation for the findings. Did the study generate evidence that seems to support the theory? If so, what does that mean? If it did not support the theory, how might that be explained? Is the theory called into question?

Finally, in the discussion, the researcher can add some commentary (where appropriate) on the issues examined in the research.

Paper's Conclusion.   The conclusion in the research paper is the final statement about the subject, the research, and sometimes the theory. It is generally no more than two or three paragraphs, and usually suggests directions for future research in this area. In some research articles, the conclusion is part of the discussion section.

Paper's References.   The final section in the research paper is the references. The goal of the reference list is to provide information that would allow an interested reader to find the cited article. A complete citation includes:

- Author's name.
- Date of publication.
- Name of the book, book chapter, or article title. Name of the publication for articles from a scholarly journal, trade magazine, or newspaper. Articles from journals and magazines usually include page numbers as well. Recall

that the goal is to be sure that any reader of the paper would be easily able to locate these sources.

References should follow the particular style, such as APA or MLA, that was used in the text of the paper. (As noted earlier, the references in this book are formatted according to APA, and offer an example of the type of information needed in an effective reference as well as an example of APA style.)

Final Review.   When the research paper is completed, it should be proofread and edited carefully, first by the author, then by a friend (or two). Students completing research projects for the same class can help by proofreading each other's work. After working on a paper for an extended period of time, the writer is often unable to catch writing or comprehension errors. Even professors ask colleagues to proof and edit papers before they submit them to journals or professional conferences (or even proposals sent internally to the dean or provost).

Students who struggle with writing should allow time for an appointment at the college writing center, to work with a tutor. Errors in the paper such as misspellings, poor grammar, and incorrect punctuation detract from its message. It is important to make sure that the paper has none of these errors in order to allow the reader—the professor—to focus on the content that the writer is presenting.

Presenting the Research Project

Students in mass communication programs generally are used to presenting their ideas in front of their classes. Many programs require classes that include public speaking skills, and even those that do not have such requirements have classes such as advertising, broadcasting, and public relations where in-class presentations are common. So it should come as no surprise that presentations are part of a theory-based course. Rosenberry and Vicker (2006) found that more than two-thirds of capstone instructors require individual and group presentations.

Since public presentations are generally covered early in the students' academic program, the notes below are meant as a reminder of some of the more salient points for a professional presentation, whether to a class of peers, a panel of professors, or a group of media professionals.

Presentation Tips

The project presentation should summarize the original research project. Regardless of how much time is allotted, it is impossible to discuss everything that is included in the written paper. At the same time, focusing on the most important components should make for a credible presentation. This should include:

- Purpose of the project
- Short statement of what has been done before

- Procedures
- Findings
- Conclusions (making sure to mention which theory was used)

Whether it is the research project or another topic that is presented, the following guidelines can help to make any presentation more professional:

Organization

- A good presentation has an introduction, body, and conclusion.
- A good presentation is well-organized and provides transitions linking the ideas.

Delivery

- Good delivery is extemporaneous, is practiced, and uses notes.
- Good delivery means the presenter does not read verbatim from notes or slides.
- Good delivery means the presenter makes good eye contact with the audience.

Visual Aids

- Visuals that accompany a presentation—such as PowerPoint slides, overheads, or posters/flip charts—should always include key words or phrases, never full sentences.
- Speakers should practice with their visuals beforehand so they know how/when to show them.
- Speakers should not turn their backs on the audience and read from their visuals.
- If video clips are shown, they should not be more than two to three minutes total of the presentation time.

Other Considerations

- Time: students should know the time requirements and practice to stay within the limits. Depending on the number of presenters and time available, most undergraduate research presentations will run between 5 and 10 minutes, with a few extra minutes for questions and discussion.
- Question and answer: Students should be prepared for the question and answer session by anticipating questions, listening carefully to the question, and answering in a concise and confident manner.

Summary

The original theory-based research project is generally longer and more complicated than work done in any prior class, which makes it a challenge for many students. By breaking it down into its components and focusing on each part individually, however, the project is far more manageable. Students who do this, and who keep on top of the project throughout the semester rather than trying to do it all in a rush in just a few days before it is due, often find that they have created something special and interesting. The majority of students are quite proud of their original research projects, because it is the key product of a course that is meant to integrate and extend the learning they have experienced throughout their college careers. Some students have even used their research projects as additions to their portfolios and in applications for graduate school programs, where the experience of having already done original research is invaluable.

QUESTIONS FOR DISCUSSION/ APPLICATION EXERCISES

1. Find an article from a scholarly journal on a topic that interests you and examine the ending of it for ideas about further research into the topic. (Sometimes, authors will even put these under a subheading that identifies this section.) One of them may provide an idea that you can use to formulate your own research project.

2. Deconstruct an article from a scholarly journal—either one you find on your own or one that your teacher provides—and analyze the various sections of it to answer questions about it such as:

   - How well does the introduction set up the article and provide the reader with an idea of where it is going?

   - Does the article explicitly cite a theory? If so, which one? How does it help to predict or explain the phenomenon that the article seeks to study? (Note: Although this book, and this chapter in particular are focused on theory-driven research, not all articles are based in theory, even those published in leading journals.)

   - What is the author's hypothesis? In a theory-based article, how does the theory relate to the hypothesis?

   - How many sources are cited in the literature review? How does the author use them to create a context for his or her present work, or justify its similarities and differences from what has already been published?

   - What methodology is used? Is it quantitative (e.g., statistics gathered from a survey or content analysis) or qualitative (e.g., a case study or textual analysis)?

   - What variables are used? Which is the dependent variable and which is the independent one? In a quantitative study, how are they operationalized? In a qualitative study, how are they evaluated and presented with textual evidence? In what ways do the variables help to prove the hypothesis? (Note: As discussed in Chapter 2, hypotheses are never definitively "proved," but the term is used in a looser sense here meaning "provide evidence or support for.")

■ In the discussion section, what does the author say about the significance of the research study's findings? Does the evidence collected and presented in the article find support for the hypothesis? What does the author say it means that the hypothesis either was or was not supported?

REFERENCES

Rosenberry, J., & Vicker, L. (2006, Autumn). Capstone courses in mass communication programs. *Journalism & Mass Communication Educator 61*(3), 267–284.

Severin, W., & Tankard, J. (2001). *Communication theories: Origins, methods and uses in the mass media* (5th ed.). New York: Addison Wesley Longman.

Shaller, J. (2006, April). *Female athletes in the media: Under representation and inadequacy*. Presented at Undergraduate Conference for Research in Mass Communication, Rochester Institute of Technology, Henrietta, NY.

Sparks, G. (2002). *Media effects research: A basic overview*. Belmont, CA: Wadsworth.

UNIT TWO

Mass Communication Theories

CHAPTER 5
Early Developments in Mass Communication Theory

CHAPTER 6
The Individual Perspective on Mass Communication Theory

CHAPTER 7
The Sociological Perspective on Mass Communication Theory

CHAPTER 8
Alternative Paradigms of Critical and Cultural Studies

5 Early Developments in Mass Communication Theory

THIS CHAPTER WILL:

- Provide a definition and description of mass communication as a social practice.
- Describe how the discipline of mass communication research is rooted in older social sciences, especially psychology and sociology.
- Describe some of the earliest research into mass communication processes by researchers in those fields (often considered the founders of communication research) and discuss how their work provided a basis for later research.
- Outline several specific early research themes of mass communication, including:
  - Bullet theory
  - Propaganda and public opinion studies
  - Information theory and cybernetics
  - Lasswell's structure-and-function models
  - Two-step flow and reinforcement theories
  - Limited effects paradigm
- Discuss how theory evolves and changes over time, and relate these historical developments to the current era of research.

In our "live-for-the-moment, what-have-you-done-for-me-lately?" culture, many people do not place much value in understanding the past. But a scene from the popular Disney movie *The Lion King* illustrates the value of using the past as an aid to understanding the present.

The wise old baboon, Rafiki, comes upon Simba as a young adult still living in the wilderness. Rafiki reminds Simba that he is the legitimate heir to the throne of the lion king and that once upon a time he aspired to take it. "That was a long time ago," Simba replies, stating that he has learned to live in the present ("hakuna matata") and that events from the past don't matter to him any more. Rafiki responds to this statement by hitting Simba over the head with his walking stick. When Simba asks, "Why did you do that?" Rafiki replies "It doesn't matter; it's in the past." He then swings the stick at Simba again. But this time, the young lion knows what is coming and ducks to avoid being hit. Simba, obviously a quick study, has learned Rafiki's lesson: knowledge of the past is vital in understanding the present (and future).

A Historical Perspective

So, any study of the current state of communication as a discipline, and the active theories that comprise it, needs to start with a look at the historical theories that preceded these modern ideas. This includes a review of theories that, over time, have been superseded by later research and in many ways made obsolete. One of the interesting aspects of communication is that its history as a formal field of study is short enough, only 80 years or so, that some of the key developments are within living memory of many people in the field today. The field has come a long way in its short history, however, as the earliest theories have evolved into newer ones that seek to predict and explain mass communication more subtly and precisely. Nevertheless, it is worthwhile to study these older theoretical approaches because they provide the "genetic material" from which contemporary theories are drawn. And because, as Simba learned the hard way, knowing about the past really does help in understanding the present.

The Evolution of Theory

To briefly recap some previously presented concepts, theory is a way to explain or predict the relationship of certain phenomena. For example, Albert Einstein's famous theory of $e = mc^2$ seeks to explain the relationship of energy to matter; Charles Darwin's theory of natural selection seeks to explain how different species of plants and animals evolved.

These examples come from physics and biology, two of the disciplines known as *natural* sciences that try to explain the physical world around us. (Others in this category include chemistry, astronomy, and geology, to name a few.) Communication theory is generally thought of as belonging to a different set of disciplines called *social* sciences, or fields of study that seek to explain how society functions and how people function within it. "Social" and "society" have the same root, the Latin word *socius*, which means "companion." The social sciences include, to name just a few, economics, anthropology, political science, psychology, and sociology.

Social science is a more recent intellectual development than natural science, which has been around for thousands of years. Natural sciences such as astronomy and chemistry trace their roots to the efforts of ancient civilizations to develop "scientific theories" to explain the natural world around them. For example, back in the second century, the astronomer Ptolemy theorized that the Sun, Moon, and planets were bodies that revolved around the Earth, a scientific breakthrough that replaced mythological explanations such as the Sun being the chariot of one of the gods. A few hundred years before that, the Greek philosopher Empedocles developed an early theory of chemistry that said matter was composed of the four elements of earth, air, fire, and water. But the social sciences are far newer. The term *psychology* was first used in the 1500s; modern economics can be traced to the publication of Adam Smith's *An Inquiry into the Nature and Causes of the Wealth of Nations* in 1776; and the term *sociology* (the study of people and their associations) is attributed to Auguste Comte, a philosopher and intellectual who coined the term in the 1830s. And communication as a distinct field of study has fully emerged only within the past several decades.

All fields of scientific inquiry, whether natural science or social science, have a history of theoretical development. All of them have evolved over time with later discoveries built upon the foundations of earlier ones. For example, chemistry has progressed from Empedocles' four elements to a periodic table consisting of more than 100 elements. An important thing to note, however, is that Empedocles' basic idea—that matter was made up of certain elemental units—has the same basis as modern chemistry. New discoveries bring more power, sophistication, and subtlety to a field of study. This kind of evolutionary development has been going on in the natural sciences for thousands of years, and in many social sciences for a few hundred years. The same dynamics can be applied to the discipline of communication, even though it is a much newer field of study.

A generally held belief that dominates thinking in a discipline is often called a *paradigm*. Various theories can operate within a given paradigm, which is an umbrella set of assumptions or ways of thinking about an aspect of the world. Ptolemy's Earth-centered universe is an example of a natural-science paradigm that held sway for hundreds of years. When a new way of thinking replaces an older one, such as the discoveries by Copernicus and Galileo that the Earth revolved around the Sun rather than vice versa, it is called a *paradigm shift*.

Even though communication theory is only a few decades old, it already has developed different paradigms. Eminent communication theorist Denis McQuail, for instance, describes the idea that information transmission has a measurable effect on recipients as the "dominant paradigm" of communication study and contrasts it with the "alternative paradigm" represented by cultural and critical studies (McQuail, 2005, p. 65). Stanley Baran and Dennis Davis discuss five "eras" of communication research, starting with the mass society perspective, followed by the social scientific/empirical perspective, the consolidation of studies done in the empirical era to create the limited effects paradigm, the emergence of the cultural and critical studies perspective, and finally the current paradigm, often described as the "moderate effects" paradigm (Baran & Davis, 2006).

This book follows a similar approach. This chapter traces the origins of mass communication theory in the direct effects/transmission model paradigm, and then describes how the limited effects paradigm emerged from scholarly investigation of this original paradigm that illustrated its shortcomings. This discussion is followed by a look at how limited effects gave way to the modern era, which encompasses both the critical theory/cultural studies approach as well as a variety of effects theories that describe significant effects of mass communication, either upon individuals, upon large groups, or upon society as a whole. But at the same time, these theories do not go so far as to suggest the broad-based, immediate, powerful, direct, and uniform influence of the media that the first historical paradigm presumed.

Definition
Paradigm: A predominant way of conceiving a situation. A number of specific theories can all be seen as valid within a paradigm.

For some students with a good memory, this discussion of the origins and definition of mass communication may seem like review from an introduction to mass communication class, but it is presented with the intent of providing a smooth transition to understanding the nature and evolution of mass communication theory.

Origins of Mass Communication

Before even thinking about mass communication as a discipline, and about the paradigms and theories that help to explain how it works, it first is necessary to consider mass communication as a human activity. One of the reasons mass communication is such a new academic discipline is that mass-mediated communication among human beings is also a relatively recent development. People have been looking at the stars and wondering what the world around them was made from since before recorded human history, so it makes sense that sciences such as astronomy and chemistry should be our most ancient ones. Humans have not engaged in mass communication for nearly as long; in fact for nearly all of human history, communication has *not* been in "mass" form, which comes from the same root as "massive," meaning in large quantities.

Arguably, the thing that makes human beings unique is our ability to engage in *symbolic* communication. The mere fact of communicating is not uniquely human because other creatures also communicate with one another. But only humans use symbols, especially spoken and written language, to convey concepts and ideas. This stands in contrast with other creatures' communication skills that are limited to simple messages rooted in instincts such as survival. For instance, bees do a "hive dance" to direct other members of the colony to food sources; birds and even whales "sing"; and anyone who owns a dog or cat can tell a playful bark from a threatening growl or a contented purr from an angry hiss. All of these are communication tools, but of a fundamentally different nature than the way humans interact with each other using symbols such as language and visual imagery.

Personal versus Mass Methods

The dominant way people have engaged in this symbolic communication throughout human history has *not* been in mass form at all. The rhetorical tradition of "mass" communication as one message to many people (as opposed to interpersonal and small group) does go back a few thousand years. Aristotle's

Rhetoric gave instruction to speakers on how to persuade an audience. But even then, the communicators were speaking personally to a crowd of people within earshot. Without the aid of microphones and amplifiers, mass communication was delivered by men with booming voices to audiences in specially designed amphitheaters that would help the sound to travel.

But as we generally use the term today, mass communication refers to communication that is mediated or enhanced by technology. It is generally one-way, communicator to audience, with little opportunity for immediate feedback from the audience, although new media technologies are changing even that.

Technology and Mass Communication

Although writing was developed in Phoenicia, Egypt, and China many centuries ago, large-scale reproduction of any individual set of symbols was not even possible until the invention of movable type about 500 hundred years ago (around 1450). Even then, the earliest printed materials had small press runs (the number of copies printed) compared to, say, a contemporary newspaper, magazine, or best-selling book. And while this technology for reproducing, preserving, and transmitting written work in large quantities (the printing press) has been around for the several hundred years since then, the technologies for recording, preserving, and transmitting sounds and moving images appeared much more recently—only within the past century and a half.

Thus, mass media are truly a modern development and, like many other modern devices, an invention of the Industrial Revolution. The first media to be produced and distributed on a large scale to massive audiences were the "penny press" newspapers that developed in American cities in the mid-nineteenth century. Prior to that, the vast majority of communication was personal and done without the aid of any sort of media. Community and family traditions took the form of oral histories or hand-written letters from one individual to another; current events were passed along among individuals through discussions in the town square or at social gatherings. Even the colonial era and early nineteenth-century press from which the penny papers evolved consisted primarily of political and business-oriented publications with narrow readerships.

The beginnings of the modern newspaper era, which can be seen as the dawn of American mass communication, are traced to the founding of the *New York Sun* by Benjamin Day in 1833. Day's success was imitated in other American cities that were growing rapidly because of both immigration from Europe and migration within the United States of people from the countryside to the cities in search of factory jobs. The expanding city populations provided the audience. The inventions of the Industrial Revolution—notably steam engines, which drove ever-larger and more sophisticated printing presses, and the telegraph, which allowed information to be sent instantly over great distances to aid in reporting—provided publishers with the means to serve those large audiences with up-to-date news (Emery, 1962). Within a few decades, newspapers had become big businesses, bringing great wealth and power to press barons such as E.W. Scripps, Joseph Pulitzer, and William Randolph Hearst.

The important point here is that within a period of about 50 years, from the middle of the 1800s to the end of that century, Americans had gone from hearing about news and events from their friends and neighbors in the town square or at the church social to reading about it in the newspaper. And as they consumed this information, so did thousands of other residents of their communities. Instead of an individualized version of an event told or written by someone the recipient knew, everyone read the same account provided by some journalist whom they did not personally know. The era of institutionalized communication to massive audiences using modern technology had begun.

This era accelerated as the twentieth century got under way. Magazines, books, and printed advertising (such as the Sears-Roebuck and Montgomery-Ward catalogues) joined newspapers in competing for American audiences' attention. Edison's phonograph (1870s), motion picture cinemas (1890s), and radio (commercialized in the 1920s) represented the dawning of electronic media. Television was first demonstrated in the 1920s but took hold in the American and European markets only after World War II ended in 1945. The technological pace and variety of mass communication methods has been growing and expanding since, introducing (among many other innovations) satellite communications; digitization of audio, video, and text files; and the Internet.

It took thousands of years for astronomy to evolve from the ancient Greeks' observation of the "wanderers" in the nighttime sky—the planets visible to the unaided eye—to current investigations of planets orbiting other stars that may be like our own. But it has taken communication only a little more than 100 years to go from Marconi's original experiments with wireless radio-wave communication to high definition television, satellite radio, and podcasts.

Defining Mass Communication

Clearly, newspapers, magazines, motion pictures, and radio and television broadcasts are methods of mass communication; in the context of communication scholarship, the messages sent through such media draw the most attention. But in a more general sense, what constitutes mass communication, and what are its characteristics? For Aristotle, it was shouting in the amphitheater. But in the contemporary era, is a teacher in front of a class "mass communicating"? Would the answer be different if it were a seminar of 15 students versus a lecture with 500?

Characteristics of the Mass Communication Process.   Although ours is a media-saturated society, and individuals absorb uncountable media messages every day, much of the communication that people engage in still is non-massive and non-mediated: conversation with friends, family, and associates, in instrumental settings such as the workplace and classroom, and in social settings such as the home or dining hall. Personal-yet-anonymous conversations with, say, a store clerk or bank teller are still commonplace, and even many "mediated" communications are of the personal variety as well, via telephone and computer network (e-mail and instant messaging).

But mass communication messages are very different from these interpersonal ones. Among the things that set mass communication messages apart are their scale, direction, impersonality, simultaneity, and transience. All of these characteristics influence the content and style of the messages and their effect on their audiences.

- **Scale:** The word "mass" indicates that the scale of a message's reach is large, much larger than one person talking to two, or four, or 14 others. Many newspapers and magazines distribute hundreds of thousands of copies; millions of people may tune in to a popular television show or listen to a popular song. Creating messages on such a large scale requires the use of technologies that tend to be large-scale themselves, and correspondingly complicated and expensive, such as printing presses and broadcast facilities. Because this technology is used to *mediate* the message—literally, to come in the middle of the sender and the recipient to help transfer the message—mass-communicated messages are frequently called mass-mediated messages, and the tools for sending them are called mass media or simply "media."

- **Direction:** Mass-mediated messages employ what is called a one-way flow. A conversation between two individuals generally contains much back and forth exchange; even a larger-group "conversation" such as a classroom lecture-discussion allows for a two-way flow of information. But in mass communication the message goes in one direction, from creator to recipient. Any feedback that is provided to the sender by the receiver is delayed and indirect, similar to a letter to the editor of the newspaper or a decline in the number of viewers of a television show as it loses popularity with its audience.

- **Impersonality/anonymity:** Related to the one-way flow, the creator of the message does not know who might receive it. And while message creators may know *some* of the recipients personally—journalists who write stories can count on their sources and colleagues reading them, for example—they cannot possibly know all of the audience members who might see or hear the message. Unlike interpersonal or small-group messages that have a small set of designated recipients, mass-communicated messages are deliberately public, meant to be accessed by anyone who may be interested in them.

- **Simultaneity:** Not only is the message large-scale, anonymous, and public, it is also sent to all the potential recipients at the same time. The messages may be received at slightly different times; some people may record a television or radio broadcast, or read the morning newspaper in the evening. But at least from the creator's standpoint, the message is released to all of the potential recipients at the same time, and most of the messages get the audience's attention within a short frame of time.

■ **Transience:** A characteristic that is related to the simultaneous nature of mass-communicated messages is that they tend to be consumed and disappear within a short time. A television or radio program has to be consumed literally as it is produced (broadcast), unless it has been recorded (which is, of course, becoming more common with digital recording devices). Some media do have more "shelf life" than others; a popular movie will stay in theaters for a few weeks, and a weekly or monthly magazine may be kept around until the next issue arrives. But in general, the nature of the message is transient, designed to be replaced by a new message from the same medium in fairly short order.

■ **Audience:** Mass media audiences have attributes that mirror these qualities of the messages and senders. McQuail identifies characteristics of the mass audience as large in number, widely dispersed, heterogeneous, and not organized to any degree, as well as non-interactive with the senders and anonymous to them (2005, p. 57).

Implications of Mediation.   The symbolic nature of communication combined with some of these characteristics of the mass process give a special importance to the study of mass media forms and practices. McQuail (2005, p. 83) notes that mass media have a number of perceived purposes, which include:

- Providing a window on events or a mirror to events.
- Filtering or serving as gatekeeper for information reaching the audience.
- Being a guide to interpret events.
- Offering a forum for the presentation of ideas.
- Disseminating information.

All of these purposes are slightly different in meaning for the audience, but what they have in common is that all of them provide a view of the world outside the audience member's personal experience. In fact, most of the contact people have with the world outside of their immediate lives comes through mediated communication, which has powerful implications for the organization and functioning of human society. This is because the reality that people experience in this way is affected by the symbols they are exposed to and the media through which those symbols come to them. The media organizations that are responsible for creating and delivering symbolic messages are social institutions themselves, with different reasons for existence and different motives for engaging in communication. This means that "mediation is unlikely to be an entirely neutral process. The 'reality' will always be to some extent selected and constructed and there will be certain consistent biases" (McQuail, 2005, p. 85).

New Media Blur the Lines.   The characteristics described above and McQuail's description of the purposes that media fulfill come from a classical view of the mass communication process. But development of the Internet has called into question some of the traditional distinctions attributed to mass communication, and in essence has blurred the lines between mass and interpersonal communication. For instance, it is no longer necessary to have access to a printing press or broadcast facility to reach thousands or millions of people with a message. A connection to the World Wide Web and some fairly simple, inexpensive software allow anyone to post messages that can be seen literally around the world by anyone else with adequate access to the network.

The development of two-way, computer-mediated technology in the mid-1990s forced communications scholars to reconsider what was, at that time, the most traditional division in the field: the distinction between interpersonal and mass-mediated communication. Traditionally, research into the connection of mass and personal communication focused on how interpersonal communication mitigated or altered effects of mass mediated communication, such as the two-step flow theory discussed later in this chapter. But Rafaeli and Sudweeks (1997) studied threaded-message groups and called them "(either) the largest form of conversation or the smallest form of mass communication." This meant rethinking the defining characteristics of each approach, especially the notion that mass media strictly consists of a one-way flow of information.

Other scholars discussed how distinctions such as number of recipients (traditionally high for mass media, low for interpersonal), and potential for feedback (low for mass media, high for interpersonal) were becoming blurred by computerized two-way communication, noting that "The new interactive technologies have certain of the characteristics of interpersonal channels, and certain of the qualities of mass media channels" (Reardon & Rogers, 1988, p. 297).

When the Internet experienced booming growth in the late 1990s, the confusion expanded along with it. The Internet "didn't fit researchers' ideas about mass media, locked, as they have been, into models of print and broadcast media," according to Morris and Ogan (1996), who added: "Computer-mediated communication at first resembled interpersonal communication and was relegated to the domain of other fields." But Morris and Ogan were among the first to propose treating the Internet as a mass medium, albeit one that "contains many different configurations of communication" and one that "plays with the source-message-receiver features of the traditional mass communication model, sometimes putting them into entirely new configurations."

Despite these "new configurations" emerging from Internet-mediated communication, plenty of media forms still operate along the traditional lines associated with mass communication. Their continued existence illustrates the importance of recognizing the difference between the sending and receiving of mass-mediated messages and those received through interpersonal or small-group channels. Furthermore, when communication research and scholarship began a few decades ago, the difference between mass and personal communication (reviewed in the historical portion of this chapter) was more pronounced than it is now. As the emerging social phenomenon of mass communication evolved and began to take hold in the early twentieth century, it was natural for people to wonder about how it was going to affect the society in which it existed. Some of that wondering turned into more serious, scholarly inquiry, which helped to create the first mass communication theories.

The Discipline of Mass Communication

The earliest evaluations of how individuals and society might be affected by mass communication came from existing social science disciplines that, not coincidentally, investigate how people act and interact on the individual level and in social organizations, namely psychology, sociology, and political science. Many of the "founding fathers" (and they were all men) of communication as a field of study were either sociologists or psychologists, and applied their knowledge and skills in those areas to this relatively new phenomenon of mass communication. (See Figure 5.1 for more information about these early scholars.)

Social Science Roots

On the psychological side, the governing principle was behaviorism, a branch of psychology often associated with Ivan Pavlov (famous for his experiments with the salivating dogs) and B. F. Skinner, who applied the principles of stimulus and response to human behavior. Behaviorists say that actions are essentially conditioned responses to external stimuli. Applied to mass communication, the stimuli naturally were thought to come through media messages. Sociology contributed the idea of functionalism, which suggests that social structures and widely adopted social values are the key determinants of a society's stability and orderly operation. In this view, media institutions are part of the social structure, and help to maintain or alter social norms.

Because they were the tools at hand, these two perspectives were used to analyze the emerging social environment in which mass media could suddenly reach millions of people with the stimuli of identical, simultaneous messages, using the power of the popular press as well as previously unfathomable technology such as radio broadcasts. This analysis led to the logical conclusion that the media must have the potential for powerful, direct, uniform (affecting everybody the same), and potentially negative effects on individuals and on the social order as a whole. Baran and Davis (2006) call this the *mass society* perspective (the first of their five eras), and describe it as centered on fears that mass media would damage existing social orders, especially by undermining the power of elite individuals within the society, and overwhelming older, traditional cultural values that contributed to keeping the social order intact.

Definition
Functionalism: A sociological theory that states that the structures of a society—its institutions and organizations, including mass media organizations—play a key role in defining the norms and values of the society and the way people behave and interact within it.

FIGURE 5.1   Founders of the Field of Communication

Four social scientists are often credited with doing the landmark research work that led to the establishment of mass communication as a discipline of its own. They were identified in a famous 1959 article by Bernard Berelson, who was himself a prominent researcher of that era. In the article, Berelson ironically—and, as it turned out, incorrectly—predicted that communication research was likely to wither and die, a prediction he made partly because he foresaw no more landmark findings coming from the research that these four icons had engaged in for the previous 30 years. These four scholars, sometimes called the "founders of the field," are:

- **Paul Lazarsfeld**, an Austrian immigrant sociologist who used survey research to measure the influences of mass media. He is especially known for his research into radio audiences in the 1930s and for his work directing the Bureau of Applied Social Research at Columbia University from the late 1940s to the early 1960s. Among the bureau's and Lazarsfeld's most noteworthy research were studies of media influences on voters in 1940 and 1948 that helped to discredit the "bullet theory" and launch the era of "limited effects."
- **Carl Hovland**, a Yale University psychologist who, during World War II, conducted experiments involving the influence of motivational films on soldiers. His conclusions that the soldiers' attitudes were not greatly affected by the contents of what they viewed also helped to undermine early theories of direct and powerful influences of media messages. However, Hovland's research did find that other factors about the films influenced attitudes, which laid the groundwork for further research into persuasive communication.
- **Harold Lasswell**, a political scientist who later became a law professor, was among the first to systematically study propaganda in an attempt to document its influences. But he is best known for an influential 1948 article in which he broke down the act of communication into a series of steps that became an organizing framework for research into this process: who says what, to whom, in which channel, with what effects. In the same article, he also identified three main functions of communication in a society: surveillance of the environment, correlation of information about the environment, and transmission of social heritage among generations.
- **Kurt Lewin**, an émigré German psychologist who was most closely associated with the field of group dynamics, is seen as a founder of the communications field largely because of his influence on the study of interpersonal and small-group communication. But he also developed the concept of gatekeeping, later applied to and widely used in mass communication research.

In addition to these four individuals, other influential early scholars included:

- **Wilbur Schramm**, who founded the first Ph.D. program in mass communications at the University of Iowa in 1943. Prominent communication theorist and historian of the field Everett M. Rogers actually nominates Schramm over any others as the true founder of the discipline because of the widespread research influence that graduates of his programs at Iowa and later at Stanford University had on the development of the field (Rogers, 1994).
- **Claude Shannon/Warren Weaver**, who in 1949 developed the mathematical theory of communication that, when combined with Lasswell's ideas (published one year earlier), really helped to define the "transmission of effects" paradigm that came to dominate the field.
- **Elihu Katz**, an associate of Lazarsfeld's at the Bureau of Applied Social Research who helped popularize the theory of the "two-step flow" and the limited effects paradigm with articles that summarized and consolidated earlier pieces of research from the Bureau that had introduced the concept.
- **Karl Marx**, a German political philosopher and intellectual who was best known for his radical ideas about economics and political science, and whose theories of ideology and power in society also form the basis for the critical theory branch of communication studies.

Even as this transmission of effects paradigm was taking hold, however, an alternative way of looking at the impacts of the media was beginning to form as well, rooted in the concept described earlier about how people interact with symbols to shape their view of the world around them.

Transmission of Direct Effects Paradigm

The widespread view that mass media could exercise a powerful and pervasive influence on those who were exposed to its messages was rooted in several characteristics of the social scene when this view took root in the middle part of the twentieth century. These factors (Curran, Gurevitch & Woollacott, 1982) were:

- The emergence of audiences larger than ever before being exposed to identical messages, through the then-new technology of radio broadcasts.
- A perception that other social changes—notably recent industrialization and urbanization that had caused confusion in social roles and changes in social structures—would leave this massive audience susceptible to outside influences.
- Anecdotal evidence that people had been powerfully affected by propaganda during World War I.

These social and technological characteristics helped bring about new ways of theorizing about the way media exposure affected individuals and society.

Bullet-Hypodermic Theory (1930s).   This process by which media would have these powerful and pervasive effects is often referred to as the bullet (or sometimes the magic bullet) or hypodermic needle theory of media effects. The bullet term is attributed to Wilbur Schramm and the hypodermic expression to David Berlo, two icons in the development of communication theory (Severin & Tankard, 2001, p. 125). Both names for this theory are simply metaphors for the type of impact a media message was thought to have on its recipients. In other words, the media could "inject" audiences with a message that would immediately, powerfully, directly, and uniformly cause them to adopt a new idea or attitude, like using a hypodermic needle and syringe to inject a substance into the body. The "bullet" image is that if the message hit the target, it would have a substantial effect, akin to a shot from a weapon hitting its target.

Implicit in this theory is the assumption that the audience is passive and vulnerable to the actions, and the messages, of the mass media. An often-cited example is the "War of the Worlds" radio broadcast on the day before Halloween in October 1938. Actor/director Orson Welles and a theater troupe created a radio drama built around a supposed invasion of the Earth by people from Mars, based on a story from noted science fiction author H. G. Wells but modified to sound as if it were a news report about an actual event. Millions who heard the broadcast believed the attack was really happening, and the ensuing panic was seen as evidence of the power of radio to affect people's beliefs about a situation.

A group of social scientists from the Radio Research Project at Princeton University investigated the incident, ultimately publishing a book-length report on it. Among their findings were that at least 6 million people heard the broadcast and that more than a million of them were frightened or disturbed by it. The researchers interviewed people who had fled their homes, rescued family members, or took other drastic actions in their terror. In a summary of the project, they wrote: "The fact that this panic was created as a result of a radio broadcast is today no mere coincidence. . . . By its very nature radio is the medium par excellence for informing all segments of a population of current happenings, for arousing them in a common sense of fear and joy, and for exciting them to *similar reactions directed toward a single objective.*" (Cantril et al. [1947], in Schramm & Roberts, eds. [1971], emphasis added). The italicized portion of the quote illustrates how the bullet theory was the operative theory behind this research, assuming that a message would have powerful, immediate, direct, and universal effects on those exposed to it.

It may be tempting to think that the bullet theory is still operating in society today. There are examples of powerful influences of the media; witnessing terrorist attacks and natural disasters do move people to action. However, scholars no longer believe that mass communication effects operate in a vacuum; that is, media effects are not thought to be so direct and so powerful that they can, all by themselves, move an individual or an entire society to action. Media effects are the result of a combination of forces, and the evolution of the theories, even at this early stage, shows how media scholars adapted to an understanding of the power of the message.

> **Application of the Bullet Theory**
>
> The fact that millions of people apparently believed that the Earth was under attack when Orson Welles's adaptation of the "War of the Worlds" was broadcast on radio in 1938 was seen as evidence of the bullet theory in action: people being powerfully and uniformly affected by a message from the mass media.

Public Opinion and Propaganda (1920s to 1940s).   Much of the concern with mass media in the era between the world wars rested with the fear that it could arouse emotions that might undermine a democratic society; the earliest systematic study of mass communication is generally acknowledged to be investigations into whether the media might damage society or threaten the social order. These included the so-called Payne studies, which in the 1920s investigated whether film violence could have an effect on children, as well as the propaganda studies conducted by Harold Lasswell and other scholars in the 1920s.

The study of propaganda is important to the history of the communication field both because it was among the first communication topics to be studied systematically, and also because it deals with two issues of ongoing interest, namely attitude change and the effects of mass communication on individuals and society. Interestingly, several of the views that led to scholarly investigation of propaganda are still held by many people, who are quick to blame the media for perceived socials ills such as permissive sexual practices and violent behavior. The notion that media institutions fulfill a propaganda function lives on in the work of many critical theorists, such as Herbert Schiller, Robert McChesney, and Noam Chomsky/ Edward Herman, whose work is discussed in more detail in Chapter 8.

An influential 1920s treatise on the topic of media sway over public opinion and its threat to the social order came not from a scholar, however, but from a journalist named Walter Lippmann. Communication scholar James Carey has called Lippmann's *Public Opinion*, published in 1922, the book that founded the field of communication study (Carey [1982] cited in Rogers [1994], p. 233). Lippmann's thesis was that the understanding people had of reality—what he called "the pictures in our heads"—was an incomplete and fallible one because any individual had a limited range of personal experience and because of the natural limitations of getting information from the media.

According to Lippmann, the volume and complexity of information that would be required to truly understand the outside world made such understanding an impossible feat for humans to achieve. Lippmann wrote strictly about the influence of newspapers because at the time radio was in its infancy, and had not at that point emerged as a news medium, and television had not yet been invented. But according to Lippmann, newspapers routinely published only a fraction of information that was available to them, and even this limited amount of information was too much for any one person to absorb. As he put it: "The real environment is altogether too big, too complex and too fleeting for direct acquaintance. We are not equipped to deal with so much subtlety, so much variety, so many permutations and combinations. And although we have to act in that environment, we have to construct it on a simpler model before we can manage with it" (Lippmann [1922], in Schramm ed. [1966]). For Lippmann, this meant people relied on simplifications such as stereotypes and developed a world view based on exposure to only a limited amount of detail. Thus, he concluded, average people could not form intelligent opinions about public policies or public leadership. The notion that we could have a democracy guided by "public opinion" was a false one, and the contemporary fears about the effects of propaganda were realistic, in his view. An alternative view was voiced by pragmatist philosopher and educator John Dewey, who said newspapers needed to move beyond purely reporting events to become vehicles for public education and debates, and should structure discussion of public issues. According to Dewey, the media's role should be "to interest the public in the public interest" (Baran & Davis, 2006, p. 86). Lippmann's ideas were a precursor to the agenda-setting theory that is discussed in Chapter 7.

Heightening these concerns in the 1920s and 1930s were the observations that mass media, especially radio, were being used as tools to sway the minds of large segments of the population in countries such as Germany under Adolf Hitler. Social science researchers concerned about the impact of the media on the social order, and the prospects for the media to undermine a liberal-democratic society based on personal and political liberty, focused their attentions on these European propaganda efforts.

Political scientist Harold Lasswell actually took an interest in propaganda well in advance of the Nazi revolution in Germany. He studied propaganda from World War I (1914–1918) from a behaviorist standpoint for his doctoral dissertation and extended the work beyond, publishing a report in 1927 that defined propaganda as "the control of opinion by significant symbols, or, to speak more concretely and less accurately, by stories, rumors, reports, pictures and other forms of social communication" (cited in Severin & Tankard, 2001, p. 109). Lasswell's view was not so much an application of bullet theory, however, as much as it was a psychological analysis based on the use of "master" symbols that have the ability to evoke emotions and actions (Baran & Davis, 2006). He took a critical view of the practice of propaganda and concluded that its strong effects posed a potential threat to democratic society (Rogers, 1994).

Research into the practices and effects of propaganda remained popular in the interwar period. In 1937, around the time that Hitler was consolidating his power in prewar Germany, the Institute for Propaganda Analysis was founded. Its stated purpose was to help educate the public about propaganda in order to make people more resistant to its effects. A book published under the auspices of the institute, *The Fine Art of Propaganda*, listed seven devices or techniques used in propaganda expression (Lee & Lee [1939], in Schramm, ed. [1966], pp. 417–418):

- **Name-calling:** Giving an idea a bad label to make people reject and condemn it without examining the evidence.
- **Glittering generality:** Associating something with a "virtue word" to make people accept and approve it without examining the evidence.
- **Transfer:** Carrying over the authority or prestige of something respected to something else in order to make it acceptable, or carrying over some sort of disapproval to make people reject and disapprove of it.
- **Testimonial:** Having a respected person say that a particular idea is good, or a hated person say it is bad.
- **Plain folks:** Attempting to convince the audience that the speaker's ideas are worthwhile because the speaker is a "person of the people/common man."
- **Card-stacking:** Selecting and using facts and logical or illogical statements to give the best (or worst) possible case for an idea.
- **Bandwagon:** Attempting to convince people that everyone of a similar group as them has accepted the idea.

Propaganda remained a popular topic for scholarly inquiry throughout the 1930s, and even into World War II, when Lasswell directed a project through the Library of Congress to do content analyses of Allied and Axis news media for evidence of propaganda (Rogers, 1994). But as the war ended, scholarly interests turned to other pursuits.

Lasswell's Structure and Function (1948).   After World War II ended, several powerful ideas that researchers had begun investigating during the war emerged, giving shape to the study of mass communication and starting to make it into a social science of its own.

Two of these ideas came from Lasswell, whose propaganda studies had a behavioral basis but whose ideas also embodied sociology's functionalist approach, (i.e., that social institutions such as the media played specific roles that contributed to the overall operation or functioning of the society). Functional

FIGURE 5.2 Contemporary Use of Propaganda Devices

Although the negative connotations of propaganda make many people think of Hitler and Al Qaeda, elements of propaganda can readily be identified in advertising and politics. One of the most obvious examples is the ongoing use of these specific propaganda devices identified by Lee and Lee in 1939:

- **Name-calling:** In the 2004 presidential election, John Kerry was labeled a "flip-flopper." Bush supporters held up flip-flops as Kerry traveled the country. The label caused some to reject Kerry without considering the evidence as to why he had changed his position on the Iraq War.
- **Transfer/Testimonial:** These two devices are the basis of celebrity endorsements. In February 2006, Nike introduced its 22nd model of the Air Jordan basketball shoe; years after Michael Jordan's retirement from basketball, fans and athletes still want to be "like Mike."
- **Glittering generality:** In the 1980s, the administration of President Ronald Reagan opposed the left-wing regime of Daniel Ortega that controlled the Central American country of Nicaragua, and sought to support rebel forces known as the "Contras" that were fighting to oust Ortega. President Reagan took to calling the Contras "freedom fighters" and at one point even compared them to the patriots who led the American Revolution against England in the 1700s.
- **Card-stacking:** When the United States invaded Iraq in 2003, the major reason given was that it was necessary to remove weapons of mass destruction from the hands of dictator Saddam Hussein, but none were ever found. It became clear many months later that the facts given to the public about these supposed weapons (including facts used in a State of the Union Address by President Bush and a speech at the United Nations by Secretary of State Colin Powell) were based on a narrow and selective interpretation of intelligence reports, with contradictory information about the presence of the weapons left out of the public pronouncements.
- **Plain folks:** This technique is especially popular in political image-making to illustrate that the individual is a man (or woman) "of the people." Politicians have been shown doing everything from carrying their own luggage (Jimmy Carter in 1976), to riding the subway to work and shopping in the "bargain basement" of a popular store (Michael Dukakis in 1988), to clearing brush at a ranch (George Bush throughout his presidency) in order to illustrate that they are just ordinary individuals like so many of the voters.
- **Bandwagon:** When advertising touts that a product is already very popular—"America's No. 1 movie;" "a *New York Times* best-seller"—the purpose is to persuade people that they should get on board as well.

analysis often focuses on how individuals are affected by broader social forces, generally through a positivist approach that applies the scientific method to human behavior. (See Chapter 2 for a discussion of positivism and communication research.) Applied to media analysis, this became a search for factors, such as message or source characteristics, that could predict or explain the effects of a message on its audience (Rubin, 1986).

In an influential article, Lasswell (1948, in Schramm & Roberts, eds., 1971), identified the media's roles as:

- **Surveillance** of the environment, which discloses threats and opportunities affecting the community and its components;
- **Correlation** of various parts of society in responding to that environment; and
- **Transmission** of cultural heritage from one generation to the next.

Building on Lasswell's work, Charles Wright later added a fourth function of **entertainment** that is usually addressed along with the first three identified by Lasswell to create a four-function typology of the functions of media in modern society. (See Figure 5.3.)

In the same 1948 article that laid out these functions of the media, Lasswell described also the basic form of "an act of communication" as having the following pattern:

- Who
- Says what
- In which channel
- To whom
- With what effects

This simple formulation was extremely influential because in it, Lasswell managed to identify various parts of the structure of communication that could be used as points of entry for scholarly inquiry on a functionalist basis: the originator of the communication (who), the message itself (what), the medium of communication (channel), the audience (whom), and, perhaps most significantly of all, the impact that these four constituents could have (effects). But Lasswell was not the only theorist in the postwar era seeking to describe the shape of the processes used for communication.

Shannon and Weaver's Information Theory. Another idea that helped to shape the emerging paradigm as one of message transmission that affected recipients came in 1949 from two researchers at Bell Labs, Claude Shannon and Warren Weaver. Their model also can be analyzed from the functionalist perspective because, like Lasswell's inventory, it seeks to break down communication into a series of steps that each contribute to the overall process and can be analyzed individually as to their implications and effects for the audience.

The Shannon-Weaver model, as it has come to be known, was really meant to apply to transmission of electronic signals, such as the electromagnetic waves that carry telephone conversations or radio and television broadcasts. (See Figure 5.4.) But it was extended to apply to the information transmission process more generally because it was a simple yet powerful way of deconstructing communication into several recognizable parts:

- **Source:** Originator of the communication
- **Message:** Content of the communication
- **Channel:** Means of carrying the communication
- **Receiver:** Recipient of the communication

FIGURE 5.3   Media Functions and Sports Reporting

When people use television, radio, print publications, and the Internet to follow their favorite sports teams, they make use of all four functions of the media as identified by Lasswell and Wright:

- **Surveillance:** Using the media to gather the basic facts about the team's performance. How did the team do last night? Did it win or lose? Were any key players injured, or did any return from injury? Did any of the fan's favorite players have a really good game?

- **Correlation:** How does the surveillance information matter to the fan's (or, in this case, the team's) position in society? How did last night's results relate to the season's overall performance? Did the team solidify its place in the standings? Secure a playoff berth?

- **Transmission of cultural heritage:** Following a team through the media teaches non-fans, casual fans, and even hard-core fans more about the sport itself, from terminology to rules to historical performances, especially when current performances break records set by great players in past seasons.

- **Entertainment:** This is perhaps the most obvious and extensive function of the media for sports fans, who watch their teams on television, follow them in newspapers and magazines, participate in blogs and other fan forums on the Internet, and maybe even take part in a fantasy league.

This was a major step forward in communication research because "more than any other theoretical conceptualization, [Shannon and Weaver's model] served as the paradigm for communication study, providing a single, easily understandable specification of the main components in a communication act" (Rogers, 1994, p. 438).

In the scientific paper that proposed this model, Shannon and Weaver introduced several other concepts that also were rapidly incorporated into the field of communication study, again extending beyond their intended purpose of describing electronic signal transmission. One was the concept of noise, which is anything that can corrupt the message along the way. In the original formulation, "noise" resulted from electromagnetic interference with the signal and a loss of signal strength over distances. Another concept Shannon and Weaver introduced is a definition of information as "reduction of uncertainty." A message with a high level of information was one that left nothing to chance—no uncertainty—on the part of the receiver. Shannon and Weaver actually sought to quantify the amount of additional "information" that the signal would need to carry in order to overcome a specific amount of interference with a mathematical formula based on statistical probability; this is why they called their idea the "mathematical theory of communication."

For a good modern example of both of these concepts, think of a poor cell-phone connection (which, of course, actually does come from corruption of the electronic signal carrying the call). Anyone who has ever had a conversation when the call signal was breaking up has experienced "noise" in the channel and a corresponding reduction of information and increase in uncertainty: "What did

FIGURE 5.4 Parts of the Process: Shannon and Weaver's Model

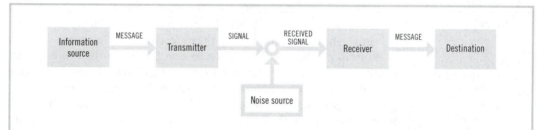

Shannon and Weaver's model helped solidify the "transmission" paradigm through the terminology it introduced that identified specific parts of the act of communication:

- **Source:** Origin of the communication.
- **Message:** Substance of the communication itself.
- **Channel:** Means through which the communication is carried.
- **Receiver:** Destination of the communication.
- **Noise:** Anything interfering with proper receipt of the communication.
- **Redundancy:** Characteristics that compensate for noise or add to information (see next definition).
- **Information:** Perhaps the most difficult part of Shannon and Weaver's model to conceptualize because "information" has nothing to do with the content of the message. Rather, it is a characteristic of the message, defined as "reduction of uncertainty" with regard to the communication. A message with high information value is one with a low level of uncertainty and thus a greater likelihood of being understood. Low information, of course, is the reverse: a message with high uncertainty because of noise or other factors.

Source of schematic diagram of Shannon's general communication system: From C. Shannon and W. Weaver, *The Mathematical Theory of Communication* (Urbana: University of Illinois Press 1999), p. 98. Copyright 1949 by the Board of Trustees of the University of Illinois. Reprinted with permission of the University of Illinois Press.

you say? When do you want to meet?" The metaphor of noise is further extended in the rhetorical tradition to anything that interferes with the reception of a message, such as a speaker's PowerPoint slide with text that is too small to be read from the back of the room, or a cell phone that rings during a lecture, distracting the audience and interrupting the speaker.

Another concept Shannon and Weaver's model used was redundancy, which was a way to overcome noise and improve the overall reliability of the message reception. In the bad cell-phone connection example, redundancy can be taken very literally, in the form of one or both parties having to deliver redundant messages—that is to say, they repeat themselves—in order to make sure all of the information they are trying to convey makes it to the other caller.

Weiner's Cybernetics (1948–1949).   Another mathematically based conception for understanding communication as a systematic process grew out of the work of Massachusetts Institute of Technology professor Norbert Weiner.

Definition
Feedback: The use of communication to either keep a system stable or make it more unstable through adjustment of future performance based on current behavior or operation of the system.

During World War II, Weiner had worked on mathematical formulas for improving the accuracy of anti-aircraft guns by using information about the trajectory and location of previous shots in relation to their fast-moving airborne targets to help predict the best place to aim future shots. More generally, this process became known as feedback, defined as "control of the future conduct of a system by information about its past performance" (Rogers, 1994, p. 397). Feedback happens when a system is changing or in flux, and it can either amplify the change or suppress it. The science of developing systems that use feedback to regulate themselves became known as cybernetics.

To get a better understanding of cybernetics, it is helpful to think of the most common cybernetic device: a home heating system controlled by a thermostat. In this conception, the "system" consists of the furnace, the thermostat, and the air inside the house, which the occupants want to keep at a constant temperature. (The technical term for this is homeostasis or use of feedback to keep the system as stable as possible). When the air temperature inside the home drops to a certain level, the thermostat detects the change and turns on the furnace. It is at this point the system starts to exhibit its cybernetic characteristics, because as the furnace runs and heats the house, the thermostat monitors the furnace's performance. Eventually, the house is warm enough, and the thermostat shuts the furnace down again. But in the process, the furnace's past actions (of providing the heat) direct its future performance (the eventual shutdown). Information about the overall system performance (the temperature of the house) is continuously monitored to guide future regulation of the system (turning the furnace on and off).

As applied to communications, cybernetics says that the communication process in a social system can lead to stability or instability of that system, whether it is a small group (such as a family), a larger group (such as a corporation), or an entire society (such as a nation, or the world). Think about the way that the feedback people personally give and receive—their responses to messages—help to either maintain the status quo or change their personal lives as they communicate with friends and family members.

Although it started out as a mathematical theory rooted in physics, sociologists from the functionalist view latched onto cybernetics as an idea that could describe the effect mass media would have on social systems. Recall that functionalism says that social structures are the key to the stability and orderly operation of a society, and that media organizations are one of the social structures that affect this stability. In this conception, the mass media can provide feedback that either keep society orderly or contribute to its disruption. Public sentiment whipped up by Nazi radio broadcasts, for example, helped lead to destabilization of the German society and overthrow of the government there by the Nazi party in the 1930s. For an example on the other side that shows media promoting or enhancing social stability, think about coverage of a major storm such as a hurricane or blizzard. News reports before the storm help individuals and institutions prepare for it—people stock up on supplies, schools may be closed, and emergency workers are put on alert. In the storm's aftermath, reports tell where destruction is the worst so that people know to avoid the area. News of the reconstruction or cleanup lets everyone know things are going back to normal. News stories about problems with the emergency response system, as was apparent with Hurricane Katrina in New Orleans in 2005, could lead to investigations and changes that could improve response the next time. At each level—preparation, cleanup, planning for future storms—information feedback through the media helps society cope with a disruptive event and return to a stable state.

On a more general level, routine news coverage of social institutions such as schools, government, businesses, and non-profit groups help people understand how these institutions contribute to a stable, orderly society. When government officials make decisions and take action, news coverage provides information about those actions to the citizens. If enough of the public disagrees with or dislikes the policies, it can lead to adjustment of the system through another form of feedback supplied by the voters at the next election that changes the status quo by voting the incumbents out of office.

Summary of the Transmission of Direct Effects Model. The idea that messages are transmitted, received, and have an effect on people was the dominant paradigm in communication theory through the middle part of the twentieth century. It started with the study of propaganda and its supposed effects on people throughout both World Wars I and II, and continued with Lasswell's formulation that separated the communication process into functions that the media served, also ending with the notion of effects. In similar fashion, Shannon and Weaver's model was based on information transmission, while cybernetics theorized that the media affected the stability of the social system by providing feedback to the system about itself. Thus, the transmission model of direct effects had all of its pieces in place, and this era stood as the high-water mark of the paradigm in which media messages were thought to have powerful and direct influences on those who were exposed to them.

Development of the Limited Effects Paradigm

As communication scholarship developed, some researchers began to question the fundamental belief about mass media being highly influential on audiences. New research questions and different methods of investigating them led to the development of new theories that created the first of the paradigm shifts described earlier.

Empirical Studies in Social Psychology. Weiner, Shannon, and Weaver brought a perspective from the natural sciences (Weiner was a mathematician, and Shannon and Weaver were engineers trained in physics) to the definitions of the communication process and its constituent parts. Lasswell was trained as a political scientist who employed the sociological theory of functionalism. But at around the same time that they were contributing their ideas to the emerging communication paradigm, some social scientists also were making investigations that applied newly emergent techniques for social science research to the task, especially from the developing area of social psychology. For the most part, these investigators were setting out to determine whether the perceived effects of mass media exposure really were as powerful as the assumptions about propaganda effects and the bullet theory/transmission theory predicted they would be. Could news in the media have an effect on who people would select as their leaders in a society? Were people truly as vulnerable to propaganda as the theories suggested? Did this mean the United States could succumb to totalitarian demagoguery as the German nation had, and undermine its stable, democratic society?

Hovland and the Experimental Section (1940s).   Perhaps the first true "test" of the effectiveness of persuasive messages such as propaganda came from a series of psychological experiments done on U.S. Army soldiers during World War II. Carl Hovland, a psychologist from Yale University who worked in the research branch of the Department of War (now known as the Department of Defense), was assigned to evaluate soldiers' reactions to motivational films called the *Why We Fight* series, a series of documentaries produced by Hollywood director Frank Capra that were designed to help new recruits (especially draftees) understand the rationale for the war.

To measure the effectiveness of the films, Hovland designed a classic experiment in which some soldiers were exposed to certain stimuli (such as certain films) while others were not; the attitudes of both groups then were measured by having them fill out questionnaires. In the end, he reached a curious conclusion, considering the prevailing theories, and what he and the Army officials thought he would find. After viewing the films, the experiment's subjects knew more about the basis of the war, so there was an effect on their knowledge level. But the films did not appear to have much impact on the men's levels of motivation to serve as soldiers, leading to Hovland's ultimate conclusion that facts do not change attitudes. In some experiments, the level of motivation for soldiers who had not seen the films was nearly identical to that of soldiers who had been exposed to them.

However, the experiments also controlled for other message characteristics, such as the credibility of the source and whether the film presented one or both sides of an argument of which it was trying to persuade the viewer, and some of these characteristics were found to affect the persuasiveness of the appeal. Hovland's wartime investigations thus helped to undermine the bullet theory and assumptions behind propaganda theory, but it also provided an intellectual and theoretical basis for studies of persuasion that persist to the present (and are discussed in more detail in Chapter 6).

Lazarsfeld and the Bureau of Applied Social Research (1940s to 1950s).   Like his contemporary, Hovland, sociologist Paul Lazarsfeld set out to measure the effects of a medium on an audience, in this case radio. Lazarsfeld's entrée to communication research was as head of the Radio Research Project of Princeton University (which also was behind Cantril's "War of the Worlds" project described earlier). After World War II, Lazarsfeld became director of the Bureau of Applied Social Research at Columbia University, which became the pre-eminent sociological research organization of its time. From 1937 through 1960, scholars associated with the bureau produced 52 books as well as 350 scholarly articles, book chapters, and other publications (Rogers, 1994). The bureau's work also contributed to the advancement of quantitative methods in social science research, especially surveys and focus groups.

Several of the bureau's projects were focused specifically on the effects of mass communication, notably studies of media influences on voters in Erie County, Ohio, during the 1940 presidential race, and in Elmira, New York, in 1948, the results of which were published in book form in 1944 and 1952, respectively. Further insight was drawn from a 1943 study in Decatur, Illinois, of what influenced homemakers' attitudes toward certain household products, the results of which were not published until 1955. Each of these projects began as a test of the influence that mass media—newspapers and radio—would have on decisions made by members of the communities under study. All of the projects concluded that the direct effects of the media were less than the researchers had hypothesized, and far less than would be predicted by the prevailing theories of the day.

Lazarsfeld designed the 1940 voting study with an assumption that media would be key influencers of people's decisions. It used a panel design, with the same people interviewed repeatedly throughout the project to evaluate their initial viewpoints and any changes they underwent. But in the end, only 54 of 600 people interviewed switched their views of the candidates from the beginning to the end of the study. "In sum," Lazarsfeld concluded, "the media had minimal effects on the 1940 presidential election campaign" (Rogers, 1994, p. 288). The Decatur study resulted in a book titled, *Personal Influence: The Part Played by People in the Flow of Mass Communication*; in it Lazarsfeld and co-author Elihu Katz concluded that "messages in the mass media provided information to many individuals, but it was when this information was transmitted from one individual to another as personal influence that individuals were motivated to make decisions and take action" (Katz and Lazarsfeld [1955] as quoted in Rogers [1994], p. 298).

Two-Step Flow and Reinforcement Theories (late 1950s). The expression "two-step flow of information" was originally used in the book about the 1940 voting study (called *The People's Choice*, written by Lazarsfeld with two co-authors). But Elihu Katz, who was Lazarsfeld's collaborator on other studies (including the Decatur study), popularized the concept later in an effort he made to provide an overall perspective for some of the work done by the Bureau of Applied Social Research. In an influential article titled "The Two-Step Flow of Communication," he sought to summarize the Ohio, Elmira, Decatur, and some other studies and said all of them demonstrated that information is gathered and analyzed by opinion leaders who pass on the information and opinions from the media to others in their social circles. In the article, Katz concluded that opinion leaders and those they led through the two-step flow process of opinion formation usually were not that different from one another. But opinion leaders were the people who would "focus the group's attention on some related part of the world outside the group, and . . . function to bring the group into touch with this relevant part of its environment through whatever media are appropriate" (Katz [1957], in Schramm ed. [1966], p. 364). It was thought that the opinion leader had greater access to mass communication, but much of the research centered on trying to discover the characteristics that distinguished these leaders from those who followed them. (See Figure 5.5.)

Another "summing up" was provided by Joseph Klapper, who said that media tended to reinforce existing ideas and attitudes rather than directly create or shape them. Klapper started by describing the current state of media research at the time (the late 1950s), noting how both researchers and the general public were confused by inconclusive and contradictory studies. He argued that this research suggested that the media were only one of many things that influenced people, saying that: "Mass communication does not ordinarily serve as a necessary and sufficient cause of audience effects, but rather functions through a nexus of mediating factors. These mediating factors are such that they typically render mass communications a contributory agent, but not the sole cause, in a process of reinforcing the existing conditions" (Klapper, 1960, p. 8).

Klapper called this the "phenomenistic" view of communication effects, because it was an "assessment of the role of that stimulus [of the media] in a total observed phenomenon" (Klapper, 1960, p. 5). It has become better known by the more recognizable term "reinforcement theory" because Klapper also concluded that research showed "mass communication is in general more likely to reinforce the existing opinions of its audience than it is to change such opinions" (1960, p. 49). (See Figure 5.6.)

Another Perspective: Symbolic Interactionism.   The early research into mass communication discussed so far in this chapter—whether touting the influence of media institutions and messages or reporting on their limitations—largely took the functionalist perspective of media organizations as social institutions that perform certain activities within society with resulting consequences for society. But another group of sociologists approached the question of how mass media affect society from a different perspective—one rooted in the idea that human communication involves symbolism, and people react to the symbols around them.

This approach looks at social organization from a perspective directly opposite that of functionalism. Rather than analyzing society "top down" from the viewpoint of social structures and their effect on people, the way functionalism does, this other approach known as *interactionism* considers the way that individual human beings react to their surroundings and others around them. It is rooted in the pragmatic philosophy espoused by John Dewey and George Herbert Mead.

FIGURE 5.5   Updating the Two-Step Flow

The two-step flow theory of Lazarsfeld and Katz has been generally discredited in modern times. (In fact, the two-step flow yielded to diffusion of innovations, which is discussed in Chapter 7.) The main reason the two-step flow fell out of favor was the increase in media access by the general public. With everyone owning a television set, people no longer relied on "opinion leaders" to receive and then spread the news.

Some interesting research of news diffusion supports this. When John F. Kennedy was assassinated in 1963, the vast majority of people found out about it from another person (Greenberg, 1964). When planes hit the World Trade Center and the Pentagon in 2001, the earliest information reaching people came directly from a news source. About 62 percent of the people who knew about the attacks within an hour of when they happened found out from television, radio, or the Internet. About 97 percent of the people surveyed learned of the attacks within three hours, and about half of them did so from the media (Kanhian & Gale, 2003).

The one area of mass communication where the two-step flow seems alive and well is in the area of public relations. The public relations practitioner is in charge of monitoring and sending messages from a company or organization to the media for dissemination to the public. The organization's spokesperson is the "opinion leader" who controls the information and the message.

FIGURE 5.6   Phenomenistic/Reinforcement Theory

Joseph Klapper's summary of a decade's worth of research concluded that the media are most successful at reinforcing attitudes people hold rather than creating new ones. The fragmentation of media offerings into niches or market segments exemplifies this theory in action. With the variety of televised sporting events, sports analysis, and talk shows on cable television and radio, and magazines and Web sites devoted to particular sports or teams, fans could spend practically all their time reinforcing their knowledge and ideas about that topic, rather than, for example, watching a concert or listening to a classical music performance to see whether they might like that type of entertainment just as well. The same can be said for aficionados of nearly any enterprise: multiple media platforms allow people who are interested in crafts, celebrity gossip, shopping, and, yes, even classical music to indulge their passion for information on a particular topic rather than developing interest in new ones.

According to this theory, most of people's reading and reacting to the world around them comes through symbolic communication. This has become known as *symbolic interactionism*, a term coined by Herbert Blumer, who studied with Mead at the University of Chicago and continued his work after Mead's death.

Lindlof defines symbolic interactionism as "the study of how the self and the social environment mutually define and shape each other through symbolic communication" (1995, p 40). In other words, the way people react with and through symbolic communication is how society and culture are formed. "The symbolic interactionist emphasizes that all that humans are can be traced to their symbolic nature. . . . We see, we think, we hear, we share, we act symbolically . . . It is through symbolic interaction with one another that we give the world meaning and develop the reality toward which we act" (Charon, 2001, p. 89). As communication theory evolved, this viewpoint would take on more significance and become the basis of a theory called the *social construction of reality*, which is described in Chapter 8.

Normative Theories of Media and Society

While social scientists were trying to ascertain how mass communication practices affected audiences and society at large, other ideas were emerging about what role and effects mass media should (ideally) have on society. These ideas fall into the realm of normative theory, which seeks to define and identify which norms or values promote optimal social progress and development.

Marketplace of Ideas

The most influential normative theory of the media in the U.S. tradition is based on freedom of expression, as embodied in the First Amendment to the U.S. Constitution. In its purest form, this is a normative theory known as *libertarianism*, or absence of restraint on the media and imposition of as few restraints as possible on other parts of society as well. The First Amendment, and its implications as a legal principle, are explored more thoroughly in Chapter 9. But the libertarian philosophical basis that led the framers of the Constitution to address freedom of the press in a legal sense is rooted in the idea that personal liberty entails various related social and political freedoms, including:

- Social mobility (as opposed to an aristocratic system of nobility and peasants).
- Self-determination (democratic representative government).
- Free and open economic systems.
- Free expression in which all voices could be heard, resulting in a marketplace of ideas among which people can choose what they wish to believe.

All of these are part of what Thomas Jefferson, in writing the Declaration of Independence, so aptly called "certain inalienable rights" summarized as "life, liberty and the pursuit of happiness."

Fourth Estate Theory

Freedom of expression is inseparable from these other social and political freedoms because it is closely related to social development and self-governance. For social systems to evolve, new ideas must be introduced into them regularly; and for people to govern themselves, they need to know about actions and policies of elected officials when it is time to vote (Kostyu, 2006). Accordingly, the media in general and journalism in particular have a special role in helping democracy to succeed. The relationship is summed up in Thomas Jefferson's frequently cited quote that "The basis of our government being the opinion of the people, the very first object should be to keep that right; and were it left to me to decide whether we should have a government without newspapers or newspapers without a government, I should not hesitate a moment to prefer the latter" (Emery, 1962, p. 167).

The media are expected to fill the Fourth Estate functions of serving as a government "watchdog" and providing accurate, credible, relevant, and sufficient information that becomes the basis for public opinion. This has been summarized by one pair of analysts as "Civilization has produced one idea more powerful than any other—the notion that people can govern themselves. And it has created a largely unarticulated theory of information to sustain that idea, called journalism" (Kovach & Rosenstiel, 2001, p. 193). As Gans (2003) summarizes it, press and politics operate within a four-part "journalism's theory of democracy": (a) journalists inform citizens; (b) citizens are assumed to be informed if they pay attention to the news; (c) better-informed citizens are more likely to participate in politics; and (d) more citizen participation will improve democracy." More succinctly, in a comment that echoes Jefferson's adage, Gans notes that "The democratic process can only be truly meaningful if citizens are informed. Journalism's job is to inform them" (p. 1).

Social Responsibility and Theories of the Press

With these historical roots, libertarian theory and the marketplace of ideas provide the dominant normative theory for how people think about media in U.S. society. But during the 1940s and 1950s—at around the same time that social scientists were investigating the effects of emerging mass media on society—debate began to arise about just how well the Fourth Estate theory was working, just how free the media ought to be, and whether there might be such a thing as too much freedom of the press. (Note that because this concerns the issue of what *should* happen or how things *could* be organized for the best results, it is considered normative theory.)

In the mid-1940s a panel of distinguished media experts was convened to consider the role of the press in American society. This body, formally known as the Commission on the Freedom of the Press, came to be known as the Hutchins Commission after its chairman, University of Chicago Chancellor Robert Hutchins. After nearly two years of meetings, it issued a book-length report in 1947 that in essence developed a new normative theory for the press that moved away from the libertarian ideal. While acknowledging that the First Amendment meant the press was supposed to be free of government controls, the commission

also said the press had a responsibility "for making its contribution to the main-
tenance and development of a free society" (Blevins, 1997). Consequently, the
commission said newspapers also should provide:

- A truthful, comprehensive account of the day's events in a context that gives
  them meaning.
- A forum for the exchange of comment and criticism.
- A means of projecting the opinions and attitudes of the groups in a society to
  one another.
- A way of reaching every member of the society by the currents of information,
  thought, and feeling that the press supplies.

These purposes for the media came to be known as a "social responsibility
theory," one of four normative theories elaborated upon a few years later by
another group of scholars. Fred Peterson, Theodore Siebert, and Wilbur Schramm's
landmark *Four Theories of the Press*, published in 1956, described a continuum of
normative theory on press freedom and social (government) control that included:

- **Libertarian model:** An absence of government control in order to foster
  growth of a marketplace of ideas.
- **Social responsibility model:** The media would exercise self-restraint to promote a diversity of viewpoints, but government regulation may be necessary to
  rein in the most dangerous impulses of a totally libertarian approach.
- **Authoritarian model:** Government controlled the press through censorship
  and licensing. Historically, this had been the most common model from the rise
  of monarchies and nation states until emergence of the libertarian model in the
  late 1700s. But authoritarian control also existed in the modern era, in countries such as Nazi Germany. Even today, countries such as Singapore are known
  for the tight rein they keep on the media, and even Russia and Venezuela are
  increasing government control of media.
- **Totalitarian model:** The media exist to serve the purposes of the state as a
  propaganda tool; sometimes called the "Soviet model" after the practices of the
  U.S.S.R. from the end of World War II to the end of the Cold War.

A key element of social responsibility theory is that if the media do not
behave responsibly for themselves, the government should have the ability to get
involved. According to Siebert, Peterson, and Schramm, "Social responsibility
theory holds that the government must not merely allow freedom; it must
actively promote it" (as cited in McQuail, 2005, p. 171). The goal should be to
develop a media system that would serve the public interest. In many respects,
the notion that broadcast regulation and licensing are designed to serve "the public interest, convenience and necessity" is an example of government involvement to help ensure the media operate in this manner. This formulation was also
noteworthy because it did not assume that the libertarian model was the only
approach, or even the best approach, to media performance in a society. Broadcast regulation and its limits are discussed in Chapter 9.

FIGURE 5.7   The Evolution of Mass Communication Paradigms

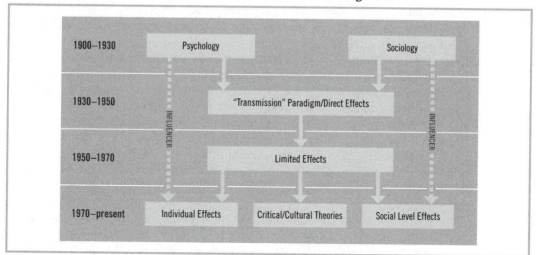

The Mass Communication
Discipline Matures

The field of communication study and the theories associated with it are relatively recent developments in the world of scholarship, and they coincide with the emergence of the electronic mass media in only the past century. The beginnings of communication study can be traced to influential work in related disciplines of psychology, political science, and sociology that sought to evaluate how mass media affected individuals and society at large.

Rogers traces the field's formal beginnings more specifically to the University of Iowa in 1943. He writes that "Inauguration of the first communication Ph.D. program in a school of journalism . . . directly led to the division of the communication field into two sub-disciplines: mass communication and interpersonal communication" (Rogers, 1994, p. 17). With its "genetic roots" in other social science fields, the new discipline took on a largely quantitative spirit focused on the effects of mass media and their messages on audiences. The emergence of a process model, effects-based paradigm of inquiry in the late 1940s amplified the empirical research trend established earlier by such founders of the field as Lasswell (content analyses), Hovland (psychological experiments), and Lazarsfeld (survey research).

The field evolved in this direction for the next 40 years to the point that in 1987, two influential researchers could proclaim that an era of "communication science" had been established. They defined this new science as one that "seeks to understand the production, processing and effects of symbol and signal systems, by developing testable theories, containing lawful generalizations, that explain phenomena associated with production, processing and effects" (Berger & Chaffee, 1987, p. 17). Berger and Chaffee acknowledged other social science fields as providing the roots for communication as a discipline, but added that "in the past two decades . . . an increasing number of communication researchers have advanced their own theories for testing instead of relying on work in allied disciplines" (1987, p. 16). Many of those theories, which emerged in the 1960s and 1970s, are the basis of the next two chapters in this book.

However, in the generation of communication research that came before the one Berger and Chaffee were describing, conclusions about the nature and power of those effects underwent a pendulum swing, or possibly an actual paradigm shift. Spurred by the work of empirical researchers over a 30-year period from the 1920s to the 1950s, the early view that media have massive, powerful, immediate, universal, and direct effects on audiences gradually shifted to the view that they have no direct effects, which is admittedly quite a contrast. Klapper (1960) concisely summarizes the principles of the limited effects paradigm as being that (1) the media rarely have a direct influence on individuals; (2) rather, this influence follows a two-step flow; (3) most people's lives have other influences upon them that cause them to reject or modify what they think about most messages from the media; and (4) when media effects do occur, they will be modest and isolated.

Lazarsfeld perhaps deserves the most responsibility for the change. "Early propaganda theorists championed the powerful mass media, but later communication scholars did not find evidence of such strong effects when they investigated the impacts of the media in voting behaviors, consumer decisions and other types of behavior change. The main scholar to begin questioning the notion of powerful media was Paul F. Lazarsfeld, and it was the Erie County study that started him questioning. The voting study launched the era of limited effects in mass communication research" (Rogers, 1994, p. 287).

But later research—in the era described by Berger and Chaffee—was successful in demonstrating that neither the direct effect posture nor the limited effects one was correct, and many modern scholars see both views as exaggerated with the truth lying somewhere in the middle (Perry, 2002, p. 29). The early view *overestimated* media effects based on assumptions without much detailed research, while the empirical view *underestimated* them, partly because of limitations inherent in the research styles. Hovland's experiments involved before-and-after questionnaires of subjects viewing 50-minute films, while many of the Bureau of Applied Social Research studies were short-term projects, lasting only a few weeks or months. Later scholars said these research designs may not have allowed enough time to fairly evaluate media effects. Media influences simply may take longer to have an effect than can be measured in a short-term experiment or snapshot survey, or these influences may be largely indirect and thus not captured by the survey instruments.

The new generation of media researchers described by Berger and Chaffee came on the scene just when it appeared that "limited effects" was taking hold as a paradigm; a famous 1959 article by Bernard Berelson said communication research was destined to become moribund and "wither away" because the research programs of the early investigators such as Lasswell and Lazarsfeld had slowed down as evidence accumulated about a lack of direct media effects, and no new ideas were emerging to replace them. But starting in the early 1960s and picking up steam in the 1970s, this new generation used some of the same empirical procedures as pioneered by the World War II generation, as well as more sophisticated ones, to demonstrate that within certain boundaries and under certain conditions, media could indeed have short-term and long-term influences on individuals and on society at large.

This is the modern era (or contemporary paradigm) of moderate effects, and consists of a large body of active and productive theories that mostly follow one of three major threads:

1. Theories associated with how people perceive, use, and understand information as it comes to them through the media as only one of many behavioral stimuli. This is related more closely to the psychological component of communication science's roots as pioneered by work of scholars such as Hovland and Klapper. It focuses on individual effects and on audiences as active users of media content, and is discussed in more detail in Chapter 6.

2. Theories associated with the effect of media outlets and institutions on social realities based on what information is presented and how it is presented. These largely extend from the functionalist perspective that drove so much of the original research in the field to describe, predict, and explain media influence at an institutional level on large groups or toward the society as a whole and are covered in Chapter 7.

3. Theories associated with audience constructions of social realities based on information they obtain from the media. This viewpoint incorporates ideas of symbolic interactionism and perspectives known as the "ritual view" of communication (Carey, 1989) and the social construction of reality (Berger & Luckmann, 1967). Research in this tradition takes a more holistic view of the media's effects on society and culture, using qualitative rather than quantitative inquiry. It takes the "critical" view that issues of power, ideology, and social reform should be first and foremost in media study and is covered in Chapter 8.

Summary

Research into mass communication and the development of communication as a scholarly discipline are relatively new. They have developed in only the past few decades, compared with natural sciences that are thousands of years old, and even with most social sciences that are a few hundred years old.

But it is noteworthy to recognize that all three of what are now the most active threads of mass communication research have their roots in the ideas developed by the founders of the field in the mid-twentieth century. The direct effects/transmission paradigm was the first to emerge, and the limited effects paradigm replaced it as researchers sought to validate the original paradigm and found they could not. The limited effects tradition, in turn, was questioned by researchers who thought that saying the media have no influence on individuals or society was too doctrinaire or too simplistic. Through research, scholars explored these theories and tried to validate them but ended up with different theories that updated the field instead. At the same time, more interpretive approaches also were emerging to challenge the dominant paradigm of mass communication research's earliest decades.

From this perspective, the field's earliest ideas (such as the bullet theory) can be seen as analogous to the Ptolemaic view of the Earth-centered universe. In other words, these theories are obsolete by current standards of knowledge, but they still deserve respect and attention because they were the best tools at hand for their times to understand the world, or predict and explain certain aspects of it. They also provided a starting point that has been built upon to help reach the current levels of understanding of the world of mass communication, and elements of the early theories can be identified in current theory and practice today.

QUESTIONS FOR DISCUSSION/ APPLICATION EXERCISES

1. What are some examples of how people sometimes presume that the bullet theory is still an operative and effective one in describing media effects on society?

2. The bullet/hypodermic theory is based on the idea that audiences are very susceptible to influence by the mass media. Are people as vulnerable—and as likely to be affected—as the theory says, or are they more resistant to media influence? Cite at least three examples from the current media and cultural landscape that illustrate or support your point.

3. Lasswell and Wright defined the four functions of the mass media as surveillance, correlation of individuals' responses to the world around them, transfer of cultural values, and entertainment. Come up with three to five different examples of each of these functions in action.

4. Give an example of a time when you served as an opinion leader—bringing a message, perhaps with interpretation, to others in your circle of friends. Or give an example of a time when you were the opinion follower, getting and possibly reacting to a media message filtered through an acquaintance.

5. Is it a fair or unfair statement to label communication efforts of the government and other powerful institutions in U.S. society to support their positions as propaganda? Why or why not?

REFERENCES

Baran, S., & Davis, D. (2006). *Mass communication theory: Foundations, ferment and future*. (4th ed.). Belmont, CA: Wadsworth.

Berger, C. R., & Chaffee, S. H. (1987). The study of communication as a science. In C. R. Berger, & S. H. Chaffee (Eds.), *Handbook of communication science* (pp. 15–19). Newbury Park, CA: Sage Publications.

Berger, P., & Luckmann T. (1967). *The social construction of reality*. New York: Anchor Books.

Blevins, F. (1997). The Hutchins Commission turns 50: Recurring themes in today's public and civic journalism. Paper presented at the Third Annual Conference on Intellectual Freedom, April 1997, Montana State University-Northern. Retrieved May 25, 2007, from: http://mtprof.msun.edu/Fall1997/Blevins.html.

Cantril, H. et al. (1947). The invasion from mars. In W. Schramm, & D. F. Roberts (Eds.), (1971). *The processes and effects of mass communication* (revised edition), (pp. 579–595). Urbana IL: University of Illinois Press.

Charon, J. (2001). The importance of the symbol. In J. O'Brien & P. Kollock (Eds.), *The production of reality: Essays and readings on social interaction* (3rd ed.) (pp. 89–96). Thousand Oaks, CA: Pine Forge Press.

Curran, J., Gurevitch, M., & Woollacott, J. (1982). The study of the media: Theoretical approaches. In M. Gurevitch, T. Bennett, J. Curran, & J. Woollacott (Eds.), *Culture, society and the media* (pp. 11–29). London: Meuthen & Co. Ltd.

Emery, E. (1962). *The press and America: An interpretive history of journalism* (2nd ed.). Englewood Cliffs, NJ: Prentice Hall.

Gans, H. (2003). *Democracy and the news*. New York: Oxford University Press.

Greenberg, B. S. (1964). Diffusion of news of the Kennedy assassination. *Public Opinion Quarterly 28*, 225.

Kanhian, S. F., & Gale, K. L. (2003). Within 3 hours, 97 percent learn about 9/11 attacks. *Newspaper Research Journal 24*(1), 78–91.

Katz, E. (1957). The two-step flow of communication. Republished in W. Schramm, (Ed.) (1966) *Mass Communications* (2nd ed.) (pp. 346–365). Urbana, IL: University of Illinois Press.

Klapper, J. T. (1960). *The effects of mass communication*. New York: The Freedom Press.

Kostyu, P. (2006). The First Amendment in theory and practice. In W. W. Hopkins (Ed.). *Communication and the law 2006 edition*. Northport, AL: Vision Press, pp. 23–41.

Kovach, B., & Rosenstiel, T. (2001). *The elements of journalism: What newspeople should know and the public should expect*. New York: Crown Publishers.

Lasswell, H. (1948). The structure and function of communication. Republished in W. Schramm, & D. F. Roberts (Eds.), (1971). *The processes and effects of mass communication* (revised edition) (pp. 579–595). Urbana, IL: University of Illinois Press.

Lee, A. M., & Lee, E. B. (1939). The devices of propaganda. In W. Schramm (Ed.), (1966). *Mass communications* (2nd ed.), (pp. 417–418). Urbana, IL: University of Illinois Press.

Lindlof, T. R. (1995). *Qualitative communication research methods*. Thousand Oaks, CA: Sage Publications.

Lippmann, W. (1922). The world outside and the pictures in our heads (Chapter 1 of *Public Opinion*). Republished in W. Schramm (Ed.). (1966). *Mass communications* (2nd ed.), (pp. 468–485). Urbana, IL: University of Illinois Press.

McQuail, D. (2005). *McQuail's mass communication theory* (5th ed.). London: Sage Publications Ltd.

Morris, M., & Ogan, C. (1996). The Internet as mass medium. *Journal of Communication 46*(1), 39–50.

Perry, D. (2002). *Theory and research in mass communication: Contexts and consequences*. Mahwah, NJ: Lawrence Erlbaum Associates.

Rafaeli, S., & Sudweeks, F. (1997). Networked interactivity. *Journal of Computer Mediated Communication 2*(4). Retrieved June 2003 from: http://www.ascusc.org/jcmc/vol2/issue4/rafaeli.sudweeks.html.

Reardon, K. & Rogers, E. (1988). Interpersonal vs. mass media communication: A false dichotomy. *Human Communication Research 15*(2), 284–303.

Rogers, E. M. (1994). *A history of communication study: A biographical approach*. New York: The Free Press.

Rubin, A. M. (1986). Uses, gratifications and media effects research. In J. Bryant, & D. Zillman, *Perspectives on media effects* (pp. 281–301). Hillside, NJ: Lawrence Erlbaum Associates.

Severin, W. and Tankard, J. (2001). *Communication theories: Origins, methods and uses in the mass media* (5th ed.). New York: Addison Wesley Longman.

6 The Individual Perspective on Mass Communication Theory

THIS CHAPTER WILL:

- Introduce the theories that focus on the individual's relationship to the mass media.
- Define key mass media theories associated with the psychological tradition.
- Focus on several key theories of the active audience, including:
  - Uses and gratifications
  - Media system dependency theory
- Examine selective processes and media effects on attitudes and behavior including:
  - Social learning theory
  - Schema and information-processing theory
  - Third-person effect
- Examine models of attitude change with special relevance to mass media:
  - Social judgment theory and source credibility
  - Maguire's information-processing model
  - The elaboration likelihood model

As Chapter 5 demonstrates in its introduction to the beginnings of research and theory in mass media, by the end of the 1950s, the field of mass communication was firmly established as a discipline. While the early theories laid the groundwork for the move from the powerful effects to the limited effects and then to the more moderate effects perspective, several paradigms were evolving at the same time. And while the discipline was attracting its own scholars and establishing its own body of research, it continued to borrow from allied fields in the social sciences.

This chapter examines the theories that focus primarily on the effect that mass media has on individuals. Some of these theories actually began as psychological or interpersonal communication theories and are only by extension related to the mass media. Others were specifically developed as a response to the impact the media were perceived to have on society. And, while these theories look at media effects on individuals, it follows that these individuals will, in turn, affect the societies in which they live. Some overlap will inevitably be apparent between these theories and those in Chapter 7, which specifically addresses the sociological perspective.

The Active Audience

Communication theory actually can be traced back more than 2,000 years to Aristotle's treatise, *Rhetoric,* which formed the basis for many theories of public address and persuasion that have evolved over the centuries since then. While Aristotle's version of mass communication involved delivering speeches to large live audiences in amphitheaters (without the benefit of microphones), significant elements of his rhetoric are evident in communication today—most prominently, the concept of persuasive communication. Aristotle was basically concerned with persuasion; that is, how speakers get an audience to agree with or buy into their message. The same central focus on persuasion is true of most communication today, particularly communication in the mass media. Advertisers try to persuade consumers to buy their products or services; public relations practitioners persuade various publics to support their organization or cause; television executives scramble to find the shows that will appeal to the largest audiences—in essence, persuading viewers that their programs are the best to watch (allowing the television folks, in turn, to persuade the advertisers to buy time on their networks). Newspapers are persuasive in their editorial content as well as in the news and features designed to attract readers. Persuasion lies at the heart of the mass media.

Also, in the tradition of Aristotle, the early theories of mass media were characterized by a focus on the messages that were sent out. Mass communication was generally viewed as a one-way form of communication: messages were sent from a source to a large or "mass" audience, which was seen as a homogeneous group of message-receivers. Message reception was thought to affect all audience members in essentially the same way. As noted in Chapter 5, propaganda theory supposed that the media would be influential in changing audience members' attitudes, and the bullet theory predicted powerful and uniform reactions to messages as was demonstrated with the "War of the Worlds" broadcast. However, when Carl Hovland researched the effectiveness of propaganda films in changing the motivations of World War II soldiers, he found little effect—although he did begin to document some of the means by which messages had persuasive effects. Lazarsfeld's voting and consumer-research studies provided further evidence that perhaps media effects did not happen in ways that the theories proposed.

A turning point in communication research came in 1959 with Bernard Berelson's famous essay, "The State of Communication Research," in which he maintained that great ideas that had given the field vitality over the previous 20 years had "worn out" and no new ideas had emerged to take their place (Berelson, 1959, p. 6). Elihu Katz responded by proposing that the field move away from its media-as-persuasion focus and instead ask the question, what do people do with the media? (Katz, 1959). This was the first formal call to a shift in focus, an active audience-centered focus.

Uses and Gratifications

Technology is shifting power away from the editors, the publishers, the establishment, the media elite. Now it's the people who are taking control.
        Rupert Murdoch, Chairman and CEO, News Corporation on the purchase
                                                of MySpace (Reiss, 2006).

Although Katz's response to Berelson is seen as a defining moment, as early as the 1940s some researchers had begun to consider the kinds of gratifications the audience received from exposure to mass media. Herta Herzog is often credited with the first such study, in which she interviewed 100 radio soap-opera fans to find out why so many housewives were attracted to soap operas. She was able to identify three primary reasons—emotional release, opportunities for wishful thinking, and obtaining advice. Herzog did not try to measure the influence of soap operas on women, just gather their reasons for listening (Lazarsfeld & Stanton, 1944, pp. 23–25). While other researchers of her time followed similar research designs with other media choices, the examination of uses and gratifications failed to dislodge the limited effects paradigm in any meaningful way. The descriptive, qualitative nature of the research, which did not examine the psychological origins of the needs that were being gratified, failed to generate much support within the research community.

In order to provide more theoretical rigor, Katz, Blumler, and Gurevitch (1974, pp. 21–22) described five elements of the uses and gratifications model:

1. The audience is conceived of as active . . . an important part of mass media use is assumed to be goal directed.

2. In the mass communication process much initiative in linking need gratification and media choice lies with the audience member.

3. The media compete with other sources of need satisfaction.

4. Many goals of mass media use can be derived from data supplied by individuals themselves . . . they can report their interests and motives.

5. Value judgments about the cultural significance of mass communication should be suspended while audience orientations are explored.

Considerable energy and controversy were directed at the first two points: the notion of the active audience and the assumption that people are very deliberate in their use of media most of the time. For example, do people consciously choose every television program they watch? Or do they sometimes use the television as background noise, or pay attention to only a fraction of what is on and ignore the rest? Some research has described television viewing as ritualistic and habitual, a passive activity requiring little concentration (Severin & Tankard, 2001, p. 298).

Several different ways of thinking about media and audiences emerged from the research and writing in the uses and gratifications perspective. Katz, Gurevitch, and Haas (1973) put the needs into five categories:

1. Needs related to strengthening information, knowledge, and understanding: cognitive needs. For example, watching the local news to find out how to dress for tomorrow's weather provides knowledge.

2. Needs related to strengthening aesthetic, pleasurable, or emotional experience: affective needs. For example, a *Harry Potter* fan pre-orders the next book in the series in order to enjoy Harry's adventures as soon as possible.

3. Needs related to strengthening credibility, confidence, stability, and status: these combine cognitive and affective needs and are known as personal integrative needs. Some women report that getting advice from *Oprah* makes them feel stronger as they face their own problems. Students read trade journals prior to job interviews, so they increase their confidence when fielding questions about the industry.

4. Needs related to strengthening contacts with family, friends, and the world: social integrative needs. For many years, groups of college students gathered in the dorm's television lounge on Thursdays to watch *Grey's Anatomy*—the experience of being together was as important as watching the program. Many sports fans also develop rituals of watching the games in groups or talking about the game in person, over the phone, and even via sports talk radio.

5. Needs related to escape and tension-release, which weaken contact with self and social roles (pp. 166–167). Students frequently report that they watch late-night comedy shows such as *The Daily Show* or *The Colbert Report* to unwind before bedtime at the end of a stressful day.

However, the research was controversial from the beginning for two reasons: The classic research methodology was based in the behavioral tradition, which meant researchers learned the answers to their questions by studying stimuli and responses. The new research model required that people respond to surveys, which seemed too subjective for the tastes of some scholars who thought it was impossible for people to accurately and objectively "self-report" on their own behaviors. Moreover, the way people's uses and needs were categorized was also seen as too descriptive and too subjective, and not based on scientific procedures (because the questionnaires suggested the categories used).

It was also controversial because research on media uses was confused with Lasswell and Wright's discussion of media functions (discussed in Chapter 5). The four elements that Lasswell and Wright labeled—surveillance, correlation, transmission of values, and entertainment—were the *functions* or *goals* of the media industries. However, the media *uses* that emerged were similar to the functions and made it difficult to focus on the active audience, rather than on the media purpose (Baran & Davis, 2006, pp. 264–265).

These concerns about uses and gratifications research have persisted over the years. However, as the limited effects paradigm waned, several developments gave the audience-centered research more credibility (Baran & Davis, 2006, pp. 268–269):

- New survey research methodologies became available that gave survey results more credibility;
- Researchers began to realize that media uses might have an impact on media effects; and
- There was a growing concern that all the effects research focused only on the negative aspects of the media.

Furthermore, the development of new media technologies has increased the control that audience members have over the media they consume, control that becomes more apparent with each passing technological development. Consider a time when there were three major television networks playing on only one television set in a typical American household—with no remote control. That was not so long ago; most college students' parents can remember a time like that. Fast-forward 30 years to the explosion in media availability and media choices available now. Beyond the presence of more television sets and more channels, audience members have much more control over their media consumption. They can use TiVo to skip through commercials. With digital-on-demand, they can watch their favorite programs whenever they want. They can download podcasts and take their favorite programs with them, and they can share their videos with the world on YouTube. Media researchers have had to adjust to the changing media landscape, and to take notice of the active audience and the role it plays in determining what it consumes and when.

However, while new media technologies have increased the complexity of doing research on media choices and the active audience, they have also allowed for some exciting new research venues. Many of the newer studies have focused on Internet-based media. For example, James, Wotring, and Forrest conducted an in-depth survey of users of electronic bulletin boards. They found that users most often used bulletin boards for gathering information as well as for socializing and meeting new people (1995, pp. 30–50).

In another study, Ferguson and Perse studied college students' use of the Web in comparison to their use of television. They found that, after using the Web for school work, students used the Web most often for entertainment, for playing games, and for browsing sites for fun. This use of the Web for diversion indicates that it might compete with or even displace television (2000, pp. 168–169). The authors suggested that television networks expand their Web presence, which has clearly happened in recent years. For example, entire episodes of television shows, such as *Lost*, can be viewed online.

Carolyn Lin has conducted research to examine how advertisers can use Internet-based venues more effectively. In two separate studies, she found that the motivation of users to access online services must be considered in deciding whether to select television versus online media for advertising dollars (1999, 2001). In fact, Lin's subjects reported that online services were capable of satisfying a wide range of needs, including surveillance, social interaction, entertainment, and escape (2001, p. 32). Lin concluded that advertisers needed to get more intentional about their research in order to better target their budgets to take advantage of online opportunities.

Thomas Ruggiero predicts that while researchers will continue to ask the same questions—such as, why do people use a particular medium and what do they get from it?—the theory will need to be expanded to include new concepts related to the transforming technology of the Internet. The uses and gratifications theory must be modernized by considering factors such as the high level of interactivity, the interpersonal aspects of this mass medium, computer-mediated social networks, and 24-hour retrieval and exchange of information and ideas (Ruggiero, 2000, pp. 28–29). It appears that this research adaptation is already under way.

Media Systems Dependency Theory

At about the same time that uses and gratifications was emerging, another theory that supports the active audience framework was being developed: the media systems dependency theory. (See Figure 6.1.)

A farmer in Kansas hears of an approaching tornado and needs to know if he should move his livestock. A school principal in Florida knows that a hurricane is brewing in the Atlantic Ocean and has to decide whether to send the children home from school early. A salesman in Chicago sees traffic backed up on I-90 for miles and contemplates whether to alter his route. A college student in Buffalo wakes up to an ice storm and needs to find out if classes are cancelled. Each of these individuals, facing a potentially life-affecting crisis, will most likely turn to the media as a source of information and advice.

In times of turmoil and uncertainty, the media become a valued source, sometimes the only source, of information. This is the basis of the *media systems dependency theory*, developed by Sandra Ball-Rokeach and Melvin DeFleur (1976). It is termed a systems theory because it examines the relationship among social systems, media systems, and audiences, and how each of these interacts and affects one another. At the same time, media systems dependency theory really focuses on the individual and how dependent he or she is on the media as a way to understand media effects (Ball-Rokeach & DeFleur, 1976, p. 5). In fact, Baran and Davis define the theory as: "the idea that the more a person depends on having needs gratified by media use, the more important the media's role will be in the person's life, and therefore, the more influence those media will have" (2006, p. 324). College students who are never without their cell phones and use instant messaging (IM) to contact their friends while doing homework (or, to their teachers' dismay, send text messages from their phones during class) because

FIGURE 6.1   Two Dependency Theory Schematics (Simple and Complex)

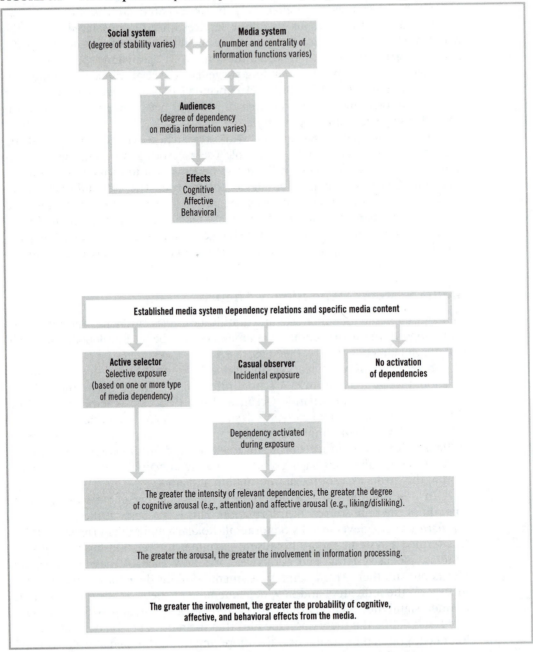

they cannot stand to be out of touch with them, can identify with a certain level of media-dependency. Similarly, most communications professors are dependent upon certain media to deliver course content, via computer projection systems, interactive Web sites, course management systems such as Blackboard, or even podcasts—all ways they depend on the media to help them perform their jobs. The key to understanding the theory, however, is realizing that the more people become dependent upon a medium, the more they will find it influential in their lives. Thus, media-dependency and media effects are inextricably linked.

Perry has noted that as society increases in complexity, media perform a greater number of functions, and people tend to become more dependent upon them. This dependency increases even more in times of conflict and change (1996, p. 60). Recall many people's use of the media on and shortly after September 11, 2001. When they first learned of the attacks on the World Trade Center and the Pentagon, most people responded by immediately turning on their televisions. Regular programming was pre-empted for days on most networks. Hindman (2004) studied public approval of both the media and the president following the Sept. 11 attacks. He found that the public tends to turn to the media in times of crisis to help resolve some of the uncertainty and ambiguity surrounding a catastrophic event. Further, the public appreciates the media's role in both providing information and communicating the human impact of the tragedy. At the same time, he found that, while the president's approval ratings soared after Sept. 11, partisan differences regarding the president also became more firmly entrenched. Even though the country became temporarily united, disruptions in the social system actually intensified the media effects (Perry, 1996, p. 40).

In a second study that examined media-dependency and Sept. 11, Lowry surveyed 507 adults in Memphis, Tennessee, regarding their use of media and interpersonal channels after the attacks (2004). He found that the degree of perceived threat was the most important predictor of an individual's dependence on

FIGURE 6.2 Media-Dependency in the Internet Age

The technology revolution has spawned a number of interesting areas for research investigation of media-dependency. Research studies are examining dependency on social-networking spaces such as MySpace and addiction to online shopping and television shopping, in addition to studies of dependency on news.

The authors' colleague who teaches in the freshmen program has noted an interesting phenomenon over the past five years: students are more frequently using social-networking sites to meet their roommates and other potential friends before they arrive at college. Whereas in the past, roommates might have exchanged a letter or a phone call to decide who would bring what to the dorm room, today's freshmen are arriving with complete information about their roommates and other students in their classes. The early association seems to help students to bond with one another more easily and ease the transition to college life. At the same time, the explosion in the use of cell phones has enabled students to keep in touch with family and high school friends more easily even after they arrive at college. Orientation leaders note that the downside of this is that freshmen are often chatting with their friends at other schools when they should be engaged in the orientation activities with their new college classmates.

the media, regardless of an individual's social status, or other demographics, except for age—younger respondents were more dependent on the media. (Interestingly, perceived threat also predicted a greater reliance on interpersonal channels of communication. Regardless of media use and availability, people still seek reassurance from other people.) Television was also the medium of choice, regardless of whether people's media habits ordinarily led them to the radio, television, or the Web (2004, pp. 353–355).

While studies using dependency theory have continued over the past three decades, it is most often studied in conjunction with other theories to determine media effects (see, for example, Matsaganis & Payne, 2005; Wang & Yang, 2007). Such a broadening of perspective has given it wider applicability and broader explanatory power, which are, after all, key functions of a good theory.

Uses and gratifications and media systems dependency theory both rely on the concept of the active audience to explain their influence. The next section will look at theories that evolved from psychology which, while still examining the effect on the individual, take a less audience-centered approach.

Individual Influences on Media Effects

Perception and Selection

Karen Kelly came to St. John Fisher College from Ilion, New York, population 8,500. The total enrollment of Ilion's combined junior/senior high school was slightly more than 800. To her, Fisher was a big school (2,500 students) in a big city (Rochester, 250,000 people). Sharif Farag came to Fisher from the borough of Queens in New York City, where he attended Forest Hills High School, with 693 in his graduating class. To Sharif, Fisher was a small school in a small city. Karen and Sharif had totally different perceptions of the exact same place. Why? It's clear that their different backgrounds and different experiences gave them different views of the same place. That is the essence of the process of perception. This section will describe perceptual processes and show how they relate to Schema Theory, Information Processing Theory, and Third-Person Effect, all of which seek to explain the way we filter information.

Perceptual Processes.   Perception can be likened to a filtering process. While thousands of stimuli vie for one's attention at any one time, humans have a finite capability for processing information from those stimuli. Thus, people employ filters that allow them to pay attention to some stimuli and not to others. Perception allows students to focus on reading their textbooks in the library and block out other stimuli such as the hum of the overhead fluorescent lights, the sensation of their bodies pressing against the chairs, the assignments in other courses waiting to be done, or the phone calls from their mothers that need to be returned. Obviously, some students are more successful at this filtering process than others.

There are some students who can write a coherent paper while chatting with friends online, listening to music from their iPods, anticipating a phone call, and enjoying a double latte; and there are others who need total freedom from distractions in order to concentrate. Whatever the tolerance of the individual, the ability to focus on specific stimuli and tune out others is one characteristic that distinguishes all humans.

But the process of perception works differently in different individuals. In addition to being from different high schools in different environments, Karen and Sharif come from different cultural backgrounds and are of different genders. These factors that account for perceptual dissimilarities include:

- biological differences
- cultural differences
- different socializing environments
- different education levels
- different religious backgrounds

The above list can probably be collapsed down to one single factor: experience. No two people perceive the world in exactly the same way because no two people (even identical twins) have had exactly the same experiences. These perceptual differences manifest themselves in a number of different ways. A student from New York City may find Rochester warm and welcoming, or may feel stifled by the "small town" environment. A student from a rural town may find Rochester big and exciting or overwhelming in its size and diversity. It all depends on the individual's perceptions. But while perception comes from personal experiences, perceptual processes also affect the way we respond to messages in the mass media. James Potter describes three different perceptual channels that might be used in responding to media messages (1999, pp. 236–237):

- **Automatic perceptual channel:** Message elements are perceived but processed automatically in an unconscious manner. For example, someone watching a football game on television becomes engrossed in a conversation and stops really paying attention to the television during a commercial. The viewer is aware that the game is in a commercial break, but the level of perception of that ad is low.
- **Attentional perceptual channel:** Message elements are processed consciously. For example, the commercial break includes a promotion for a new reality show. The viewer notes the commercial but is not a fan of reality television, and therefore does not take any note of the new program.
- **Self-reflexive perceptual channel:** The audience member is consciously aware not only of the elements in the message, but also of processing those elements. For example, during the break, the viewer sees a teaser for the local news that reports a huge accident that has closed down a local highway, pays conscious attention to that because he needs to use that highway to visit a friend after the game, and reminds himself to watch the news after the game before leaving.

Potter's typology of perceptual channels is difficult to verify empirically through research. Psychologists have, however, described several selective processes that can have an effect on how individuals are influenced by the media. Joseph Klapper, whose work with the limited effects perspective is discussed in Chapter 5, was among the first media scholars to describe them in terms of mass communication. In 1960, Klapper wrote:

> . . . People tend to expose themselves to those mass communications that are in accord with their existing attitudes and interests. Consciously or unconsciously, they avoid communications of opposite hue. In the event of their being nevertheless exposed to unsympathetic material, they often seem not to perceive it, or to recast and interpret it to fit their existing views, or to forget it more readily than they forge sympathetic material (p. 19).

Klapper was describing selective exposure, selective retention, and selective perception. By and large, people choose media messages that are in agreement with their prevailing attitudes and interests: *selective exposure*. A politically conservative student might watch Fox News, while a politically liberal student might read the *New York Times*. People also seem to remember media messages that agree with their attitudes and interests: *selective retention*. A student whose brother is fighting in Iraq would be more likely to remember the locations of the various hot spots in that country, and not to remember the location of the specific battles in the Israel-Palestinian conflict. A student with a cousin on an Israeli kibbutz near the country's border might treat news from those two conflicts exactly the opposite way. And lastly, people also tend to perceive messages in a way that fits with their attitudes and interests: *selective perception*. A student from a rural area might perceive the new Wal-Mart as bringing more goods and lower prices to her area, while another student from a more urban area might see Wal-Mart as the exploitation of low-wage workers and a threat to mom-and-pop retailers.

Schema Theory.   So far, the topic of perception has been discussed as a psychological construct, but without attaching a theory to it. One theory that relates to the process of perception and the way people filter information is known as the *schema theory*.

Robert Axelrod is a political scientist who used the concept of information-processing to build schema theory. (See Figure 6.3.) He borrowed Jerome Singer's definition of a schema as a "pre-existing assumption about the way the world is organized" (Axelrod, 1973, p. 1248). So when new information becomes available, an individual tries to interpret it based on the way he has always interpreted information about the same situation. It explains how an individual tries to make sense out of a complex world (Axelrod, 1973, pp. 1248–1249). For example, consider the college student working on a current events assignment for journalism class late one evening. He flips on the television and comes upon *The Colbert Report* on Comedy Central. Based on his past experience, he knows that *The Colbert Report* is not a serious news show, but a parody of Bill O'Reilly on Fox News. If he were looking for a serious analysis of a news event for his journalism assignment, he would know, based on his past experience, that his professor would not accept *The Colbert Report* as a source. While he might appreciate the entertainment value of Stephen Colbert, he would have to turn to PBS or another serious news source for information. This is an example of using a schema to process information—the schema is prior knowledge of *The Colbert Report* and knowledge of source credibility, which is the basis for the decision not to use it as a source for a journalism assignment.

Another scholar noted for her work on schema theory is Doris Graber. She describes schemas as "cognitive structures consisting of organized knowledge about situations and individuals that have been abstracted from prior experiences . . . used for processing new information and retrieving stored information" (1984, p. 23). If the concept of a schema is still confusing, another way to think about it might be as a pattern of existing knowledge, interests, and attitudes that an individual has, similar to a partially completed jigsaw puzzle. The schema is the backdrop or the outline. Information is received from the environment and filtered through the schema. If the new information is the right size, shape, and color, it fits into that jigsaw puzzle to help complete the picture. The more complete the puzzle, or schema, the more ability the person has to process that information.

Graber notes that schemas perform four major functions:

1. They determine what information will be noticed, processed, and stored, so it becomes available later for retrieval from memory.
2. They help individuals organize and evaluate new information so that it fits into their established perceptions.
3. They make it possible for people to go beyond the immediate information presented and fill in missing information.
4. They help people solve problems because they contain information about likely scenarios and ways to cope with them (p. 24).

For example, consider a task that college students must master at many schools—registering for classes through an online interface. A first-year student might find that this registration can be a complex and scary process. The course registration schemas of freshmen are very limited, because most of them were scheduled into high school classes by their guidance counselors. The college student must make course selections, be sure the times do not conflict, schedule classes around work and other activities, be sure prerequisites are fulfilled, meet with their advisor to get their PIN (personal identification number), and then navigate the secure Web site where registration is done online. The first time through is pretty challenging. Skip ahead to registration for senior year, which still may be anxiety producing, but not because seniors do not know the process. By now, their schemas are more complete and the registration process is easy to accomplish (provided the classes they want at the times they want with the most popular professors are not closed out). Those seniors who choose to go on to graduate school will undoubtedly be able to negotiate a new registration system more easily because their schemas have successfully accommodated a working knowledge of online registration at the undergraduate level.

FIGURE 6.3 Schema Theory and Information Processing

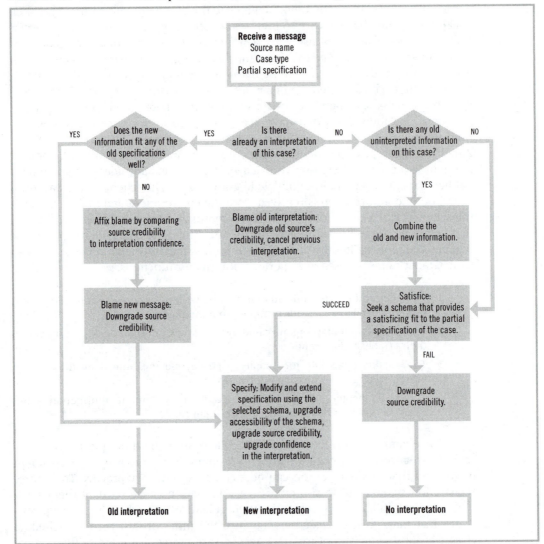

While this example may help to illustrate how schemas work, it may not be a pure mass communication example. However, individuals use schemas all the time to respond to messages in the mass media. Most students who receive an e-mail informing them that they can partake in a million-dollar windfall from a benefactor in Nigeria will recognize an e-mail scam and know to delete the message without responding. Students know that the *Wall Street Journal* is more difficult to read than the *National Enquirer*. They know they will be more likely to find their college friends on Facebook than on MySpace, and they can evaluate invitations from others in social-networking spaces based on their past experience and decide whether or not to respond.

It is important to remember that schemas represent social learning (Graber, 1984, p. 147). People acquire schemas over time by learning from and observing others as well as by having direct experience. The mass media play a role in schemas in the same way that they play a role in social learning theory: while some schemas develop from personal contact and face-to-face interaction, schemas can also evolve from exposure to mass media. Social learning theory is discussed in greater detail later in this chapter.

Information-Processing Theory. The work of Axelrod and Graber points out an inextricable link between the concept of schemas and another theory, information-processing theory. Baran and Davis note that information-processing theory is actually a large set of diverse and different ideas about how people interpret and process all the information they receive (2006, p. 286). It has been a complex field of study for cognitive psychologists. However, among mass media scholars, research on schemas and information processing in mass communication has generally focused on how individuals process news stories. One prominent media scholar, Doris Graber, maintains that people are overwhelmed by too much information, so they need processing mechanisms to help them pull out the information they want to get. Graber (1984, p. 125) took Axelrod's model and related it to how individuals process a news story:

> First comes the reception of a message. The integration process starts the series of questions to determine whether and how the new information relates to stored concepts and whether it is worth processing. . . . If the information is worthwhile and is reasonably well related to established schemas that can be brought to mind, it is integrated into them. If not, the new information or its source may be discredited or rejected or the new information may alter or replace the previous schema that has been called into question.

For example, suppose that a student receives an e-mail from the student activities board notifying the campus that the administration is planning to cancel the annual spring festival, which in the past has featured a concert, picnic, and other activities near the end of the school year. Graber offers four questions that should be answered in the application of the model to a specific situation:

1. Does this cover a topic the individual already knows about? Yes, the festival has been an annual event that the entire student body looks forward to each year.
2. Is it a familiar or predictable occurrence, based on previously stored knowledge? Maybe, because the administration has been trying to limit the incidence of underage drinking on campus, and drunken behavior at the festival has been a problem the previous two years.
3. Does it make sense or contradict past experience? It could do either, because the funds are from the student government but the administration could veto plans if they do not approve.
4. How can the credibility of the source be evaluated? Credible, because the campus group that sent the e-mail is the planning committee for the festival.

Further, Graber's research revealed that people process news stories using one of three different strategies:

1. Straight matching of a news story to a schema: the administration always wants to spoil students' good times, so they are doing it again.
2. Processing through inferences: deducing that this is like when they cancelled the drag show.
3. Multiple integration of a story with several schemas: it could be framed as taking control from students, as a safety issue, as pressure from the board of trustees, as distrusting students, or as treating students like they are still in high school (pp. 123–137).

Graber also maintains that news stories are processed with schemas as a result of what she calls *media cueing*, which means that the pictures, headlines, and graphics that accompany a story will link it to a particular schema (p. 124). So a television or newspaper story on snowfall might show children happily sledding in a park, or angry motorists stuck in traffic, or the city's emergency command center. Each image would evoke a different schema for the consumers of that medium and would prompt different responses. (Chapter 7 explains how this concept of media cueing is similar to the concept of framing.)

The results of other research reveal three dimensions of news information-processing strategies that people consistently use:

1. selective scanning, skimming, and tuning out items
2. active processing, going beyond or reading through a story to reinterpret it according to the person's needs
3. reflective integration, replaying the story in the person's mind and using it as a topic of discussion (McLeod, Kosicki, McLeod, 1994, p. 148).

For an example of McLeod et al.'s strategies, consider a typical college student scanning Yahoo News. She skims over and tunes out information about the cyclone about to hit China, the controversy over the presidential elections in Pakistan, the latest doping scandals to hit baseball . . . and then she comes across a story about the price of textbooks. As a college student, she is likely to read the story through and process it, to interpret it according to her needs. Her state representative is pushing to have textbook sales become exempt from state sales tax; that is news she can use. Part of her schema helps her determine how to find the cheapest textbook (in the bookstore or online) and how she feels about her elected officials (she might vote for the person proposing the sales-tax break in the next election). Further on in the news report, she comes across a story about the new vaccine for women to halt the spread of the human papilloma virus (HPV), which causes cervical cancer. She reads this even more carefully and reflects on whether she should consider asking her doctor about it. She brings it up with her suitemates in the dorm that evening. After discussing it, they decide to ask the staff at the college wellness center if they should talk to their doctors about the new vaccine. This is reflective integration of the news story into her schema, which will affect future evaluation of information about the same topic.

In applying information-processing theory to mass media, however, the research has focused primarily on how people process television news, and how the broadcast news media hinder rather than help people's understanding of news stories (Baran & Davis, 2006, pp. 290–292). This is done because the average newscast tries to cover too many stories in too short a time period, condensing complex information into short segments and human interest scenarios that confuse the viewer. Also, the extensive visual images are often overwhelming and actually detract from understanding of the content. At the same time, viewers do not give television news stories their full attention and rely on routine activation of schemas to process news stories, rarely engaging in reflective processing. Given that television news is no longer the dominant medium it once was, it is likely that further research on information processing will need to expand its focus to other forms of mass media messages.

Third-Person Effect. Another theory that is also closely linked to perceptual processes is the *third-person effect*. Davison identified the third-person effect as one in which an individual who is exposed to mass media messages believes the messages have a greater impact on others than on himself (1983, p. 4). Davison did several small experiments in which he gauged people's perceptions of the influence of mass media messages on other people. His topics included presidential elections, newspaper strikes, and the effect of television commercials on children. In each instance, he found that people perceived that others would be more influenced by mass media messages than they themselves would be (1983, pp. 1–15). One of the more interesting applications of this phenomenon came in the area of censorship—the censor rarely admits that he is affected by a mass media message but maintains that he must protect others from being affected by these messages (Davison, 1983, p. 14). This issue played out in 2007 in upstate New York, when the Monroe County executive threatened to withhold funds from the public library if patrons were allowed to view pornography in the library. The concern expressed most often was that children would walk by, see the pornographic material, and be affected by it.

As might be expected, a lot of the strength of the third-person effect comes from messages that are seen as negative or socially undesirable. For example, McLeod, Eveland, and Nathanson found that college students perceived that the effects of antisocial language in rap music would be more likely to affect others than themselves. Those with the strongest third-person effect were also most likely to favor censorship of rap music (1997). David and Johnson (1998) investigated the impact that television programming and advertising had on perceived body image in a study of 144 female college students. They found that the third-person effect was stronger for those with high self-esteem (i.e., women who felt good about themselves thought that other women would be more affected by television's depictions of ideal body size than they would). Lo and Wei (2000) surveyed more than 2,600 Taiwanese high school and college students about their attitudes toward Internet pornography. They found that women perceived that pornography had a greater impact on men than on women, and that women were more likely to support restrictions on Internet pornography.

More recently, Huge, Glynn, and Jeong (2006) posited that the third-person effect was more complicated than originally assumed. Their study, which examined the response to the priest sex abuse scandals in the Roman Catholic Church, looked not only at the perceived effects on self and others for the respondents, but it also explored their interest in the issue, the relevance of the issue for their social group, and the relevance of the issue for the target group. The third-person effect was greater in a group that was more interested in the issue (i.e., Roman Catholics were more interested in this issue than non-Catholics), found to be perceived as bigger for the out-group (i.e., Roman Catholics thought non-Catholics would be more influenced by the news on the issue than they were), and members of the out-group estimated that they would be influenced more than members of the in-group (i.e., non-Roman Catholics thought they would be more influenced by the story than Roman Catholics). The authors conclude that social distance and relevance of the topic must be considered in research on the third-person effect.

While it has not been a pivotal theory of mass media, many current studies are tying in third-person effect as one of several theories that explain how people respond to mass communication. And, in an era in which censorship, FCC regulations, and wiretapping are recurring concerns, the third-person effect may explain many phenomena around us.

Thus far this chapter has considered the ways that people use and interpret the messages they receive from the media. But the media play another important role in the formation and change of individual attitudes. The next section examines several key theories that look at of the concept of attitude change; in other words, persuasion.

Information and Attitude Change

Early Theories: Social Judgment Theory and Source Credibility.   As mentioned earlier, information on persuasion and attitude change has been part of interpersonal communication for centuries. In the 1930s, Sherif's research on social norms led to his social judgment theory, which examined the impact that other people have on developing norms of behavior. Individuals are dependent upon their social groups to help formulate standards for how to behave in society—better known as social norms. For example, students know to wear clothing to class, even in extremely warm weather. Our social norms, and our laws, prohibit individuals from strolling through society naked. In fact, this norm is so ingrained that most people would not even consider going out without clothing in any weather. We learn this social norm from the people around us as we are growing up. Similarly, we learn other norms that help society function smoothly; for instance, waiting in line at the grocery store, raising a hand to ask a question in class, stopping at a red light, returning books to the library. Sometimes people

FIGURE 6.4   Gangsta Rap and the Third-Person Effect

In April 2006, Rochester, New York's daily newspaper, the *Democrat and Chronicle*, embarked on a crusade it called "Rebuilding, Restoring Rochester Thru Music." The initiative was aimed at decrying the culture of violence, drugs, and degradation of women depicted in gangsta rap music. Frequent editorials invited citizens to clip out a coupon to send to radio stations and record companies threatening to boycott this type of music. On its Web site (www.DemocratandChronicle.com), the newspaper listed the initiative's accomplishments within its first 14 months:

- In March 2005, nearly 40 people participated in a community forum on the hip-hop culture sponsored by the *Democrat and Chronicle* Editorial Board. The event helped launch our anti-gangsta rap campaign.
- Over the past year, the *Democrat and Chronicle* published 25 editorials and columns on the subject.
- More than 50 readers and public officials, including Senator Hillary Rodham Clinton, wrote essays and letters.
- Members of the Editorial Board made more than 20 public appearances to discuss gangsta rap.
- City Councilman Adam McFadden, who initially defended gangsta rap, said the newspaper's campaign helped him change his mind.
- Gangsta rap's negative influence was cited in then-Mayor William Johnson's anti-violence plan in 2005.
- Community educator Nate Brown organized a series of student forums.
- A coalition was organized to seek state funding for a music education program serving city youths.
- More than 4,000 "Take a Stand" coupons were collected. These coupons asking readers to pledge their opposition to gangsta music were published alongside essays and editorials on the issue; readers were urged to fill them out and mail them to the newspaper, which promised to forward them to music companies that sold gangsta rappers' albums.

The initiative clearly is an example of the third-person effect. The campaign decries the influence that gangsta rap music has on the youth culture in the city. Interestingly, some citizens responding to the permanent link on the Web site ask for evidence that this type of music has negative effects. One comment reads, "There was this exact same argument in the Fifties about Rock and Roll."

Source: www.democratandchronicle.com/apps/pbcs.dll/article?AID=/20060430/OPINION04/604300302. Retrieved May 29, 2007.

do violate these norms, but if they do, sanctions generally are imposed upon the violator.

However, while people may learn directly from others, at the same time many social norms, trends, customs, and even language come from the mass media. Fashion magazines dictate the styles in many high schools and colleges; political campaigns focus more and more on the appearance of a candidate and the 10-second sound-bite to make an impact; Internet bloggers have been responsible for forcing the government to address political scandals even leading public officials to resign; new words such as "disinformation," "punked," and "blogosphere" have become part of our language as a result of media influence. Thus, even though the early research on social norms focused on the influence of people, the mass media are also a powerful source of social norms and behaviors.

Chapter 5 describes how Carl Hovland did some of the early research on persuasion when he examined the role that films played in soldiers' motivation to fight in World War II. In addition to this area, Hovland also collaborated with Sherif in a number of studies of social pressure and persuasion. Among them were his studies of *source credibility*. Hovland discovered that where a message comes from and who delivers it can be major factors in whether that message is perceived as credible and persuasive by the recipient. A clear illustration of this can be found in celebrity endorsements. Manufacturers are willing to pay millions of dollars for being able to market their products with celebrities as spokespersons. Basketball icon Michael Jordan is one of the most famous athletes of all time, turning his superstardom into contracts with Nike for his Air Jordan sneakers, as well as financial institutions, underwear companies, and others. The concept behind this is *source credibility*.

The three main components of source credibility are knowledge, trustworthiness, and charisma or dynamism. To be believable, a source must demonstrate each of these characteristics.

For example, another sports icon, skateboarder Tony Hawk, has endorsed a line of skateboards, clothing, shoes, and video games that bear his name. In terms of source credibility, Hawk has good knowledge of the sport of skateboarding and what it takes to be successful—by age 16, he was considered the best skateboarder in the world. Hawk is credited with inventing over 80 aerial skateboard tricks and landed the first-ever 900 (two and a half mid-air spins) at the X-Games, a feat that solidified his reputation as the best skateboarder ever. Is Hawk trustworthy? Since he retired from active competition, Hawk has established the Tony Hawk Foundation, which provides financing for public skateboard parks in low income areas (by 2007, 366 such parks have been financed). He also founded the public charity, Athletes for Hope, and, as of this writing, has no major scandals attached to his name or business enterprises. Finally, Hawk comes across as a charismatic personality in person, in his DVDs, and in media interviews. Thus, Tony Hawk exhibits a high degree of source credibility in the sport of skateboarding. At the same time, Hawk might not rate as high in endorsing a particular brand of computer or soft drink. So credibility is tied to the topic as well as to the source.

The components of credibility can be extended to sources in person as well as in the mass media. The president's press secretary, a hospital spokesperson, the city police chief, the local news anchor, the college professor—all exhibit characteristics of source credibility in their topic areas. The college professor who teaches media law would have little credibility in a thermodynamics class. Similarly, the physics professor would have low credibility in a media law class. Additionally, sources might be evaluated differently by different individuals. The Republican president's press secretary may have high credibility among members of his party, but low credibility among Democrats. The Reverend Jerry

Falwell may have spoken for many Christians during his time as the leader of the Moral Majority, but his credibility among gays and lesbians was always low. Understanding the components of source credibility helps media practitioners to craft the most persuasive messages, while recognizing that they cannot persuade all the people all the time with a single message.

Theories of Behavioral Change

Social Learning Theory. How does a child learn to tie her shoes? Throw a baseball? Speak confidently in an interview? Social learning theory, also referred to as *social cognitive theory* in the psychology literature, addresses these questions.

Chances are that these things and many others were learned through the use of role models. The concept of role models is really the basis behind social learning theory. Individuals are creatures of imitation and learn to do things by watching and copying the behavior of others. It is also possible to learn what *not* to do by watching others: For example, a child who sees his little sister burned by a hot stove learns not to put his hand there; a son who watches his father struggle with emphysema vows not to smoke; a student whose roommate fails for cheating resolves to do all her own class work.

Albert Bandura is the name most frequently associated with social learning or modeling theory. Bandura is a Stanford University psychologist who first achieved a measure of fame for the Bobo doll experiments in the 1960s. Children were exposed to an adult who either played gently or aggressively with a Bobo doll, an inflatable doll that was rounded on the bottom with a weight in the base so it bounced back up when it was knocked down. Children who saw the doll treated aggressively behaved in an aggressive manner, thereby validating the social learning theory.

But Bandura's research went far beyond this experiment. In fact, he is considered one of the top five most influential psychologists of the twentieth century, in company with the likes of Sigmund Freud, B. F. Skinner, and Jean Piaget (Haggbloom, 2002, p. 146). Bandura observed that not all learning can be *directly* experienced, that learning comes from a variety of sources. One of those prominent sources is the mass media. Bandura (1994, pp. 70–71) maintained that the media teach people in three main ways, through:

1. **Observation:** Individuals can learn how to do things they have never done before because they have seen it in the media. For example, the popular Food Network and cooking shows on television have instructed people on new food preparation techniques that they may use in their own kitchens;

2. **Inhibition:** Seeing the negative consequences of behavior in the media can teach people not to engage in such behaviors. For example, seeing media icon Martha Stewart go to prison for insider trading might encourage others to be more diligent about their financial dealings; or seeing Rosie O'Donnell censored for her antiwar rants may encourage others to be more cautious about expressing their opinions; and

3. **Disinhibition:** People are not afraid of some things because they have seen them being dealt with in the media. For example, children and adolescents have been injured trying risky stunts that they see on professional wrestling shows or on the television program *Jackass*. In a more positive vein, victims of childhood sexual abuse have found the courage to come forward when they see examples of others who have faced their abusers and found closure.

Baran and Davis also note that Bandura's concept of vicarious reinforcement is central to social learning in the mass media. This means that people can learn from reinforcement that is observed and not directly experienced. While learning can occur without reinforcement, individuals choose to engage in the observed behavior based on the positive or negative reinforcement seen (Baran & Davis, 2006, p. 198). For example, seeing the bad guys get caught on television will reinforce the learning that crime does not pay, even if the observer is not the one being punished. Or seeing the sexual behavior depicted on *Sex in the City* may lead young professionals to the conclusion that all single women sleep around with multiple partners.

Bandura is clearly in sync with other mass media researchers: for example, with George Gerbner, because he sees the media as "cultivating" a certain view of the world; and with Everett Rogers, because he sees the role that the media play in diffusing innovation and ideas through society (Bandura, 1994, pp. 75–85). Gerbner and Rogers are discussed in more detail with the sociological theories in Chapter 7. The key to understanding Bandura's ideas is noting the complexity of factors that account for human learning and behavior. Media messages are a large and important factor, to be sure, but are not the only means by which learning and understanding occur.

FIGURE 6.5   Foul Language on Television: An Application of the Social Learning Theory

In a study that directly looked at the media and social learning theory, Kaye and Sapolsky examined the incidence of obscene words and their context on seven television networks during the 8 to 11 p.m. viewing hours. The researchers found that profane words and phrases were heard once every eight minutes on prime time, an increase from once every 13 minutes four years earlier. The highest incidence of profane language occurred during the first hour of prime time. While much of the coarse language was mild in nature, the researchers believe the repetition is the factor that will most influence young viewers. Further, Kaye and Sapolsky found that 60 percent of obscene language was met with a neutral response by other characters on television, and a full 25 percent was met with a positive response, indicating a general acceptance of obscene language used by the television characters. According to social learning theory, viewers would be influenced by behaviors they view most often and the consequences of those behaviors. Many educators and parents fear that increased use of obscenity has led to an increase in rudeness and overall decline in civility in society.

Source: Kaye, B.K. & Sapolsky, B.S. (2004) Talking a "blue" streak: Context and offensive language in prime time network television programs. *Journalism and Mass Communication Quarterly 81*(4) 911–927.

Information Processing and Attitude Change.   While earlier in this chapter, the discussion of schemas and processing of news was closely associated with the mass media, psychologist William McGuire suggested his own "information-processing theory" that dealt with attitude change. McGuire's persuasive model laid out specific steps that needed to be followed sequentially before attitude change could occur. While he expanded and revised his model several times, McGuire's eight-step model (1976, pp. 303–313) for attitude change included:

1. Exposure to the message.
2. Perception of the message.
3. Comprehension of the message.
4. Agreement with the message.
5. Retention of the message.
6. Retrieval of the message (when needed).
7. Decision-making related to the message.
8. Action in accordance with the message.

In an application of McGuire's model for planning and conducting public health campaigns, Huhman, Heitzler, and Wong (2004, p. 5) write:

> McGuire's model posits that the impact of persuasive communication is mediated by three broad stages of message processing: attention, comprehension, and acceptance. Attention depends on exposure and awareness; comprehension is predicated on understanding the message; and acceptance includes intention and, finally, behavior change. In McGuire's model, because of the inherent variability in how people process media messages, a percentage of the audience is lost at each stage. Thus, high levels of exposure and awareness are needed to create measurable population effects.

For example, a public relations practitioner with the Cystic Fibrosis Society is planning a fund-raising event, a stair-climb up to the top of the tallest building in the city, to raise funds for research for a cure for cystic fibrosis. She first needs to get people's attention to the event and the cause. She can do this through a variety of means including news releases, media alerts, celebrity endorsements, and so on, which make the public aware of the event. In the second stage, she needs to get people to understand the cause and the importance of the event to this cause. This will require her to separate her message from the other health-related organizations in town and their fund-raisers going on at or near the same time. By emphasizing the strides that have already been made in cystic fibrosis research, she may be able to increase comprehension. In the final stage, the public will accept the message by either participating in the event or sponsoring a participant. She might get this acceptance by enlisting the support of local athletic teams and health clubs, by gaining endorsements from local celebrities affected by the disease, or by offering desirable prizes for the top fund-raisers.

While McGuire's theory was not originally developed for mass communication, it does point to the need for persuasive messages to follow a sequential format in order for them to be successful. Perry notes that, in the way that the theory views people as processing information in a rational, linear way, it is similar to social learning theory, described earlier (1996, p. 101). But what if people are not persuaded through a rational, systematic way? The next theory elaborates on that perspective in considering alternative ways that persuasion occurs.

Elaboration Likelihood Model.   A second model that deals with attitude change is the elaboration likelihood model, developed by Petty and Cacioppo (1986), who, actually building on McGuire's work, asked what happens during the message processing part of the persuasion process (Perry, 1996, p. 115). (See Figure 6.6.)

The elaboration likelihood model (ELM) states that there are two routes through which information is processed that can lead to attitudes being changed:

1. The central route, in which the information is actively processed and the individual evaluates it in a rational manner, and

2. The peripheral route, in which the receiver does not actively process the information in a cognitive sense, but instead relies on peripheral cues, such as the style of the message, the credibility of the source, her own mood, and so on.

Elaboration refers to how much cognitive work is involved in processing the information. When people process information in the central route, they are high in elaboration, relying on their prior experiences and knowledge to analyze the situation, evaluate arguments, and think through their own position. With peripheral processing, individuals are low in elaboration, and they form attitudes or change ideas based on simple inferences or associations, such as in the case of a celebrity endorsement. Attitudes formed on the basis of the central route last longer and are more resistant to change (Perry, 1996, p. 116).

Of course, which route becomes the persuasive one varies depending on several factors related to the individuals, starting with their degree of involvement. Individuals are more likely to process via a central route when they are highly involved in the subject and the information coming to them. For example, a student is more likely to process choice of an internship or a job via the central route, while the brand of breakfast cereal purchased at the grocery store could be a more peripheral decision. Second, the ELM is more likely to be engaged when an individual perceives the message as personally relevant. This would suggest that a senior looking for a job after graduation would be more interested in the messages of the college career center than classmates who are planning to attend graduate school or freshmen just completing their first semester at school. And third, the ELM suggests central processing requires a degree of attention and the ability to elaborate on the message. Distractions can weaken the strength of the central message and allow for peripheral cues, such as the attractiveness of a celebrity endorser, to weigh more heavily in the persuasion (Perry, 1996, pp. 116–117). For example, Tiger Woods endorses golf equipment, but also puts his celebrity stamp of approval on automobiles, credit cards, watches, and even a Japanese broadcasting company. While his expertise in recommending golf equipment may justify his endorsement (and lead a serious golfer to process Tiger's endorsements via the central route), advertisers of watches, automobiles, and credit cards are looking for peripheral route persuasion.

FIGURE 6.6   Elaboration Likelihood Model

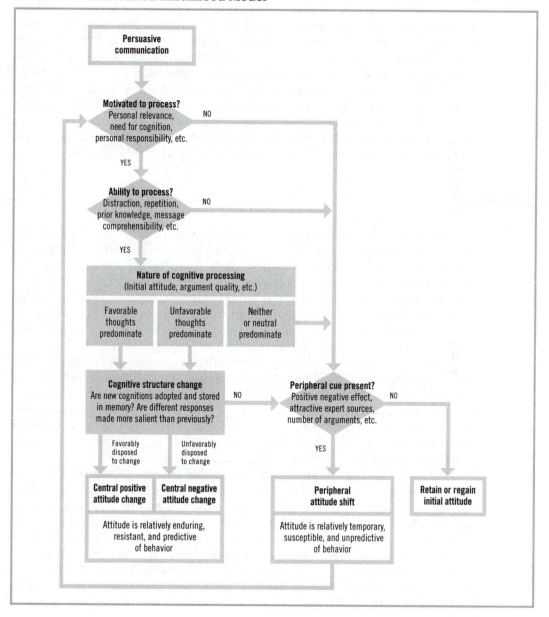

Although the ELM suggests that the two routes are mutually exclusive, Petty and Caccioppo stress that they are really points on a cognitive processing continuum that show the degree of effort a person expends when confronted with a message. The more people work to evaluate a message, that is, the more *elaboration* they employ with it, the less they will be influenced by factors not related to the message content (Griffin 2003, p. 187).

The elaboration likelihood model brings together a number of attitude-change theories. It has excellent application to mass media because mediated messages have the potential to provide both central and peripheral cues. Research has tested ELM most specifically in advertising. Petty and Priester report that studies have shown people are better able to use the central route when processing print sources than those that are more controlled, such as radio and television (1994, p. 104). They note that an important goal of any persuasive strategy aimed at changing attitudes is to increase people's motivation to think about the message. This is true whether one is looking for a long-lasting attitude change (e.g., safe sexual practices) or those where a short-term change is acceptable (e.g., donating to the dance marathon) (Petty & Priester, 1994, p. 116).

Summary

The individual effect theories of mass media illustrate clearly how the discipline has borrowed from allied fields in the social sciences. Social learning theory, perception, and schema theory all came directly from the psychological tradition, and students still study these ideas in introductory psychology classes. Additionally, the theories of persuasion and attitude change, such as social judgment, source credibility, Maguire's information-processing theory, and the elaboration likelihood model, have their roots in theories of psychology, even though they have been adopted as part of mass communication's theoretical foundation.

Advertisers, public relations professionals, and journalists are not the only individuals interested in opinion formation and attitude change. In fact, most of the early work in this area (indeed, dating all the way back to Aristotle), focused on how persuasion takes place in interpersonal, group, or face-to-face encounters. These theories can be adapted to the mass media, however, because the same dynamics can occur whether an encounter takes place face-to-face, over television, on talk radio, or via the Internet.

The uses and gratifications and the media systems dependency theories underscore the importance of considering the role of the audience. Researchers are still debating the concept of the active audience, and how purposeful one's media choices actually are. The value of this perspective, however, is the consideration that has been given to the audience, as a key player in the media landscape. As choices increase and users get more control, the uses and needs of the audience must be taken into account by the media practitioners. Further, they need to continue to find ways that they can engage the audience in the media forums, giving them a chance to participate. Web logs, talk radio, reality shows in which the audience votes, reader contributions to online news sites—all of these are indicative of the growing role of the user of mass media in determining programming and content.

These theories are focused primarily on the relationship of mass media with the audience at the individual level, although it is assumed that this collection of individuals will affect the larger society. In Chapter 7, theories that specifically focus on larger-scale or group effects are examined.

QUESTIONS FOR DISCUSSION / APPLICATION EXERCISES

1. Consider some of the media you utilize in the course of a day—print, broadcasting, and online sources. Looking at the categories of needs in the uses and gratifications theories, how well do the needs match up with your uses?

2. Can you identify your level of dependency on various mass media? Consider a catastrophic occurrence you personally experienced. How did your media use and dependency change as the news emerged?

3. Using Graber's tenets of information-processing theory, what factors influence how students read the campus newspaper? Watch campus television?

4. What sources can you identify as the most credible as you make major decisions—picking your major, looking for an internship, buying a car? Can you distinguish the impact that personal versus mass media sources have on your major decisions?

5. In social learning theory, Bandura maintains that the media teach us in three ways: observation, inhibition, and disinhibition. Find examples of how each of those may be operating to produce learning in children, college students, and adults.

6. As a future media practitioner, what lessons would you take away from the elaboration likelihood model in terms of crafting persuasive appeals?

REFERENCES

Axelrod, R. (1973). Schema theory: An information processing model of perception and cognition. *American Political Science Review 67*, 1248–1266.

Ball-Rokeach, S. J., & DeFleur, M. L. (1976). A dependency model of mass media effects. *Communication Research 3*, 3–21.

Bandura, A. (1994). Social cognitive theory of mass communication. In J. Bryant & D. Zillman (Eds.), *Media effects: Advances in theory and research* (pp. 61–90). Hillsdale, NJ: Lawrence Erlbaum Associates.

Baran, S. J., & Davis, D. K. (2006). *Mass communication theory: Foundations, ferment, and future* (4th ed.). Belmont, CA: Thomson/Wadsworth.

Berelson, B. (1959). The state of communication research. *The Public Opinion Quarterly 23*(1), 1–6.

David. P., & Johnson, M. A. (1998). The role of self in third-person effects about body image. *Journal of Communication 48*(4), 37–58.

Davison, W. P. (1983). The third-person effect in communication. *Public Opinion Quarterly 47*(1), 1–15.

Ferguson, D. A., & Perse, E. M. (2000). The worldwide web as a functional alternative to television. *Journal of Broadcasting & Electronic Media 44*(2), 155–174.

Graber, D. A. (1984). *Processing the news: How people tame the information tide.* New York: Longman.

Griffin, E. (2003). *Instructor's manual for a first look at communication theory.* New York: McGraw-Hill.

Haggbloom, S. J. (2002). 100 most eminent psychologists of the 20th century. *Review of General Psychology* 6(2), 139–152.

Hindman, D. B. (2004). Media system dependency and public support for the press and the president. *Mass Communication and Society* 7(1), 29–42.

Huge, M., Glynn, C. J., & Jeong, I. (2006). A relationship-based approach to understanding third-person perceptions. *Journalism & Mass Communication Quarterly 83*(3), 530–546.

Huhman M., Heitzler C., & Wong F. The VERB™ campaign logic model: A tool for planning and evaluation. *Preventing Chronic Disease* [serial online] 2004 July. Retrieved Aug. 15, 2006 from: http://www.cdc.gov/ pcd/issues/2004/jul/04_0033.htm.

James, M. L., Wotring, C. E., & Forrest, E. J. (1995). An exploratory study of the perceived benefits of electronic bulletin board use and their impact on other communication activities. *Journal of Broadcasting & Electronic Media, 39*(1), 30–50.

Katz, E. (1959). Mass communication research and the study of popular culture. *Studies in Public Communication 2*, 1–6.

Katz, E., Blumler, J. G., & Gurevitch, M. (1974). Utilization of mass communication by the individual. In J. G Blumler & E. Katz (Eds.), *The uses of mass communication* (pp. 19–32). Beverly Hills, CA: Sage Publications.

Katz, E., Gurevich, M., & Haas, H. (1973). On the use of the mass media for important things. *American Sociological Review 38*, 164–181.

Klapper, J. T. (1960). *The effects of mass communication.* New York: The Freedom Press.

Lazarsfeld, P. F., & Stanton, F. N. (1944). *Radio research 1942–1943.* New York: Essential Books, Distributed by Duell, Sloan, and Pearce.

Lin, C. A. (1999). Online-service adoption likelihood. *Journal of Advertising Research 39*(2), 79–89.

Lin, C. A. (2001). Audience attributes, media supplementation, and likely online service adoption. *Mass Communication and Society 4*(1), 19–38.

Lo, V. H., & Wei, R. (2000, April). *Third-person effect, gender and pornography on the internet.* Paper presented at the annual meeting of Broadcast Education Association, Las Vegas, Nevada.

Lowry, W. (2004). Media dependency during a large-scale social disruption: The case of September 11. *Mass Communication and Society* 7(3), 339–357.

Matsaganis, M. D., & Payne, J. G. (2005). Agenda setting in a culture of fear: The lasting effects of September 11 on American politics and journalism. *American Behavioral Scientist 49*(3), 379–392.

McGuire, W. J., (1976). Some internal psychological factors influencing consumer choice. *Journal of Consumer Research 2* (4), 302–319.

McLeod, D. M., Eveland, W. P., Jr., & Nathanson, A. I. (1997). Support for censorship of violent and misogynic rap lyrics: An analysis of the third-person effect. *Communication Research 24*, 153–174.

McLeod, J. M., Kosicki, G. M., & McLeod, D. M. (1994). The expanding boundaries of political communication effects. In J. Bryant & D. Zillman (Eds.), *Media effects: Advances in theory and research* (pp. 123–162). Hillsdale, NJ: Lawrence Erlbaum Associates.

Perry, D. K. (1996). *Theory and research in mass communication.* Mahwah, NJ: Lawrence Earlbaum Associates.

Petty, R. E., & Cacioppo, J. T. (1986). The elaboration likelihood model of persuasion. *Advances in Experimental Social Psychology 19*, 123–205. New York: Academic Press.

Petty, R. E., & Priester, J. R. (1994). Mass media attitude change: Implications of the elaboration likelihood model of persuasion. In J. Bryant & D. Zillman (Eds.), *Media effects: Advances in theory and research* (pp. 91–122). Hillsdale, NJ: Lawrence Erlbaum Associates.

Potter, W. J. (1999). *On media violence.* Thousand Oaks, CA: Sage Publications.

Reiss, S. (July, 2006). His space. *Wired* magazine 14.07, Retrieved Aug. 16, 2006 from: http://www.wired. com/wired/archive/14. 07/.

Ruggiero, T. E. (2000). Uses and gratifications in the 21st century. *Mass Communication and Society 3*(1), 3–37.

Severin, W. J., & Tankard, J. W. Jr., (2001). *Communication theories: Origins, methods, and uses in the mass media* (5th ed.). New York: Addison Wesley Longman.

Wang, C. C., & Yang, H. W. (2007). Passion and dependency in online shopping activities. *CyberPsychology & Behavior 10*(2), 296–298.

7 The Sociological Perspective on Mass Communication Theory

THIS CHAPTER WILL:

- Introduce mass media theories that affect society as a whole.
- Consider the impact of agenda setting.
- Trace the development of diffusion of innovation.
- Review the issues associated with the knowledge-gap hypothesis.
- Examine the effect of the spiral of silence.
- Distinguish a variety of cultivation effects, including the effects of television violence.

The evening of Friday, June 17, 1994, found millions of Americans watching the National Basketball Association finals on the NBC television network. Coverage was interrupted to report on a developing story: Former football star O. J. Simpson, who was accused of the murder of his wife and another man, had failed to surrender to police that afternoon. He was riding in a white Ford Bronco driven by his friend Al Cowlings on a California freeway, holding a gun to his own head. Thus began a low-speed chase, followed live by news crews on the ground and aloft in helicopters, that held the national attention for several hours and pre-empted all network programming. More than a decade later, college students shown a videotape of the O. J. Simpson chase were able to recognize the event in fewer than five seconds. Many recall watching the basketball game that evening when news of the chase broke in and pre-empted that coverage.

Was this a critical event in American life? Was this the most important news event occurring at the time? Did the network coverage give more importance to the event than perhaps was warranted? These questions and the role of the media in choosing to portray what it deems the most newsworthy events are examined in a theory known as *agenda setting*.

Agenda setting is one of the pivotal theories from the sociological perspective, that is, theories that examine the ways in which the media have been shown to be influential on large groups or society in general. Chapter 6 examines the psychological theories of the mass media—the theories that look at how media influences people at the individual level. The sociological perspective takes the theoretical view a step further to ask how media influences groups and society. While there is some overlap between these two perspectives, this chapter will focus primarily on the sociological or group perspective.

In strict chronological terms, agenda setting was not the first sociological theory of mass communication because other researchers were examining broad social impacts before McCombs and Shaw's seminal work defining agenda setting in 1972. But agenda-setting's origins actually can be traced to Walter Lippmann's *Public Opinion*, written in 1922 (McCombs, 2005, p. 157), so that theory will begin this chapter.

Agenda Setting

How important is a presidential election? The war in Iraq? National health care? Immigration reform? The paternity of Anne Nicole Smith's baby? Paris Hilton's legal troubles and Lindsay Lohan's alcohol abuse? These are all stories that have received extensive and prolonged coverage by the media, leading the public to know about them and think about them. This is, very simply, agenda setting. Severin and Tankard describe the agenda-setting function of the media as "the media's capability, through repeated news coverage, of raising the importance of an issue in the public's mind" (2001, p. 219). And it is clear that the media do this. Twenty-four hour cable news channels have led the media to cover more issues in greater detail than ever before and to deem even relatively minor events as newsworthy. To fill all those hours, news channels are covering even relatively "minor" news events. For example, even a news organization as prestigious as the BBC dedicated a reporter to the Michael Jackson child molestation trial. And, when 2006 Kentucky Derby winner Barbaro broke his leg in the Preakness Stakes, all major news outlets camped out at the New Bolton Center at the University of Pennsylvania where he was being treated. the public is inundated with news coverage and the sheer amount affects their perception of what is important.

But agenda setting is not a recent phenomenon. Chapter 5 notes that as early as 1922 Walter Lippmann was discussing how the press contributed to "The World Outside and Pictures in our Heads." Princeton University's Bernard Cohen further refined the concept in 1963 when he noted that the press "may not be successful much of the time in telling people what to think, but it is stunningly successful in telling its readers what to think *about*" (Baran & Davis, 2006, p. 316). While neither Lippmann nor Cohen actually used the term "agenda setting," the concept was essentially the same when mass communication researchers began a systematic study of the influence of the news media on its audience (McCombs, 2005, p. 157).

The seminal research that formally defined a theory of agenda setting, known as the Chapel Hill studies, took place during the presidential election of 1968. Maxwell McCombs and Donald Shaw surveyed 100 undecided voters in Chapel Hill, North Carolina, about the issues they considered most important in the upcoming election. They then compared the responses with the stories covered by newspapers, television, radio, and news magazines. The researchers found almost a perfect correlation between the issues that voters thought were the most important and the issues that were most prominently featured in the news media, which they described as "agenda setting" (McCombs & Shaw, 1972). They used the term "salience" to describe the level of importance that becomes attached to an issue. For example, a highly salient issue is one that gets a lot of media attention and that the audience therefore comes to believe is very important. Hundreds of research studies since that time have confirmed this influence.

Agenda-Setting Processes

How does agenda setting actually work? There are three main factors that lead to agenda setting: priming, obtrusiveness of issues, and framing.

Priming.   In a study of how television newscasts affect presidential elections, Iyengar, Peters, and Kinder found that the media use a process known as *priming*, "by ignoring some problems and attending to others, television news programs profoundly affect which problems viewers take seriously" (1982, p. 855). When the media prime an issue, such as gasoline prices, over another issue, such as families without health insurance, it affects the attention the public gives to the issue and how important it seems to the audience. Iyengar and Simon (1993) investigated priming related to the first Persian Gulf crisis in 1990. The more the story was covered on the news, the more important it appeared in public opinion polls. Further, the research revealed that the first President Bush's approval ratings were more strongly tied to his handling of the war than to any domestic issues. More recently, Holbert et al. (2003) investigated the effect of viewing the television program *The West Wing* on college students' perceptions of the U.S. presidency. In a survey of almost 200 students, the researchers found that viewing the television program about a fictitious president primed more positive images of the presidency, more positive images of the current president and his predecessor (George W. Bush and Bill Clinton), and highlighted the importance of the president appearing to be engaged as important to presidential success. (At the same time the research also determined that President Joshua Bartlett, the character on the show, was seen as more popular than either Bush or Clinton by viewers.)

Issue Obtrusiveness.   A second factor related to agenda setting involves the obtrusiveness of issues. When Zucker examined whether agenda setting would take place for all issues, he discovered that it is more likely to occur with issues that the public has not directly experienced, which are known as *unobtrusive* issues (Severin & Tankard, 2001, p. 228). For instance, high gasoline prices would be considered an obtrusive issue—one that people who regularly purchase gas for their automobiles experience directly. Contrast that with an issue such as global warming, the effects of which may be less obvious in people's daily lives. Agenda setting is more powerful in bringing issues that are unobtrusive to the public's agenda. The price of gas will be important to people whether or not the news media cover it, but the topic of global warming attracted noticeably more interest after the release of Al Gore's movie, *An Inconvenient Truth*, and still more after Gore won an Academy Award for the film. Another example of an obtrusive issue is parking on college campuses, which is something most students have directly experienced. By contrast, most students probably would not be aware that they could have holds placed on their academic records due to unpaid parking tickets, unless the college newspaper brought it to their attention.

Framing.   Still, a third factor that affects the public's agenda is the framing of an issue. Tankard defines a frame as "the central organizing idea for news content that supplies a context and suggests what the issue is through the use of selection, emphasis, exclusion, and elaboration" (Sparks, 2001, p. 156). A news frame can be thought of as a picture frame or a photographer "framing" a shot. The camera viewfinder can capture only a portion of the scene, so the photographer has to decide what belongs in the scene and what does not. In a similar way, journalists decide what information to include and what to exclude from a news report, and which details deserve the greatest emphasis.

Some theorists question whether frames are consciously placed in a story by the journalist. But whether framing is deliberate or not, it is clear that frames affect the public's perception of an issue. Is flag burning an expression of free speech or an unpatriotic act? Is stem cell research the killing of human life or research to cure disease? Is Barry Bonds the greatest home-run hitter of all time or a cheat who should be banned from baseball's Hall of Fame for using steroids? Do people who live in coastal areas hit by hurricanes deserve insurance protection or are they foolish for choosing to live in an unsafe area? A news story about any of these issues could be framed either way, depending on the facts and language choices that are used to compose the article.

A variety of research studies have shown that the way an issue is framed affects how the public interprets the issue, and who the audience members think is responsible for fixing problems. For example, Maher looked at the effects of newspaper frames of local environmental problems in Austin, Texas. For his Ph.D. dissertation, Maher did a content analysis of the local paper and then surveyed local residents about their perceptions of the cause of the problem. He found that the public was influenced by the newspaper coverage of the events, even though a number of causes of the problems had not been highlighted by the press (Severin & Tankard, 2001, pp. 279–280).

More recently, a significant number of media scholars have begun to look at frames in different contexts. Chyi and McCombs examined the *New York Times'* use of frames in coverage of the shootings at Columbine High School.

They found that the *Times* kept the story alive for more than 30 days and published 170 articles by supplying different frames for the same story—for example, community frame, future frame, and society frame (2004). Bronstein (2005) examined frames used to describe the new feminist movement to see whether journalists were recycling frames from the 1970s. Christopher Martin wrote an entire book on the way the media has framed labor unions. In *Framed: Labor and the Corporate Media,* he maintains that journalists have framed organized labor stories as consumer issues, while ignoring the actual concerns of the union workers (Roush, 2005). And Shaffer (2006) examined how frames were used in reporting the case for installation of a municipal wireless local area network, or Wi-Fi, in Philadelphia. The project was framed as something for the public good by a citizens' group, and as risky and unnecessary by the telecommunications industry.

It is worth noting that a lot of public relations work is essentially about framing, trying to get the news media to emphasize certain aspects (i.e., employ certain frames) in the news coverage of an organization or an issue. This is a good example of how mass media theory explains a practice used by media professionals.

Influences on Agenda Setting

So who is responsible for agenda setting? The public agenda comes from the press—but who sets the press agenda? According to McCombs, the press agenda comes from "the traditions of journalism, the daily interactions among news organizations, and the continuous interactions of news organizations with

FIGURE 7.1   The Framing of 9/11

Tony Palmeri of the Department of Communication, University of Wisconsin, Oshkosh, participated in a panel discussion that examined media frames shortly after the Sept. 11 terror attacks. Palmeri looked at mainstream media frames depicting the United States and the intervention in Afghanistan. He was able to identify the following frames:

1. Freedom versus terror: the issue of whether we will permit evil to destroy civilization and rule the world; based on catch phrases such as "You are with us or you are with the terrorists." Depictions of the United States as the protector of freedom and al Qaeda, the Taliban, and Bin Laden as evildoers; and visual images such as Ground Zero, the Pentagon, and the celebration of the Palestinians after Sept. 11.
2. Humanitarian intervention: the issue is whether the United States will help the suffering Afghan people; catch phrases such as "bombs and bread" and "Our war is with the Taliban, not with the Afghan people"; and visual images such as food drops and grateful Afghans.
3. Quagmire: the issue of whether the United States will get itself stuck in another costly war; catch phrase: another Vietnam; images: Vietnam soldiers returning in body bags.

Source: "The Love/Hate Relationship with the United States: Media Framing" http://www.uwosh.edu/faculty_staff/ palmeri/commentary/frames.htm.

numerous sources and their agendas, especially including policy makers in government" (2005, p. 164). These influences include:

- The monitoring of what happens at other news organizations. Journalists have always looked to their competitors, as well as to standard-bearers, such as the *New York Times.* Students who intern at television or newspaper newsrooms immediately notice the bank of television monitors tuned to all the other stations in town. But 24-hour news coverage and breaking stories on the Web have heightened the sense of competition and monitoring even further.
- Prominent news sources who are public officials, government officeholders, administrators, and public relations personnel. These routine sources have significant press access and can be very influential. During elections, especially national elections, political campaigns are particularly successful at setting the press agenda (and the increase in candidate advertising probably adds to this agenda-setting effect on the public).
- The increase of public relations activities in both the public and private sector that has had a significant effect on the press agenda. The recent attention to the controversy over video news releases highlights the press's reliance on business, government, and trade organization sources that sometimes produce stories that look like real news and get aired by television stations (McCombs, 2005, pp. 164–165).

In the early days of agenda-setting research, Ray Funkhouser (1973) identified five mechanisms that also influence the amount of media attention an issue might receive. These mechanisms help to explain how the media sets the agenda:

1. Adaptation of the media to a stream of events: For example, after a time, the plight of the Hurricane Katrina victims and the devastation in New Orleans just seemed to be more of the same and ceased to be considered news.
2. Over-reporting of significant but unusual events: For example, when Vice President Dick Cheney shot his friend in a hunting accident, the media reported the story continuously for days.
3. Selective reporting of the newsworthy aspects of otherwise non-newsworthy situations: For example, when 18-year old Samantha Larson reached the summit of Mt. Everest, she became the youngest climber to have scaled the highest peak in each of seven continents. Hundreds of people reach the summit of Mt. Everest every year, but it was the age of this climber that made the story so newsworthy.
4. Pseudo-events, or the manufacturing of events such that they appear to be newsworthy: For example, in March 2006, more than 1,500 middle and high school students in Virginia and Maryland walked out of school to protest proposed federal legislation that would crack down on illegal immigrants. Even though it was a manufactured demonstration, the press showed up to cover it, and thereby gave attention to the issue.
5. Event summaries, or situations that portray non-newsworthy events in a newsworthy way: For example, when the president of the United States has his annual physical, the results are released to the press. Television generally

FIGURE 7.2   Student Research on Agenda Setting

One enterprising college student at the authors' institution conducted her original research project by asking the question of whether the campus newspaper actually set the agenda for the students on campus. She enlisted two groups of students: one group promised not to read the campus newspaper for six weeks; the other group promised to read the campus newspaper each week for six weeks. To ensure that the second group received the newspaper, the student personally delivered the paper to the students' rooms. At the conclusion of the six weeks, she surveyed both groups on what issues they thought were most important on campus. True to the agenda-setting theory, those who read the campus newspaper were more likely to name issues that were featured prominently on the front page of the campus paper.

Another student conducted his research project in a similar way, but with two different newpapers. He had one group of students read the city's daily newspaper and the second group read the alternative news weekly. At the conclusion of the study, he interviewed each group and found that their perceptions of the most important issues in the city of Rochester were definitely influenced by the publication they read.

shows the president going to and from Walter Reed Army Hospital, and sometimes includes a sound bite of the president saying he feels great. Since a sitting president has not had any major health issues for many years, this may be reassuring to the American public, but it is not particularly newsworthy.

McCombs concludes that because of its role in agenda setting, the press does exert a major influence on public opinion (2005, p. 166). At the same time, the public also has a role in its interpretation of the media messages. An understanding of information processing (discussed in Chapter 6) may help to explain how public agendas are set. In addition, as the media landscape expands and changes, the nature of agenda setting may also be changing. Bloggers, citizen journalists, and independent media all are adding more voices that help to set the agenda in society. Some control has been taken from the press, since anyone with Internet access can disseminate a message. New research is considering these venues for further influence on agenda setting.

Diffusion Theory and Research

The discussion in Chapter 5 concludes with the two-step flow theory as part of the limited effects paradigm. To recap, the two-step flow theory maintains that information flows from the media to opinion leaders, who share the information as well as their perspective with their relevant social contacts. Thus the media are seen as having more of an indirect effect than a direct effect on society.

For more than two decades, researchers studied diffusion of political news, social issues, news stories, even fashion and movie reviews, in an attempt to define the nature and function of these opinion leaders. It became clear, however, that there were serious flaws with the two-step flow theory. Among the flaws was the realization that the media were becoming more and more pervasive; in particular, more people had access to more extensive media coverage as television sets became more popular. Thus, it was discovered that people were more likely to receive information directly from the media, rather than from other people. While the two-step flow still may be a valid consideration in special circumstances, such as in public relations (where the PR professional serves as an opinion leader for her media contacts) or in small-town news, the research evolved into an examination of how information actually traveled through society, which is called *diffusion research*.

The name most closely associated with diffusion research is Everett Rogers, but the seminal research on diffusion was actually done by Ryan and Gross, who studied the diffusion of hybrid seed among Iowa corn farmers (1943). The Iowa corn studies were pivotal because they not only looked at the difference between mass media channels and interpersonal channels in spreading news about innovations, but they also identified those people who were likely to be early adopters of an innovation and those who would lag behind (Rogers, 1995). Following from this early research and working for more than three decades, Rogers reviewed a wide range of research studies to demonstrate that, when new innovations are available to a population, they will pass through a series of stages on their way to becoming adopted (Rogers, 1995):

- First, people will become aware of the innovation, often through the media; For example, many people learned about high definition television from seeing television promos that stated, "this program is being broadcast in HDTV."
- Second, a small group of early adopters will try out the innovation; Because of the cost involved and the relatively few number of shows broadcast in high definition, only a small group originally invested in the high definition televisions to watch HD programming.
- Third, opinion leaders learn from the early adopters and try the innovation; For example, the chair of the mass media program at a college may report on his experience with HDTV and invite his colleagues over to see how much better programs are in comparison to traditional broadcasts.
- Fourth, if the opinion leaders like the innovation, they may encourage their associates to try it; so the college professors might encourage their friends and students to give it a try.
- Fifth, after most people have adopted the innovation, a group called laggards will also make the change; In the future, all television programming will be in high definition as per federal legislation, so even the laggards will have to update their televisions eventually.

The rate of adoption and number of adopters is often depicted as an S-shaped curve relating number of adopters to the passage of time, as shown in Figure 7.3.

FIGURE 7.3   Diffusion of Innovations Curve

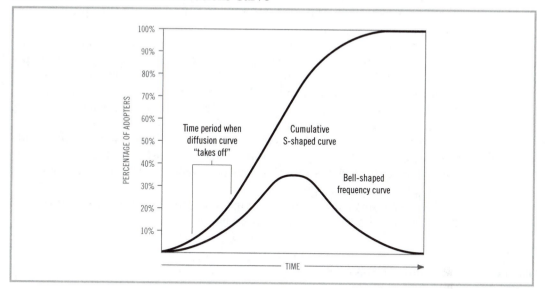

Rogers (1995) notes that the innovation decision process proceeds generally through five discrete stages:

1. Knowledge of the innovation: becoming aware of HDTV.
2. Persuasion by forming an attitude toward the innovation: seeing that HDTV is superior to regular television.
3. Decision to accept or reject the innovation: everyone agrees that HDTV is better but individuals will need to decide whether they can make the financial investment.
4. Implementation or trying out the innovation: actually purchasing a high definition television.
5. Confirmation, or reinforcing or reversing the decision about the innovation: confirming that this is the best way to watch television, or returning it to the store after deciding it was not worth the investment.

While diffusion of technological innovations is one way that diffusion theory can be applied, media practitioners are often more concerned with how news is diffused through society. Melvin DeFleur summarized more than 40 years of studies about how news flows from media sources through society. Among his findings were that most people get their news directly from a news medium, as opposed to another person. At the same time, news events of deep concern to large numbers of people will move faster and further within a population, regardless of the source (Severin & Tankard, 2001, pp. 212–213). Events such as the September 11, 2001, terrorist attacks and Hurricane Katrina are examples of news stories that moved swiftly through the population by both media outlets and the two-step flow, with the personal-contact part of that process often including the message, "turn on your TV."

The research on diffusion is also valuable to media practitioners in marketing and advertising. The increased use of viral advertising, word-of-mouth (WOM) advertising, and stealth advertising are all based on Rogers's theory (Center for Interactive Advertising, n.d.). Advertisers have realized that interpersonal contact, even if it is done electronically, is a valuable means of reaching potential customers. And with the explosion in the use of cell phones, e-mail, instant messaging, and text messaging, it does not take very long to contact individuals with a promotional pitch. Some colleges are using such technologies to spread the word to students about campus emergencies, particularly through text messaging to students' cell phones.

The way information moves through a society is also a significant component of the next theory examined in this chapter.

FIGURE 7.4   Diffusion and the iPod

Everett Rogers examined characteristics that influence whether or how quickly an innovation is adopted. These factors can be applied to a fairly recent technological innovation, the iPod music player.

1. Relative advantage: the degree to which an innovation is perceived as better than the idea it supersedes: The iPod replaced the portable CD player . . . it is smaller, holds more music, and it is easier to download music directly onto the player. At the same time, it is more expensive than a CD player, easier to lose, and takes more technological understanding to use.

2. Compatibility: the degree to which an innovation is perceived as being consistent with the existing values, past experiences, and needs of potential adopters: The iPod is appealing to people who use Walkmans or portable CD players and like to choose their own music instead of listening to the radio. It gives them greater flexibility and more ability to customize their listening habits.

3. Complexity: the degree to which an innovation is perceived as difficult to understand and use. The iPod is considered easy to use by tech savvy college students who were already downloading music onto their computers. The iPod is probably perceived as more difficult to use by older listeners or those without computer experience.

4. Trialability: the degree to which an innovation may be experimented with on a limited basis. A friend or coworker can demonstrate an iPod to a potential user, and it can be borrowed and tried out. In some electronic stores, customers can try out demo models. However, an iPod is more costly than other portable music technologies, and unless it is defective, probably cannot be returned.

5. Observability: the degree to which the results of an innovation are visible to others. It is easy to find many people walking across campuses, through city streets, and in shopping malls to witness the popularity of this device. In fact, in 2006, it is difficult to purchase a portable CD player and finding a cassette tape player is almost impossible.

Knowledge-Gap Hypothesis

Most college students today grew up watching the television program *Sesame Street*. At some point, they might have learned it was educational, but they enjoyed it for the entertainment value as well (actually, whenever one of the authors brings a clip from *Sesame Street* into the classroom for demonstration purposes, the class always protests when the segment ends).

What many students do not know is that *Sesame Street* was actually part of an educational experiment designed to help disadvantaged children become better prepared for kindergarten. The program's original design was aimed at narrowing what was seen as a knowledge gap between children of high and low socioeconomic status. However, the results of extensive research studies and data analysis showed mixed results in terms of its success in meeting that goal. All preschoolers who watched *Sesame Street* on a regular basis did seem to learn from the show, but the program alone did not erase the gap between lower income and higher income children in terms of preparing them for school (Katzman, 1974). In fact, children from better-off families seemed to benefit more from the show than those from poorer homes. Thus, the phenomenon of *Sesame Street* became a significant part of the discussion around the knowledge-gap hypothesis.

Chapter 2 notes that a hypothesis is a research question. The researcher needs to ask questions and answer them in order to formulate theory. The term hypothesis is often used to describe a theory that is still in the development stage or that has not been fully researched and verified. Because of the somewhat tenuous nature of the research findings, the knowledge-gap has not yet achieved theory status and is still known as a hypothesis.

The names most often associated with the knowledge-gap hypothesis are Tichenor, Donohue, and Olien. They stated the knowledge gap in the following way: "As the infusion of mass media information into a social system increases, segments of the population with higher socioeconomic status tend to acquire this information at a faster rate than the lower segments, so that the gap in knowledge between these segments tends to increase rather than decrease" (1970, pp. 159–160). Why might there be such a gap in knowledge or information between segments of society at different levels of the socioeconomic scale? Tichenor and his colleagues posited five reasons why this might be so:

- Higher level of communication skills: people with higher socioeconomic status tend to be better educated, so they are better able to read and comprehend material at a high level; for example, in the issue of deciding among health care options, people with higher levels of communication skills may be better able to interpret complex information about health care options, and seek out additional information, even if it is of a technical nature.
- A greater amount of stored information: accumulated prior information helps this better educated population act more capably on new information; for example, the better educated person probably has already made health care decisions in the past and can relate any new information about the program to past experience.

- Relevant social contacts: people from a higher socioeconomic status probably know others who they can call for advice on health care options. They also may have more access to the information and skill at researching topics, especially online—for example, college students and employees have access to databases with more information through their schools' libraries.
- Selective exposure, acceptance, and retention of information; for example, someone who thinks she cannot afford health care may not pay attention to relevant information or remember details of programs, since she considers it so far out of her ability to pay.
- The nature of the mass media system, which has been shown to be aimed at a higher education level (p. 162). One of the authors had a student who did a readability analysis of forms and instructions from the New York State Department of Social Services. He found that the forms were written at a graduate school level, yet they were intended for lower-income people who often had only a high school education—or less.

The knowledge-gap hypothesis can be viewed as a somewhat disturbing theory, pointing up differences of class and privilege in our society and proposing that the media contribute to widening the gap. It is true that some of the information gaps are clearly visible today in terms of access to information and technology. Most middle and upper-middle class families have at least one computer and Internet access, usually high speed access at that, which poorer families cannot afford. Similarly, high schools in prosperous communities generally have more computers in the classrooms than their inner city counterparts. This technology gap is sometimes known as the "digital divide."

At the same time, later research looked at the impact that this information gap actually had on communities in terms of diffusion of information and issues of local impact. In a follow-up piece of research, Donahue, Tichenor, and Olien (1975) found that the knowledge gap declines when an issue has strong local impact and when there is conflict in a community—for example, a community that becomes home to a registered sex offender finds ways to spread that information quickly through the society to all members of the community, particularly parents of children. Additionally, the knowledge gap is likely to be less in smaller communities where there are limited media channels and much information is shared through informal channels—for example, in a small town where everyone meets at the local diner, information about a newcomer with a questionable background will be shared quickly. In larger communities, with many media outlets for information, the divide among segments of the population is likely to be larger.

Tichenor, Donahue, and Olien also studied conflict in 19 different cities that were experiencing conflicts over environmental issues (such as wilderness logging and environmental pollution). Their findings regarding the knowledge gap were somewhat reassuring, in that they found all segments of society will become informed when there is an important local issue and increased news coverage from local or outside sources provided more and better access to information (Baran & Davis, 2006, pp. 313–314).

More recently, in a study of the knowledge gap and presidential elections, Holbrook found that the knowledge gap does not necessarily grow over the course of the election and that forums such as debates actually do help to narrow the knowledge gap among segments of society (2002). Liu and Eveland found that there was not a clear-cut knowledge gap when voters used newspapers versus television as their main source of news (2005). However, in a study of the knowledge gap in transitional democracies' elections (Brazil, Mexico, and Russia), McCann and Lawson found that the knowledge gap widened or stayed the same. While the media resources were there for interested voters, the results were ascribed to the failure of the campaigns and the media to engage the citizens in the process (2006).

But while researchers still try to pinpoint the role of the knowledge gap using traditional media, another segment of the research population is looking at the impact of the digital divide, Internet use, and new media. For example, Prior (2005) argues that greater media choice makes it easier for people to find the content they prefer the most. In a survey of more than 2,300 adults, he found that people who like news and people who like entertainment each take advantage of the increasing media channels to watch what they like. As a result of these choices, knowledge gaps have actually widened; those who are interested in the news know more about politics and are more likely to vote, while those who are interested in entertainment know little about politics and are less likely to vote.

In spite of obvious knowledge gaps due to technology, some media initiatives may contribute to an attempt to narrow this gap. Some examples include:

- Public television shows such as *Homework Hotline*, where middle school students can call in by phone and get help with their homework when they do not have a parent or after-school program available to assist them.
- High school test review shows, which are broadcast for recording during the overnight hours. In New York state, public television stations produce and broadcast review shows before the Regents exams each spring.
- GED programs are available online or on television, so that parents or shift workers can earn a high school diploma without having to attend classes in person.
- Distance and online classes offered by many colleges and universities.
- Partnerships between television stations and newspapers to increase coverage of election issues through candidate debates, interviews, profiles, and citizen forums.

Whatever the forum for research into the knowledge gap, the issue of accessibility must play a significant role. The explosion in technology has further highlighted the differences between those with access and those without. Knowledge gaps are partly a function of motivation and interest, but also a function of access to the technology that houses the information.

Spiral of Silence

It would be difficult to get through high school without some experience of the impact of peer pressure — to drink, to smoke, to dress like one's social group, to go along with the crowd. However, every student who has taken introductory psychology knows that this peer pressure extends far beyond adolescence. Individuals are pressured by others to conform to standards of dress, behavior, and attitudes in a wide range of circumstances, even when the groups are not part of their usual social circle. Elisabeth Noelle-Neumann took the idea of group pressure to conform and added an additional component: the influence of the media. Noelle-Neumann posited that public opinion is formed by a process in which individuals try to determine whether their opinions are in the majority, a process that involves the media because the media is the way that people gauge public opinion.

It is clear that opinion polls, as reported by the media, play a large part in determining further public opinion. Noelle-Neumann maintains that media reporting helps individuals decide which opinions they might express without being seen as social outcasts and which opinions are in the minority. As individuals self-censor the minority opinions, those opinions do not get expressed, and thus do not get reported in the media. Thus, a spiral effect occurs, when the majority expresses a dominant opinion and the minority keeps silent, which makes the majority opinion seem even *more* dominant and makes the minority view seem even further outside the mainstream.

For example, a student from a rural area is a recreational hunter, a member of the NRA, and opposed to a ban on assault weapons. It is likely that his social group, his friends and family, will also be opposed to such a ban. However, this student will also use information from the media to gauge whether public opinion is for or against gun control. He will then use the knowledge of the public's opinion when he is with a group outside his own social circle, and that will help him decide whether or not to express his pro-gun opinion. The media publicize which opinions are dominant, which opinions are on the increase, and which opinions may cause social isolation if they are stated in public (Severin & Tankard, 2001, p. 273). So, according to the spiral of silence theory, if this student finds out the public opinion favors a ban on assault weapons, and he is involved in a discussion on the topic in his political science class, he will be hesitant to express his opinion which is opposite of the majority view.

Glynn and McLeod (1984) supported the spiral of silence in their study of 98 Wisconsin voters during the presidential election of 1980 (when Ronald Reagan defeated Jimmy Carter and John Anderson ran as a third-party candidate). They found that individuals were influenced by polls in their willingness to express an opinion that was in the minority; however, even though they did not speak out, they still maintained their minority opinions.

But not all research on the spiral of silence has supported its view. In 1997, Glynn, Hayes, and Shanahan conducted a review of the research studies that had been done on the spiral of silence. They concluded that the evidence supporting the spiral was actually quite weak. The researchers recommended that survey questions that ask individuals if they would hypothetically be willing to express a deviant opinion should be replaced by observations of individuals actually speaking out. However, no studies reviewed for this book followed that recommendation and continued to rely on self-reporting surveys.

In 2001, Moye, Domke, and Stamm examined the spiral of silence in relation to people's views on affirmation action. This is considered a sensitive topic, probably more sensitive than election candidates, because it affects efforts to promote diversity in education and hiring, but also has discriminated against people in the majority. Moye and her colleagues found that fear of isolation did influence individuals' willingness to speak out with a minority opinion; however, they found that those with a higher level of education were more likely to speak out in any circumstances. They also found that the most important reference was the opinion of the close circle of friends and family in determining willingness to speak out against the perceived majority opinion (2001, pp. 7, 16–17).

Noelle-Neumann viewed the spiral of silence as reflecting a powerful effects model of the media. She maintained that this happens because the media are virtually everywhere, the media tend to repeat stories and perspectives, and the values of journalists influence the content of the news they report (Baran & Davis, 2006, p. 322). This was an almost prophetic observation: at the time when it was made (in the early 1970s), the three news networks (ABC, NBC, and CBS) were still dominant and Ted Turner had not yet launched CNN.

More than three decades later, Noelle-Neumann's assertions about media proliferation are more true than ever. Multiple 24-hour cable news channels struggle to fill the hours with repetitive news, an increasing number of opinion pieces, and a focus on features and celebrities; talk radio surpasses music stations in many markets and has been shown to influence voter opinion during elections and catastrophic events; pollsters such as Norm Ornstein from the American Enterprise Institute and Andrew Kohut from the Pew Research Center appear regularly on news programs and offer the "pulse" of the country, usually ascertained through overnight polling; and networks and newspapers frequently team up to conduct polls and report their findings—even visitors to Web sites such as Fox News, CNN, and the BBC can participate in polls and see how their views compare to those of others on the site. The result often is what Eric Alterman called an "echo chamber" of reinforcing opinion from an assortment of media all elaborating on the same idea (Alterman, 2003).

Baran and Davis also provide an example of news coverage in early 2003 as an example of the spiral of silence working to quell public dissent in the run-up to the Iraq War that began in March of that year. In 2004, the editors of the *New York Times* addressed their own inadequacies in investigating and reporting on the Bush administration's claims that Iraq had weapons of mass destruction, the link between Iraq and the September 11 terror attacks, and the assertion that the war would pay for itself with Iraqi oil revenues. The media's unwillingness to challenge the Bush administration's claims on these issues before the war led to public opinion against the war being discouraged or even stifled. Questioning the need for war was seen as unpatriotic and not supporting the troops. The *Times'* acknowledgement that it failed to challenge controversial claims and to investigate reports more aggressively showed that the press had helped to lead the country to a spiral of silence that suppressed dissent on the issue of the war (Baran & Davis, 2006, p. 325).

Over the years, the spiral of silence has been somewhat controversial, with studies employing a variety of research designs and producing inconsistent results. Scheufele and Moy reviewed 25 years of research on the spiral of silence and made several observations and recommendations. Most important, they contend, is the need to consider cultural differences when examining the spiral. Cross-cultural factors are a key variable in the decision to speak out on an issue, and they recommend returning to a more macroscopic view of the theory (2000).

It would be inappropriate to leave the discussion of the spiral of silence without noting the controversy surrounding its originator, Elisabeth Noelle-Neumann. Noelle-Neumann worked as a journalist in Nazi Germany in the 1940s and later became a Nazi apologist. Some critics feel that her early views were influential in her writings, including the formation of the spiral of silence. Simpson notes that her writings show hostility toward ethnic and racial diversity in societies and support political reforms that would disenfranchise large segments of the population (1996, p. 166). Simpson also claims that her writings characterize the general population as "ignorant, passive, and incapable of self-rule" and that it is up to the "political and cultural elites . . . to enforce stability and defend their values and traditions from the onslaught of vulgar democracy" (pp. 166–167). It is questionable whether the personal views of a theorist should affect academic judgment of her theory, but the controversy over this one researcher is noteworthy in its intensity.

Cultivation Theory

How likely is it that you will be the victim of a violent crime? How safe is your neighborhood? Is crime on the increase in society? Are women more likely to be victims of crime? These were some of the questions that George Gerbner's research team asked individuals who were considered light, moderate, or heavy viewers of television (with "heavy" defined as more than four hours of television time per day). His subjects included U.S. as well as Canadian citizens of all backgrounds, education, and income levels. Gerbner discovered that heavy viewers of television were more likely to drastically overestimate the likelihood that they would be victims of a violent crime, the safety of their own neighborhoods, and the overall increase of crime in society (Gerbner et al., 1980, pp. 222–225). Gerbner called this skewed perception "The Mean World Syndrome." People who watch a lot of television inhabit a world that they perceive as meaner and more dangerous than people who watch less television.

George Gerbner has been called "The Man Who Counts the Killings" (Stossel, 1997). The former dean of the Annenberg School of Communications at the University of Pennsylvania became famous for keeping track of the violence on television and projecting how this violence was affecting our society. Gerbner had already been studying violence in the media when, in 1968, President Lyndon Johnson's National Commission on the Causes and Prevention of Violence tapped him to analyze the content of television news. Thus began the longest running media research project ever (Stossel, 1997), called the Cultural Indicators Project. This project consisted of two components: message system analysis, which is the monitoring of violence in prime time television; and cultivation analysis, which is the investigation of viewer conception of social reality associated with their television viewing (Gerbner et al., 1980, p. 212).

Over the more than 30 years of the project, researchers and the public continued to be astounded at the level of violence shown in television programming, and the amount of television that average Americans consumed. For example, in 1992, the American Medical Association reported that the average child watched television for 27 hours a week and would see more than 40,000 murders by the age of 18 (Stossel, 1997). However, of special interest to mass media researchers, and what Gerbner really wanted to focus on, is how that television viewing affected the perceptions of the viewers.

The central tenet of this cultivation theory is that heavy television viewing literally *cultivates* a common view of the world. Just as a farmer cultivates crops to make them develop and grow, media influences also grow and develop in people and in society over time. Thus, cultivation is not the result of a single television program or any short-term exposure to a media message. And, while Gerbner's research focused exclusively on television violence, there is no reason to think that this cultivation effect would not hold true for other media and other experiences. Newspapers also are often criticized for reporting nothing but bad news, such as crime and scandals, that makes it seem like their communities are dangerous places in which to live. Such coverage over time, critics contend, creates a poor image of an area that is nowhere nearly as bad as the reality. Journalist and press critic James Fallows says the same thing happens with coverage of the political process, where emphasis on candidates' weaknesses helps make the public jaded and cynical about politics. By presenting public life as "a depressing spectacle" Fallows says that "the message of today's news coverage is often that the world cannot be understood, shaped or controlled" (1996, p. 140).

Cultivation Processes

Later in the development of the theory, and in response to some of his critics, Gerbner identified two processes that helped to explain the reactions of different people to the violence they viewed on television. The first was *mainstreaming*, which describes how people from very different social groups come together to share a common perception as a result of their exposure to television; television is the common factor that brings people of different backgrounds and experiences together, that cultivates common perspectives and overrides differences among individuals (Gerber et al., 1986, pp. 30–31). Indeed, heavy television viewers share high scores on the Mean World Index, which indicates that they think most people are looking out for themselves, a person cannot be too careful out there, and most people will take advantage of others if they had the chance (p. 31). Factors such as age, gender, race, or socioeconomic status would not matter, according to Gerbner. All people who watch a lot of television would share the same perceptions.

The second process Gerbner identified to further explain the theory was *resonance*, which describes how some images have an even greater impact for people whose real-life situation mirrors that of what happens in the media. Gerbner says "when what people see on television is most congruent with everyday reality (or even perceived reality), the combination may result in a coherent and powerful 'double dose' of the television message and significantly boost cultivation . . . the congruence of the television world and real life circumstances may 'resonate' and lead to markedly amplified cultivation patterns" (Gerbner et al, 1980, p. 217).

For example, everyone who watches the television show *Law and Order* gets the impression that there is a significant amount of violent crime in New York City (mainstreaming). However, for people who live in New York City, the familiar locations and local characters in the show make the level of crime seem more real to them (resonance). Female viewers may have an even higher degree of resonance, since they feel more vulnerable and more likely to be victims of a violent crime. (It is worth noting that, in reality, crime has fallen in New York City, so that it now has one of the lowest per capita crime rates of any city in the country.)

Gerbner notes that one significant issue that increases the cultivation effect is that the violence that we see on television is "swift, painless, and effective . . . and always leads to a happy ending." Thus, we see violence solves many problems without many serious consequences (Stossel, 1997). Gerbner theorizes that this leads people, especially youth, to cultivate a culture of violence and a jaundiced view of the world in which violence is the basis of power as well as the solution to our problems.

Potter and Chang (1990) demonstrated that television viewing does have an impact, but it also matters what type of programming a person is watching. They disagreed with a general cultivation effect for heavy television viewers, but supported a cultivation effect that took into account the type of programming. According to this argument, someone who watched a lot of crime shows would have a different cultivation effect from someone who watched a lot of game shows.

In an application of the theory to international students living in the United States, Woo and Dominick (2003) found very strong support for the cultivation effect. International students who watched a lot of daytime talk shows that featured topics such as adultery and other dysfunctional personal relationships had more negative perceptions of human relationships in the United States and overestimated the incidence of undesirable behaviors in romance, marriage, and families. Even when they eliminated the softer talk shows such as *Oprah* from their analysis, the cultivation effect was still strong. This was especially true for international students who were new to the United States and had little other experience with Americans before coming to study in this country (pp. 122–123).

Research on violent content in support of cultivation theory continues today, even after the death of George Gerbner. However, not everyone supported Gerbner's work and conclusions. Critics faulted his research design, and the fact that he did not differentiate between types of violence. In the Cultural Indicators Project content analyses, cartoon violence and slapstick comedy were counted the same way as a brutal murder, without regard to context. Critics maintained that this all-inclusiveness inflated the violence index. In addition, Gerbner was unable to demonstrate a causal link between watching violence and viewers' violent behavior (Baran & Davis, 2006, p. 331).

But perhaps most controversial of all is that Gerbner's research attempted to use quantitative methods to measure a cultural indicator. In so doing, he used empirical methods to study humanistic assumptions, actually combining social science and humanities (Baran & Davis, 2006, pp. 333–335). This unorthodox approach drew criticism from researchers in both camps. However, as Newcomb noted, Gerbner was the first to move his study out of a laboratory setting and examine what was happening in the real world as well as the impact that television was having upon the culture (Baran & Davis, 2006, p. 333). And some maintain that what was once a criticism is actually becoming a reality among media scholars. In describing the cultural indicators, the parallels between Gerbner and Marshall McLuhan will become apparent in the next chapter.

Other Theories of Media Violence

As cultivation theory illustrates, there is considerable controversy around the issue of media and violence. While Gerbner decried the amount and level of violence in television and the movies, his critics often faulted his failure to show the impact this violence had in terms of society's behavior. And yet, thousands of studies have examined the impact of media violence on behavior, much of it focusing on children. Recall that Chapter 6 includes a review of Albert Bandura's social learning theory, which posited that children imitate role models that they see on television, including aggressive role models. One of the earliest scholars to research the impact that television has on behavior was Leonard Eron, who was the first to do longitudinal research on the effect of television on a population. In 1960, Eron studied third-graders (8- and 9-year-olds) in a suburban community north of New York City. In addition to watching them in the playground, he had their parents fill out questionnaires that included how much and what types of television the child watched. Eron observed that the more violent television the children watched, the more aggressive they seemed to be in school. He returned when the children were 19 and found that the boys who watched a lot of television were more likely to get in trouble with the law. Finally, Eron returned to the community in 1982, when his subjects were 30. He found that children who had watched the most violent television programming in their youth were more likely to use violence against their own children, were more likely to be convicted of a crime, and were reported to be more aggressive by their spouses than those who watched less television (Stossel, 1997). In testifying before a U.S. Senate committee on television programming in 1999, Eron estimated that 10 percent of all youth violence can be attributed to television (Eron, 1999).

What mass media theories actually help explain the impact that violent programming may have on behavior? There have been many, but three stand out.

■ **The catharsis hypothesis:** *Catharsis* is a Greek word that means purification or cleansing. It has also been used to mean tension release. So the catharsis hypothesis would argue that watching television helps to release tension. Under the uses and gratifications perspective (described in Chapter 6), this was seen to be true. Students report watching *American Idol, Real World,* or *CSI* as a way to relax, especially during times of extreme stress such as finals or the week a major research project is due. But the catharsis hypothesis as applied to media violence would indicate that watching violence on television would help to release violent tendencies in the viewer. Seymour Feshbach was one of the first researchers to propose that viewing television violence might have a positive effect. Feshbach posited that watching other people behave in an aggressive manner would allow angry and aggressive individuals to cleanse their pent-up feelings of anger, calm down, and actually let them act out aggressive fantasies, so they would be less likely to act on their anger (Sparks, 2002, p. 82). The research in support of this was based on a study done at a detention facility for young boys. The youths in the group that watched the nonviolent programming had higher levels of aggression than the group that watched the violent programming. While the findings initially seemed to support the catharsis hypothesis, it was later discovered that those who weren't allowed to watch their favorite programs were angry and acted out because of this (Sparks, 2002, p. 83). While the initial premise might have made intuitive sense, the catharsis hypothesis is not considered a valid explanation of the impact of media violence.

■ **The disinhibition hypothesis:** A second view of media violence implies desensitization to violence from repeated exposure. Individuals who watch a lot of violence on television are less affected by it, and thereby more likely to behave in an aggressive manner (Perry, 1996, p. 159). This hypothesis has some support from both anecdotal evidence as well as research studies. For example, Gerbner has noted that the first *Die Hard* movie had 18 deaths, while the second had 264. The first *Robocop* movie had 32 deaths and the second 81 (Stossel, 1997). The implication is that it will take more violence to satisfy the viewers who came to see more of the same in the sequels. But the findings are more blatant in the research studies. Potter (1999) reviewed more than five decades of research on the effects of exposure to media violence. Among the effects he noted that were strongly supported were (1999, p. 26):

■ Exposure to violent portrayals in the media can lead to subsequent viewer aggression through disinhibition—for example, seeing a television character use violence to solve a problem, like fighting with the classroom bully, will make the viewer more likely to try violence to solve the problem of the classroom bully in his own school.

■ Exposure to violence in the media can lead to desensitization—for example, seeing graphic depictions of dead bodies on crime investigation shows may desensitize a person to be less affected by a crime scene in his own neighborhood.

■ Long term exposure to media violence is related to aggression in a person's life—aggression becomes a way to solve all problems.

■ Media violence is related to subsequent violence in society—viewers will translate that violence to their lives.

■ People exposed to many violent portrayals over a long time will come to be more accepting of violence.

■ **Priming:** Recall that earlier in this chapter priming was described as a function of agenda setting and a way to describe how agenda setting works. The same term is used in relation to media violence effects as a process of associations. Leonard Berkowitz believed that the mass media are a potent source of images or ideas that can prime people's thoughts and actions. Thus, viewing images of media violence can prime thoughts of hostility and affect the way viewers see others and interpret their actions. It might also prime thoughts that lead one to believe that aggressive behavior might be warranted in certain situations and might bring benefits, and it

FIGURE 7.5   Are Copycat Crimes Explained by Cultivation Theory?

Four youths who shot two Las Vegas police officers claimed they had been motivated by Ice-T's rap song "Cop Killer." A boy who killed his mother told the judge he got the idea from the movie *Scream*. The film *Menace II Society* has been cited on more than one occasion for providing a plan for car jacking and killing motorists.

Juvenile offender expert Ray Surrette of the University of Central Florida has done extensive research on motivations for young criminals, particularly those who commit copycat crimes. Surrette reports that juvenile offenders find influence from both the media and peers for committing their criminal acts. However, for both juvenile and adult copycat offenders, the use of the media is more pragmatic, which means that they use ideas in the media to help with crimes they were already contemplating. They see the media as one of a number of sources of information. Surrette also found that the amount of media consumption is not related to the likelihood that offenders will commit a copycat crime.

Thus, an examination of copycat crimes would not be considered an example of cultivation theory. It might, however, fit as an example of social learning theory and/or uses and gratifications, since the young offenders see the media as a model for how to behave and use the media as a source of information.

Source: Surrette, R. (2002). Self-reported copycat crime among a population of serious and violent juvenile offenders. *Crime and Delinquency* 48(1) 46–69.

might prime action tendencies that cause people to be more inclined to act violently (Sparks, 2002, p. 83). Research has discovered that priming can affect the individual for some time after exposure. Also, it can operate automatically and even without awareness (Berkowitz & Rogers in Bryant & Zillman, 1986, p. 59).

While the theories of media violence may not be considered sociological theories in the strict sense that they affect populations as a whole, they are considered an extension of cultivation theory. While society may be concerned with the individual who views a violent movie and then copies that crime in real life, media theorists generally study the question of media violence in terms of the impact it has on a society or culture as a whole.

Summary

This chapter and the previous one have sought to organize what are known as the effects theories of mass communication according to the level at which they mostly seem to operate, either affecting individual message consumers or affecting larger groups such as members of a community following an election or heavy watchers of television, up to the level of an entire society. Obviously, there is some overlap in the nature and results of media effects because large groups and society as a whole are composed of individuals. The effects theories, however, are not the only way in which researchers seek to explain the influence of the media on modern society. An entirely different way of looking at such influences is discussed in the next chapter.

QUESTIONS FOR DISCUSSION/ APPLICATION EXERCISES

1. What sorts of topics are on the agenda of students at your university? How effective are the campus media (newspaper, radio station, television station, etc.) in setting the students' agenda?

2. How does news spread through your social group? Think of critical news in your life and how you found out about it—which messages came from the media and which came from people?

3. Can you think of a new product that you have adopted in the past six months? How did you find out about it? How were you persuaded to try it and use it?

4. What is the responsibility of the mass media in narrowing the knowledge gap? Are there things that the media is doing or should be doing that help narrow the gap?

5. Can you cite some current examples of how the spiral of silence operates to maintain the majority viewpoint and silence the minority?

6. With the explosion in media choices today, is there really a cultivation effect? Can society as a whole be moving toward a common view when everyone is consuming something different?

REFERENCES

Alterman, Eric (2003). *What liberal media?: The truth about bias and the news.* New York: Perseus Books.

Baran, S. J., & Davis, D. K. (2006). *Mass communication theory: Foundations, ferment, and future* (4th ed.). Belmont, CA: Thompson Wadsworth.

Berkowitz, L., & Rogers, K. H. (1986). A priming effect analysis of media influences. In J. Bryant & D. Zillman (Eds.), *Perspectives on media effects* (pp. 57–81). Hillsdale, NJ: Lawrence Erlbaum Associates.

Bronstein, C. (2005). Representing the third wave: Mainstream print media framing of a new feminist movement. *Journalism & Mass Communication Quarterly 82*(4), 783–804.

Center for Interactive Advertising (n.d.). Retrieved Aug. 16, 2006 from http://www.ciadvertising.org/.

Chyi, H. I., & McCombs, M. (2004). Media salience and the process of framing: Coverage of the Columbine school shootings. *Journalism & Mass Communication Quarterly 81*(1), 22–35.

Donahue, G. A., Tichenor, P. J., & Olien, C. N. (1975). Mass media and the knowledge gap: A hypothesis reconsidered. *Communication Research 2*, 3–23.

Eron, L. D. (1999). Effects of television violence on children. Testimony before Senate committee on Science, Commerce and Transportation Regarding Safe Harbor Hours in TV Programming. May, 18, 1999.

Fallows, J. (1996). *Breaking the news: How the media undermine democracy.* New York: Pantheon Books.

Funkhouser, G. R. (1973). Trends in media coverage of the issues of the '60s. *Journalism Quarterly 50*, 533–538.

Gerbner, G., Gross, L., Morgan, M., & Signorielli, N. (1980). The "mainstreaming" of America: Violence profile no. 11. *Journal of Communication 30*(3), 212–231.

Gerbner, G., Gross, L., Morgan, M., & Signorielli, N. (1986). Living with television: The dynamics of the cultivation process. In J. Bryant & D. Zillman (Eds.), *Perspectives on media effects.* Hillsdale, NJ: Lawrence Erlbaum Associates.

Glynn, J. C., & McLeod, J. (1984). Public opinion du jour: An examination of the spiral of silence. *Public Opinion Quarterly 48*(4), 731–740.

Glynn, J. C., Hayes, F. A., & Shanahan, J. (1997). Perceived support for one's opinions and willingness to speak out: A meta-analysis of survey studies on the "spiral of silence." *Public Opinion Quarterly 61*(3), 452–463.

Holbert, R. L., Pillion, O., Tschida, D. A., Armfield, G. G., Kinder, K., Cherry, K. L., & Daulton, A. R. (2003). *The West Wing* as endorsement of the U.S. presidency: Expanding the bounds of priming in political communication. *Journal of Communication 53*(3), 427–443.

Holbrook, T. M. (2002). Presidential campaigns and the knowledge gap. *Political Communication 19*, 437–454.

Iyengar, S., Peters, M. D., & Kinder, D. R. (1982). Experimental demonstrations of the "not-so-minimal" consequences of television news programs. *American Political Science Review 76*(4), 848–858.

Iyengar, S., & Simon, A. (1993). News coverage of the gulf crisis and public opinion. *Communication Research 20*, 365–383.

Katzman, N. (1974). The impact of communication technologies: Promises and prospects. *Journal of Communication 24*(4), 47–58.

Liu, Y. I., & Eveland, W. P. (2005). Education, need for cognition, and campaign interest as moderators of news effect on political knowledge: An analysis of the knowledge gap. *Journalism & Mass Communication Quarterly 84*(2), 910–929.

McCann, J. A., & Lawson, C. (2006). Presidential campaigns and the knowledge gap in three transitional democracies. *Political Research Quarterly 59*(1), 13–22.

McCombs, M., & Shaw, D. (1972). The agenda-setting function of mass media. *Public Opinion Quarterly 36*, 176–185.

McCombs, M. (2005). The agenda-setting function of the press. In G. Overholser & K. H. Jamieson (Eds.), *The press* (pp. 156–168). New York: Oxford University Press.

Moy, P., Domke, D., & Stamm, K. (2001). The spiral of silence and public opinion on affirmative action. *Journalism & Mass Communication Quarterly 78*(1), 7–25.

Perry, D. K. (1996). *Theory and research in mass communication.* Mahwah, NJ: Lawrence Erlbaum Associates.

Potter, W. J., & Chang, I.C. (1990). Television exposure measures and the cultivation hypothesis. *Journal of Broadcasting and Electronic Media 34*(3), 313–333.

Potter, W. J. (1999). *On media violence.* Thousand Oaks, CA: Sage Publications.

Prior, M. News versus entertainment choice: How increasing media choice widens gaps in political knowledge and turnout. *American Journal of Political Science 49*(3), 577–592.

Rogers, E. (1983). *Diffusion of innovations* (3rd ed.). New York: Free Press.

Rogers, E. (1995). *Diffusion of innovations* (4th ed.). New York: Free Press.

Roush, C. (2005). Book review: Framed: Labor and the corporate media. *Journalism & Mass Communication Quarterly 82* (2), 460–461.

Ryan, B., & Gross, N. (1943). The diffusion of hybrid seed corn in two Iowa communities. *Rural Sociology 8*, 15–24.

Scheufele, D., & Moy, P. (2000). Twenty-five years of the spiral of silence: A conceptual review and empirical outlook. *International Journal of Public Opinion Research 12*(1), 3–28.

Severin, W. J., & Tankard, Jr., J. W. (2001). *Communication theories: Origins, methods, and uses in the mass media* (5th ed.). New York: Addison Wesley Longman.

Shaffer, G. (2006). Frame-up: An analysis of arguments both for and against municipal wi-fi initiatives. Paper presented at the Annual Convention of the Association for Education in Journalism and Mass Communication, San Francisco.

Simpson, C. (1996). Elisabeth Noelle-Neumann's "Spiral of Silence" and the historical context of communication theory. *Journal of Communication 46*(3), 149–171.

Sparks, G. G. (2002). *Mass media effects research*. Belmont, CA: Wadsworth Thomson Learning.

Stossel, S. (1997). The man who counts the killings. *The Atlantic Monthly 279*(5), 86–104.

Tichenor, P., Donahue, G., & Olien, C. (1970). Mass media flow and differential growth in knowledge. *Public Opinion Quarterly 34*, 159–170.

Woo, H. J., & Dominick, J. R. (2003). Acculturation, cultivation, and daytime TV talk shows. *Journalism & Mass Communication Quarterly 80*(1), 109–127.

8 Alternative Paradigms of Critical and Cultural Studies

THIS CHAPTER WILL:

- Compare and contrast the more traditional communication-science paradigm with the "alternative paradigm" of interpretive and critical views of the way media institutions and media content affect society and culture.

- Define some of the key terms and concepts used in this area of inquiry, such as ideology, hegemony, and institutional reinforcement of the elite power structure.

- Describe how these different approaches to media study require different research methods and techniques for formulating theory.

- Provide an overview of some of the most popular approaches within this paradigm, including political economy, the Frankfurt and Birmingham (British) schools of thought, post-modernism, and Marshall McLuhan's technological determinism.

The theories of the effects paradigm investigated through communication science (as described in Chapter 6 and Chapter 7) are the predominant way of theorizing about and researching mass communication today. Two studies of academic research trends both found that theories such as agenda setting, uses and gratifications, cultivation, and diffusion of innovations were among the most-used ones in published research (Bryant & Miron, 2004; Kamhawi & Weaver, 2003).

But communication science is not the only way to evaluate how the mass media affect audiences and shape society. Many researchers prefer a non-empirical approach to the topic that comes in different varieties with different labels that share some common underlying themes. It is what theorist Denis McQuail refers to as the "alternative paradigm" (2005, p. 65), which is perhaps the most all-inclusive term. Encompassed within this paradigm are related, but distinct, approaches including the critical paradigm (also called critical theory or critical studies) and cultural studies. Notably, critical theory also was among the "top five" theories documented in the studies by Kamhawi and Weaver (2003) and by Bryant and Miron (2004), in the form of "Marxist theory" on one list and "hegemony theory" on the other.

The prevailing theme in this alternative paradigm branch of communication inquiry is that knowledge is a form of power, and groups within a society use media institutions to help them exercise and maintain power. This happens through mass media promoting a set of ideas associated with a society's powerful interests, which frequently marginalize or drown out other, non-mainstream ideas. Researchers in this alternative paradigm say that the effects approach is incapable of addressing this issue adequately, because effects research tends to be constructed too narrowly and is incapable of looking beyond the status quo toward any sort of reformist stance. According to advocates of critical theory, communication science actually reinforces the status quo and its power arrangements by emphasizing quantitative measurement of the existing situation.

Another characteristic of the interpretive tradition is that its proponents believe theories and research projects should advocate action, specifically actions directed at improving society by helping "outsider" groups overcome the marginalization and domination they face. As one scholar expresses it, the dominant theme in critical and cultural studies is giving voice to oppressed groups within the society (Littlejohn, 1999, p. 247).

This idea of reform is why the approach is so often called a *critical* one. To understand this better, think about the words "critical" and "criticism" in a generic sense. If a person is being critical of someone or something, what is he doing? Well, he is probably pointing out shortcomings, and possibly also suggesting improvements about whatever it is he is criticizing. This is similar in concept to the "constructive criticism" or "critical feedback" teachers make on students' assignments. In a communication setting, critical theorists say that is exactly what they are trying to do with regard to the mass media: offer constructive criticism about both content and control systems for contemporary commercial media. The goal of theory and research in this tradition is to identify ways in which the media system is falling short of its best performance and to suggest ways in which better performance might be attained.

A Response to Limited Effects

Critical and cultural inquiry has its roots in European sociology, and really took hold as a reaction to the limited effects paradigm based in social science research and popularized in the United States in the 1950s and early 1960s.

The concept of limited effects came about when social scientists such as Paul Lazarsfeld tried to use quantitative methods to test ideas about the powerful, direct, and uniform effects of media associated with propaganda and the bullet theory (as described in Chapter 5). However, the results of these tests seemed to indicate that mass media messages behaved in a way opposite to what theories of powerful effects would predict. According to this research, the media apparently did not strongly or directly influence audience members. Rather, researchers from this era found evidence that the influence of media messages was affected by the audience members' contact with other people (two-step flow theory) and that media messages tended to support ideas that media consumers already had (reinforcement theory). When Katz, Klapper and other theorists argued for a view of limited effects, some other media scholars disagreed because they thought that the findings understated the media effects. One of these reactions was further social science investigation, such as agenda setting and cultivation research (discussed in Chapter 7) that sought to document circumstances under which some type of direct and meaningful effects *could* take place.

But another reaction was a more interpretive analysis that took a broader view of media and society together—recognizing how mass media had become a key part of the way ideas were communicated and culture was maintained within modern society. "These new perspectives argued that the media might have the power to intrude on and alter how we make sense of ourselves and our social world. . . . media affect society because they affect how culture is created, shared, learned and applied" (Baran & Davis, 2006, p. 227). This was the critical/cultural paradigm.

Positivist/Interpretive Differences

Definition
Positivism: This style of inquiry uses investigative methods of the physical sciences, such as experiments and objective measurement of specified criteria, to address and understand social phenomena. It is associated with the communication science tradition, (whose research is based largely on quantitative measurement of hypotheses drawn from the theories explained in Chapter 6 and Chapter 7) but is rejected by critical and cultural theorists.

The social science approach used in the investigations by scholars such as Lazarsfeld, as described in Chapter 5, is sometimes called the "positivist" or "neo-positivist" method: a term taken from the nineteenth-century writings of August Comte, a philosopher, intellectual, and early sociologist. In Comte's positivist philosophy, the only way "true" knowledge can be developed is through real-world observations. The scientific method and its use as a source of knowledge (as described in Chapter 1 and Chapter 2) are very closely related to this philosophy. From the positivist perspective, "meaning and truth are derived using logical, analytical or empirical rules of verification" (Melody & Mansell, 1983, p. 106).

But interpretive theorists reject the idea that knowledge must always come from scientific proof; they believe that this makes it impossible to consider the context of a situation as part of the research. Additionally, they view human behavior as something that is so complex that it is hard to draw meaningful conclusions about society from behavior that can be empirically observed and measured (Melody & Mansell, 1983, p. 108).

Consequently, in terms of research style, critical and cultural scholars lean heavily toward qualitative methods rather than quantitative ones. (See Chapter 3 for a comparison of both methods.) In essence, critical and cultural theorists say that studying people requires a different approach than quantitative measurement; they contend it is more important to go in-depth with individual situations than to collect and manipulate statistics from large samplings.

Critical researchers believe that this inability of quantitative research to reach accurate conclusions about the effect of media on culture is especially true over the long term. "One of the major problems in that type of [limited effects] research has been that the empirical instruments used were often too crude to note small changes that could be of great significance as they were compounded over time. For instance, it might be hard to detect short-term attitude changes in an audience that result from the content of the network evening news; yet, compounded over years, those effects might be profound" (DeSola Pool, 1983, p. 259). Thus, the critical scholar would maintain that long-term effects of mass communication are best analyzed within individual cases examined over time, rather than through data collected by surveys, content analyses, and experiments that count the instances of people engaging in particular behaviors at one moment in time.

In fact, some within the critical school go further, saying that empirical research into human behavior is so narrow and mechanical that it is basically pointless. In this view, "positivists do not merely base their work on that evidence, they enshrine it, making measurable data the definitive goal of research. The result of this slavish devotion to fact is, at best, a narrowing of research sights and, at worst, a view that what is real is measurable and what is measurable is real" (Mosco, 1983, pp. 244–245).

(At the same time, it should be noted that an equally negative view of interpretive research is expressed by supporters of traditional social science research, who criticize the critical/interpretive approach as being nothing more than subjective opinion that produces essays instead of research or discovery of new knowledge. "If intelligently applied, the [interpretive] approach may result in brilliant verbal descriptions and analyses that strike the reader as having an inherent quality of obvious truth. However, it does not allow for precision, falsification and replication. Any talented scholar can come up with a radically different interpretation, seemingly equally plausible, but the criteria are usually vague" [Rosengren, 1983, p. 199]. Some positivist social scientists also say that rather than being truly reform-minded, critical researchers push a narrow and biased agenda based on utopian views that ignore reality and end up merely attacking media without any realistic suggestions for reform.)

Goals of Critical and Cultural Research

In addition to disagreeing about methods of inquiry, quantitative social scientists and critical or cultural theory adherents differ in their research goals as well, regarding whether to "take sides" in doing research. The scientific method is meant to be a form of objective inquiry. The social scientist should have a hypothesis or a prediction about how certain variables are related. But objectivity means that the scientist does not have a viewpoint or idea about how the variables *should* be related or what relationship among them would be the *best* type of relationship. The goal of social science in the positivist tradition is to investigate and document things *as they are*, not to offer opinions about how they *should be*.

A Reformist Perspective

Critical research takes exactly the opposite stance, dropping the pretense of objectivity; cultural studies seeks out a middle ground of more objective analysis through the use of qualitative data analysis. Adherents to the critical tradition deliberately have viewpoints about how they believe the social system should operate and, through their research, set out to illuminate why and how the actual situation varies from their conception of the way things ought to be. Critical research has the goal "to reshape or invent institutions to meet the need of the relevant social community" (Smythe & Van Dinh, 1983, p. 118). Or, as similarly expressed by another scholar from the critical tradition, "Critical research offers an alternative way of seeing the place of communication in society by focusing on the transformation of social relations" (Mosco, 1983, p. 244). Researchers in this tradition say that research has no real value unless it takes a viewpoint. They further claim that a great deal of empirical research is nothing more than measurement of activities for the sake of measuring them, with findings that serve no real purpose. Rather, as Baran and Davis point out, "Those who develop critical theories seek social change that will implement their values" (2006, p. 231).

Exploring Ideology and Hegemony

Two concepts that lie at the heart of these reform-minded approaches are ideology and hegemony. Ideology refers to a dominant way of thinking about how society should be organized, featuring the ideas of those who hold power in the society. A more technical definition says ideology is "culturally constructed and institutionally reinforced understandings of the world which privilege the positions of the powerful" (Lye, 2004). Hegemony takes the concept of ideology and goes a step further to describe how ideology can be used as a tool for social control by undermining or crowding out ideas from outside of the mainstream that threaten those privileged positions of the powerful.

Hegemony was first defined by Antonio Gramsci, a leftist Italian journalist, who used the term to describe a situation in which a large portion of society becomes compliant and consents to the dominant ideology without even realizing it is being imposed on them. This happens because the dominant ideology is made to seem so convincing that even those who end up being exploited by the powerful interests (whom the ideology protects and supports) "buy in" to its ideals. In the critical view, the media play a part in promoting this consent and compliance. "The concept of hegemony suggests that the ideas of the ruling class in society become the ruling ideas throughout society. The mass media are seen as controlled by the dominant class in society and as aiding in exerting the control of that class over the rest of society" (Sallach, 1974, as quoted in Severin & Tankard, 2001, p. 282).

Definitions

Ideology: Dominant way of thinking about how society should be organized, based on the ideas of those who hold power in the society and promoted by those social elites as a way to maintain power.

Hegemony: Consent to a dominant ideology by a whole social system, even by those who are adversely affected by it and who therefore should be resistant to that ideology being imposed on them.

Focus on Power Structures

To summarize, critical discussions of ideology, hegemony, and reform of the social structure generally take the form of examining power relations within the communication of a society by examining topics such as:

- Which groups hold power, and by what means.
- Which groups are marginalized, oppressed, or cut off from power, and how the more powerful groups keep them marginalized.
- What role communication systems (especially mass media organizations) have in these power relationships.
- How communication structures could be set up differently to address these issues.

The methodological distinctions described earlier are related to these differing goals because quantitative social science focuses exclusively on what currently exists, not how things could be, and by doing this it tends to reinforce the existing power structure (McLeod & Tichenor, 2003, p. 99). "The real basis for the dichotomy between critical and traditional social science research lies in the allegiance of the researchers to the status quo vs. change in existing political and economic institutionalized power relations. . . . For most administrative research the existing power structure can do no wrong; for most critical research it can do no right" (Melody and Mansell, 1983, p. 106). Clearly, the answer must be somewhere in the middle. But it is easy to see, given the different perspectives and goals, how the divide became so wide.

Types of Critical and Cultural Research

So far the critical, cultural, and interpretive traditions have been described as a single entity, and there are some common goals regarding "communication in the exercise of social power" (Slack & Allor, 1983, p. 215). But even within the tradition, some approaches examine these social relationships from different perspectives. The fundamental difference is the level of analysis, either at a macroscopic (large-scale) level focusing on social institutions; or at a microscopic level about how the culture of everyday life is created and how that culture affects individuals and groups in more personalized ways (Baran & Davis, 2006, p. 230). The first of these approaches, dealing with social institutions and the structure of society, is more closely aligned with critical theory and the second approach is more common in cultural studies.

Critical Theory

Critical theory's philosophical basis comes from the ideas of Karl Marx, best known for his radical theories of politics and economics. Marx was perhaps the original "critical theorist," with criticisms directed at the political and economic power structure of nineteenth-century Europe. In his view, the working class (proletariat) provided the true source of wealth in the newly industrialized society, but the social structure oppressed the workers and allowed that wealth to be unfairly monopolized by the capitalists (bourgeoisie) who owned the factories. Scholars at the University of Frankfurt in Germany were among the first to apply variants of Marx's ideas, mixed with psychologist Sigmund Freud's ideas that unconscious impulses are a key part of human behavior, to the operation of mass media and its relation to powerful forces in society in the 1930s.

Political Economy. Classical Marxism, with its critique of the control of the industrial system by the bourgeoisie or upper class, focuses on how control of the production system becomes a tool that these powerful elites use to enhance their power within society. Control of the economic base or "structure" is enhanced and reinforced by these same elite individuals controlling the "superstructure," or social and cultural institutions such as churches, schools, and the media. Broadly considered, political economy theory is about how the forces within a society help to determine how its economic and social systems operate together.

As applied to mass communication, political economy theory maintains that "economic institutions shape the media to suit their interests and purposes" (Baran & Davis, 2006, p. 241). Economic control of the means of media production—that is, the ownership of newspapers, magazines, television, radio, movie studios, and so on, by huge corporations—limits or alters the forms of mass culture distributed through those media. One example of this is the predominance of songs and music videos produced to be just three to five minutes long to meet the programming needs of commercial radio and television (Kellner, n.d.)— meaning they are produced at a length that leaves the most flexibility for fitting commercials around them. Another common theme in critical theories of media is that content production is so constrained that it reinforces the status quo and undermines prospects for social change (Baran & Davis, 2006, p. 241). Consider, for example, the 90-second news package. Perhaps that is enough time to cover a fire in an old warehouse, but it is not enough to effectively deal with complex issues such as education reform or the intricacies of government health policies. Yet the economic realities of working for news operations at stations owned by large media corporations force reporters to cover even complicated stories in a compressed time period, and viewers learn to take their news in 90-second doses. Many adults get used to the shortened format and grow impatient with longer reports on public television or on the BBC.

Commodification of Culture. Herbert Schiller, a political economist whose ideas seem particularly meaningful right now, predicted that corporate control of media would have substantial effects on the content that media organizations produced. He further stated that this would become more significant as the economic system shifted toward a greater emphasis on production and use of information over production of industrial goods (such as steel and autos), which is exactly the trend the world economy has been following for the past several

FIGURE 8.1   Political Economy Theory in Action

Media reformist Robert McChesney has referred to the practice of advertisers pushing their goods on media audiences as "carpet-bombing." Such domination of the American media by advertising can be explained by the theory of political economy, which holds that media content is dictated by the financial needs of organizations behind the content. This would explain newspapers that devote 60 percent of their space to ads, or television and radio stations that give up 20 minutes or more out of an hour to commercials.

decades. "The accelerating effort to transform information into a good for sale and not primarily for social use is centered directly on its production, accumulation, storage, retrieval and distribution" (Schiller, 1983, p. 253). It is worth noting that Schiller, who died in 2000, wrote those words before the current explosion of media and expansion of telecommunications offerings such as satellite television, satellite and HD radio, digital distribution of video and music, or even the Internet and cellular phones. If anything, the "production, accumulation, storage, retrieval and distribution" of information has even more economic value and is controlled by even larger (and fewer) corporations than when he wrote this passage in the early 1980s.

Schiller's ideas are referred to as the *commodification of culture* theory. In economics, a commodity is a basic material, such as crude oil or unprocessed grain, which is essentially the same no matter what its source and is therefore sold in large quantities on the basis of price alone. According to Schiller, treating information as a commodity and "selling" it through the mass media explains the simplistic, escapist, and copycat tendencies of television, film, and music. One barrel of oil is identical to another, which is what makes it a commodity. Likewise, many media offerings are so similar that they might as well be identical. Sitcoms, dramas, and reality shows on television; action movies and romantic comedies in the theater; and sound-alike pop singers on the radio all are cited as evidence that media productions have become a commodity, too. Such commodity-like offerings are created to appeal to the largest audiences possible, which, according to Schiller's theory, makes commodification very lucrative for corporate owners of the media production system. But this trend also leads to a less-diverse, lower-value set of cultural offerings for the society because the commodified goods crowd out higher-quality material, such as important public affairs information, that could lead to social improvement.

Herman and Chomsky's Propaganda Model.   Another theory that is covered under the umbrella of political economy is the *propaganda model* of Edward Herman and Noam Chomsky, which describes how powerful government and business interests influence the media. These theorists describe a system in which cultural offerings mostly are produced by for-profit media businesses that derive most of their profit from advertisers that are also commercial enterprises. Besides these powerful commercial interests, the power of the government affects the content

FIGURE 8.2 Television Shows as Commodities

After CBS scored a surprise hit with *Survivor* during that show's first season, it spawned a host of reality programming on broadcast and cable networks. When ABC's *Who Wants to Be a Millionaire?* became a smash success, the network soon had it on the air several nights each week. When the crime dramas *Law and Order* and *CSI* developed large followings, their producers rolled out variants to use the original shows' popularity to reach more viewers (or, more likely, to reach the same viewers for more hours in the week).

Shows that bear such striking similarities to each other exemplify what Herbert Schiller called *commodification*. The term comes from economics: a commodity is a good that is identical no matter who the producer is, such as a barrel of oil or a bushel of wheat. So Schiller used that metaphor to refer to media offerings that are so similar in form and purpose that they might as well be identical and are valuable to their producers more for their quantity than their quality.

of the media through the role of government officials as news sources and through tools such as broadcast regulation and licensing.

The model as constructed by Herman and Chomsky outlined five influences, which they called filters, that help to determine what makes it into the news when news media are controlled by large commercial media businesses (Herman & Chomsky, 1988, p. 2). The filters are:

- **Ownership**: News and entertainment content tends to be pro-business (or at least favorable to the capitalist system) because media owned by large corporations are not going to report information that would question the basis or legitimacy of how they themselves operate.
- **Advertising**: Media organizations are dependent on advertising, so they tend to avoid coverage that would upset advertisers and are inclined to present information that will draw the largest possible audience to maximize potential advertising revenue. Simple concepts, lots of visuals, and sensational content draw such an audience, especially on television, while long, complicated public affairs coverage does not.
- **Sourcing**: A large volume of news comes from government and business sources (public information officials and public relations representatives) whose job is to present information in terms most favorable to their organizations. To make their point, Herman and Chomsky describe the extensive public relations apparatus of the U.S. Defense Department and how it portrays a particular, and favorable, view of the military.
- **Flak**: Chomsky and Herman use this term to describe the tendency of government and business interests to vigorously object to any information that does not serve their best interests and that seeks to offer an opposing view.
- **Anti-communist ideology**: A dominant us-versus-them ideology is used as an organizing scheme for news presentations because powerful interests of government and business want to show the public that they need and deserve its support. In Chomsky and Herman's original formulation, written during the end of the Cold War era in the 1980s, this theme was anti-communism; arguably today the term "anti-terrorism" could easily be substituted.

With this theory, Chomsky and Herman sought to update some of the original research into communication and society as described in Chapter 5—investigation of persuasive communication or propaganda as disseminated by powerful interests in society. Controversies over the use of video news releases by television stations without disclosing their source—corporations or the government—is also an example of what this theory would predict. But it remains a controversial view because its position that the government and large businesses engage in propaganda goes against the perception that the U.S. media system operates (or at least *should* operate) with freedom of expression as its purpose and goal.

A contemporary media political economist whose work builds on that of Herman and Chomsky is Robert McChesney, who has written extensively on the effects of ownership of media by large conglomerates. In his view, those effects are highly negative, so he also is active in promoting media reform that emphasizes independent media outlets (such as community radio and Internet campaigns); watchdog groups that confront corporate media; and mobilization of citizens to petition the FCC and other government groups for change. McChesney and some of his associates maintain a Web site, www.freepress.net, with information about these issues and ideas for reforms.

Frankfurt School.   Political economy theories focus on issues of ownership and control of media operations and how they are used in hegemonic ways to promote a dominant ideology. They deal with what Marx called the "base" or "structure" of society; that is, ownership of the means of production. This is why they sometimes are called structural theories. But in Marxist theory, the structure exists along with a "superstructure" of other social systems, including schools, churches, and cultural outlets, which also help to spread ideology.

The first individuals to apply this "superstructure" and its resulting "structures of oppression" portion of Marxist thought to media-generated culture were a group of scholars in Frankfurt, Germany, whose ideas have come to be known as the *Frankfurt School* of thought (Littlejohn, 1999, p. 9). They sought to keep Marxist theory alive during the 1920s and 1930s, at a time when it appeared to be declining because the Communist revolution had not spread from Russia and, in fact, was threatened by the rise of an alternate political/economic philosophy known as fascism that closely aligned government and commercial interests. These developments of European history helped to bring the "revolutionary" appeal of Marxism under control (Bennett, 1982). But using the Marxist view of *superstructure* or control of cultural institutions in society, the Frankfurt scholars theorized that mass culture created by powerful elites was imposed on the masses as a means of social control that would help maintain the authority of those powerful individuals by keeping the mass of people distracted and disorganized. Rather than having a cultural system that invites and allows people to participate in the decisions of society, the result is "a generally alienated (rather than emancipated and activated) audience" (Rosengren, 1983, p. 193).

Many of the Frankfurt School's most influential intellectual thinkers were Jewish and had fled Germany as it came under Nazi control in the 1930s. As a result, some work of what is called the "Frankfurt School" actually was done in the United States by these exiled scholars, notably Theodor Adorno, Max Horkheimer, and Herbert Marcuse. Adorno and Horkheimer's definitive book on how mass culture promotes social control, *The Dialectic of Enlightenment,* was written in the middle of World War II (1944) while they were living in New York City. The book "offers a vision of society that has lost its capacity to nourish true freedom and individuality" (During, 1993). For Adorno and Horkheimer, this loss occurred when production of cultural artifacts shifted from an individual-artist basis (e.g., painters such as the Impressionists or musical composers such as Mozart) to an industrial one (e.g., Hollywood movies and radio musical programming). In Adorno and Horkheimer's view, "the modern culture industry produces safe, standardized products geared to the larger demands of the capitalist economy. It does so by representing 'average' life for purposes of pure entertainment or distraction as seductive and realistically as possible" (During, 1993, p. 31).

Adorno and Horkheimer described a market/capitalist-based set of culture "industries," especially producers of Hollywood films, who were not interested in producing art but rather just serving up distractions to help create a conformist society that would accept the values of the capitalist system that produced them. "From every sound film and every broadcast program the social effect can be inferred which is exclusive to none but shared by all alike. The culture industry as a whole has molded men as a type unfailingly reproduced in every product . . . The might of industrial society is lodged in men's minds" (Adorno & Horkheimer, 1944, in During, 1993).

The ideas of the Frankfurt School thinkers are seen as an important and influential development in the analysis of media and society because they went beyond pure issues of media ownership to describe how ownership, content production, and social influence mutually reinforced each other with a hegemonic result (i.e., one that supports the continued domination of the elite and the powerful). The Frankfurt School's ideas put ideology at the center of the media-social influence debate and suggested that the media "occupy a critical position within the more general Marxist debates concerning the way in which the economic, political and ideological levels of the social formation should be construed as relating to one another" (Bennett, 1982, p. 49).

Cultural Studies

The Frankfurt School examined culture, but it is generally grouped with critical theory because of its Marxist approach. But by emphasizing the importance of ideology, it set the stage for a cultural studies tradition to follow that would move even further away from structural political economy theory to more closely examine the role of ideology in creating and controlling culture. Cultural studies is defined by Kellner (n.d.) as "a set of approaches to the study of culture and society . . . [that] provides some tools that enable one to read and interpret one's culture critically." These sometimes have neo-Marxist influences but often do not.

FIGURE 8.3   The Frankfurt School and "Indie" Film Producers

In their devastating critique of popular culture (*The Dialectic of Enlightenment*, 1944) Theodor Adorno and Max Horkheimer wrote that cultural offerings produced by large businesses are all style, with no substance, made with the goal of creating a conformist society. They compared mass-produced pop culture goods (such as Hollywood movies) very unfavorably to the work of individual artists, such as fine art paintings or symphonies. In a modern adaptation of their thoughts, it could be said that the contemporary music and movie industries' emphasis on turning out look-alike and sound-alike productions that will have the greatest popular appeal, and these businesses' associated refusal to distribute the more avant-garde works of independent filmmakers or non-mainstream musical groups, is an example of the same process at work.

In a typical cultural studies perspective, multiple ideologies exist, generally including a dominant or hegemonic one. A society's mass media help to keep this ideology dominant through repetition and through emphasis of certain points of view and exclusion of others. One of the scholars most closely associated with contemporary cultural studies, Stuart Hall, has described this as a process of cultural meanings being constructed through the use of symbols, especially language. What matters to a cultural scholar is what kinds of meanings become attached to descriptions of people, organizations, or situations. "In order for one meaning to be regularly produced, it has to win a kind of credibility, legitimacy or taken-for-grantedness for itself. That involves marginalizing, downgrading or delegitimating alternative constructions" (Hall, 1982, p. 67).

A major goal of cultural studies research is to counteract these marginalizing portrayals and offer alternatives to them. "The chief aim of cultural studies is to expose how ideologies of powerful groups are unwittingly perpetuated and ways they can be resisted to disrupt the system of power that disenfranchises certain groups" (Littlejohn, 1999, p. 236). Such research employs qualitative research techniques, emphasizing evidence gained through examination of human subjects and/or texts, through a process of analyzing large amounts of qualitative data combined with inductive reasoning (making broader generalizations from patterns found in the data). Two key tools for this are the research processes known as semiotics and rhetorical analysis, both of which are explained in Chapter 3.

Symbolic Interactionism and the Social Construction of Reality.   In its emphasis on symbols and signification, cultural studies draws heavily on theories of symbolic interactionism and social construction of reality to examine the influence of ideology. Chapter 5 describes how the earliest developments of mass communication theory focused on what became known as the transmission model, exemplified by Harold Lasswell's functional model (*who* says *what* to *whom* through which *channel* with what *effects*) and Shannon and Weaver's source-message-channel-receiver model. But some theorists proposed an alternative to the functionalist transmission model, which they called interactionism. This was based on the idea that the key determinant of social behavior is the way people react to their surroundings and other people around them.

This is literally the opposite perspective of the functionalist theory, which says that large-scale social structures and institutions are the driving forces behind how people behave and react as social beings. Rather, in this alternative view, media messages become a part of this reaction arena (or social environment) through a process of *symbolic interactionism*. This theory is associated with the work of Herbert Blumer, who coined the term in the 1930s. For Blumer and those who have built upon his work, social behavior—how people act and interact with one another—depends on the meanings people infer from messages or how they interpret what other people say and do. Making these interpretations and attaching these meanings happens entirely through symbolic communication. "We share ideas, rules, goals, values (all symbolic), and these allow us to continue to interact cooperatively with others" (Charon, 2001, p. 90).

The process of interacting and giving meaning to the world around them through reading and interpreting symbolic communication means that people are responsible for constructing the social world that they end up living within. "The human being, because of the symbol, does not respond passively to a reality that imposes itself but actively creates and re-creates the world acted in" (Charon, 2001, p. 90).

Sociologists Peter Berger and Thomas Luckmann built upon this idea with a theory they called the *social construction of reality* that describes how situations created by social interaction come to be seen as "objective" and "real"—in other words, come to be seen as if they were something other than human creations. In an influential essay titled "The Social Construction of Reality" (1967), Berger and Luckmann define objective reality as something outside of human control, something that "cannot be wished away." Over time, the ongoing interaction of individuals with one another builds up social institutions, in the form of habits, values, and roles that people come to adopt. This results in an institutionalized social reality based on shared meanings and understandings that come about through symbolic communication—a world that is seen as "objectively" real, even though it was created by people (Berger & Luckmann, 1967, p. 60).

Since people created this reality, they should be able to change it—but that does not happen, according to Berger and Luckmann. "The institutions are now experienced as possessing a reality of their own, a reality that confronts the individual as an external and coercive fact . . . A world so regarded attains a firmness in consciousness; it becomes real in an ever more massive way and can no longer be changed so readily" (1967, p. 59). This idea that symbolic expression defines the reality that human beings experience is a central feature of the cultural studies branch of the interpretive paradigm.

British Cultural Studies. One of the first, and most significant, places to develop an alternative paradigm or counterpoint to the limited effects theories generated by U.S. social science researchers was the Centre for Contemporary

Cultural Studies at the University of Birmingham, England, in the 1960s. (The name of the research center, in fact, gives this branch of the alternative paradigm its name.) This collection of British scholars in many ways built upon the work of their counterparts in the Frankfurt School. Both sets of researchers were interested in theorizing about how mass culture and mass media help to create a hegemonic ideology that keeps the lower classes of society from challenging the elites who control society. Both schools of thought also believed in the need to construct a critique of the way in which this hegemony was created.

But a major difference between the two was that, while the Frankfurt School dismissed the idea of mass culture being any sort of positive force in society, the British Cultural Studies school actively focused on ways to "correct" mass culture so that it could counter oppressive ideology. This tradition recognizes the power of elites to promote ideology but says that elite domination is not inevitable if an egalitarian and culturally pluralistic approach is pursued, meaning that people who are not in the highest socioeconomic status or are in so-called marginalized groups still can be organized and can change the system. The Birmingham scholars started out with a focus on the oppression of working class people in Great Britain, again similar to the Frankfurt scholars' focus on the class divisions described in Marxist thought. But while the Frankfurt school kept its work focused on class struggle, the British school of cultural studies soon expanded to include analysis of texts that were seen as marginalizing women and people of differing races, ethnicities, and sexual orientations.

The Frankfurt School was thoroughly Marxist in its approach, while the British School was less clearly so. One description of the British school of thought said that it used Marxism and semiotics (the study of how symbols impart meaning; see Chapter 3) "to understand the nature of contemporary social life and the central place of communication within it" (Grossberg, 1996). But a longtime leader of the British school—Stuart Hall, who was its director from 1969 to 1979—has said that the goal of its research was not to be avowedly pro-Marxist, as the Frankfurt scholars were. Instead, the British scholars just happened to be concerned about the same issues that Marxism helped to highlight: the power and reach of capital in society, relationships between those with social power and exploitation of those without it, and a general theory that would connect different domains of life such as economics, politics, and culture.

In an essay describing the work of the Centre, Hall wrote that application of Gramsci's ideas about hegemony and ideology came closest to describing what the organization was really trying to accomplish (Hall, 1996, p. 267). He summarized the Centre's work as a consideration of questions of culture through the metaphors of language and textuality, and of creating theories about power, history, and politics as matters of representation through language. The British Cultural Studies scholars sought to understand how symbols become a source of cultural power and a way in which people identify themselves. In Hall's words, "Culture is the struggle over meaning, a struggle that takes place over and within" the way things are symbolized (Hall, 1984, as quoted in Grossberg, 1996, p. 157).

A great amount of work in cultural studies concerns the ways in which words, images, symbols, and meanings are used to portray groups that are outside of the mainstream of social power—especially women and people of different races, ethnic backgrounds, and sexual orientations. It also deals with how these groups can reclaim that power. For an example of how symbols and meanings can affect portrayals—something Hall calls the "struggle over the sign"— consider the difference between calling someone a "woman" or a "lady" versus calling her a "chick," a "honey," or a "babe." Or think about descriptions of individuals as "black" or "African-American" versus any one of an unfortunately large number of racial epithets used to describe dark-skinned people. Radio personality Don Imus found himself embroiled in a controversy that ended up costing him his job for a time in mid-2007 when he used a combination of racial and sexual insults to refer to African-American women from a college basketball team. This is an excellent example of how the symbols used to describe people and the meanings those symbols convey can matter to an individual or group and affect how others see them, and the impact that those symbols can have when they are part of a mass media message. Cultural studies seeks to better understand how this process of attaching symbolic meaning works and what it means for the individuals and groups involved, for the media that use those symbols, and for the society as a whole.

Other Approaches

Much of what McQuail has called *alternative paradigm*, generally referred to here as the interpretive paradigm, can be organized under critical or cultural theory approaches. But, appropriately for a research tradition that celebrates the personal, subjective nature of scholarly investigation, this paradigm also encompasses other ideas and approaches that cannot be lumped into either of those categories. A description of some of these approaches follows.

Postmodernism. *Postmodern* is a term with broad applications in the arts and other areas of contemporary society. It is possible students have encountered the term in coursework in English or other humanities subjects. Applied to communication theories, postmodernism describes the fundamental differences in the alternative communication paradigm. Theories that use a structural orientation, such as political economy, are sometimes called *modernist* approaches because they have to do with traditional organizations of society using the principles of modernity. They are contrasted with the postmodern, sometimes even called "post-structural," views of the cultural studies tradition (Baran & Davis, 2006, p. 8).

But to really understand the term *postmodern* as it applies to social structures, it is necessary first to understand the concept of *modernity*, because postmodernism is fundamentally a critique of the modernist ideal and a set of ideas that offer alternatives to that ideal. Defined in this way, *modernity* is a theory of social organization associated with principles of the eighteenth-century movement called the *Enlightenment*, which advocated that intellect and reason could be used to understand the universe and solve the problems facing humanity. According to Enlightenment philosophy, knowledge and ideas produced by the rational and knowing self can lead to progress and continuous improvement of human institutions and the human condition. Auguste Comte's positivism and the scientific method (discussed earlier in this chapter) are direct outgrowths of this perspective.

Most of the ideas used to organize Western society—including capitalism, representative democracy, personal liberty, the rule of law, and the advance of technology—come out of the Enlightenment's social ideals. What Europeans and (especially) Americans think of as "progress" over the past three centuries—the Industrial Revolution, the Information Age, technology-based invention and innovation—all are part of modernity.

But *post*modern thinking questions the benefits of modernity and the philosophy of the Enlightenment that lies behind it. This is because while the modern developments of the past couple of centuries have brought a technologically advanced, more comfortable lifestyle to a portion of the world's inhabitants, notably in North America and Western Europe, most of the planet has not shared in the benefits.

Modernity has brought about advanced medical procedures that have saved lives, taken humans to the Moon, and given us the Internet. But it also has led to two world wars in which millions of people died horrible deaths caused by technologically advanced weapons (e.g., machine guns, aircraft bombs). It has not ended starvation, poverty, or the tendency for some people to be inhumane or cruel to each other. It *has* created pollution; given us nations presided over by brutal dictators who use modern technology to oppress, torture, and kill the people they rule; and, for the first time in history, made it possible for human beings to literally obliterate life on the planet through the incredible destructive power of nuclear weapons.

So postmodernist thinking asks: Can this really be called *progress*? As a social philosophy (or theory), the Enlightenment predicts that humans can use their intellect and rationality to eventually create a perfect society by ultimately finding the single best approach to human social organization. But is this view a legitimate one? Is there a single "right" way to organize an economy or a political system? Will science and technology provide all the answers? Can humans continuously improve themselves and their social systems far enough that the benefits of modernity will outweigh the problems it has created? Postmodernists say that at present the answer to all of these questions is "no," and they doubt that it ever will be possible to answer them "yes."

The general outlines of postmodern thinking are attributed to several French intellectuals, starting with Michel Foucault. Foucault argued that modern life that is organized around the principles of reason and rationality would necessarily have to exclude from full participation in the social system anyone not capable of being a fully functional, rationally directed member of the society. Those who are incapable of this—the infirm, disabled, those who chose alternative lifestyles—have no value in the "rationalist" society. Thus, in Foucault's view, rationality and modernity will never lead to the "perfect" society. By definition, they will be unjust and dismissive toward a portion of humanity.

Jean Francois Lyotard built upon this foundation (and popularized the word "postmodernism") in a 1979 book in which he argued that the "grand narrative" of modernity no longer had universal value, largely because of the shortcomings of modernist social organizations and some of the negative effects of modernity as described earlier. Rather, he argued that contemporary society should adopt a postmodern view that rejects grand narratives and gives respect and attention to smaller, more individualized narratives with no overall organizing principle. Postmodernism from Lyotard's perspective has been described as "the critique of grand narratives, the awareness that such narratives serve to mask the contradictions and instabilities that are inherent in any social practice" (Klages, 2003).

Thus, postmodernism has come to be defined as a way of looking at society in which there is no unifying, singular way of interpreting any given text, practice, or human behavior. There is no "correct" form of government or economic system, no single "correct" way to set up social institutions—and no "correct" (or universal) interpretation of a media message or description of its effects. Knowledge is situationally based and understanding is in the eyes of the beholder.

In the context of the interpretive paradigm, Lyotard's view of postmodernism is very closely associated with cultural studies, which emphasizes the contributions that "marginalized" groups can make to society with their small narratives providing a counterweight to the dominant ideology ("grand narrative") that works to keep them oppressed and marginalized. This is further reflected in the differences between proponents of empirical and qualitative research methods as described earlier. Modernity equates knowledge with science and the use of the quantitative, positivist perspective. It dismisses the value of individual, subjective narrative. Postmodernism, on the other hand, celebrates such narrower and individual views. This is a fundamental reason why scholars who take a critical or cultural view use methods that reject positivism and instead rely on interpretation and the search for meaning.

For the postmodernist, context is everything and nothing is absolute. However, this attitude that "everything is relative" and everything is open to interpretation opens postmodernism to some criticism as well. If everything is subject to interpretation, every viewpoint in scholarly inquiry is potentially valid. If that is the case, then two completely different conclusions drawn from the same set of facts could both be considered equally valid. If that is so, then what is the value of inquiry in the first place? If nothing is ever "wrong," how can anything be "right"? Thus, while postmodernism has many adherents, it also has many detractors who dismiss it as a theory with little value or validity.

McLuhan's Technological Determinism.   As the interpretive or alternative paradigm was growing in popularity in the early 1960s, one of the people identified with it was Marshall McLuhan, a Canadian media scholar. McLuhan became famous for his analysis of the role of pop culture in society; and for his formulation of memorable phrases to describe that society, such as "the global village" and "the medium is the message." McLuhan built on the ideas of his mentor, Harold Innis, who theorized that forms of communication were directly related to structures in society, a process that Innis called "the biases of communication." This was a classic critical theory/political economy view in that he related social structures used in the exercise of power to structures of information control. McLuhan, however, was not a structural theorist in exactly the same way as Innis. Rather, he adapted Innis's ideas to come up with his own theories about how media technologies affect patterns of human thinking and human beings' ways of relating to the world around them.

McLuhan's central idea is that historical eras of social structure each have been the product of the dominant communication medium of the time. As communication technology and methods have changed over the course of human history, social organization has changed accordingly (Sparks, 2002).

According to McLuhan, the earliest form of human organization was the *tribal paradigm*, an era before printing technology was developed when communication was dominated by oral transmission conveyed in chronological order. The only things people knew about were either from their own experience or from talking to other people about events that they had not personally witnessed. Either way, communication experiences happened chronologically—in the order in which a person lived his life. When this is the main way people communicate, according to McLuhan, the resulting culture is going to be based on how things in the society relate to one another, which he called a tribal view.

This tribal paradigm was replaced in the early-modern era (about 600 years ago) by the *print paradigm*, which fostered linear thinking instead of relational thinking and also ended the need for chronological communication. Unlike oral messages that cannot be preserved, something that is written down can be communicated to someone an hour later, a day later, or many years later. But it also creates a need for order and structure in messages; written communication makes sense only if components of the message are in the proper order. In the process of imposing order, linear communication undermines the relational and communal characteristics of tribal-era communication. As a result, the Enlightenment, the rise of modernity, and the print paradigm are closely related in both time and function.

The linear communication-print paradigm lasted several hundred years until the twentieth century, when it was supplanted by the *electronic paradigm*, which extends the ability for people to see and hear at distances, and allows them to experience communications "real-time," even if those activities are not live but were recorded earlier. Communication in this electronic era also uses multiple senses and therefore is not as linear as the print style, which gives it something in common with the tribal paradigm, according to McLuhan. For example, someone watching television can hear the telephone ring, and can continue watching the show even as they take the call and talk to the person on the other end. Contrast this with the idea of trying to read a letter and read the newspaper simultaneously. It cannot be done. They would have to be read sequentially, in accord with McLuhan's notion of a linear print paradigm.

McLuhan cannot really be described as a postmodernist, but his description of the course of history has a great deal in common with the development and ascendance of modernity and the mid-twentieth-century development of post-modernism. McLuhan's description of a linear, mechanistic print era roughly overlaps the era of modernity, from the Renaissance to the mid-twentieth century, and is based on the same principle of structured rationality that the Enlightenment used as a social organizing principle. McLuhan proposed that this era was fading into history and being replaced by a less-directed, less-organized form of social structure. At around the same time—the late 1960s/early 1970s—Lyotard was describing the replacement of grand narratives with personalized, local ones. Lyotard said the beginning of the postmodern era was the post-World War II reconstruction of Europe in the 1950s; McLuhan's electronic era took hold with the spread of television, also in the 1950s. So, in a way these two thinkers were espousing the same idea from slightly different perspectives about a historical evolution of the social structure.

The focal point of McLuhan's ideas is that a society dominated by electronic media will differ from a print-dominated one because people relate to the world around them according to which senses they use to learn about it. This was expressed in one of his well-known sayings about communication styles, that media are "the extensions of man." By this he meant that the media are a tool for communication that, like other tools, extend human capacities. One of the examples he uses in explaining this is that a person can dig a hole with his hands or dig it with a shovel; the tool of the shovel extends the capacity of the hands and creates conditions under which the hole can be dug faster and more efficiently (McLuhan, 1964, in Hanson & Maxcy, 1999). In a similar way, media extend the senses by creating an ability to see and hear things at a distance and to experience them at times other than when they were created. According to McLuhan, this "extension" of the senses changes the way people relate to their environment and to each other, altering the social structure in the process.

A related concept is summed up in what is probably McLuhan's best-known saying about how media relate to culture: "the medium is the message." In other words, what really matters is not whether or how people are changed by the content of the messages they receive (as in the effects paradigm), but rather how society is organized by the dominant way in which messages are communicated (oral, print, or electronic). Here McLuhan departs dramatically from the effects theorists of the social science tradition and even from most critical and cultural thinkers. In McLuhan's view, it did not really matter what an individual was watching on television (comedy, violence, news, etc.) or even who controlled the content of the broadcast. What mattered was that he was watching television rather than reading a book or talking to other people about events. The effect on the individual and the social system came from the way the message was mediated, not from the content. Contrasted with, for example, Gerbner's cultivation theory (from Chapter 7) about the effect of message content, the difference in perspective is dramatic.

FIGURE 8.4   What Would McLuhan Say about Facebook?

The crux of Marshall McLuhan's approach is that the dominant way of communicating in a society will affect the way social interactions and social organizations develop and evolve. The Internet in general and the development of social networking sites such as MySpace and Facebook in particular can be seen as applications of what his ideas would predict. Mobile communications (via voice and, increasingly, text and video-enabled cellular phones) are another example. The tools of communication that extend human senses (of seeing, speaking, and listening) dramatically influence how people relate to one another and how ways of interacting across society at large develop.

A third famous McLuhan-ism combines these ideas. He stated that the electronic media could create a "global village." Even in the 1960s, when these ideas were first presented, technology allowed people to see and hear things from around the world as easily as those nearby. In McLuhan's view, this allowed people to interact in almost the same way as they did in the pre-print tribal era, but without the geographical limitations. So, he theorized that a new worldwide social order could emerge as the electronic media linked up the world.

In his time, McLuhan faced stinging criticism from fellow academics, not only for his radical ideas but also because he took his views about media into the popular arena, where he became a celebrity of sorts by giving interviews and appearing on entertainment programs. As things he predicted came to pass, however, his ideas earned more respect and an entire media ecology movement has evolved from his work. McLuhan died in 1980, but his idea of a new social order based on the media and means of communication has renewed interest because of the globalization of information through the Internet, satellite delivery of media messages, and myriad other technologies.

Summary

The alternative paradigm incorporating critical and cultural studies offers a stark contrast to the communication-science/effects tradition in its methods, its goals, and its conclusions about how media and society interact. In many respects, the two traditions "talk past" each other and find little common ground for agreement. Positivist communication scholars say that critical and cultural theories are opinions without verification; critical and cultural scholars say that empirical research is measurement without meaning. To put it another way, it has been said that quantitative social science emphasizes reliability over validity, while the alternative approach focuses on validity at the expense of reliability. In both cases, the results are incomplete. Yet the divisions often seem difficult to reconcile because they lie at the core of what each tradition believes.

But both have a contribution to make to communication study. Critical theory and cultural theory raise interesting and important questions about the role of the media and its effect on culture in contemporary society, even if they lack the means to answer them definitively. In the process, cultural studies has diverged somewhat from the critical paradigm. It has increasingly turned to empirical qualitative analysis of media texts and text-audience interaction in the interpretation of meaning, using interviews, focus groups, and ethnography to better understand these influences in modern society. Yet its focus on interpretation and understanding still limits its ability to make definitive general claims about the nature of media effects. The traditional paradigm of quantitative social science, on the other hand, consists of tools that can provide verifiable, credible evidence to answer questions. But its detractors from the critical paradigm are correct in saying that social scientists frequently are content with narrow, quantifiable research projects that seldom even ask important questions, much less try to answer them (Rosengren, 1983).

Using all of these perspectives, however, paints a more comprehensive picture of media and culture than might be provided by only using one paradigm. For example, a common theme in cultural studies is the tendency of the media to promote a hegemonic male perspective, by offering sexualized portrayals of women in movies, television, and magazines; or by concentrating audience attention on topics geared toward a male perspective. (Consider the prominence given to professional sports in television broadcast scheduling, for example.) A political economy analysis would look at the impact of corporate control on creating these outcomes; a cultural theorist's concern would interpret meanings of the messages on the screen or printed page.

The same issue can be addressed, however, through social science theories such as Bandura's social learning (e.g., are the body-image problems many young women face developed through what they learn from sexualized images in the media?); or agenda setting (how many male-oriented topics do the mass media present compared to female-oriented ones?). Identifying issues such as these and describing why they matter to society can best be analyzed from a critical perspective. Once that problem definition is made, such topics also can be investigated using quantitative social science methods such as attitude surveys or content analyses.

Using all of these perspectives could be likened to creating multi-channel sound for music and video production, which provide more audio information to create a fuller, richer, and more complete reproduction of the movie's soundtrack by literally surrounding the viewer with audio. Likewise, the interpretive and social science paradigms, when used in harmony with each other, can offer a more complete picture of the impact of media on society and culture. Increased richness and detail are developed when multiple paradigms are applied to an analysis, similar to the increased richness and detail that a multi-channel home theater system can provide, as opposed to a conventional two-channel stereo system.

QUESTIONS FOR DISCUSSION/ APPLICATION EXERCISES

1. Students who have done internships at media outlets can probably identify ways in which they were confronted with the political economy model. Can you identify specific examples of filters identified by Herman and Chomsky that you have experienced?

2. After considering the contributions of Marshall McLuhan described in this chapter, visit the following Web site from the Canadian Broadcasting Corporation: http://archives.cbc.ca/IDD-1-69-342/life_society/mcluhan/. After viewing some of the links in the archives, how has your opinion of McLuhan changed? Is there a lesson for today's media practitioners in his message?

3. Identify some areas of mass media or issues involving the media that might be addressed more appropriately by the critical or cultural perspective than by the effects tradition described in Chapters 6 and 7. Then take one or two issues and identify specific research questions that would use a critical or cultural approach to investigate them.

REFERENCES

Adorno, T., & Horkheimer, M. (1944). The culture industry: Enlightenment as mass deception [Chapter 1 of *The Dialectic of Enlightenment*]. In S. During (Ed.), *The cultural studies reader* (2nd ed.) (pp. 31–41). New York: Routledge.

Baran, S., & Davis, D. (2006). *Mass communication theory: Foundations, ferment and future* (4th ed.). Belmont, CA: Thompson Wadsworth.

Bennett, T., (1982). Theories of the media, theories of society. In M. Gurevitch, T. Bennett, J. Curran, & J. Woollacott (Eds.), *Culture, society and the media* (pp. 30–55). London: Methuen & Co., Ltd.

Berger, P., & Luckmann T. (1967). *The social construction of reality*. New York: Anchor Books.

Bryant, J., & Miron, D. (2004, December). Theory and research in mass communication. *Journal of Communication 54*(4), 662–704.

Charon, J. (2001). The importance of the symbol. In J. O'Brien & P. Kollock (Eds.), *The production of reality: Essays and readings on social interaction* (3rd ed.) (pp. 89–96). Thousand Oaks, CA: Pine Forge Press.

DeSola Pool, I. (1983, Summer). What ferment? A challenge for empirical research. *Journal of Communication 33*(3), 258–261.

During, S. (1993). Introduction. In S. During (Ed.), *The cultural studies reader* (2nd ed.) (pp. 1–30). New York: Routledge.

Grossberg, L. (1996). History, politics and postmodernism: Stuart Hall and cultural studies. In D. Morley & K.-H. Chen (Eds.), *Stuart Hall: Critical dialogues in cultural studies* (pp. 151–173). New York: Routledge.

Hall, S. (1982). The rediscovery of ideology: Return of the repressed in media studies. In M. Gurevitch, T. Bennett, J. Curran, & J. Woollacott (Eds.), *Culture, society and the media* (pp. 56–90). London: Methuen & Co., Ltd.

Hall, S. (1996). Cultural studies and its theoretical legacies. In D. Morley & K.-H. Chen (Eds.), *Stuart Hall: Critical dialogues in cultural studies* (pp. 262–275). New York: Routledge.

Herman, E., & Chomsky, N. (1988). *Manufacturing consent: The political economy of the mass media*. New York: Pantheon Books.

Kamhawi, R., & Weaver, D. (2003 Spring). Mass communication research trends from 1980 to 1999. *Journalism & Mass Communication Quarterly 80*(1), 7–27.

Kellner, D. (n.d.) Cultural studies, multiculturalism and media culture. Retrieved June 15, 2006 from: http://www.gseis.ucla.edu/faculty/kellner/papers/SAGEcs.htm.

Klages, M. (2003). Postmodernism. Retrieved June 15, 2006 from: http://www.colorado.edu/English/courses/ENGL2012Klages/pomo.html.

Littlejohn, S. (1999). *Theories of human communication*. Belmont, CA: Wadsworth.

Lye, J. (2004). Who controls the media and their meanings? Retrieved June 12, 2006 from: http://www.brocku.ca/english/jlye/control.html.

McLeod, D., & Tichenor, P. (2003). The logic of social and behavior science. In G. Stempel, D. Weaver, & G. C. Wilhoit (Eds.), *Mass communication research and theory* (pp. 91–110). Boston: Allyn & Bacon.

McLuhan, M. (1964). Understanding media: The extensions of man. Excerpt republished in J. Hanson & D. Maxcy (1999), *Sources: Notable selections in mass media* (2nd ed.) (pp. 117–123). Guilford, CT: Dushkin/McGraw-Hill.

McQuail, D. (2005). *McQuail's mass communication theory* (5th ed.). London: Sage Publications Ltd.

Melody, W., & Mansell, R. (1983, Summer). The debate over critical versus administrative research: Circularity or challenge. *Journal of Communication 33*(3), 103–116.

Mosco, V. (1983, Summer). Critical research and the role of labor. *Journal of Communication 33*(3), 237–248.

Rosengren, K. (1983, Summer). Communication research: One paradigm or four? *Journal of Communication 33*(3), 185–207.

Schiller, H. (1983, Summer). Critical research in the information age. *Journal of Communication 33*(3), 249–257.

Severin, W. J., & Tankard, J. W. Jr. (2001). *Communication theories: Origins, methods, and uses in the mass media* (5th ed.). New York: Addison Wesley Longman.

Slack, J., & Allor, M. (1983, Summer). The political and epistemological constituents of critical communication research. *Journal of Communication 33*(3), 208–218.

Smythe, D., & Van Dinh, T. (1983, Summer). On critical and administrative research: A new critical analysis. *Journal of Communication 33*(3), 117–127.

Sparks, G. (2002). *Media effects research: A basic overview*. Belmont, CA: Wadsworth.

UNIT THREE

Bridge to the Real World

Media Law

THIS CHAPTER WILL:

- Describe key terms and principles of the legal system, and principles of the First Amendment.
- Discuss specific areas of media law that practitioners must be familiar with, including:
  - Libel
  - Privacy
  - Copyright
  - Commercial speech
  - Broadcast regulation.

An important aspect of the U.S. political system is that, as second President John Adams said, it is "a government of laws, not of men" (Bartlett, 1980, p. 381). This means that no individual—king, queen, dictator, or president—can be solely responsible for operation of the government and exercise of its power. Rather, a standardized set of rules is used to define, and frequently limit, the scope of government authority. These rules are called laws.

A dictionary definition of the word "law" might read something similar to "a rule of conduct established and enforced by some authority." In the U.S. system of representative democracy, that authority comes from those who are affected by the law: the citizens. In other words, the lawmakers—elected and appointed legislators, judges, and executive officials—should answer to the citizens as they operate a system of creating, interpreting, enforcing, and periodically changing the law.

The legal system reaches into most aspects of modern life. Criminal laws seek to establish a baseline of civilized behavior in society, with prohibitions on killing or injuring other people, and on stealing or damaging their property. When individuals have a dispute, one or both parties may file a lawsuit to settle the matter. Even everyday tasks of life come into contact with the law; the simple act of driving to work or school is governed by traffic laws, for instance. Businesses in particular face many legal limits on their operations. Some of these are general and applied to all types of companies (wage-and-hour laws, tax laws) and some are more specific (such as health codes for restaurants or safety-equipment requirements for construction work).

Media organizations also face specific legal principles centered on their function of disseminating information for public mass consumption. These rules apply largely to organizations whose primary focus is communication—newspapers, television stations, or advertising agencies, for example. But it is worth noting that any business or institution that conducts public relations activities as well could face media law issues related to that PR work.

The Legal System

Both in the specifics of media law and in a more general sense, the U.S. legal system is a complicated one. Understanding some of the key terms and fundamental aspects of the system are a necessary starting point.

Levels and Types of Courts

Our nation has a dual court system, with different sets of courts operated by states and by the federal government. State courts handle more cases, and more high-profile cases. An important murder trial, for instance, would be a state-court trial in most cases because the definition of what constitutes murder, which types of punishments someone convicted of the crime could face, and so on are defined by state governments.

Both the federal and state systems have three levels of courts:

- Trial courts (also known as courts of origination)
- Appeals courts
- Second level appeals court (usually the so-called highest court)

The appeals courts review the decisions of trial courts and may reverse them if some error is found in how the law was applied. But having a second level of appeal—that third layer of the system—means that a party that loses an appeal has another opportunity to make the case. In the federal system, the levels are District Courts (origination), Circuit Courts of Appeals (with each circuit overseeing a number of district courts), and the U.S. Supreme Court, the highest court in the United States. State systems vary, especially in what the courts at each level are called. In New York state, for instance, "Supreme Court" is the lowest level of courts, not the highest.

Appeals take place within either a state or federal system and generally do not cross out of that system, with one exception. This is when the U.S. Supreme Court is called upon to review a decision of a state court, which is how some of the most famous cases in the history of constitutional law developed, such as

Gideon v. Wainwright (right to counsel), *Roe v. Wade* (right to an abortion), and *Times v. Sullivan* (constitutional defense for libel). The Supreme Court, however, will not review a case from a state court unless the justices can determine that the case has something called a "federal question," or something that the Constitution says is a matter for the federal government to decide on.

Civil versus Criminal Law

When most people think of law, criminal law is the area that generally comes to mind first. This area consists of the arrest, adjudication, and possible punishment of people who violate laws that prohibit certain types of behavior called crimes. Crimes can range from such minor and common offenses as traffic tickets, to more serious issues such as theft, up to very serious violations such as assaults, robberies, and murders.

Criminal Law. Criminal law refers to a society's definition of activities, called crimes, that are prohibited in the interest of keeping society safe and orderly. These behaviors are outlawed because they injure other people personally (e.g., assault, rape, murder), violate their property rights (e.g., vandalism, burglary, or larceny), or endanger public safety in general (e.g., violating traffic laws, inciting a riot). Crimes are defined by statute at the state and federal level, but most criminal behavior is covered by state law and is adjudicated by state courts.

Because even crimes against individuals are a threat to public order, the government becomes involved as a party to the incident when someone is accused of criminal behavior. Criminal cases are framed as "The people v. the defendant," with the government literally taking a side to help protect the public welfare. The reason the government becomes involved is because only the government has the legitimate power to take away liberty and even life (through capital punishment). Only by application of this unique power through criminal law can a person be sent to prison, or, in the ultimate penalty, be executed. Because of this power, criminal law has many procedural safeguards to help prevent people from being unfairly accused or punished. These protections include treating defendants as innocent until proven guilty, requiring guilt to be proved "beyond a reasonable doubt," giving the accused party the right to a jury trial, and other rules that help people defend themselves.

Civil Law. The other major category of law is civil law, when the government is not involved directly as a party. In civil law, the power of the government is exercised through the courts to mediate disputes between individuals. This actually is the area where most legal activity takes place because it involves a vast number of routine matters such as divorces, personal-injury lawsuits, and contract and property disputes. Civil law also is the arena for most communications law, including issues of libel, privacy, and intellectual property enforcement or infringement.

Civil actions typically seek one of two remedies. In other words, the party that initiates the action wants the court to force the other party to do one of two things:

■ Pay money to compensate for some sort of injury or harm. A good example of this is money demanded in a personal-injury lawsuit.

■ Compel some sort of action or behavior, or force an action to stop. For example, in a divorce, which is a civil action, the parties use the court to specify certain actions regarding child custody (how the parents should act with regard to where the children live, visitation rights, etc.). In a copyright-infringement case, a party found guilty of violating a copyright most likely would be ordered to stop doing whatever is causing the infringement, as well as being directed to pay a fine and/or monetary award to the copyright owner.

Most media law tends to be civil in nature, such as an individual suing a newspaper or broadcast organization for a libel infraction or breach of privacy. Media law actions can involve government, but an important thing to note is that even this usually proceeds as a civil action rather than a criminal prosecution.

In such a case, a government organization such as the Federal Communications Commission, the U.S. Justice Department, or even a judge or other key individual from the government might be a party to a civil suit. For example, with First Amendment issues (such as imposing or removing a prior restraint on publication), the government enters into the action not as a criminal prosecutor but usually as the respondent in a civil action brought by a media organization as the plaintiff to stop the alleged First Amendment violation. When the American Civil Liberties Union wanted the Child Online Protection Act thrown out on First Amendment grounds, for example, U.S. Attorney General Janet Reno was named as the defendant and the case became known as *ACLU v. Reno*.

One situation in which criminal law may enter a media-governmental dispute, however, is when a reporter or media organization refuses to honor a court order and thus may be found in contempt of court, which is a crime. This has happened, for example, when reporters refused to testify in a case even though a judge had ordered them to do so. Judith Miller, a reporter for the *New York Times*, spent 85 days in jail for contempt of court in 2005 for refusing to disclose her sources in the Valerie Plame CIA leak case.

First Amendment

The First Amendment consists of only 45 words, but it is the well from which much of the law that affects media organizations flows. The text of the amendment is:

"Congress shall make no law respecting an establishment of religion or prohibiting the free exercise thereof; or abridging the freedom of speech or of the press; or the right of the people peaceably to assemble, and to petition the government for redress of grievance."

Understanding the First Amendment is crucial for media practitioners because it underpins so much in media law. For example, the famous libel case of *Times v. Sullivan* (covered later in this chapter) essentially said that false statements were inevitable and in some cases should not be punished because free and open discussion on the conduct of public officials is protected by the First Amendment.

The principle of expressing opinions about the government is the main rationale behind the First Amendment. As this country's founders believed, for a democracy to function correctly, people must be able to talk freely and frankly about issues of public concern and share that information. In other words, not only the popular ideas or those that are favored by those who control the government can be openly discussed or debated, but all ideas deserve to be discussed and debated in a public forum. This was a very radical view for the late eighteenth century, the period of history when the U.S. Constitution was written. At the time, most governments around the world were still monarchies over which the rulers had absolute power—including the power to prevent people from criticizing them.

The First Amendment in its literal form applies only to Congress ("Congress shall make no law . . .") but later was extended to states under the Fourteenth Amendment, which truly made the U.S. Constitution the law of the land. The Fourteenth Amendment was passed in the post-Civil War Reconstruction era to ensure that states could not take away the rights of newly freed slaves. But once it was a part of the Constitution, it was used in a variety of contexts to extend protection of that document by permitting state laws to be overruled when they violated the U.S. Constitution. In one famous media-related example of this, a state law allowing censorship of newspaper publication was found to be an unconstitutional violation of the First Amendment (*Near v. Minnesota*).

First Amendment Limits

While the First Amendment sounds absolute in its wording (the word "no" in the phrase "Congress shall make *no* law" is unequivocal), in practice it does not provide for unlimited freedom of expression. In fact, it can be seen as offering different tiers or layers of protection to different types of expression.

The first of these layers covers political and social expression, which are granted the strongest measure of protection—almost absolute protection, in fact. The next level is commercial and indecent expression, which are defined as protected speech but can be restricted to a greater degree by the government than political or social expression. The third level is unprotected speech, which applies to such practices as obscenity, false advertising, and threatening speech.

Often, a First Amendment controversy arises because people disagree about just which of these levels applies to a particular act of expression. Photographer Robert Mapplethorpe once put together an exhibit that showed erotic photos of homosexual activity and what one news article described as "children in questionable poses" (Associated Press, 2000). This raised the question of whether the display of the work of an artist deserved complete First Amendment protection as in the first of these three layers. Or was it indecent expression, meaning that a government body could put limits on it such as prohibiting it from being exhibited where anyone younger than 18 could view it? Or was it actual obscenity, and therefore subject to being banned or shut down by the local authorities because it falls in the category of unprotected speech? A Hamilton County (Ohio) grand jury indicted a Cincinnati museum and its director on obscenity charges over just such an exhibit in 1990, but a jury acquitted them of the charges (Associated Press, 2000).

Examining the characteristics that make a particular form of expression into unprotected speech is helpful in defining the boundary between protected and unprotected speech. For instance, threatening speech is based on the concept that some statements are not really an expression of ideas so much as a threat or personal attack, what are known as "fighting words," and they therefore do not deserve to be "protected" as a form of speech. The interest of society in maintaining peace and keeping people from threatening each other is balanced against the individual right of free expression—and in this case, public peace wins out.

But determining whether an expression deserves to be put in the category of fighting words relies on what is called a strict scrutiny test. For a statement to be classified this way (and thus be considered unprotected speech), the statement must be especially violent and obnoxious and must be directed at specific individuals. So there is a distinction between what is called "hate speech" and "fighting words." In general, the ideas expressed at a white supremacist rally against black people or Jews would be protected speech, even though it is hateful and vile, unless the comments were directed at violence against particular individuals, in which case it might cross the line to become fighting words. Similarly, distinctions between indecency, pornography, and obscenity help to define the line because indecent and pornographic expressions are protected speech but obscenity is not.

Restrictions of Expression

Government controls over freedom of expression proceed in three primary ways: neutral regulation; punishment after the fact for something that has been published; and prior restraint, or censorship.

Neutral Regulation and Time/Place Restrictions.   One way expression can be restricted without facing First Amendment issues is when regulations are neutral with regard to content. For example, the operation of media organizations can be regulated through procedures such as local building codes, state wage and hour laws, and federal Occupational Safety and Health Administration guidelines about working conditions without concern for infringing on their freedom of the press. While having a city government shut down a newspaper and take over its building could be seen as a serious First Amendment violation, theoretically that could happen to a newspaper operating in a condemned building. If the government could show its actions met the criteria for what it does with condemned buildings and that it would have regulated any other business in the same way, the action cannot be opposed on free-speech grounds. And, of course, the newspaper could just move to a building that met the proper codes and continue publishing. This is the concept of neutral regulation.

From the same principle, people generally have the right to stand in a public place, such as a street corner, to express their views. But should they have the right to step into traffic and make it stop so that people would have to listen to them? Would it be abridging their free-speech rights to prohibit them from doing that? Or take the example of a noise ordinance. Should someone have the right to crank up his home theater system and blast his favorite politician's speech on C-SPAN as loud as he can make it at 3 a.m. when his neighbors are sleeping? Would a city regulation that prohibited this practice by forbidding loud stereos from playing in the middle of the night violate his free-speech rights? These restrictions—called time, place, and manner regulations—do not control the content of the expression, just the circumstances under which it can reasonably be expressed. Such restrictions can be enforced without violation of First Amendment rights.

One form of time-and-place restriction that has received attention in recent years is expression in the workplace. Do companies have the right to punish employees who criticize or embarrass the company in public, such as on a Web log, or should the employees' statements be considered protected speech? In 2004, a Delta Air Lines flight attendant was fired after posting pictures on the Internet of herself in her flight uniform, taken onboard a Delta plane, which the company said were inappropriate. (She was fully clothed in all of them, but they included ones with her skirt hiked up very high and another with her blouse partially unbuttoned.) In general, courts have sided with companies because the restrictions are not being made by the government, which is what the First Amendment is designed to prevent.

Prior Restraint/Subsequent Sanction. But although content-neutral regulation and time-place-manner-of-expression limits are generally not controversial, prior restraint and subsequent sanction are another matter entirely. Prior restraint is when the government censors or prevents publication of an idea while subsequent sanction occurs when the person or organization that makes the expression is punished after it happens.

The concept of freedom of expression and the ideas behind the First Amendment really grew out of resistance to prior restraint. The idea of censorship developed in the Middle Ages, around the time that secular governments developed apart from ecclesiastical (church-run) governments. Churches have strict controls on expressions of ideas that run counter to their major belief system, and those who express views opposite of that dogma are called heretics. So, government censorship of political thought was just the secular version of churches banning heresy. When the Constitution's framers developed the First Amendment's wording, they clearly had prohibiting prior restraint in mind with the wording: "Congress shall make no law abridging freedom. . . . "

But courts have ruled that post-publication punishments, however, also can be seen as abridgement of free speech through what is known as a "chilling effect." If a particular type of expression is punished, then other people will avoid expressing themselves in the same way because they fear facing the some sanction.

Prior restraint by government order is seen as the most serious threat to freedom of expression (Blasi, 1981, as quoted in Helle, 2006) because:

■ Time and delay are on the side of the government. If something is held out of the public sphere while its fate is being debated, the censorship is already happening while the deliberation takes place. There is no incentive on the part of the censoring authority to resolve the situation because while it is unresolved they are achieving what they have set out to do—that is, prevent publication.

■ It is accomplished too easily. It is difficult and messy to punish after the fact, but making a prior restraint only takes one statement.

■ It is biased in favor of restricting ideas. A censor's job is to keep information away from the public, not find reasons to let it out.

Prior restraints are presumed to violate the First Amendment (and therefore are unconstitutional) unless the government meets a heavy burden to prove otherwise, which is called First Amendment due process. Rather than the individual having to prove that speech should be protected, the government must show that it is unprotected by presenting evidence that:

■ Allowing the expression to go forward would create a danger that is serious and imminent, a term that means the danger is both immediate and inevitable.
■ Stopping the speech will end the dangerous situation.
■ Restraining the speech is the only way to avoid the danger, and no alternatives exist.
■ The terms of prior restraint for a particular situation are neither so vague nor so overly broad that they could be used to limit speech in other circumstances.

The most commonly known example of this is the language used by Justice Oliver Wendell Holmes, who said that free speech does not allow someone to shout "fire!" in a crowded theater.

Libel

Libel is a published, false statement that harms a person's reputation. A libel claim is a civil action of one person against another, or frequently against the corporate "person" of a media organization that the plaintiff claims has committed the libel. The elements of libel—six things the plaintiff must prove—are:

■ **Publication**: The libelous statement must be distributed in some way, which does not necessarily mean mass media dissemination. Of course, in the context of discussing *media* law, the major concern is a libelous statement published in mass media venues such as newspapers and magazines, television broadcasts, and on

Internet sites. But in a technical sense, memos, photocopied letters, notices on a bulletin board, group e-mails, or story drafts circulated to colleagues at a newspaper or magazine could constitute "publication." Anyone involved with communication of any kind should be careful about what they say on paper or in electronic form that could be damaging to other individuals.

■ **Identification**: Libel is usually limited to an individual party, and the plaintiff must show that the publication identified him and that the statement applied to him. Identification does not have to be by name, however; it can be by circumstantial facts. A college newspaper that published a libelous statement about the campus "dean of students" or "director of student life," without naming the person, could still be guilty of libeling them, because there is usually only one person with such a job or title on a campus. So he or she would be identified by the title even if the name never appeared.

■ **Defamation**: This is defined as an assertion of fact that exposes someone to hatred, ridicule, or contempt (classical definition), or harms a person's reputation by things such as: lowering the subject in the esteem of others, causing them to be shunned, or injuring them in their business or career.

■ **Injury**: The plaintiff must demonstrate some loss of money, reputation, or standing in the community, or evidence of mental anguish and suffering.

■ **Falseness**: This is part of the definition of libel—true statements cannot be considered libelous—but demonstrating falseness also is part of the proof. The plaintiff must show just how the statement was a false one.

■ **Fault**: Libel is a tort, or claim of injury, and such claims can be made only on the basis of some mistake or error on the part of whomever caused the injury. So the libel plaintiff must show that whoever published the libelous statement did something wrong or made some kind of mistake that led to the libel. Fault standards differ for private versus public figures, which is covered at greater length in the discussion of the constitutional defense. But fault generally is defined as negligent behavior with the two most common standards being (a) failure to do what an average, prudent person would have done in the situation to ascertain the truth or investigate the facts behind the defamatory statement; or (b) failure to do what a prudent *professional* in the field would have done.

It is up to a judge or jury at the libel trial to determine whether the person (such as a newspaper reporter) acted prudently. Among the things that go into this consideration are whether the person who was defamed was contacted for a comment, whether the information was verified based on the best sources available, and whether the reporter tried to verify any contradictions between sources that could have helped to get to the truth of the matter. Usually, following generally accepted principles of news reporting to verify information is the best way to guard against a libel plaintiff's claim of negligence.

Constitutional Defense

The law of libel began at the state level, with different states stipulating different defenses against libel. There was no federal law of libel until the Supreme Court decided the case of *New York Times v. Sullivan* in 1964. In this case, the court established a limited constitutional defense from libel charges.

The background of the case was that L. B. Sullivan, a police commissioner in Montgomery, Alabama, sued newspapers including the *New York Times* because of an advertisement taken out by a civil rights advocacy group that had false statements about the treatment of black citizens by police officials during civil rights protests of the era. The ad, which was published in 1960, did have some incorrect facts. For example, the ad said students were arrested for singing at the capitol building in Montgomery, but they actually were arrested at a lunch-counter sit-in. And the ad got the song wrong; in the incident at the capitol they sang the "Star Spangled Banner," not "America" ("My Country 'tis of Thee"). Police units were there but did not "ring" the campus as the ad said.

Understanding this case requires some understanding of the historical time and place in which it originated. It came from the deep South in the early 1960s, as the civil rights movement was growing and spreading, which white government officials in the South did not like. The protests also were drawing media coverage, which white government officials in the South also did not like. A libel tort (lawsuit) was a way to strike back at some of the people and institutions that were causing the government officials all this bad press.

So the tort was filed under Alabama state law, and Sullivan and other police officials who were suing won at the trial level. The newspapers appealed and the verdict was upheld in all the Alabama courts. But when it was appealed to the U.S. Supreme Court, the state court's verdict awarding damages to the police officials for the false statements was overturned.

In ruling that the advertisement was not libelous, the Supreme Court specified two groups of people—public officials and private individuals. Public officials, because of their greater ability to access forums in which they may dispute potentially libelous utterances, were required to show a fault standard of *actual malice* on the part of the defendant, which was in this case the *New York Times*. Actual malice is defined as either:

- Knowing the statement is false when it is published; or
- Not caring whether or not it is true or false and publishing it anyway, which the court called "reckless disregard for the truth." Usually, this means a lack of even trying to verify the information.

What the court did by defining this term "actual malice" was create a new, harder-to-meet fault standard that replaced ordinary negligence. Because it is a more difficult fault standard to meet, it became harder for public officials to win libel cases. It applied only to public officials; the ordinary negligence standard still applied to private individuals. The court's rationale for creating two fault standards for two categories of libel plaintiffs was that one important function of the media in a democracy was to provide a check on the conduct of public officials. So, actual malice is called a "constitutional" defense because it is based in the First Amendment's protection of the ability to express ideas about the government.

According to Justice William Brennan, who wrote the court opinion in *Times v. Sullivan*, fear of libel could lead to timid coverage of public officials and their misconduct; what was at issue was "commitment to the principle that debate on public issues should be uninhibited, robust and wide open, and that it may well include . . . attacks on government and public officials" (Youm, 2006, p. 96). In other words, constitutional protections of free speech could be undermined too easily by actions of state courts in making libel awards. The media must be allowed to make innocent errors in order to avoid a chilling effect of self-censorship that would deprive the public of information that can lead to truth about government. Establishing the standard of actual malice for public officials therefore reduced the pressure on the media and made aggressive reporting on government conduct easier to perform.

Over time, other cases have helped to refine who has to meet the tougher "actual malice" standard. One of the most important decisions came only three years after the original decision. In *Associated Press v. Walker* and *Curtis Publishing Company v. Butts*, the Supreme Court decided two cases together and created the public figure doctrine. In both cases, the libel plaintiffs were not government officials but were still well-known individuals. While protection of political speech is the First Amendment's most important aspect, it does not protect *only* political speech, but other expressions as well. So the court said that First Amendment protection should extend to errors made in reporting on prominent individuals even if they were outside the political arena, and because of their fame the actual malice standard should still apply.

In its current formulation for libel purposes, a public official is defined as more than just a public employee. It is someone who has substantial responsibility over the conduct of government affairs and occupies a position that invites public scrutiny, such as elected officials and high-level government bureaucrats. But these are relative terms; "substantial responsibility" and "high level" seems to imply presidents and members of Congressional representatives, but local town officials would qualify as public officials in coverage by a local newspaper or radio station.

"Public figure" is a harder definition to make, but it has come to be thought of as people who voluntarily expose themselves to the public spotlight by putting themselves in a prominent place. As such, it applies to many celebrities and also people who voluntarily involve themselves in controversial issues. (See Figure 9.1 to trace the expansion and contraction of the categories of plaintiffs to whom the actual malice standard should be applied.)

Other Defenses against Libel Suits

Aside from the important constitutional defense, libel law includes other defenses known as common law defenses. They include:

- **Consent**: If a person knows a libelous statement is going to be published and gives his assent, he cannot sue for libel later.

FIGURE 9.1   History of the Constitutional Defense for Libel

Several Supreme Court decisions have both expanded and contracted the number of libel plaintiffs to whom the constitutional defense for libel and actual malice standard would apply:

- 1964: Actual malice standard created with definition that it applies to public officials (*Times v. Sullivan*)
- 1967: Actual malice standard extended to public figures as well as public officials (*Associated Press v. Walker, Curtis Publishing v. Butts*)
- 1971: Actual malice extended to all libel suits in which the defamatory communication relates to matters of public concern (*Rosenbloom v. Metromedia*)
- 1974: Actual malice standard contracted somewhat as the court pulls back from standard in Rosenbloom and further clarifies public figure category (*Gertz v. Welch*).
- 1976: Actual malice standard contracted further in *Time v. Firestone*. The court ruled that a woman who was a public figure in one aspect of her life—a socialite who was well known in her community—nevertheless did not have to meet actual malice standard for a libel suit over a story that was not related to her public life (about her divorce). For coverage of that topic, the court ruled, she should be treated as a private figure.

- **Truth**: Most state laws provide that truth is a complete defense in libel cases. True statements are not actionable, even if they damage someone's reputation. The issue, though, becomes whether truth or falsity can be proved in court. In general, plaintiffs must prove the falsity and defendants do not have to prove truth. But libel lawyers generally advise defendants that it is helpful if they *can* prove the truth of any facts in a controversial statement that might be made the subject of a libel case.

- **Qualified privilege**: News media cannot be sued for libel if they publish statements that—taken at face value—seem defamatory so long as the statements come from official proceedings (such as those of a legislature or court) and meet certain requirements. The three requirements such reported statements must meet to earn what is called a qualified privilege against being libelous are:

  - Information must be obtained from a record or proceeding recognized by the state as official. Good examples are trials and other open court proceedings, court documents that are open to the public (such as motions and briefs), and official records or minutes of legislative and executive proceedings.
  - The media report must be fair and accurate. Reporters should be careful that information is not taken out of context.
  - The source of the statement must be clearly noted in the media report.

It is important to note that qualified privilege must be based on neutral reporting of what happened at the official proceeding. If there are factual errors, insertion of opinions, or unnecessary additions of irrelevant facts, the qualified privilege can be destroyed. Perhaps the most common example in which qualified privilege is used comes in court reporting, when witnesses frequently make highly defamatory comments about the conduct of those on trial; qualified privilege allows the testimony to be reported as it occurs without fear of a libel case.

■ **Fair comment**: In general, there is no such thing as a false opinion. Opinions cannot be proved true or false, so claiming that an opinion statement is libelous is impossible because a plaintiff cannot satisfy one part of the claim: the need to prove falsity. But the key to fair comment is that the statement must be understood as an opinion, and should relate to a person's performance of duties, not to their character or reputation. Similarly, someone cannot hold an opinion about whether or not something is a fact. A commentator, for instance, could not write "It is my belief that the mayor has embezzled money from the sewer fund." Either the mayor is an embezzler or he is not; that fact cannot be changed by anyone's opinion. And if he is not, such a statement would be a false, defamatory statement (and therefore a libel) even though it involves a public official and even though it is preceded by the words "my belief."

Privacy

The history of privacy as a legal right can be traced to Louis Brandeis, who became a famous Supreme Court justice in the early 1900s. But in the1890s, before he was a member of the Supreme Court, he and a colleague wrote an essay that helped to define the legal status of privacy. This came about because there is no "right to privacy" in the Constitution the way other rights are enumerated in the Bill of Rights. But starting with Brandeis and extending through other legal opinions, including ones issued by the U.S. Supreme Court, the idea has evolved that several elements of the Bill of Rights including the Third Amendment (which says the Army may not take over people's houses against their will to quarter troops), the Fourth Amendment (protection against unreasonable search), and the Fifth Amendment (protection against self-incrimination) in effect add up to a constitutional principle that people are entitled to privacy.

Four "Common Torts" of Privacy Infractions

Privacy becomes an interesting issue in media law through balancing the individual right of privacy with public rights, such as the right to know, the right to be informed, and freedom of the press. The media have a substantial First Amendment right to disclose facts about people. But using the right of privacy, courts have ruled individuals are entitled to a certain level of control regarding disclosure of information about themselves. The major boundaries between what is fair game for publication and what falls in the private realm are expressed through four torts that help to specify what it takes for an individual to pursue a privacy claim.

Public Disclosure of Embarrassing Private Facts.   For individuals to successfully claim that disclosure of certain facts was an unwarranted invasion of privacy, they must be able to demonstrate several characteristics about those facts. Under this tort the facts must be proved to be:

■ **Sufficiently intimate**: Personal details that a person does not ordinarily reveal such as personal medical history, financial history, or details of relationships with family members.

■ **Sufficiently private**: The facts are closely known to only a few people and were never voluntarily revealed in a public domain. Things that happen in public or are part of the public record generally lose the aura of privacy. Also, once a person voluntarily discloses information and it is published in one place, it is considered in the public domain and cannot be taken back or made the subject of a privacy claim in a future situation.

■ **Highly offensive**: To the point of being humiliating, not just mildly embarrassing, if the private information becomes known.

■ **Not a matter of public concern** (sometimes called the *newsworthiness* defense): The question becomes, what makes something a public concern? People who voluntarily put themselves in the public light, for example, celebrities, give up some of their right to privacy because their actions become by definition a "matter of public concern." Many highly newsworthy events are by definition a matter of public concern, so people caught up in a police activity (such as a hostage situation) or a disaster that generates extensive news coverage who have facts about themselves revealed in the media as a result, will have a more difficult time claiming that their privacy has been invaded.

An example could be some of the less-than-flattering coverage of Hurricane Katrina disaster victims being rescued in a state of half dress or in their underwear. Generally, such an image on television or in the newspaper would seem to meet the standards of private, intimate, and humiliating. But because the image depicts the person's involvement in a newsworthy event, it might not be sufficient grounds for winning a privacy claim.

Intrusion.   Application of this tort generally concerns *how* the information was gathered, rather than *what* was gathered or reported; the accepted standard is that if the information was gathered in ways that a reasonable person would consider offensive, it constitutes an intrusive practice. The three most common types of intrusion are:

■ **Trespass**: Going onto private property without the owner's consent.

■ **Misrepresentation**: To the point of offensive deception: Undercover reporting is not necessarily an invasion of privacy as long as the disguise is not used as way to trespass or to engage in an activity that would not otherwise be allowed, such as someone who was not qualified to be a nurse dressing up as a nurse to do undercover reporting in a hospital.

■ **Surveillance** by extraordinary means: Laws vary by state, but as a general rule reporters can legally observe (and report on), photograph, or record anything from a public area, such as a sidewalk. They cannot, however, use technology to improve upon what an unaided person would be able to see or hear from that public place, such as using powerful telephoto lenses to spy on and photograph people in secluded places on their private property.

Misappropriation of Name or Image. Misappropriation is the unauthorized use of a person's name, photograph, likeness, voice, or endorsement to promote the sale of a commercial product or service. Misappropriation is most common and most likely to occur in advertising. To avoid problems, those involved in advertising creative work should routinely have subjects sign a model release form written in simple, straightforward language when using their name or likeness in a commercial ad. Regardless of whether or not a release form has been signed, however, courts have generally allowed the media to reuse editorial photos or clips in its own self-promotion provided there is no suggestion that the person actually endorsed the publication. Further, there are special dispensations when the appropriation occurs in the context of satire or comedy.

False Light. This privacy violation is defined as depicting someone in an inaccurate way. It often applies to misuse of photos, such as a photo showing people sitting in a bar that accompanies a story about alcohol abuse. Such a photo could imply that everyone in the photo is an alcohol abuser, and anyone who was identifiable might then claim they were portrayed in a false light. Out-of-context quotes can lead to false-light situations as well. One of the authors once had a student in a journalism class who did a class assignment feature story on the problems of plagiarism and cheating in light of reports about how the Internet and other technology helps students to cheat. In one place in the story, she quoted a student on the topic and the context of the quote almost made it seem like he was admitting to being a cheater. He was not really admitting that, and a careful reading of the quote showed that. But the placement of the quote near other information about cheating practices could have left the reader with a false impression about the quoted student—it could have placed him in a false light.

In general, the elements of false light are:

- The portrayal must be "highly offensive to a reasonable person;" and
- The person making the portrayal had knowledge of how it would misrepresent the person or acted in reckless disregard about it.

This makes false light and libel somewhat similar. The distinction between false light and libel is that in false-light claims, one need not prove injury or damage to reputation, but only prove that the statement was highly offensive. Courts in some states have refused to recognize false-light claims because of their similarity to libel.

Copyright

Protection of property rights is a key aspect of the law. For example, criminal statutes prohibiting burglary (illegal entry of a building) and larceny (theft of money, goods, or services) protect the right of owners to keep and control their property. Many actions that involve torts and contracts also are disputes over money or other valuable property. In all of these cases, however, the property is physical, or at least tangible (such as a certain amount of money). But not all property fits this description, and so a body of laws exists to protect the rights of people who have created what is called intellectual property, or products of the mind.

Intellectual Property's Unique Nature

Intellectual property is treated differently under the law because of a fundamental difference in its character from physical property, a characteristic known as rivalrous versus nonrivalrous use. Physical property is subject to rivalrous use, which means it cannot be used by multiple people for equal benefits. If one person eats a sandwich, no one else can eat the same sandwich. If the owner of a car lends it to a friend, the owner is deprived of its use while the friend has it. But if one person reads a good book then loans it to a friend, both can get the same enjoyment from it. A third, fourth, and fifth person could get the same benefit, even if they cannot enjoy it simultaneously.

Or consider the situation when four friends decide to share a pizza and a movie. A typical pizza shared four ways will provide everyone with an adequate share; likewise, when all four watch the movie together one person's "consumption" of it does not affect the other three. All can enjoy it equally. But suppose the group grew to 20 people, or 200. Would one pizza adequately feed that many people? Certainly not. But can 20 people watch the same showing of a movie without any one person's use of it affecting the others? Yes, they can. Could 200 people watch it? If the seating and projection system were adequate, the answer again is "yes."

Clearly, sandwiches, pizzas, and cars are subject to rivalrous use; all potential users are rivals for the benefit and as the pool of users grows, some people get shut out of those benefits. But movies and other intellectual property do not face the same rivalries because benefits come from *use* of the good rather than *possession* of it. This forces the law to treat intellectual property differently. Theft statutes and contract enforcement address physical property with rules about possession and consumption. But with intellectual property, the focus is on its use.

Principles of Copyright

Three main categories of intellectual property protection, dealing with three different things, are:

- Patents, which protect devices and inventions
- Trademarks, which protect identifying devices used in business (e.g., a company name or logo)
- Copyright, which protects literary and artistic works.

With regard to the media, the most important of these is copyright because it specifically protects the work of people who publish literary and artistic works such as books, magazines, newspapers, musical recordings, movies, and television shows. One side of this is that anyone in a communication business has to be careful about how they use material produced by other people, lest they infringe upon someone else's copyright. But copyright law also is interesting and important to media practitioners because it is what allows the media to exist as a business. Its protections are what make it possible for creative works to be sold profitably because it grants those who create a literary or artistic composition exclusive control over their work.

In order to provide an incentive for producing "works of the mind," such as inventions and literary compositions, the authors of the U.S. Constitution included language protecting intellectual property. Article 1, Section 8 of the Constitution gives Congress the power to give people who have created something the right to use it exclusively as a means of promoting "science and the useful arts." But "nonrivalrous use" presents two sides to this right. The protection is designed to provide an economic incentive for people to invent devices and processes, and to produce literary and artistic works. Intellectual property rights mean the inventor (who holds a patent) or author (with a copyright) has protection against somebody with a bigger factory or faster printing press getting their hands on the creation and using it to make money, denying creators the fruits of their labor.

But at the same time, particularly when it comes to literary works, there is a social benefit from having information passed from person to person. If authors had 100 percent control over their work, they could control to whom it should be circulated, which is not what the framers of the Constitution had in mind when they wrote the First Amendment. So, copyright has both exclusive uses for its holders as well as limitations that are designed to help ideas reach the public domain.

Copyright can be applied to creative works of original authorship fixed in any tangible medium of expression. Things that are not "fixed" cannot be copyrighted. But the key word in the definition is *original*. An expression does not have to be terribly creative—there is no test for artistic merit—as long as the expression is original. It also does not have to be novel. Something could be conceptually very similar to a work that someone else has done, but still can be original enough and creative enough to be copyrighted. For example, this is surely not the only chapter in a communications book that addresses media law, but the fact that other authors have included similar chapters in their books does not prevent the current authors from including it here, nor does it prevent the publisher from copyrighting this presentation of the material.

Some things cannot be copyrighted, notably facts and ideas. To extend the example above, Chapter 5 reports on certain historical facts about the development of communication research, including the names of important contributors to the field and dates of their works. These basic facts cannot be copyrighted and in fact they have appeared in many books about communication theory and research. But a particular arrangement of facts can be copyrighted because the way they are selected and presented create original authorship, so the same sets of facts have been used in any number of works that each were copyrighted by their authors or publishers (including this one). Previous authors of other texts about communication history could not say the authors of this book infringed upon their work by simply using the same facts, or just by having the idea of writing a history chapter even though it has been done before. This reflects another central aspect of the field, which is that ideas cannot be copyrighted either.

Exclusive Uses.   Copyright is enforced by giving the owner five exclusive rights to the work:

- **Reproduction**: The right to copy, duplicate, transcribe, or imitate the work in fixed form.
- **Modification** (also known as derivative works): The right to modify the work to create a new work, such as a second edition of a book.
- **Distribution**: The right to distribute copies of the work to the public by sale, rental, lease, lending, or even giving it away.
- **Public performance**: The right to recite, play, dance, act, or show the work at a public place or to transmit it to the public. This applies more to artistic and literary expressions such as paintings, photos, and musical performances than to written work.
- **Public display**: The right to show a copy of the work directly or by means of a film, slide, or television image at a public place or to transmit it to the public.

Limitations.   But in the interest of balancing public and private benefits, these "exclusive" rights are balanced off or limited because of the concept of free flow of information in a society. These limits are:

- **First sale**: People who buy a book, CD, or other tangible piece of intellectual property can do what they want with it. Owners can lend, sell, or give these items to other people; libraries can lend them out. The idea is that the holder of the copyright would benefit economically from that first sale but after that the ideas could circulate freely.

- **Time limits**: Having exclusive-use rights expire after a period of time is another way to "balance" the idea that the copyright-holder should benefit from the creation of the intellectual property while still promoting the circulation of ideas throughout a society. This provision of copyright law says works enter what is called the *public domain* and become free for use by anyone after a set amount of time. Originally, that time was set at 28 years. Later changes in the law expanded that time frame, most recently in 1998 when it was expanded to the life of the author plus 70 years for some works, to a straight 95 years for others.

■ **Fair use**: Allowing others to use part of a creative work for other purposes, such as criticism, commentary, news reporting, teaching, scholarship, or research, is another device for promoting wider circulation of ideas. Fair use is how a news reporter can excerpt a book in a book review and how television news can show part of a concert or sporting event whose broadcast is copyrighted by whatever organization has paid the musical group, team, or the league for the exclusive rights to show the event. It is how college professors can show their students television interviews and movies in their classes, and how textbook authors can quote excerpts from other scholars.

Whether something has been "fairly used" depends on a balance among four factors stipulated in the copyright act. Copyright law does not define "fair use"; it only says that fair use depends upon some combination of these four factors:

■ **Purpose and character of use**: Use of an excerpt for educational purposes is different from republishing a portion of a work for commercial gain. This guideline addresses the issue of whether re-use of the work serves the purpose of the public interest and promotion of the marketplace of ideas as the constitution and copyright law intend.

■ **Nature of copyrighted work**: Some types of work would suffer more damage to their value by a copyright infringement than others, For example, copying parts of a workbook designed to be "consumable" would be considered more harmful than copying some types of materials, such as a few pages from a textbook, because unlike a used but clean textbook, a used workbook has no resale value. By providing photocopies of the exercises in the book, the value of the books produced by the publisher is completely undermined.

■ **Amount and substantiality of portion used**: The concept of fair use is predicated on using a small part of a work, not the entire piece.

■ **Effect on market value of copyrighted work**: Copying text from an out-of-print book presumably is less harmful to the author and publisher than copying an in-print book because original copyright holders have decided not to sell it any longer. The same idea would apply to photocopying a clipping from a week-old newspaper; newspapers do not republish articles, so a week-old article has no market value to be affected. However, a newspaper story could not be reproduced verbatim in a book such as this without permission from the copyright holder.

Commercial Speech

Recall that in the earlier discussion of the First Amendment, three levels or tiers of expression were discussed, the middle of which was indecent and commercial speech. The point made in that discussion was that this tier is protected speech, but nevertheless one that faces more restrictions than some other types of expression.

Exploring ideas about commercial speech starts with an interesting legal proposition: a corporation is, under the law, treated in the same manner as an individual person would be. "Incorporation" is essentially the act of creating an entity that can act under the law in the same manner as an individual can with many of the same rights and responsibilities as individuals. The corporation has the right to enter into contracts—with individual people and other corporations. It has the right to own property. It can sue, and be sued. Thus, many of the rights attributed to people also are attached to corporations.

But does the corporate "person" have First Amendment rights? The idea that it might, and legal decisions addressing the issue, are a fairly recent development, dating to the mid-1970s. Maybe not surprisingly, the concept of applying First Amendment principles to commercial speech came not from pitches for cars or cat food but out of advertising with a public-affairs aspect to it. *Times v. Sullivan* is remembered for the landmark libel doctrine that came out of it, but a footnote to the case is that it was probably the first time the importance of freedom of expression was attached in some way to an advertisement.

One of the landmark cases in developing commercial speech doctrine was *Bigelow v. Virginia* (1975). The background of the case is that the state of Virginia tried to ban ads for an abortion service in New York state. At that time, abortion was legal in New York but had not yet been legalized in Virginia. Bigelow established the "principle that commercial advertising enjoys a degree of First Amendment protection" (Gower, 2006, p.152). An interesting aspect of this case is that even though it was a commercial ad, trying to get people to come and use a paid service in New York state, it still had public-issue overtones to it because the ad was about abortion and the case came about only one year after the Supreme Court decision on *Roe v. Wade*.

The next year, another Virginia case, *Virginia Board of Pharmacy v. Virginia Citizens Consumer Council*, came before the Supreme Court concerning ads that contained prices of prescriptions at a time when advertising such prices was banned under state law. This is generally considered to be the first time the Court addressed something that was purely commercial speech—that is, in an ad without political overtones—in a First Amendment context. In this case the court said regulating the ability of pharmacists to advertise their prices violated the pharmacists' First Amendment rights because that was information that deserved to be part of public discourse, part of the "marketplace of ideas." One line of reasoning the court used was that the decisions people make about how and where to spend their money affect the operation of the economy and economic policy, which are as important to the functioning of society as purely political discourse.

But the Virginia Pharmacy opinion said explicitly that government still was free to restrict advertising speech to do things such as prohibiting false and misleading ads, or to prohibit advertising of products and services that are illegal. The principle is that regulation is legitimate when it serves a "substantial government interest," although that wording was not used until a later decision.

Prohibiting false and misleading advertising qualifies as one of those "substantial interests" for society, but is also a good example of how commercial speech can be regulated more tightly than other types of expression. It would be impossible to picture the Supreme Court ruling that it is legitimate for states or the federal government to outlaw false newspaper stories, or to put limits on stories that did not serve a "substantial interest" of the government or society. In fact, *Times v. Sullivan* said exactly the opposite; it said libel—by definition a false statement—must be tolerated in some circumstances involving statements about activities of public officials. But such limits on truth and falseness are allowed in commercial speech; the Federal Trade Commission and Federal Communications Commission both have a deep body of regulations about truth in advertising.

Another key case involving these limits to regulation was the *Central Hudson Gas and Electric Corp. v. the New York State Public Service Commission* (1980). In this one, the PSC, which regulates public utilities such as gas and electric providers, tried to tell Hudson Gas it could not run ads encouraging people to use more electricity during the energy crisis of the 1970s. The corporation claimed it had a First Amendment right to advertise and promote the use of its product. The Supreme Court ruled that the PSC regulation indeed was overly restrictive but at the same time the court did not completely bar such limits on advertising and commercial speech. Instead, it set up a four-part test for use in future rulings over whether a restriction was a legitimate one or went too far. The test was:

1. Is the ad accurate, and does it promote a legal product/service? If the ad is either (a) false/misleading or (b) promotes illegal activity, it is does not fall in the protected speech category and could therefore be restricted or censored.
2. Is there a substantial government interest at stake in the information that would be regulated? Does it deal with important issues? If the issues are not substantial, the government has no business regulating them.
3. Does the regulation directly advance the government interest?
4. Is the regulation narrow enough only to address the direct government interest involved? A regulation that was too broad would fail the test and be deemed illegitimate by the court.

The main authority enforcing limits on what is allowable in advertising is the Federal Trade Commission, whose main concern is untruthful and deceptive advertising. For advertising to be considered deceptive it does not have to make blatantly false statements; a false reference or implication is enough. Such deception can relate both to information that is included and things that are omitted. Failure to include important qualifiers about claims that are made, such as not identifying possible problems or risks, can be seen as a deception. This is why so many ads have disclaimers, such as statements in toy commercials that say "all items sold separately," warnings that the driving stunts seen in car commercials are done by "professional drivers on a closed course," and disclosure of side effects in pharmaceutical ads. To omit the important information that a drug had side effects could be seen as a deceptive practice.

The FTC oversees an extensive body of administrative law and enforcement measures that define misleading or false advertising, summarized in a four-point test of its own that addresses whether an ad is deceptive or false:

■ The ad contains either a representation or an omission that is likely to mislead consumers.

■ The misleading detail is likely to affect the consumer's decision.

■ It must be likely to mislead a reasonable consumer. The audience is taken into account in determining "reasonable," so different standards apply, for example, to children's advertising.

FIGURE 9.2   False Advertising Claims

Matters that the Federal Trade Commission has pursued as allegations of false or deceptive advertising have included:

■ A national restaurant company in 2007 settled FTC charges that it had engaged in deceptive practices in advertising and selling its gift cards. According to the FTC, it failed to give purchasers adequate notice that if the cards were not used within a certain amount of time, their value would be reduced. The restaurant chain agreed to restore the value to cards purchased between 2004 and 2006 that had the limits on them.

■ A magazine-subscription telemarketing firm was cited by the FTC in 2007 on grounds that it had called consumers and told them they were eligible to receive "valuable coupons" for groceries and other items, when in fact the telemarketers were signing up consumers to purchase unwanted magazine subscriptions.

■ Two companies that marketed oral sprays that were supposed to help users lose weight, reverse the aging process, and prevent or treat diseases by containing or causing the body to produce human growth hormone also faced action by the FTC. The companies reached settlements with the regulators in 2007 that involved one company paying $172,500.

■ An exercise-equipment manufacturer alleged to have falsely claimed that use of the equipment would cause users to trim inches of fat from their bodies without reducing calories. In 2003, the company was accused of further falsely stating that these claims were based on a clinical study proving that product worked.

■ A computer manufacturer's claims of a "money back guarantee" with a "full refund" and free "on-site service" to consumers upon request, when such was not the case, according to the federal regulators. The company paid a $290,000 fine in 1998.

Source: Federal Trade Commission Office of Public Affairs news releases, available at: www.ftc.gov/opa.

- The representation or omission must be likely to cause harm—to consumers' health, safety, or to their finances. In other words, it must be a claim that would cause them to spend money on something they probably would not have bought if they had not seen or heard the false claim.

Broadcast Regulation

The basic rationale behind broadcast regulation is physical or technological, based on the limits of the broadcast spectrum or airwave frequencies. The government has decided, and the courts have supported the idea, that spectrum management justifies government licensing of broadcasters and that in return for being able to use a piece of the broadcast spectrum, broadcasters can be required to serve the public interest.

However, this also leads to a situation in which broadcasters can face government regulations of content that would violate the First Amendment if they were applied to print media. For example, consider the sanctions for broadcasting "indecent" material. *Playboy* and many other magazines show full and partial nudity in their pages, with no threat or fear of government regulation. Yet when singer Janet Jackson's breast was shown for only a couple of seconds during the televised halftime show of a Super Bowl game, it led to a fine of several hundred thousand dollars against the broadcaster, CBS, and its parent corporation (which was Viacom at the time). Similar fines have been made against Howard Stern and other radio personalities for use of language on the air that can commonly be found in print.

Note that none of this material is considered obscenity, which would be unprotected speech. It all falls in that second-tier category of indecency, which is still protected speech. But broadcast regulations, administered and enforced by the FCC, can prohibit the exact same words or images that could be never be banned from a book or magazine except in violation of the First Amendment. The primary reason behind this is that broadcasters are seen as using a public resource—the airwaves—which gives the government a legitimate interest in protecting the public interest.

History of Broadcast Regulation

The initial regulatory authority for broadcasting came not out of mass broadcasting, such as today's network television, but what is called point-to-point broadcasting, specifically ship-to-shore communications. In the early years of radio, there were no standards, and it was common for interference and static to be created if several people in a given area were trying to communicate on the same frequency. So the government's first legal authority to regulate wireless broadcasting was by allocating different parts of the electromagnetic spectrum for different uses to prevent this interference, and then setting up a system of licensing use of different parts of the spectrum. The Radio Act of 1927 set up the Federal

Radio Commission. In 1934 a new piece of legislation replaced that agency with the Federal Communications Commission (FCC). This is an agency that practices administrative law, with a variety of powers that cross the whole body of judicial, legislative, and executive authority. In other words, it can:

- Make regulations that broadcasters have to obey, the same as if they were statutes passed by a legislature.
- Hold hearings that are judicial procedures, very much like trials, the way the judicial branch of government does.
- Enforce regulations, such as imposing indecency fines, and make decisions, such as issuing broadcast licenses, as the executive branch is empowered to do.

Granting and denying licenses are the most significant powers that the FCC has. But it also has other powers—regulations that it can make broadcasters obey and policies that broadcasters must follow—that provide some of the most interesting areas of media regulation and policy. Although most of these rules and policies come under the guise of regulation of broadcast technology, over time they have taken on some First Amendment implications. The result is unequal and in some ways inferior treatment of broadcasters' First Amendment rights in comparison with newspapers and other print media. Two interesting cases from the early days of broadcast regulation highlight this.

In *Near v. Minnesota* (1931), an early case about prior restraint in print media, the state passed a law to prohibit a newspaper's publication of malicious personal attacks on public officials. However, the Supreme Court ruled that publication could not be stopped without causing an unconstitutional prior restraint. But in *Trinity Methodist Church v. FCC* only a year later, the FCC denied renewal of a radio station license owned by a church because of broadcast attacks on public officials—and the Supreme Court upheld the decision. In these two cases, the kind of things said in the attacks was very similar but the court came to completely opposite conclusions about whether regulation was permissible just because one was print and the other was broadcast.

The first case in which the Supreme Court in a very direct way dealt with the issue of whether broadcast regulation was constitutional was not until 1969. In this case, a radio station owned by the Red Lion Broadcasting Co. challenged an FCC regulation requiring it to give reply time for a personal attack on an individual. The company claimed that forcing the station to carry such a reply infringed on its First Amendment rights. However, the court ruled that the FCC policy did not violate the broadcaster's First Amendment rights and was consistent with 1934 Communications Act's provisions about broadcasting being in the public interest. The reasoning was that those who have broadcast licenses do not automatically get a broader First Amendment right than those who do not have them; the real First Amendment protections belong to the public and its right to have access to information. So, according to the court it was not unconstitutional to require licensees to share the frequency with others who have different views; the fact that the broadcast spectrum is limited makes it acceptable for the government to adopt regulations consistent with the First Amendment's underlying goal of keeping the public informed.

An important case on the indecency issue was *Pacifica Foundation v. FCC* (1978). A New York City radio station broadcast comedian George Carlin's routine about the "seven words you can't say on television" during the afternoon. At a subsequent hearing, the FCC did not impose any sanctions on Pacifica but did threaten to impose them if the radio station ever engaged in "indecent" programming in the future. The radio station appealed that finding from the FCC into the courts, but ultimately the Supreme Court upheld the FCC decision based on the agency's authority to regulate licensees in the public interest. The "pervasive nature" of broadcasting and the "public interest" in protecting children from exposure to the kind of programming in the Seven Words routine made the threat allowable even though it is by definition at least a chilling effect if not a form of prior restraint. The principles established by Pacifica were still in force 25 years later when the FCC issued its fines over the language of Howard Stern and the behavior of Janet Jackson during the 2004 Super Bowl halftime show.

Summary

The law was one of the first areas of human activity to emerge as a profession—an endeavor based on specialized knowledge of those who practice it. The U.S. legal system is a complicated one, and it seems to get more complicated with the passing of time. Through the First Amendment language regarding "freedom of the press," the media are the one business or social institution that are specifically addressed by the U.S. Constitution, and special aspects of media law affect anyone who plans a career as a media practitioner.

Does that mean it is necessary to be a legal scholar just to be a newspaper reporter, broadcast journalist, advertising writer, or public relations practitioner? No, but it does mean that individuals in those and other areas of media practice need a basic understanding of the laws that affect them. These vary by area. Broadcasting and print journalists face the most concern with libel, for instance, although advertising and public relations professionals should note that libel cases do happen in their area of practice as well. (The most famous and important libel case in history, *Times v. Sullivan*, came from an advertisement.) The purpose of this chapter has been to provide a basic overview and awareness of the various areas from a practitioner's point of view.

QUESTIONS FOR DISCUSSION/ APPLICATION EXERCISES

1. Look at the list of First Amendment cases under consideration by the Supreme Court at the Freedom Forum's First Amendment Center (www.firstamendmentcenter.org). Pick one that interests you, write a short synopsis of the facts of the case, and pretend you are a member of

the Supreme Court who will decide the case. How would you rule, and what interpretation of the First Amendment would you use to make that ruling?

2. Author Charles Mann has written (in an *Atlantic Monthly* article in 1998) that "Copyright is the regulatory authority for the marketplace of ideas" and law professor Eben Moglen (interviewed in "Tollbooths on the Digital Highway" in 2003) refers to the "copyright bargain" to describe the idea that copyright allows producers of intellectual property to benefit from their ideas, but within limits so that society has access to all of the ideas that are produced. But digital technology is changing both sides of the equation by allowing faster, more efficient copying of copyrighted materials, yet also creating conditions for producers to control their distribution in ways not previously possible (tunes that play only on an iPod, for example). Overall, which do you think constitutes technology's greater threat: copying tools that undermine the ability of authors to control their work, or the digital controls that Mann describes as "lock[ing] up the raw materials, of culture"? For more background on this issue, you may want to look at the resources listed below. Mann's article can be accessed through databases such as Lexis/Nexis, while Moglen's comments about copyright can be found in the transcript of a show available on the PBS Web site:

- Mann, Charles C. (1998). "Who will own your next good idea?" *Atlantic Monthly* 282:3 (September 1998), 57–75.
- "Tollbooths on the Digital Highway." (2003). This report from the PBS newsmagazine *NOW* can be found online at: http://www.pbs.org/now/transcript/transcript_copyright.html.

REFERENCES

Associated Press (2000, April 8). Mapplethorpe controversy reverberates in Cincinnati 10 years later. Retrieved May 29, 2007, from: http://www.freedomforum.org/templates/document.asp?documentID=12172.

Bartlett, J. (1980). *Familiar quotations* (15th ed.) (p. 381). Boston: Little, Brown and Co.

Gower, K. K. (2006). Regulating advertising. In W. W. Hopkins (Ed.), *Communication and the law 2006 edition* (pp. 151–162). Northport, AL: Vision Press.

Helle, S. (2006). Prior restraint. In W. W. Hopkins (Ed.), *Communication and the law 2006 edition* (pp. 53–70). Northport, AL: Vision Press.

Mann, Charles C. (1998, September). Who will own your next good idea? *Atlantic Monthly* 282(3), 57–75.

Tollbooths on the Digital Highway. (2003, January). *NOW, with Bill Moyers*. Public Broadcasting System. Transcript available at: http://www.pbs.org/now/transcript/transcript_copyright.html.

Youm, K. H. (2006). Defamation. In W. W. Hopkins (Ed.), *Communication and the law 2006 edition* (pp. 87–116). Northport, AL: Vision Press.

10 Media Ethics

"Whenever the term media ethics is introduced into polite conversation, someone is bound to ridicule the reference as an oxymoron."

Day, 2003, ix

THIS CHAPTER WILL:

- Describe the relationship between law and ethics, and why mass media students need to be aware of ethical behavior in the field.
- Present some ethical models for analyzing real-life cases.
- Provide an overview of the ethical guidelines offered by professional media associations.

When the topic of ethics in the mass media is raised, people inevitably think of Jayson Blair of the *New York Times* or Jack Kelley at *USA Today*, both of whom resigned in disgrace from premiere jobs in the field because they fabricated information in their news stories. Blair and Kelley became symbols of everything that the public thinks is wrong with the media today, and these high-profile cases undoubtedly helped to fuel some of the public's mistrust of journalists. Indeed, a 2004 Gallup poll found that only 21 percent of Americans believe that journalists have high ethical standards; tying them with politicians and ranking them lower than auto mechanics (Maier, 2004).

Looking at cases such as Blair and Kelley, however, is not very helpful for students who are studying journalism ethics. What these journalists did was so far wrong that these cases are not useful ones in determining which behavior standards are acceptable and where the line between acceptable behavior and unacceptable behavior lies. It is never acceptable to fabricate information or characters to write a story or make breaking news, so even the most cursory look at the Kelley or Blair cases leads to obvious conclusions.

Ethics becomes an especially important issue in the workplace, however, in those gray areas where the journalist, the advertiser, or the public relations professional can see both sides of an issue, and where they have to choose one course of action over another. This is when the study of ethics and ethical decision making comes into play, not in the black and white, but in the gray.

In point of fact, newly graduated media practitioners often are protected from making such ethical judgment calls by the nature of the work environment and the tendency to work as part of a team. And much of ethical behavior in the workplace revolves around the simple concepts of honesty and truthfulness. Most of the time, it really is black and white: it is wrong to lie; it is right to tell the truth. But learning about ethics means getting some experience evaluating those shades of gray and figuring out the location of the line that should not be crossed.

Mass communication educators are clearly concerned about ethics. Between 1983 and 1993, the number of media ethics courses in mass communication increased by 86 percent (Lambeth, 2006, p. 3). The field's accrediting body recommends as one of its professional values and competencies that students "demonstrate an understanding of professional ethical principles and work ethically in pursuit of truth, accuracy, fairness and diversity" (ACEJMC, 2003). The discipline has its own ethics journal, *The Journal of Mass Media Ethics*, which began publication in 1985. And Rosenberry and Vicker (2006) found that more than 57 percent of capstone courses in mass media programs include some instruction on ethics. Clearly the profession is concerned about its credibility and each of the media professions has its own ethical guidelines.

While one chapter will not completely prepare a student to face the ethical challenges of her profession, this overview will provide the prospective media professional with the tools to help examine difficult work situations and determine the most ethical course of action.

What Are Ethics?

Larry Leslie defines ethics as moral principles for living and decision making (2004, p. 6). The word *ethics* comes from the Greek word *ethos*, denoting image or credibility. In the rhetorical tradition of Aristotle, the image or credibility of a speaker would determine the likelihood that he could persuade his audience. Even in the modern-day classroom, students of persuasion learn that a speaker's ethos is an important factor in imparting a message. The ethos generally consists of an individual's knowledge, trustworthiness, and charisma. Thus, a speaker with high ethos would have a good command of the subject matter (knowledge), would be telling accurate and truthful information (trustworthiness), and would be able to deliver that information in an articulate and dynamic way (charisma).

While ethics are important for all professionals, and while most professions (e.g., accounting, law, medicine, etc.) have their own codes of ethics, it is easy to see why ethics is a crucial issue for mass media professionals. Their job is, in essence, crafting and delivering messages, whether that message is written or spoken, in a newspaper, over the airwaves, in person, or via the Internet. Without credibility, their ability to deliver that message effectively is greatly diminished. Media practitioners have a special responsibility to be sure their messages are based on knowledgeable facts, are accurate, and are delivered in a well-crafted and articulate manner.

Media Ethics and Media Law

Johan Retief notes that it is important to distinguish between media ethics and media law because they are not the same thing. Just because something is legal does not make it ethical, and an illegal action is not always unethical (Retief, 2002, p. 25). He integrates some of Louis Alvin Day's writings to examine the relationship between ethics and laws with the following considerations (pp. 25–26):

1. All laws should be morally just.
2. If a law is unjust, a case can be made for acts of civil disobedience. For example, journalists generally try to avoid using deceptive or undercover reporting techniques, but the BBC has traveled to Zimbabwe undercover to record human rights abuses because journalists have been banned from that country.
3. All citizens, including journalists, have a moral responsibility to obey the law.
4. Ethical questions cannot be resolved merely by looking at the legal issues. For example, even if it is legally permissible to publish the name of a rape victim, is it ethical to do so?
5. A just law may be violated only in emergency situations or when a higher moral obligation is involved.
6. Violations of the law involve prescribed penalties; ethical violations do not (although journalists, politicians, and business executives have lost their positions and been blacklisted from their professions because of ethical violations).
7. Media freedom places a greater responsibility on media practitioners to consider the ethical implications of their behavior.

With regard to the final point, Englehardt and Barney argue that professional communicators have a critical role in preserving a democratic society and must accept responsibility for their professional actions. They assert that:

> . . . The argument for communicators maintaining moral autonomy is made compelling by the rights granted to them in the First Amendment. However, when some communication professionals unthinkingly follow conventions, rules, or orders, they actually give up their First Amendment freedoms. In order for the First Amendment to be a valid protection of free speech, its defenders must themselves accept responsibility for the effects of their actions, rather than shift responsibility to others (2002, p. 5).

Ethical Models

While ethical guidelines are helpful, Englehardt and Barney argue for a thoughtful consideration of professional situations that challenge ethical principles. One way to systematically examine these dilemmas is through the use of ethical models. Remember that models are like theories in that they are representations that attempt to explain a particular phenomenon. Applying a model to an ethical dilemma can help the media practitioner better understand the situation and choose the appropriate course of action. The next section will consider three models that can serve as frameworks for ethical decision making.

The SAD Formula: A Model of Moral Reasoning

Louis Alvin Day has developed a model that he maintains works well for the "moral-reasoning neophyte," a label that generally fits the recently graduated media practitioner. Based on the work of Ralph Potter (who is discussed later in this chapter), Day's model includes three sequential categories of consideration: the situation definition, the analysis of the situation, and the decision, or ethical judgment (Day, 2003, p. 64). The components of the model—situation, analysis, decision—provide the acronym that gives the model the label "SAD." (See Figure 10.1.) In detail, these stages are:

- **Situation Definition**: In this step, the media practitioner should identify the facts of the situation and the conflicting values and principles that make the situation an ethical dilemma (Day, 2003, p. 65). Some of these may be obvious, but some may require additional investigation, discussion, or thought to reveal. The three separate components that should emerge during this step are: description of facts, identification of principles and values, and a statement of the ethical issue or question (2003, p. 67).
- **Analysis of the Situation**: Day maintains that the most important step in this model is to examine the situation and evaluate ethical alternatives (p. 65). Within this step, he recommends considering four actions:

  1. Thoroughly discuss the relative weight given to each of the conflicting values and principles.
  2. Examine factors external to the case that might influence the direction of moral judgment.
  3. Examine various groups and individuals who are likely to be affected by the ethical judgment.
  4. Apply ethical theories or principles (p. 66).

- **Decision**: In the final step, the decision is made and must be defended (p. 66).

A good example of an ethical dilemma that new journalists sometimes face early in their career is accepting gifts. Print and broadcast organizations generally discourage journalists from accepting gifts from sources or advertisers, although

FIGURE 10.1 SAD Model

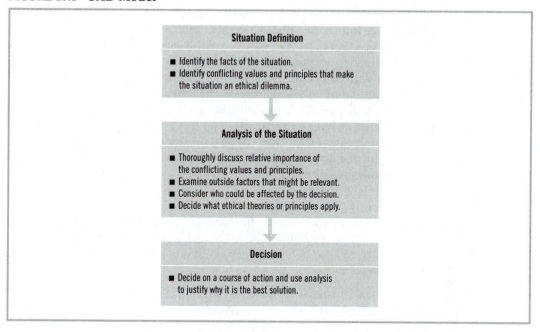

Situation Definition

- Identify the facts of the situation.
- Identify conflicting values and principles that make the situation an ethical dilemma.

Analysis of the Situation

- Thoroughly discuss relative importance of the conflicting values and principles.
- Examine outside factors that might be relevant.
- Consider who could be affected by the decision.
- Decide what ethical theories or principles apply.

Decision

- Decide on a course of action and use analysis to justify why it is the best solution.

some have established limits—for example, reporters might accept a coffee mug or a modest lunch, but not a golf outing or box seats at the Super Bowl. But a newly graduated graphic designer reports that the area of gifts is grayer in her department, the specialty publications division of a large newspaper company that creates "vendor publications" for paying clients. When the client dictates which photos, content, advertising, and so on should be used, do the same rules apply as for journalists in the newsroom upstairs who are supposed to work at arms-length distance from their sources? Using the SAD model, the young journalist might go through the following steps to apply reason to the situation:

1. Definition of the situation: The situation is that a vendor/client wants to meet at the local country club to discuss the publication and buy a nice dinner for the designer in the process. The value is that a journalist should remain objective and not accept any sort of gift that would prejudice her toward this client. However, it is already clear that the designer is not an unbiased entity working on this publication. The work she is doing may be journalistic in form, but it is more like advertising or public relations in function. The question is whether going out to an expensive dinner with the client would be ethical.

2. Analysis of the situation: This analysis would include a consideration of whether the relationship with the client is more important than the need to stay objective as a journalist. Other external factors might include a very specific company policy and what others in her department have done in

the past. A further consideration might be whether the designer is likely to be working with the client's competitors in the future on a different publication. Other journalists, photographers, and designers in the office may be influenced or affected by the behavior of this one designer, and other clients might be affected by the knowledge that this one client was allowed to curry favor with one of the designers who works on other accounts.

3. Decision: The young designer reports that this was a topic of considerable debate in her department. Most of the workers concluded that it was not worth the risk to accept gifts of any type from clients or vendors to ensure that no impropriety took place. (In fact, during a heat wave, one photographer even turned down the offer of an ice cream sundae from a client when they were out on a photo shoot.)

Another young journalist reported that, while the newsroom at his paper never accepts gifts of any kind, after September 11, 2001, they were allowed to keep some of the food baskets because the reporters were working so many hours. Retief might call this an emergency situation or an instance when a higher moral principle was involved.

Larry Leslie's Decision-Making Model

Larry Leslie's decision-making model is actually a lot like the classic decision-making processes that groups go through in dealing with a task (define the problem, list the solutions, choose the best solution, implement the solution, and so forth). Leslie maintains that postmodern thought (which is defined in Chapter 8) needs to be rejected in the case of ethics. Postmodernism has moved away from the rules and the structures that reason produces, and yet Leslie says that reason—meaning carefully structured consideration—needs to be employed for successfully dealing with an ethical dilemma (Leslie, 2004, p. 21). Thus, the decision-making model (shown in Figure 10.2) requires that the media practitioner carefully and logically consider each of the steps and alternatives in order to come to an ethical solution to a dilemma.

First, however, it must be determined that one is indeed dealing with an ethical issue. Issues of concern may not be ethical at all, or may not be primarily ethical in nature. Other types of issues may include legal problems (is this an issue of criminal or media law?), social problems (are these problems that affect groups or relationships in society at large or within an organization?), policy problems (are these problems of corporate or government regulations?), and economic problems (are these problems of finances?). For example, a media relations professional whose client is embroiled in a financial scandal may be faced with legal and economic issues, as well as ethical ones. Those components must be considered and evaluated before moving on to ethical concerns. Leslie stresses that it is important to ascertain first whether the problem or issue is indeed an ethical one and to proceed through the prescribed decision-making steps only if it is one (Leslie, 2004, pp. 22–26). The steps he recommends are:

FIGURE 10.2 Larry Leslie's Decision-Making Model

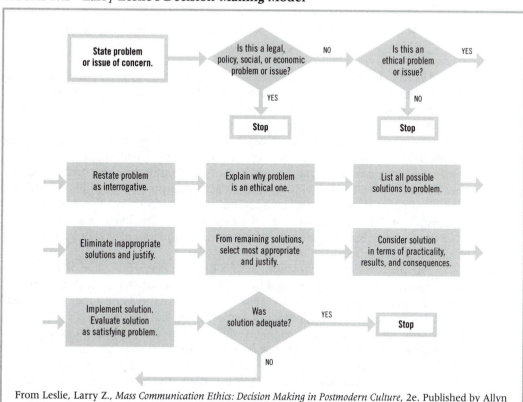

From Leslie, Larry Z., *Mass Communication Ethics: Decision Making in Postmodern Culture*, 2e. Published by Allyn and Bacon, Boson, MA. Copyright © 2004 Pearson Education. Reprinted by permission of the publisher.

1. Restate the issue as a question. This will enable the practitioner to focus on the problem and provide an answer that will lead to a satisfactory solution.

2. Explain *why* it is an ethical problem. For example, "This problem deals with issues of behavior that are right and wrong, or positive and negative," and so forth. If it is not possible to explain the ethical ramifications, then that is a clue that it might not *be* an ethical problem and some other solution may be needed.

3. List all possible solutions to the problem. It is important to generate as many solutions as possible, even those that seem obvious or extreme, using a technique similar to brainstorming. The solution will be somewhere on that list.

4. Examine the list of solutions, eliminate inappropriate solutions, and justify the choices. Justification means being able to explain why the potential solutions that remain were kept and explain why the others were not.

5. Examine the remaining solutions, select the most appropriate solution, and justify this choice.

6. Consider this solution in terms of practicality, results, and consequences (i.e., can it work, what will happen, what will be the long-term effects of this solution?).

7. Implement the solution. After it has been implemented and given a chance to work, evaluate to see if the solution solved the problem.

8. Was the solution adequate? If the problem was not solved, go back through the steps to work further on the problem (Leslie, 2004, pp. 27–31).

Leslie's model points out that making ethical decisions can be complicated. Sometimes there is only one solution to an ethical problem, an absolute ethical principle. Others are flexible or variable, and only a thorough evaluation of the issue will reveal the most ethical decision (2004, p. 30).

The decision-making model can be used effectively in the example of the public relations practitioner engaged in crisis communication. A client who is embroiled in a scandal of any type presents a dilemma for the media relations professional, whose job it is to keep the client and the organization viewed in a positive light. Consider a university's communications office. What are some of the issues that must be dealt with when students are involved in a scandal, such as, for example, the allegations of rape against members of the Duke University lacrosse team in the spring of 2006?

The university public relations staff is hired to keep the image of the university a positive one in the press and to the various publics, which include students, parents, alumni, donors, and the general public. At the same time, the PR staff must acknowledge wrong-doing and demonstrate that perpetrators of any criminal actions will be held accountable to the law and the university's standards for student conduct. Further, any factors that helped to foster the incident must be dealt with, such as the culture of entitlement that seemed to be part of the team. Because the incident involving the Duke players involved criminal charges, this was a legal issue as well as an ethical one. Additionally, universities have legal and policy restrictions with regard to the disclosure of information about students, all of which need to be figured into the equation of how to respond to this incident. Public relations guidelines, such as those offered by the Public Relations Society of America, also help to provide a framework for the media relations department to address this issue.

In the Duke incident, the university provided an entire Web site with information and extensive media coverage at http://www.dukenews.duke.edu/mmedia/ features/lacrosse_incident/. The following year the Duke lacrosse players were exonerated and the charges dropped, while the district attorney who prosecuted the case was sanctioned and disbarred for a rush to judgment. However, because of the way the PR team handled the crisis, this case will undoubtedly serve as an example of open and full disclosure in crisis communications and media relations for future PR students.

The Potter Box

Several media scholars (including Louis Alvin Day, described earlier in this chapter) have built models of ethical decision making based on the work of Ralph Potter. As a doctoral student in theology at Harvard University, Potter began outlining his ideas in his dissertation, and then refined and expanded them over several decades (Backus & Ferraris, 2004, p. 223). The Potter Box (shown in Figure 10.3) is divided into four equal quadrants, with each quadrant containing one of the components for moral reasoning. The four components are:

1. Situation definition (establishing the facts of the case).
2. Values (establishing values, both moral and non-moral).
3. Principles (identifying competing principles).
4. Loyalties (determining stakeholders) (Land, 2006, p. 31).

While the Potter Box is one of the most widely used and applied ethical models across disciplines, it has been applied to the mass media to analyze ethical issues in print and broadcasting news coverage (see, for example, Williams, 1997, and Park & Park, 2000). Backus and Ferraris note that one of the best attempts to clearly define each step came from Guth and Marsh, who applied the Potter Box to public relations. The steps are operationalized as follows:

1. Define the situation as objectively as possible, with detailed information related to the ethical dilemma.
2. State and compare the merits of the different values, notions of what is right and what is wrong, different beliefs, and questions of facts versus values.
3. State a principle for each value, for a broader idea of justice.
4. Consider other ethical principles.
5. Decide to whom you are being loyal.
6. Examine whether there are others to whom you should feel loyal. Does this suggest another principle to consider? Are there some to whom you feel no loyalty?
7. Select a course of action that embraces the most compelling principles and loyalties. Does this seem like the best course of action? If so, implement it.
8. Evaluate the impact of the decision (Backus & Ferraris, 2004, pp. 226–227).

FIGURE 10.3   Potter Box

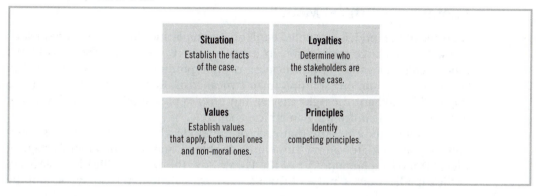

Media scholar Mitchell Land has adapted the Potter box into a "Point of Decision Pyramid," which he feels moves the components of the box more systematically toward making a decision (Land, 2006). The bottom of the pyramid is the philosophic base upon which moral reasoning is always built. The next three panels that sit upon the philosophic base are facts, principles/values, and stakeholders/loyalties. Land explains how to approach this part of the pyramid:

> First, list the case facts that give rise to the ethical dilemma as "bullet points," cutting through the details to expose the essential facts of the moral crisis. The second panel should list principles that emerge from an elaboration of the facts and consideration of stakeholders. The third panel considers stakeholders, who should be prioritized in terms of competing rights, claims, and loyalties. This system allows the media practitioner to move between the panels in considering the point of decision, which is at the top of the pyramid (Land, 2006, pp. 31–35).

One of the significant features of the Potter Box and the Land Pyramid is the consideration of the stakeholders in an ethical issue. Stakeholder analysis is an important component of many ethical models because it asks questions such as:

- Who is involved in this issue?
- Who has the most to gain?
- Who has the most to lose?
- Who is the media practitioner most responsible to?

For example, an advertising professional has a duty to represent his client, the person or company that is paying him to craft a message on their behalf. The media professionals must consider the client as the most important stakeholder in the analysis of an ethical issue. However, if the client is asking the practitioner to misrepresent a product or to use unethical tactics, the advertising practitioner must consider the other stakeholders in the situation: the audience, the competitors, and even himself, because his own reputation is on the line. It is a combination of these factors that determine the decision the professional must make.

Summary of Ethical Models

All three of the models presented earlier have similarities in terms of certain variables. They all urge progression in a systematic way through the steps in the model; consider values and principles as underpinnings; and stress the need to consider more than one solution to an ethical crisis. Remember, a model is not a theory that explains the right answer, but it is a representation that helps to sort out issues when confronting an ethical challenge.

It is important to note that each of the models has a stage that talks about applying appropriate values. These include steps 1 and 4 of the analysis stage of the SAD model, component 2 of the Potter Box, the two "justification" stages of Leslie's model, steps 3 and 4 of Guth and Marsh's eight-step framework, and the middle panel of the second layer of the Land pyramid. Advice provided to media practitioners by their professional associations is a valuable source of the values and principles that can be applied in the decision models for each appropriate area.

Professional Codes of Ethics

This section looks at the main concentrations within the mass media disciplines and provides the guidelines for ethical behavior as stipulated by their professional organizations. This is not an inclusive list, but a representative sample, because some concentrations have more than one professional association. It is interesting to note that some of the associations go into more detail than others—for example, the Public Relations Society of America even includes an ethics pledge that members are encouraged to sign. However, there are common threads of ethical behavior related to honesty, independence, and concern for stakeholders that run through all the professions.

The Poynter Institute: A School for Journalists

The Poynter Institute calls itself "a school for journalists, future journalists, and teachers of journalists" in St. Petersburg, Florida. While its focus is almost exclusively on print and broadcast journalists, it is recognized as the leading repository of commentary and education on ethical issues in the profession. Its guiding principles and 10 questions to ask for making decisions (listed in Figure 10.4) are included here as helpful tools to media practitioners for any field.

> *Guiding Principles for Journalists*
> - **Seek Truth and Report It as Fully as Possible**
>   - Inform yourself continuously so you in turn can inform, engage, and educate the public in a clear and compelling way on significant issues.
>   - Be honest, fair, and courageous in gathering, reporting, and interpreting accurate information.
>   - Give voice to the voiceless.
>   - Hold the powerful accountable.
> - **Act Independently**
>   - Guard vigorously the essential stewardship role a free press plays in an open society.
>   - Seek out and disseminate competing perspectives without being unduly influenced by those who would use their power or position counter to the public interest.
>   - Remain free of associations and activities that may compromise your integrity or damage your credibility.
>   - Recognize that good ethical decisions require individual responsibility enriched by collaborative efforts.

FIGURE 10.4   10 Questions for Good Ethical Decision Making

1. What do I know? What do I need to know?
2. What is my journalistic purpose?
3. What are my ethical concerns?
4. What organizational policies and professional guidelines should I consider?
5. How can I include other people, with different perspectives and diverse ideas, in the decision-making process?
6. Who are the stakeholders? Who are those affected by my decision? What are their motivations? Which are legitimate?
7. What if the roles were reversed? How would I feel if I were in the shoes of one of the stakeholders?
8. What are the possible consequences of my actions? Short term? Long term?
9. What are my alternatives to maximize my truth-telling responsibility and minimize harm?
10. Can I clearly and fully justify my thinking and my decision? To my colleagues? To the stakeholders? To the public?

Source: Posted by Bob Steele on February 29, 2000, at http://www.poynter.org/column.asp?id=36&aid=4346.

- **Minimize Harm**
  - Be compassionate for those affected by your actions.
  - Treat sources, subjects, and colleagues as human beings deserving of respect, not merely as means to your journalistic ends.
  - Recognize that gathering and reporting information may cause harm or discomfort, but balance those negatives by choosing alternatives that maximize your goal of truth-telling.

The Poynter code closely resembles one used by the Society of Professional Journalists, which can be read in full at: http://www.spj.org/ethicscode.asp.

The American Society of Newspaper Editors (ASNE)

According to its Web site, http://www.asne.org, "the American Society of Newspaper Editors is a membership organization for daily newspaper editors, people who serve the editorial needs of daily newspapers and certain distinguished individuals who have worked on behalf of editors through the years." The organization serves a number of functions, including taking stands on ethical issues that confront journalists. For example, the organization supports the right of journalists who reported on the steroid scandal in baseball to protect their sources.

ASNE Statement of Principles
ASNE's Statement of Principles was originally adopted in 1922 as the "Canons of Journalism." The document was revised and renamed "Statement of Principles" in 1975.

- **Preamble**: The First Amendment, protecting freedom of expression from abridgment by any law, guarantees to the people through their press a constitutional right, and thereby places on newspaper people a particular responsibility. Thus journalism demands of its practitioners not only industry and knowledge but also the pursuit of a standard of integrity proportionate to the journalist's singular obligation. To this end the American Society of Newspaper Editors sets forth this Statement of Principles as a standard encouraging the highest ethical and professional performance.

- **Article I**: Responsibility. The primary purpose of gathering and distributing news and opinion is to serve the general welfare by informing the people and enabling them to make judgments on the issues of the time. Newspapermen and women who abuse the power of their professional role for selfish motives or unworthy purposes are faithless to that public trust. The American press was made free not just to inform or just to serve as a forum for debate but also to bring an independent scrutiny to bear on the forces of power in the society, including the conduct of official power at all levels of government.

- **Article II**: Freedom of the Press. Freedom of the press belongs to the people. It must be defended against encroachment or assault from any quarter, public or private. Journalists must be constantly alert to see that the public's business is conducted in public. They must be vigilant against all who would exploit the press for selfish purposes.

- **Article III**: Independence. Journalists must avoid impropriety and the appearance of impropriety as well as any conflict of interest or the appearance of conflict. They should neither accept anything nor pursue any activity that might compromise or seem to compromise their integrity.

- **Article IV**: Truth and Accuracy. Good faith with the reader is the foundation of good journalism. Every effort must be made to assure that the news content is accurate, free from bias and in context, and that all sides are presented fairly. Editorials, analytical articles and commentary should be held to the same standards of accuracy with respect to facts as news reports. Significant errors of fact, as well as errors of omission, should be corrected promptly and prominently.

- **Article V**: Impartiality. To be impartial does not require the press to be unquestioning or to refrain from editorial expression. Sound practice, however, demands a clear distinction for the reader between news reports and opinion. Articles that contain opinion or personal interpretation should be clearly identified.

- **Article VI**: Fair Play. Journalists should respect the rights of people involved in the news, observe the common standards of decency and stand accountable to the public for the fairness and accuracy of their news reports. Persons publicly accused should be given the earliest opportunity to respond. Pledges of confidentiality to news sources must be honored at all costs, and therefore should not be given lightly. Unless there is clear and pressing need to maintain confidences, sources of information should be identified.

These principles are intended to preserve, protect, and strengthen the bond of trust and respect between American journalists and the American people, a bond that is essential to sustain the grant of freedom entrusted to both by the nation's founders.

Radio and Television News Directors Association (RTNDA)

The Radio and Television News Directors Association "represent[s] local and network news executives in broadcasting, cable, and other electronic media in more than 30 countries," according to its Web site, http:/ /www. rtnda. org. RTNDA offers information and workshops to television executives and also takes stands on media issues, including the use of video news releases and reporters' shield laws. These guidelines were adopted at the group's annual conference in September 2000.

RTNDA Code of Ethics and Professional Conduct

The Radio-Television News Directors Association, wishing to foster the highest professional standards of electronic journalism, promote public understanding of and confidence in electronic journalism, and strengthen principles of journalistic freedom to gather and disseminate information, establishes this Code of Ethics and Professional Conduct.

- **Preamble**: Professional electronic journalists should operate as trustees of the public, seek the truth, report it fairly and with integrity and independence, and stand accountable for their actions.
- **Public Trust**: Professional electronic journalists should recognize that their first obligation is to the public. Professional electronic journalists should:
  - Understand that any commitment other than service to the public undermines trust and credibility.
  - Recognize that service in the public interest creates an obligation to reflect the diversity of the community and guard against oversimplification of issues or events.
  - Provide a full range of information to enable the public to make enlightened decisions.
  - Fight to ensure that the public's business is conducted in public.
- **Truth**: Professional electronic journalists should pursue truth aggressively and present the news accurately, in context, and as completely as possible. Professional electronic journalists should:
  - Continuously seek the truth.
  - Resist distortions that obscure the importance of events.
  - Clearly disclose the origin of information and label all material provided by outsiders.

  Professional electronic journalists should not:
  - Report anything known to be false.
  - Manipulate images or sounds in any way that is misleading.
  - Plagiarize.
  - Present images or sounds that are reenacted without informing the public.
- **Fairness**: Professional electronic journalists should present the news fairly and impartially, placing primary value on significance and relevance. Professional electronic journalists should:
  - Treat all subjects of news coverage with respect and dignity, showing particular compassion to victims of crime or tragedy.

- Exercise special care when children are involved in a story and give children greater privacy protection than adults.
- Seek to understand the diversity of their community and inform the public without bias or stereotype.
- Present a diversity of expressions, opinions, and ideas in context.
- Present analytical reporting based on professional perspective, not personal bias.
- Respect the right to a fair trial.
- **Integrity**: Professional electronic journalists should present the news with integrity and decency, avoiding real or perceived conflicts of interest, and respect the dignity and intelligence of the audience as well as the subjects of news. Professional electronic journalists should:
  - Identify sources whenever possible. Confidential sources should be used only when it is clearly in the public interest to gather or convey important information or when a person providing information might be harmed. Journalists should keep all commitments to protect a confidential source.
  - Clearly label opinion and commentary.
  - Guard against extended coverage of events or individuals that fails to significantly advance a story, place the event in context, or add to the public knowledge.
  - Refrain from contacting participants in violent situations while the situation is in progress.
  - Use technological tools with skill and thoughtfulness, avoiding techniques that skew facts, distort reality, or sensationalize events.
  - Use surreptitious newsgathering techniques, including hidden cameras or microphones, only if there is no other way to obtain stories of significant public importance and only if the technique is explained to the audience.
  - Disseminate the private transmissions of other news organizations only with permission.

  Professional electronic journalists should not:
  - Pay news sources who have a vested interest in a story.
  - Accept gifts, favors, or compensation from those who might seek to influence coverage.
  - Engage in activities that may compromise their integrity or independence.
- **Independence**: Professional electronic journalists should defend the independence of all journalists from those seeking influence or control over news content. Professional electronic journalists should:
  - Gather and report news without fear or favor, and vigorously resist undue influence from any outside forces, including advertisers, sources, story subjects, powerful individuals, and special interest groups.
  - Resist those who would seek to buy or politically influence news content or who would seek to intimidate those who gather and disseminate the news.
  - Determine news content solely through editorial judgment and not as the result of outside influence.
  - Resist any self-interest or peer pressure that might erode journalistic duty and service to the public.
  - Recognize that sponsorship of the news will not be used in any way to determine, restrict, or manipulate content.

- Refuse to allow the interests of ownership or management to influence news judgment and content inappropriately.
- Defend the rights of the free press for all journalists, recognizing that any professional or government licensing of journalists is a violation of that freedom.
- **Accountability**: Professional electronic journalists should recognize that they are accountable for their actions to the public, the profession, and themselves. Professional electronic journalists should:
  - Actively encourage adherence to these standards by all journalists and their employers.
  - Respond to public concerns. Investigate complaints and correct errors promptly and with as much prominence as the original report.
  - Explain journalistic processes to the public, especially when practices spark questions or controversy.
  - Recognize that professional electronic journalists are duty-bound to conduct themselves ethically.
  - Refrain from ordering or encouraging courses of action that would force employees to commit an unethical act.
  - Carefully listen to employees who raise ethical objections and create environments in which such objections and discussions are encouraged.
  - Seek support for and provide opportunities to train employees in ethical decision making.
- In meeting its responsibility to the profession of electronic journalism, RTNDA has created this code to identify important issues, to serve as a guide for its members, to facilitate self-scrutiny, and to shape future debate.

Public Relations Society of American (PRSA)

According to its Web site, http://www.prsa.org, the Public Relations Society of America is the largest professional organization for public relations with more than 20,000 members. PRSA's ethical statements include a code of provisions, statement of professional values, and a code of ethics pledge that members are encouraged to sign to guide their professional behavior.

PRSA Code of Ethics 2000
- Professional Values
- Principles of Conduct
- Commitment and Compliance

This Code applies to PRSA members. The Code is designed to be a useful guide for PRSA members as they carry out their ethical responsibilities. This document is designed to anticipate and accommodate, by precedent, ethical challenges that may arise. The scenarios outlined in the Code provision are actual examples of misconduct. More will be added as experience with the Code occurs.

The Public Relations Society of America (PRSA) is committed to ethical practices. The level of public trust PRSA members seek, as we serve the public good, means we have taken on a special obligation to operate ethically.

The value of member reputation depends upon the ethical conduct of everyone affiliated with the Public Relations Society of America. Each of us sets an example for each other—as well as other professionals—by our pursuit of excellence with powerful standards of performance, professionalism, and ethical conduct.

Emphasis on enforcement of the Code has been eliminated. But, the PRSA Board of Directors retains the right to bar from membership or expel from the Society any individual who has been or is sanctioned by a government agency or convicted in a court of law of an action that is in violation of this Code.

Ethical practice is the most important obligation of a PRSA member. We view the Member Code of Ethics as a model for other professions, organizations, and professionals.

PRSA Statement of Professional Values

This statement presents the core values of PRSA members and, more broadly, of the public relations profession. These values provide the foundation for the member code of ethics and set the industry standard for the professional practice of public relations. These values are the fundamental beliefs that guide our behaviors and decision-making process. We believe our professional values are vital to the integrity of the profession as a whole.

- **Advocacy**: We serve the public interest by acting as responsible advocates for those we represent. We provide a voice in the marketplace of ideas, facts, and viewpoints to aid informed public debate.
- **Honesty**: We adhere to the highest standards of accuracy and truth in advancing the interests of those we represent and in communicating with the public.
- **Expertise**: We acquire and responsibly use specialized knowledge and experience. We advance the profession through continued professional development, research, and education. We build mutual understanding, credibility, and relationships among a wide array of institutions and audiences.
- **Independence**: We provide objective counsel to those we represent. We are accountable for our actions.
- **Loyalty**: We are faithful to those we represent, while honoring our obligation to serve the public interest.
- **Fairness**: We deal fairly with clients, employers, competitors, peers, vendors, the media, and the general public. We respect all opinions and support the right of free expression.

PRSA Code of Provisions
Free Flow of Information
Core Principle
Protecting and advancing the free flow of accurate and truthful information is essential to serving the public interest and contributing to informed decision making in a democratic society.

Intent
- To maintain the integrity of relationships with the media, government officials, and the public.
- To aid informed decision making.

Guidelines
A member shall:

- Preserve the integrity of the process of communication.
- Be honest and accurate in all communications.
- Act promptly to correct erroneous communications for which the practitioner is responsible.
- Preserve the free flow of unprejudiced information when giving or receiving gifts by ensuring that gifts are nominal, legal, and infrequent.

Examples of Improper Conduct under This Provision
- A member representing a ski manufacturer gives a pair of expensive racing skis to a sports magazine columnist, to influence the columnist to write favorable articles about the product.
- A member entertains a government official beyond legal limits and/or in violation of government reporting requirements.

Competition
Core Principle
Promoting healthy and fair competition among professionals preserves an ethical climate while fostering a robust business environment.

Intent
- To promote respect and fair competition among public relations professionals.
- To serve the public interest by providing the widest choice of practitioner options.

Guidelines
A member shall:

- Follow ethical hiring practices designed to respect free and open competition without deliberately undermining a competitor.
- Preserve intellectual property rights in the marketplace.

Examples of Improper Conduct under This Provision
- A member employed by "a client organization" shares helpful information with a counseling firm that is competing with others for the organization's business.
- A member spreads malicious and unfounded rumors about a competitor in order to alienate the competitor's clients and employees in a ploy to recruit people and business.

Disclosure of Information
Core Principle
Open communication fosters informed decision making in a democratic society.

Intent
To build trust with the public by revealing all information needed for responsible decision making.

Guidelines
A member shall:

- Be honest and accurate in all communications.
- Act promptly to correct erroneous communications for which the member is responsible.
- Investigate the truthfulness and accuracy of information released on behalf of those represented.
- Reveal the sponsors for causes and interests represented.
- Disclose financial interest (such as stock ownership) in a client's organization.
- Avoid deceptive practices.

Examples of Improper Conduct under This Provision
- Front groups: A member implements "grass roots" campaigns or letter-writing campaigns to legislators on behalf of undisclosed interest groups.
- Lying by omission: A practitioner for a corporation knowingly fails to release financial information, giving a misleading impression of the corporation's performance.
- A member discovers inaccurate information disseminated via a Web site or media kit and does not correct the information.
- A member deceives the public by employing people to pose as volunteers to speak at public hearings and participate in "grass roots" campaigns.

Safeguarding Confidences
Core Principle
Client trust requires appropriate protection of confidential and private information.

Intent
To protect the privacy rights of clients, organizations, and individuals by safeguarding confidential information.

Guidelines
A member shall:

- Safeguard the confidences and privacy rights of present, former, and prospective clients and employees.
- Protect privileged, confidential, or insider information gained from a client or organization.
- Immediately advise an appropriate authority if a member discovers that confidential information is being divulged by an employee of a client company or organization.

Examples of Improper Conduct under This Provision
- A member changes jobs, takes confidential information, and uses that information in the new position to the detriment of the former employer.
- A member intentionally leaks proprietary information to the detriment of some other party.

Conflicts of Interest
Core Principle
Avoiding real, potential, or perceived conflicts of interest builds the trust of clients, employers, and the publics.

Intent
- To earn trust and mutual respect with clients or employers.
- To build trust with the public by avoiding or ending situations that put one's personal or professional interests in conflict with society's interests.

Guidelines
A member shall:

- Act in the best interests of the client or employer, even subordinating the member's personal interests.
- Avoid actions and circumstances that may appear to compromise good business judgment or create a conflict between personal and professional interests.
- Disclose promptly any existing or potential conflict of interest to affected clients or organizations.
- Encourage clients and customers to determine whether a conflict exists after notifying all affected parties.

Examples of Improper Conduct under This Provision
- The member fails to disclose that he or she has a strong financial interest in a client's chief competitor.
- The member represents a "competitor company" or a "conflicting interest" without informing a prospective client.

Enhancing the Profession
Core Principle
Public relations professionals work constantly to strengthen the public's trust in the profession.

Intent
- To build respect and credibility with the public for the profession of public relations.
- To improve, adapt, and expand professional practices.

Guidelines
A member shall:

- Acknowledge that there is an obligation to protect and enhance the profession.
- Keep informed and educated about practices in the profession to ensure ethical conduct.
- Actively pursue personal professional development.
- Decline representation of clients or organizations that urge or require actions contrary to this Code.

- Accurately define what public relations activities can accomplish.
- Counsel subordinates in proper ethical decision making.
- Require that subordinates adhere to the ethical requirements of the Code.
- Report ethical violations, whether committed by PRSA members or not, to the appropriate authority.

Examples of Improper Conduct under This Provision
- A PRSA member declares publicly that a product the client sells is safe, without disclosing evidence to the contrary.
- A member initially assigns some questionable client work to a non-member practitioner to avoid the ethical obligation of PRSA membership.

American Advertising Federation (AAF)

The American Advertising Federation is the trade association for 50,000 professionals in the advertising industry, including advertisers, agencies, and media companies, and 210 college chapters. According to its mission statement, "The American Advertising Federation protects and promotes the well-being of advertising. We accomplish this through a unique, nationally coordinated grassroots network of advertisers, agencies, media companies, local advertising clubs and college chapters." (http://www.aaf.org/about/index.html). AAF members work together to advance the field of advertising in business, government, and in the community. They educate members on the latest trends and recognize advertising excellence. Their Board of Directors adopted their statement of ethics and principles in March of 1984.

AAF Advertising Ethics and Principles
- **Truth**: Advertising shall tell the truth, and shall reveal significant facts, the omission of which would mislead the public.
- **Substantiation**: Advertising claims shall be substantiated by evidence in possession of the advertiser and advertising agency, prior to making such claims.
- **Comparisons**: Advertising shall refrain from making false, misleading, or unsubstantiated statements or claims about a competitor or his/her products or services.
- **Bait Advertising**: Advertising shall not offer products or services for sale unless such offer constitutes a bona fide effort to sell the advertising products or services and is not a device to switch consumers to other goods or services, usually higher priced.
- **Guarantees and Warranties**: Advertising of guarantees and warranties shall be explicit, with sufficient information to apprise consumers of their principal terms and limitations or, when space or time restrictions preclude such disclosures, the advertisement should clearly reveal where the full text of the guarantee or warranty can be examined before purchase.
- **Price Claims**: Advertising shall avoid price claims which are false or misleading, or saving claims which do not offer provable savings.
- **Testimonials**: Advertising containing testimonials shall be limited to those of competent witnesses who are reflecting a real and honest opinion or experience.
- **Taste and Decency**: Advertising shall be free of statements, illustrations or implications which are offensive to good taste or public decency.

Summary

It is undoubtedly a positive sign that many media professionals, when asked to give students an example of an ethical dilemma they have faced in the workplace, have to pause and think for some time. Sometimes they have an example, but frequently they do not. Ethical dilemmas just do not come up for them because their professional behavior is guided by a set of principles that make moral decisions easy. A commitment to an honest representation of the truth, regardless of whether it is advertising, public relations, print, broadcasting, or any allied field, is what matters most.

The tools are available in the form of ethical models and professional association guidelines to help deconstruct an ethical conundrum, but most of the time, ethics should not be an issue. It may be difficult to dispel the negative image that the public has of sleazy public relations practitioners, unscrupulous advertising executives, and exploitative journalists. (And some media "professionals" who distort and slant the news to appeal to a target audience contribute to that negative image.) But student interns are generally heartened to learn that the vast majority of media professionals work hard to do their jobs, to maintain strict ethical standards, and to model those standards for future media practitioners.

QUESTIONS FOR DISCUSSION/ APPLICATION EXERCISES

1. Find a case related to your field of interest in the media such as journalism, advertising, or public relations. Analyze the case and make recommendations based on one of the ethical models presented in the chapter. Use the principles from the appropriate professional organization (as dictated by the model) to assess the situation and reach a decision. A variety of media ethics cases may be found at the following Web sites:
   - www.poynter.org/content/content_view.asp?id=31889&sid=32#Studies
   - www.journalism.indiana.edu/gallery/ethics/
   - support.comm.psu.edu/∼ethics/casestudies.html
   - www.scu.edu/ethics/practicing/focusareas/cases.cfm

2. In conducting informational interviews with professionals in the field or attending panel discussions, ask them what kinds of ethical issues they have faced on the job, and the process they have used for resolving the ethical dilemma.

REFERENCES

ACEJMC (Accrediting Council on Education in Journalism and Mass Communications) Accrediting Standards. Retrieved August 4, 2006, from: http://www2.ku.edu/∼acejmc/PROGRAM/STANDARDS.SHTML.

Backus, N., & Ferraris, C. (2004). Theory meets practice: Using the Potter box to teach business communications ethics. Proceedings of the 2004 Association for Business Communication Annual Convention, pp. 222–229. Retrieved August 17, 2006, from: http://www.businesscommunication.org/ conventions/Proceedings/2004/PDFs/21ABC04.PDF.

Day, L. A. (2003). *Ethics in media communications: Cases and controversies* (4th ed.). Belmont, CA: Thompson Wadsworth.

Englehardt, E. E., & Barney, R. D. (2002). *Media and ethics: Principles for moral decisions*. Belmont, CA: Thompson Wadsworth.

Lambeth, E. (2006). Elements of media ethics instruction. In M. Land & B. Hornaday (Eds.), *Contemporary media ethics* (pp. 3–13). Spokane, WA: Marquette Books.

Land, M. (2006). Mass media ethics and the point-of-decision pyramid. In M. Land & B. Hornaday (Eds.), *Contemporary media ethics* (pp. 15–38). Spokane, WA: Marquette Books.

Leslie, L. (2004). *Mass communication ethics: Decision making in postmodern culture* (2nd ed.). Boston: Houghton-Mifflin.

Maier, T. W. (2004). New media's credibility crumbling. *Insight Magazine* May 8, retrieved August 19, 2006, from: http://foi.missouri.edu/mediacredibility/nmcredcrumbling.html.

Park, J., & Park, J. (2000). How two Korean newspapers covered the Starr report. *Newspaper Research Journal 21*, 83–98

Retief, J. (2002). *Media ethics: An introduction to responsible journalism*. Cape Town, South Africa: Oxford University Press South Africa.

Rosenberry, J., & Vicker, L. (2006, Autumn). Capstone courses in mass communication programs. *Journalism & Mass Communication Educator 61*(3), 267–284.

Williams, R. B. (1997). AIDS testing, Potter and TV news decisions. *Journal of Mass Media Ethics 12*, 148–159.

RESOURCES FOR ETHICAL GUIDELINES

American Advertising Federation
http://www.aaf.org/

American Society of Newspaper Editors
http://www.asne.org/index.cfm

The Poynter Institute
http://www.poynter.org/

Public Relations Society of America
http://prsa.org/

Radio-Television News Directors Association
http://www.rtnda.org/

Society of Professional Journalists
http://www.spj.org/ethicscode.asp

CHAPTER

11 Media Economics

THIS CHAPTER WILL:

- Provide an overview of principles from economics, especially at the firm and industry level (microeconomics). Special attention will be focused on:
  - Market structures
  - Competition
  - Integration
- Describe and illustrate, through examples, how these principles can be used to better understand the contemporary media landscape.

President Calvin Coolidge once famously remarked that "The business of the American people is business." Interestingly, although he made this statement during an address to the American Society of Newspaper Editors (Bartlett, 1980, p. 736), it came at a time when the media really were not major business operations. When Coolidge made his speech in 1925, television had not been commercialized and radio, an industry of local operators, was in its infancy. Even among the dominant mass medium of the day—newspapers—most were family-owned single enterprises serving local markets.

Since Coolidge's day, media industries have become larger, more diversified (as new technologies created new media forms), and more commonly under the control of corporations rather than individual owners. Large corporations often control dozens or hundreds of media outlets nationwide, encompassing many different genres (newspapers, magazines, television, radio, Internet sites, etc.) under one ownership structure. So media have become "big business," and understanding the media landscape requires an understanding of economic principles.

How big is big when it comes to the media? According to a report prepared for the International Intellectual Property Association, the "core" copyright industries of newspapers and periodicals, radio and television broadcasting, book publishing, musical recording, motion pictures, and computer software contributed $819 billion to the U.S. economy, or 6.6 percent of U.S. gross domestic product, in 2005. Nearly 5.4 million people worked in these industries, or 4 percent of the total U.S. workforce (Siwek, 2006).

A prominent scholar in the field, Robert Picard, defines media economics as "the study of how economic and financial pressures affect a variety of communications activities, systems, organizations and enterprises." But he also notes that a separate definition for media economics is somewhat pointless "because it implies that the economic laws and theories for media are different than for other entities" when actually "media economics is a specific application of economic laws and theories to media industries and firms" (Picard, 2006, p. 23). Thus, principles of general economics can be used to better understand contemporary, commercially based media.

Additionally, the way media firms follow these economic principles is intertwined with production of the media goods that help to create a society's culture, as various types of critical theory suggest (as described in Chapter 8). According to this critical-theory-based approach, content decisions made with business operations in mind can lead to content provided by the media that differs from what the organizations could (or even should) produce as creators and purveyors of culture. This provides a second good reason for trying to understand how economic principles affect media operations.

Market Principles

Definition
Economics: The study of how people and societies make choices among scarce resources to produce goods and distribute them for consumption.

Any study of economics must begin with a study of markets because of their role in allocating what a society produces. No economy produces enough to serve every need and desire of every individual within it. In the theory of economics called free-market or capitalist economics, the market is regarded as the best device for answering the question of who gets what, and how much, when there are not enough resources for everybody to have everything they want.

Free-market economics asserts that markets are the best tools for the distribution of wealth because of their ability to allocate resources efficiently. (Critical theory takes the opposite view, at least with regard to cultural goods. Chapter 8 describes how critical theory maintains that a market model leads to decisions about production of cultural goods according to the goals of powerful interests in society.) The U.S. business system is generally market-based, including the media businesses within it. So understanding how markets work is a necessary part of understanding the media landscape, too.

Definition
Market: A forum of exchange that allocates economic resources.

Supply and Demand

The fundamental rule that economic theory uses to explain allocation of resources is the principle of supply and demand. Supply is the amount of a good that will be provided for consumption at a given price. Demand is the amount that consumers in the market will be willing to purchase at a given price. The theory of supply and demand in allocating the output of a society's economy is based on three principles (which also are illustrated in Figure 11.1):

1. Demand declines when prices rise, and vice versa (i.e., demand increases when prices are lower). This is largely based on the "auction" effect. When so many people want a good that supplies of it begin to run short, prices are "bid" to a higher level. This is a major factor in the high cost of oil and high gasoline prices of recent years. At the same time, lower prices bring out more buyers. More people can be found wanting to buy Hondas or Toyotas than BMWs or Rolls Royces because more people can afford Hondas and Toyotas. Lower prices also result in additional purchases by individual buyers. For example, if someone had $50 available to spend on a trip to the clothing store, she could afford five shirts that cost only $10 each but would only be able to buy three if they were priced at $15 each. So, overall, the quantity of a good demanded is higher at lower prices.

2. Supply increases as prices rise, which is the complete reverse of the demand relationship. The major reason is that higher prices tend to "coax out" more supply. A classic example that can be found in any basic economics text is agricultural goods. Suppose wheat and corn are selling for the same price per bushel but then for some reason the price of wheat doubles. The higher price leads to more supply because some farmers will plant wheat instead of corn because they can earn more from it.

3. Supply-demand equilibrium determines prices, and quantity produced and demanded. When they are compared or "overlaid" on each other, the supply and demand relationships together determine the amount of goods

FIGURE 11.1   Principles of Supply and Demand

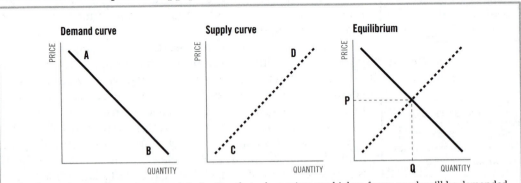

The demand curve slopes downward, indicating that when prices are higher, fewer goods will be demanded (A). As the price drops, the quantity demanded rises (B). The supply curve slopes upward, indicating that fewer goods will be produced at lower prices (C) than when prices are higher (D). An equilibrium point at the intersection of the supply and demand curves shows that at price P, quantity Q will be produced and consumed in the market.

that will be produced and consumed, and also the price at which the exchange will be made. According to this theory, the free-enterprise market economy follows this model to efficiently allocate resources and determine how much of a given good will be produced using the scarce resources available.

Utility and Substitution as Factors in Determining Demand

While this model is the basis of studying a market economy, it also is oversimplified because it ignores other factors that enter the equation, especially on the demand side. Most importantly, while price may be the most significant thing that determines demand, it is not the *only* thing that determines demand.

Another crucial factor in demand is utility, which is how much satisfaction or usefulness the consumption of a good provides. A good example of utility can be drawn from end-of-the year purchases of calendars. A nice calendar for the coming year might cost $5 to $15 at a bookstore or gift store, and many people willingly pay it because the calendar is functional, attractive, makes a good holiday gift, and so forth. In other words, the calendars have high utility and so people are willing to pay a reasonable price for them. But how much would these buyers pay for a copy of the ending-year's calendar? Most likely, they would not want it at any price (even for free) because it is obsolete, so the purchase would have zero utility. Higher utility can foster greater demand, sometimes without regard to price.

Another principle behind demand is that it is influenced by availability and costs of substitute goods, which are those that serve the same or substantially the same function. Different flavors or brands of soft drinks in a vending machine are substitutes for one another, and what economists call "perfect" ones at that

Definition
Utility: The level of satisfaction or usefulness that the consumption of a good provides.

because they are very close in form and function. Someone might prefer cola to lemon-lime, but if she were really thirsty and the machine was sold out of cola drinks, she probably would purchase another flavor because it would provide the same utility of quenching her thirst. Prices of substitutes matter, too. If the thirsty student notices a water fountain near the vending area where she could get a drink for free, it could affect her level of demand for the $1.25 bottled water from the machine.

Price, Utility, and Media Goods. Utility and substitution are especially relevant to evaluating demand for media goods. A subscription to a running magazine might have high utility for a college student whose hobby is training for marathons, and have no utility for his neighbor who does not care at all about that topic, and instead is into model railroading. The second student, on the other hand, might subscribe to a model railroad publication that the runner would have no interest in reading. And most likely neither of them would subscribe to *Disney Adventures*, even though both might have younger siblings who read it.

This illustrates that the contents of a media good are strongly related to its utility; people will not consume media goods—whether a book, magazine, television show, or Web site—on a topic in which they have no interest. Price is still a factor, though. The typical price of a monthly magazine is $15 to $20 for a one-year subscription, and the marathoner probably would pay something like that because of the utility the magazine brings him. But he probably would not pay hundreds of dollars a year for it; at some point, the price would affect his demand for the product even if he found it interesting and useful.

As for substitution, people can get news and entertainment from many sources, but to what degree are media outlets substitutes for each other? The evening news broadcasts from one network to another are close, nearly *perfect substitutes*. They provide a similar amount and type of information in a similar format. Television news and a newspaper are also substitutes for each other, but they are called *imperfect substitutes*. They have a similar function—providing the news—but do so in such different ways with different characteristics that they do not replace each other as perfectly as, for example, one brand of cola replaces another. Going a step further, many college students substitute *The Daily Show* for a newspaper or a television news show to get their news. Such a substitution is certainly less than perfect, offering a skewed view of the political landscape. But it is better than no news at all, because at least its viewers are aware of major issues of the day.

In a similar vein, various magazines, such as *Time*, *Newsweek*, and *U.S. News and World Report* summarize the week's news in comparable ways, which is another way of saying they are good substitutes for each other. When various substitutes are available, a reader might then make a decision about which to choose based on price: which one offers the best subscription deal? For example, if someone subscribed to *Elle* magazine and its price went up beyond what she was willing to pay, she might start buying *Vogue* or *Marie Clare*. But at the same time, she would not be likely to buy *Disney Adventures*, or the running or model railroad magazines in place of her fashion magazine, at any price. Those just are not close enough substitutes to provide the same utility.

> ### Definition
>
> **Substitutes:** Different goods that serve identical or substantially the same functions.
>
> - Perfect substitutes are very close in nature and function, such as two different brands of cola (or another soft drink flavor).
> - Imperfect substitutes have the same general nature and function but differ in certain noticeable ways, such as soft drinks versus fruit juices, milk, or water.

Scale Economies and Other Supply-Side Factors

A key consideration in the production cost of many goods is whether they are subject to economies of scale, which reduce the cost of each unit as more goods are produced. For example, if it costs $10 million a year to operate a factory, and the factory produces just 10 units a year, they each would have to sell for $1 million just to break even. If the factory produces 1 million units they could be sold for just $10 each; the higher levels of production drive down the cost of each unit.

Some goods can be produced profitably with low economies of scale. For example, military and commercial aircraft tend to be produced in relatively small numbers and sell at a price of millions of dollars for each unit. But no one would pay $1 million for a television set or a toaster, so manufacturers of these goods (and most others) pay attention to economies of scale—producing enough units to bring the cost of each product down to a reasonable level.

Most media businesses are powerfully affected by these economies of scale. It costs millions of dollars to set up a printing facility or a broadcast station. If that press were used to produce just a few newspapers, each of them would need to be sold for a huge sum just to cover the cost of running the press to make them (not to mention paying the reporters, photographers, and editors to create the content). Or if that radio station reached just a few dozen listeners, the cost that advertisers would be paying to reach each listener would be extremely high. This is why even small radio stations have several thousand listeners, or why a network television show has millions of viewers. It is why newspapers print thousands of copies each day, and millions over the course of a year. Because of the large initial cost or set-up cost (the press, the broadcast facility, the people to generate the content), large production numbers are necessary or else it would cost so much to produce each unit that no one would pay to buy them. Without proper economies of scale, media businesses could not exist.

Definition
Economy of scale: A decline in average cost per unit as more units are produced.

Market Structures and Competition

Principles of supply, demand, and allocation are based on the assumption that some sort of rivalry or competition exists in the market for a good or service. The competition among consumers vying for access to goods defines the principle of demand. But more significantly, suppliers or producers compete for consumers. The nature of this competition is called the market's structure. Economists distinguish among four basic market structures: monopoly, oligopoly, imperfect competition (sometimes called monopolistic competition), and perfect competition.

■ **Monopoly** occurs when the market has a single producer of a unique product without close substitutes. In this case, that single producing firm dominates the market with substantial control over price because consumers have no other place to turn. In media, for example, many daily newspapers are monopolies—the sole such product of their kind in the market, with no close substitutes.

■ **Oligopoly** is defined as a market with a few producers of products that are close substitutes for each other but not quite perfect ones. A classic example is the automobile industry. Cars differ by make, model, and design but are nearly identical in form and function; a standard six-passenger car from any manufacturer will be pretty much like another. Plus, nearly all cars are built and sold by a dozen or so companies from the United States, Germany, Japan, and Korea. So the worldwide auto industry is an oligopoly, selling largely similar products at similar prices. Just as daily newspapers provide a good example of a media monopoly at the local level, local television markets provide an oligopoly example at the same level. A medium-sized television market might have three or four stations affiliated with the major commercial networks and provide similar offerings in daytime, prime time, and local programming, including news.

■ **Monopolistic competition** is defined as having many producers of products with enough differences to make them distinct from one another even if they may serve the same purposes. In economic terms, this makes them close substitutes. This describes the market for many consumer goods, including personal care products (shampoos, soaps, etc.), home care products (laundry detergent, other cleaning supplies), and packaged foods (cookies, candy bars, breakfast cereal, soft drinks, beer). A good example of monopolistic competition in local media might be radio broadcasting. Even a medium-sized market will have quite a few stations; the authors' home market has more than 20 stations even though it is ranked just 79th nationally for ratings purposes. These stations are differentiated by their formats: rock, pop, oldies, jazz, and country music, news-talk, sports-talk, religious, and so forth. Beyond the formats, each tries to distinguish its image with its on-air personalities, promotions, and community appearances. While there is some variation from station to station, one classic oldies station is much like another, as cross-country travelers observe. (With media consolidation, some of these stations are *exactly* alike because they all come from the same place with the same content.)

Another important point for communication students to note regarding monopolistic competition is the significance of advertising to contribute to product-differentiation. Fundamentally, there is very little difference in American-brewed lager beers (e.g., Budweiser, Coors, and Miller) or soft drinks (Coke and Pepsi). These competing products are very close to one another in taste, price, packaging, and other product attributes. But their manufacturers spend hundreds of millions of dollars each year on advertising and promotion trying to convince beer and soda drinkers that they are different, in order to encourage sales by making them seem more unique. And judging by some of the very strong preferences observed among students and faculty, these manufacturers have been very successful in this differentiation.

Definitions
Market structures: Monopoly: A single producer of a unique product without close substitutes, which allows that single producer to dominate the market. Oligopoly: A limited number of firms with products that are undifferentiated (close but not quite perfect substitutes for each other). **Monopolistic/ imperfect competition:** Many producers of products with differences that help make the products distinct, although they may serve the same functions. **Perfect competition:** Many producers of undifferentiated (identical) goods.

■ **Perfect competition** is a market structure in which there are many producers of undifferentiated (identical) goods. The classic example that economists use is agricultural production: a bushel of wheat is a bushel of wheat, and thousands of farmers each produce wheat that is identical no matter where it is produced.

Market Structures, Competition, and Integration

Definition
Differentiation: An effort to make it seem as if a product is unique (the way a monopoly product is) to help expand demand for it.

In classic market theory, more competitive markets—those closer to perfect competition and furthest from monopoly—are the markets that price goods as closely as possible to the costs of producing them (which efficiently allocates resources). They also are more innovative, including innovations in the production process that can make goods cheaper or deliver them more efficiently as well as innovations in the products themselves to make them more attractive to users. Which market structure best describes the U.S. economy? There are some differences among industries, but it is primarily a mix of oligopolistic competition (recall the auto example from earlier) and imperfect (i.e., monopolistic) competition, such as the beer and soft drink example. As seen in the examples, different media businesses fall at different places along the competitive spectrum.

But another characteristic of the U.S. economy has been a greater tendency toward integration, which is control of different aspects of production and distribution of goods. This is related to structure and competition, because greater integration reduces competition, thereby allowing highly integrated firms to behave something like monopolists, by limiting sources for a product. Market integration comes in two varieties, known as horizontal and vertical integration.

Horizontal Integration. Horizontal integration occurs when a single entity controls multiple outlets that provide a common function in the production chain to the consumer. For example, picture the following simple "industry" for the production and sale of bread:

- 10 farmers produce the wheat.
- 10 millers turn the wheat into flour.
- 10 bakeries turn the flour into bread.
- 10 grocery stores sell the bread to individual consumers.

Definitions
Horizontal Integration: A single entity controlling multiple outlets that provide a common function in the production chain to the consumer.
Vertical integration: A single entity controlling multiple levels of the production chain.

This is a competitive marketplace, because if one farmer tried to raise his prices, the millers would just turn elsewhere for their supply. At the same time, no single miller could pressure farmers to sell their wheat for an unfairly cheap price because another miller in the market could offer a fairer price. In similar fashion, the price that millers can charge the bakers is controlled because if one person raised prices too high the baker would just choose another miller as his supplier. And so on, up the production chain to the consumers. Competition promotes economic efficiency and fair prices throughout the industry.

Suppose one enterprising miller bought her neighbor's mill, and then the next one down the road, and the next, until she owned all 10 mills? This is horizontal integration: one entity controlling various outlets at a single level of the production/distribution chain to create a monopoly. This monopoly mill owner has total control over both the price she will pay to the farmers for their wheat and the price she will charge to the bakers for the milled flour because in both cases they have no alternative except to do business with her. Horizontal integration is a way of seeking greater market control by creating a less-competitive, more monopolistic market structure at one level in the production process.

Vertical Integration. One of the characteristics of a production chain such as the one in this example is that profits are made at every level. Suppose the selling price at each level was:

- Raw wheat to make enough flour for one loaf of bread: 40 cents
- Milled flour for one loaf of bread: 80 cents
- Wholesale price for one loaf of bread (baker's price to grocer): $1.20
- Retail price for one loaf of bread (grocer's price to consumer): $1.60

The value that is added at each stage of the process is 40 cents. Not all of that is pure profit because the 40 cents extra that the miller charges over what he paid for the wheat must also cover the production costs of running the mill. Similarly, the baker must cover costs such as power to heat the ovens, rent on the building where the bakery is housed, and so on.

Now, suppose rather than buying other mills, the enterprising miller has a different idea to get more control over the market. She decides to buy a farm to ensure her supply of wheat. Then she also buys a bakery and a grocery store, so that she owns an operation at every level of the supply chain. The miller goes from earning 40 cents for every loaf of bread a consumer buys to earning the entire $1.60. Even after subtracting the production costs, she is making far more profit from each loaf sold than her original 40 cents.

When profits through multiple levels of the production chain are captured by one entity, it is called vertical integration. In addition to capturing profit at every level, vertical integration insulates the organization from competition. If farmers raise wheat prices, the miller does not have to worry so much about it because she has her own farm to supply the business. Integration has had a powerful effect on the operation of media businesses as well.

Markets and Media

How does all of this apply to media? Well, as Picard's definition at the beginning of the chapter illustrates, media organizations exist as individual firms and as parts of industries that operate according to the principles described throughout this chapter. Understanding concepts such as competition, market structure, and integration are important starting points for understanding the operation of media businesses in the contemporary economy.

Dual Markets

One of the unusual features of nearly all media businesses is their need to serve two markets simultaneously, namely audiences and advertisers. Economic principles affect both of these markets, but not always in the same way. Media managers tend to view this as a complementary matter. They say that producing high-quality content attracts the audiences, whose attention is then sold to advertisers. The advertising revenue pays for the costs of producing that quality content.

But the heart of critical theorists' critiques is that audience needs and advertiser needs are not as compatible as the media moguls contend; rather, the dual-market arrangement frequently creates situations where one side must be favored over the other. Most often that means catering to advertisers because of the need to make profits. According to this argument, based on the theory of political economy, the drive for the largest possible audience means that the "public interest" ends up being defined as "whatever interests the public." This in turn leads to sensationalistic news coverage rather than quality public affairs programming, violent and sexualized movie and television content rather than more responsible offerings, and so on. Defenders of the market system counter that the only logical alternative to the advertising-supported market model is a "deep pockets" model, which essentially means government funding (and possible control) of the media. But the issue of operating in two markets simultaneously is one of the unusual aspects of media economics, and undeniably can affect content decisions in some cases.

Revenues and Costs. In classical economic theory, the demand curve and the amount of revenue that a business collects are very closely related to one another. In the equilibrium diagram in Figure 11.1, note that Q amount of goods will be sold at price P. If Q equals 1 million units and P equals $5, then the revenue the firm would earn is $5 million (multiplying P times Q). If the average cost of producing a single unit is $4, then the total cost of production would be $4 million. And the profit would be $1 million ($5 million total revenue minus $4 million total production cost).

But a major implication of the dual-market structure is that media businesses have two sources of revenue, one from the audience and one from the advertisers, and they are not weighted equally. Most media businesses rely more heavily on advertising, and some rely on it exclusively (as illustrated in Figure 11.2).

On the cost side, the physical cost of goods sold is minimal with many media. With broadcast media, in fact, there is no physical cost of the goods. A newspaper or magazine contains only a few cents worth of paper; the laser disc that contains a music CD or movie DVD is similarly inexpensive. Rather, the costs come from *producing the content* itself—paying reporters and editors to produce the news; paying actors, writers, directors, and production technicians to create a motion picture; or compensating musicians for the songs they create. In other words, most of the cost is the intellectual property of the goods, not the physical property of the medium. Costs also arise from *distributing* and *delivering* the content, including the fixed costs of a

FIGURE 11.2   Media Revenue Sources

Medium	Audience Revenue	Advertiser Revenue
Newspapers	Y[1]	Y
Magazines	Y	Y
Broadcast television	N	Y
Cable television	Y	Y
Broadcast radio	N	Y
Satellite radio	Y	N[2]
Musical recordings	Y	N
Motion pictures	Y	Y/N?[3]
Internet	Y?	Y?[4]

[1]This applies to most newspapers, although some, especially weeklies and those with limited news content (called "shoppers" or "pennysavers") do not have audience revenue. They are distributed for free and earn all their revenue from advertising.

[2]Satellite radio is generally ad free as of this writing, though some services have started to accept advertising on some channels.

[3]The movie presentation itself is not interrupted by ads the way television shows are, but movies can include product placements and tie-ins, which are a source of advertiser revenue for movie producers. Also, at many showings, patrons must watch advertising before the feature presentation airs, so a trip to the movies is not ad free.

[4]The Internet business model is perhaps the most complicated of all and is still evolving. Access to the Internet generally comes via a subscription fee of some sort, though many people actually have a "bundled" service that provides this access in combination with their telephone or cable television service. Others access the Internet "free" through their school, their employer, or a public service such as a library or Internet café that offers wireless access. But while the service appears free to the user, in those cases someone else is paying for the access. On the advertising side, some Web sites and organizations such as Google and Yahoo earn large amounts of revenue from advertising. Many media-related sites such as the Web versions of newspapers and broadcast/cable news outlets carry advertising, too. But the vast majority of Web sites do not feature ads.

press for a newspaper or magazine, terrestrial or satellite broadcast facilities for a television or radio station, wiring for a cable system, or equipment to make CDs or DVDs.

Market Structures as Units of Analysis.   These three levels in the supply process—production, distribution, and final delivery—form an effective framework to analyze media industries. The three levels exist distinctly in the television industry, for example, with television production studios creating shows and series, networks (broadcast or cable) distributing them, and either the local television station (broadcast) or local cable system delivering the signal to the end user. For movies, however, the studio is usually both producer and distributor, with local theater chains and video rental stores providing delivery. In music, artists produce the songs but most of the market power is with the record labels (distributors) who supply the local radio stations (deliverers) that play the songs. Newspapers, however, tend to control every stage of the process, from the writing of the stories to the printing of the product to the delivery to the doorstep.

Recall the earlier discussion about integration and note that what is being described here is how different types of media are vertically integrated. An important feature of integration is market control; the amount of integration found in a particular media segment provides an idea of how much control firms within that sector have in their marketplaces. In the three examples given, different types of vertical integration can be found in different types of media businesses, and it is no coincidence that the tightly integrated newspaper is the most monopolistic, at least in local markets.

However, horizontal integration also is equally important as a determinant of market structures, especially among broadcast media. For example, what do the following groupings of media properties have in common?

■ Nickelodeon/Nick at Nite, BET, TV Land, MTV, VH1, Spike TV, CMT, Comedy Central, Showtime, the Movie Channel, Sundance Channel

■ CNN, HBO, TBS, TCM, Cartoon Network

■ ABC Family, the Disney Channel, SoapNet, ESPN, A&E, the History Channel, Lifetime Television, Lifetime Movie Network, E! Entertainment

Most readers will recognize these as various cable networks, and may even recognize the common thread. At the time of this writing (a needed disclaimer because of the frequency with which holdings change), the first set was owned by the Viacom Corporation, the second by Time Warner, and the third largely by Disney, though some properties were partially owned by other companies in partnership with Disney. So, as cable watchers surf through the television channels, they may look at some or all of these 25 different stations, but really are looking at properties owned by just three media organizations. This is an example of horizontal integration used to exercise a greater degree of market control, especially through attention to content offerings for different demographics. Each corporation, for instance, has an option for children (Nickelodeon, Cartoon Network, Disney Channel) and for movie watchers (the Movie Channel, TCM [Turner Classic Movies], Lifetime Movie Network).

Returning to vertical integration for a moment, the large media conglomerates also integrate themselves vertically along the production-distribution-delivery axis. Disney at this writing had nearly a dozen production subsidiaries under its control for creating movies and television shows. At the distribution level it had not only the cable networks listed above but also the ABC broadcast network. And at the delivery level it owned and operated 10 local television stations, including ones in the nation's largest markets. Time-Warner was similarly integrated with several movie and television production units, a large number of cable networks, and the nation's largest cable delivery system, though it lacked a strong over-the-air broadcast presence of either a broadcast network or owned/operated local stations.

The large media conglomerates—not only Time Warner, Disney, and Viacom/CBS but also News Corporation, NBC-Universal, and a small number of others—operate in an oligopoly market for the production and distribution of much media content. Dozens of studios create movies and television shows and even more dozens of cable/broadcast networks exist to distribute them, but nearly all of these entities are controlled by a relative handful of corporations. Likewise, there are hundreds of magazines but a few large companies are responsible for publishing most of them.

Definition
Conglomerate: A large corporation that controls different types of businesses.

Other firms focus more on a strategy of horizontal integration, such as Clear Channel, which at the time of its purchase by a private equity company in early 2007 owned more than 1,200 radio stations around the country, controlling multiple stations in most of the markets in which it did business. (These numbers are subject to change based on what the new owners decide to do with their portfolio of stations.) Citadel Communication and Entercom Communications pursued the same strategy, although neither was as large as Clear Channel. In many cases, the end result is an oligopoly situation in local broadcasting. Clear Channel at this writing owns several stations in the authors' home market, and also formed a partnership with the local daily newspaper to share stories and content both on the air and on their respective Web sites, another way of horizontally integrating. However, the company's strategies also have become more vertical in recent years, with Clear Channel using a centrally produced satellite feed to provide the same content to many radio stations around the country.

Earlier, radio broadcasting was described as a medium where imperfect or monopolistic competition defined the market structure. But in many of those medium-sized markets with a dozen or more radio stations, most or all of them may be owned by just a couple of national conglomerates. This is a good example of the "split" between audience and advertiser markets because it might be fair to describe the radio industry as monopolistically competitive for *listeners* with its various formats (country, modern rock, soft pop, news-talk, etc.) but more like an oligopoly when it comes to *advertisers*, who have limited alternatives for getting their spots on the radio. These market structures are also an example of the impact that government regulation can have on a marketplace, because they emerged only after the rules for ownership of multiple broadcast outlets in a single market were changed by the Telecommunications Act of 1996.

For another example, the Gannett Corporation at this writing owns more than 100 newspapers in markets across the country, ranging from the nation's largest-circulation paper, *USA Today*, to papers a fraction of its size in small markets such as Elmira, New York, and Chillicothe, Ohio. While Gannett and a few other firms (New York Times Co., Tribune Co., McClatchy Co., Community Newspaper Holdings Inc., Lee Newspapers, Media General, and some others) could be said to constitute a horizontally integrated oligopoly of the U.S. newspaper industry at the national level, at the local level they generally operate as monopolies, in markets that have only one daily newspaper. A recent trend in the industry is for these firms to acquire several newspapers in a particular region forming a "cluster," a horizontal integration strategy designed to create more control of local markets for news and advertising (Layton, 2006).

Understanding the concepts of product substitution and differentiation also offers insight into how the media landscape is constructed. Some media products are very close substitutes, such as the weekly news magazines. Their editorial approaches and writing styles may differ slightly, but *Time* and *Newsweek* offer pretty much the same utility to readers and to advertisers. Likewise, the four major broadcast networks all are pretty close substitutes. Individuals may have a favorite show that is on one particular network, but across their schedules, offerings of each network (dramas, sitcoms, reality shows, movies, sports, daytime talk shows and soap operas, nightly half-hour news shows) are quite similar.

The major cable news networks are also substitutes for one another. But it could be argued that cable news networks as product substitutes are not as close as the ABC, NBC, and CBS nightly news shows. This is because some cable news stations have abandoned the objectivity to which journalists should ascribe in their reporting. For example, Fox News Channel deliberately seeks to differentiate itself with a more pro-Republican viewpoint. This differentiation is enough to attract some viewers who want their news flavored in such a way and repel others who do not.

Similarly, on a delivery level cable television was extremely lucrative during its heavy-growth phase from the mid-1970s to early 1990s because of its monopolistic character. Cable-franchise installations, such as electric utilities and telephone wiring, were seen as a natural monopoly because of the cost of running wire to each user's house. But more recently, satellite companies such as DirectTV have begun to offer similar *distribution* channels—familiar networks such as ESPN, Nickelodeon, and MTV—through an alternative *delivery* system, breaking cable's stranglehold on reaching consumers. In many markets, this has led to competition of satellite and cable companies seeking customers on the basis of content offerings, service, and price, reflecting the benefits of competition described earlier in the chapter.

Summary

Comprehending the relationship between market theories and structures and the different kinds of competition allows for a clearer understanding of the media landscape. Media offerings are produced and sold—supplied and demanded—according to the principles of classical economics. But demand for media "products" is more significantly affected by factors such as utility (based in media content/audience interest) and product substitution than demand for other goods such as soft drinks or breakfast cereals is.

As described at the beginning of the chapter, the goal of economics is allocation, or determining what gets produced and who benefits by it. In a capitalistic society, markets are the main way this allocation takes place. According to free-market or capitalist economic theory (as opposed to, say, Marxist theory) competition is seen as a good thing. According to classical market theory, competition helps promote the most efficient allocation of resources and the best prices for consumers.

Competition also helps spur technology and innovation as firms try to improve a product or invent ways to serve customers better. Or they seek to do something better or cheaper—especially cheaper. In electronic media, innovation has been centered on advancing technology, such as going from black and white television to color television to high-definition and digital broadcasting, or from AM to FM to satellite distribution of radio signals. But in many media markets and industries, horizontal and vertical integration have undermined competition by creating oligopolies or monopolies at certain points in the production system, thus reducing the benefits that competition can bring to a marketplace.

The purpose of this chapter has been to introduce some terminology and principles of economic theory at a very basic level that help in explaining the current landscape of media organizations, and to offer some examples and illustrations about how these principles can be applied (such as seeing Fox News Channel's conservative slant as a means of product differentiation). A more thorough treatment would require a much more in-depth discussion of the theory of the firm (microeconomics) as it relates to markets, structures, pricing, competition, substitution, and other topics. Likewise, a more complete discussion of how these principles apply to all media operations at every level would take far more elaboration than the few simple examples presented here. The concepts presented here are meant to provide a starting point, particularly for understanding the impact of the market model on content, and the influence of the media organization (producer/distributor/delivery system) over the media user/consumer.

This understanding is important for students who plan careers in media because they may face the realities of media economics in their internships and entry-level jobs. Internet news has become an effective product substitute for the daily newspaper for many people, leading to declines in newspaper circulation and fewer jobs for would-be reporters as the industry retrenches. Or, in another example, a generation ago radio stations generally had local staffs for on-air production. But in the corporately controlled, horizontally and vertically integrated situation of the contemporary radio industry, many local stations have been converted to automated operation with content fed from a central source owned by the parent corporation. This means that jobs for the people who make that content, such as on-air hosts and producers, may be physically located far from a student's home city. It also means that the actual number of jobs in the field may be greatly reduced. The student who wants to break into radio may find it difficult because of these situations. These are just two examples of how larger-scale economic trends and principles can affect the local media landscape and have an impact on those who work in it as well as the audience members.

QUESTIONS FOR DISCUSSION/ APPLICATION EXERCISES

A good starting point for the investigations suggested in these exercises is the "Who Owns What" portion of the Web site operated by *Columbia Journalism Review*, a magazine that covers media issues and trends. It can be found at: http://www.cjr.org/tools/owners/.

1. Determine who owns the newspaper, radio, and television stations in your hometown or the town where your college is located (or a nearby city if you are in a rural area or small city with no truly "local" media).

2. Analyze the cable television offerings in your community to see what level of horizontal integration exists, that is, how many of the channels are owned by the same conglomerates? Also, determine who owns the local cable distribution franchise. Is there much overlap of the distributors (network ownership) with the deliverer (owner of the cable system)?

3. Analyze the vertical production chain of a few popular television shows. See if you can find one that is produced, distributed, and delivered all by the same company. (Hint: Delivery might be the hardest link in this chain to establish, at least in your home community. But you may be able to find that the producer/distributor of a show owns the final delivery stage somewhere, such as a local cable system or local broadcast station in another town or city in your state.)

REFERENCES

Bartlett, J. (1980). *Familiar quotations* (15th ed.). Boston: Little, Brown.

Layton, C. (2006, June/July). Surrounded by singleton. *American Journalism Review 28*(3), 44–49.

Picard, R. (2006). Historical trends and patterns in media economics. In A. Albarran, S. Chan-Olmsted, & M. Wirth (Eds.), *Handbook of media management and economics* (pp. 23–36). Mawah, NJ: Lawrence Erlbaum Associates.

Siwek, S. (2006). *Copyright industries in the U.S. economy: The 2006 report*. Washington, D.C.: International Intellectual Property Alliance. Retrieved May 23, 2007, from: http://www.iipa.com/pdf/2006_siwek_full.pdf.

12 Preparing for a Career in the Mass Media

THIS CHAPTER WILL:

- Provide a framework for a job search in the mass media.
- Offer guidelines for a job search strategy, including writing resumes, assembling portfolios, getting internships, networking, and interviewing.
- Discuss the issues around attending graduate school.

Few students face the prospect of their senior year in college without some significant concerns and questions about the future. Where should they begin their job search? Should they consider graduate school now? How will they be able to pay back their loans while working at an entry-level position? What is it they really want to do with their lives? This chapter responds to these concerns by supplying guidelines and strategies tailored to the needs of a student preparing for a career in mass media.

Most colleges, through their career center and/or academic departments, encourage students early on to start building a resume that will attract potential employers. This is certainly true in the mass media field, where a portfolio of work is often expected, internships are routine, and networking is the key to finding employment. Waiting until senior year to begin working toward a career can be a risky strategy. Nevertheless, some students do reach senior year with little on their resumes. To these students, the adage "better late than never" applies, and they certainly will find more success starting a career hunt *before* rather than *after* graduation.

The Job Market in Journalism and Mass Communication

Each year, the Association for Education in Journalism and Mass Communication (AEJMC) surveys graduates of mass media programs across the country and publishes the findings in its November newsletter. The *Annual Survey of Journalism*

& Mass Communication Graduates reports the job rates and salaries of graduates from the year before. As of this writing, the Association reported employment information for the class of 2006 in November 2007.

For the class of 2006, about 76 percent of the graduates reported at least one job offer. This is an improvement over the previous year, but still lower than the year 2000, when more than 82 percent of the graduates had at least one job offer. By October 31 of their graduation year, about 64 percent of the class of 2006 was working full-time, with slightly less than 60 percent indicating that the job was "in their field" (Becker, Vlad, & McLean, 2007).

The salaries for recent graduates also showed improvement in 2006, rising by about $1,000 over the previous year to a median salary of $30,000. This is a lower rate than graduates of other degree programs and, even when adjusted for inflation, is lower than the rate graduates made in 2000. Graduates who took jobs in radio, television, and with weekly or daily newspapers made the lowest salaries, while those in advertising, Web-based media companies, and cable television made the most.

While the job market has looked good for recent graduates, there is not a huge amount of optimism about the potential for future growth. Much will hinge upon advertising spending, which drives the rest of the media economy.

Job Search Strategies

Although mass communication graduates do not have control over the future health of the mass media industry, they need to be prepared more than ever before in order to compete for jobs in the fields of their choice and to help position themselves for competitive salaries. The key strategies students may employ as they prepare for and execute a job search are described in this section and are especially effective if used in conjunction with visiting the career center and using other campus resources.

Researching the Field

Students planning their spring break trips become travel experts. They investigate the various destinations, determine what their budgets will allow them to do, and carefully plan all aspects of their trips, including travel, lodging, meals, and entertainment. They also manage to do this during an academic semester while juggling classes, homework, and jobs. And yet, these same students frequently wait until May of their senior year to utilize their college's career center, often with the excuse that they just did not have the time to get started on their job search. At the very least, the job search plan should be at least as detailed as a spring break trip. Just as students would not show up at the airport without a ticket and try to board a plane, they should not just sign up for on-campus interviews or send out resumes at random without thoroughly researching the field and figuring out just what they want to do.

Potential applicants should be looking for information such as:

- How big is the job market in this field?
- What are job titles and duties of typical entry-level jobs?
- What are the turnover and prospects for advancement like in the field?
- What salaries might a new graduate expect?
- What qualities and experiences are required of people entering this field?

In addition to doing research on the Internet and in the college career center, these questions are most easily answered by conducting informational interviews with individuals currently working in the field. Professionals are generally responsive to requests from college students to discuss their careers and career paths, and to offer advice for someone interested in that field. Informational interviews (explained in greater detail in the networking section later) not only provide some of the information that is helpful in career planning, but they also help students build their professional network, which is a rich source of employment opportunities. More than 70 percent of professional positions are never advertised but are found through networking.

Research and informational interviews also help students to steer their job search and/or confirm their focus in the field. Without a core message that is integrated throughout the job search, a student will have a much tougher time making contacts, obtaining interviews, and landing job offers.

Writing a Resume

While some students wait until senior year to think about their resumes, most have spent time on this important document before then to get summer jobs, apply for internships and scholarships, and the like. During the last year of college, students should be refining and updating the experiences on their resumes, reviewing it with the career center staff and relevant professors, and taking advantage of resume reviews offered by professionals in the field. Many colleges have networks of alumni who volunteer to review resumes and conduct mock interviews. These volunteers are a rich and ready source of job information and are also valuable additions to a professional network. Even an individual not working directly in the field probably has a list of contacts in related areas.

A resume is sometimes called a 15-second advertisement. This is because the average recruiter spends fewer than 15 seconds reviewing a resume before deciding to pursue it further or sending it to the recycling bin. The purpose of a resume is to get an interview, so it clearly must indicate what the employer may expect from the applicant in the interview process.

Resumes can be organized chronologically or functionally, with most recent college graduates choosing the former. A resume should include the following components:

1. Heading: The heading should not say "Resume" but rather have the name, address, phone number, and e-mail address of the applicant.

2. Job objective. While some career experts disagree as to whether a job objective is necessary, most students will want to indicate the type of job they are interested in, the type of company or industry, and the location. (One recruiter was overheard saying he wanted to see the objective on the resume because "If students do not know what they want to do, it is not my job to figure it out for them.")

3. Education: For most college seniors, their academic degree can be their most valuable asset. This should be highlighted, along with GPA (if it is a good one), any minors or concentrations, and awards and honors received.

4. Work experience: The employer is generally not interested in the time a student spent in the produce department of the local supermarket or taking care of a neighbor's child. Rather, the experience section should focus on jobs that provided the most transferable skills that can be applied to the position for which the student is applying. Internships, even unpaid ones, should be highlighted as most relevant to the career field of interest.

5. Optional topics: Additional experience, such as volunteer activities, student activities, special skills or training, and honors, should be included. A resume should not include personal information such as marital status.

In formulating the resume, the following guidelines are recommended:

1. A resume should be flawless. Proof it multiple times, get a friend to proof it, ask professors to proof it, and take it to a career counselor for review. Errors are noise in the communication process, and a mistake as minor as a single misspelling will send a resume to the recycling bin.

2. In the field of mass media, education is important, but experience tops it. Any firsthand knowledge of the job for which a student is applying should be prominently highlighted. For example, under the heading of "Relevant Experience," a student who is applying for a reporting job might include an unpaid internship at the local paper, work as a reporter or editor on the campus newspaper, and any freelance reporting done for the hometown newspaper.

3. Keep the resume simple and professional. Use classic fonts such as Times New Roman and Arial, do not mix font types, and use white, off-white, or light gray heavy-weight paper. A resume that is sent as a fax should be printed on plain copy paper, because that will come through more clearly than embossed or watermarked paper. Ideally, if an electronic resume is requested, it should be sent as a PDF file to minimize any formatting changes that may occur when the recipient opens the file.

4. At all times, keep the needs of the reader in mind. While the student wants the job, the employer wants to fill a position in the company or organization. Focusing on the needs of the employer will make it more likely that this resume will lead to an interview.

An example of a resume with these characteristics is provided in Figure 12.1.

FIGURE 12.1   Sample Resume

Dorothy N. Toto
123 Yellow Brick Road
Oz, New York 12345-6789
585-333-4444
dnt4321@sjfc.edu

Objective:	A position in special events or media relations with a nonprofit health care organization.	
Education:	B.A., Communication/Journalism	Anticipated May, 2008
	St. John Fisher College, Rochester, New York	
	Minor: Marketing	
	GPA: 3.44 Major GPA: 3.75	
	Service Scholar	

Relevant Experience: Public Relations Intern   September–December, 2007
Highland Hospital, Rochester, NY
Planned special events for the opening of new bariatric unit including media alerts, event planning, press kits, and publications.

AIDS Rochester, Rochester NY   September, 2005–May, 2006
Service Scholar Placement, helped coordinate fund-raising events, wrote all PR pieces related to AIDS Walk that raised $10,000.

Cardinal Courier, St. John Fisher College   January, 2004–Present
Responsible for weekly health column in award-winning campus newspaper. Recognized by New York Press Association for series on STDs among college students.

Other Work Experience: Computer Lab Assistant
Office of Information Technology
St. John Fisher College   September, 2005–Present

Work-study job of 10/hours per week during school, full-time in summer. Help students in computer lab with questions or problems. Proficient in lab software and research databases.

Resident Advisor, St. John Fisher College   January 2006–Present
Responsible for 30 first-year students in residence halls. Plan educational programming, maintain group cohesiveness, resolve conflicts.

Software: MS Office, Dreamweaver, Photoshop, InDesign.

Assembling a Portfolio

In addition to resumes, many mass media jobs require that students present a portfolio of their work. One student, when asked before an interview to bring "his clips," put articles cut from the campus newspaper into a manila envelope and handed this to the interviewer. Needless to say, he did not get the job.

For print journalism, advertising, and public relations majors, a portfolio means a collection of writing samples—newspaper stories, ad copy, news releases, and media alerts. The examples can come from classes, internships, the campus newspaper, and volunteer activities. They are kept in a single portfolio, generally a black binder with plastic sheets protecting the samples. As with the resume, the portfolio samples should be flawless, consisting of only the best work a student has. The first page of the portfolio should be a resume. Reference letters may also be included. A portfolio is taken to interviews, but should not be left behind.

In print journalism, however, it is a good idea to bring a smaller work sample that can be left behind, or submitted in advance with a resume and cover letter. Many newspaper and magazine editors will schedule an interview only if they have had the opportunity to review some clips first, so if clips are not included in the initial contact, the candidate may not get an opportunity to show off the portfolio. Candidates should not expect editors to return these clips, so the originals should not be sent. Editors will be satisfied with high-quality photocopies.

For broadcasting and new media students, a portfolio is likely a DVD containing work samples. These may include television news and feature packages, radio spots, production examples, or other electronic work such as Web sites and online newsletters. The DVD should always begin with an electronic resume and biographical information. Because these electronic presentations are easily duplicated, they may be sent ahead (with a hard copy of the resume) to prospective employers and/or left behind after interviews. More and more students are creating personal Web pages where they stream their video examples as an alternative to recording the work on a DVD. Still, it is the responsibility of the applicant to make it as easy as possible for a prospective employer to see their work, so a hard-copy resume and cover letter may still be the initial contact; however, many employers now prefer electronic applications.

Finding Internships

There is no doubt about it: internships are the surest route to finding jobs in the communications field. When students do internships, they are networking with professionals and getting real-life experience in an area that may be a possible career choice. The word "possible" is used intentionally here: internships are valuable to help students decide what they want to do—and also what they do *not* want to do. The most valuable experiences are ones that help students more clearly define their career goals.

Some communications programs require internships of all their students; for others, an internship is strongly recommended. Whatever the policy, all students should take advantage of the internship experience as a valuable route to finding a job.

Actually, finding an internship is a lot like finding a job and seeking one is a good way to practice the job-search strategies described earlier. A student needs to prepare a resume, contact possible internship sites, go on interviews, and accept the internship that will provide the best experience. Proceeding in a systematic way in the internship search will provide excellent experience for the job search. In ideal circumstances, the internship can even lead directly to a job.

Once it is obtained, an internship should be treated as a real job—because it is. Successful interns practice the following strategies:

1. Take the commitment seriously. Show up on time, do not cancel unless it is a true illness or emergency, and complete all required hours.

2. Show an interest in the company, the position, and the field. Supervisors most often report that they are impressed with students who ask a lot of questions and show an ongoing interest in the job and the company.

3. Demonstrate initiative. During slow times, successful interns find things to work on, visit others in related departments, and ask if they might shadow these people or assist them on their projects. Interns, as representatives of a desirable media demographic, may also be welcomed to make suggestions or offer opinions on new and ongoing projects.

4. Make sure they are getting enough responsibility. There is a familiar stereotype of the "intern" who only gets coffee and makes copies, just for the opportunity to be in the media business. (David Letterman and Stephen Colbert frequently make fun of the menial jobs their interns do.) However, accepting a situation where a student will not get any samples for a portfolio or any meaningful experience to put on the resume cheats the student. Students who feel they are not getting responsibility typical of an entry-level position in their internships should speak with the internship director at their school.

5. Always practice the most ethical behavior. While ethics are generally a part of all journalism education, students do occasionally get into internships where they feel uncomfortable about things they are asked to do. Interns should not have to tolerate situations where they are asked to engage in dishonest behavior, are confronted with having to support the unethical practices of others, or are the recipient of unwanted personal advances. Many organizations that appreciate and value mass media interns can be found, so interns should never feel that they are stuck at one site. Any questionable ethics should be reported immediately to the internship director at the student's school.

At the conclusion of the internship, student interns should request reference letters from their supervisors and others with whom they have worked closely. They should also conduct informational interviews with key individuals at their site to be sure these people can be included in their professional networks. And they should never leave the internship without writing appropriate thank-you notes to all who have helped them during the internship. Small gifts, such as a mug from the student's school, are also appropriate for an internship supervisor who has shown outstanding support.

Networking

Students might be surprised to learn that the majority of jobs are never advertised in classified ads, on company Web sites, or on Internet job-search sites. Some studies report that 75 to 80 percent of professional positions are found through networking. What is networking? Networking is talking to people for information and advice, and using those contacts to meet others who can help in a job search. Throughout the process, a student never asks for a job, just for information and advice.

It is easiest for a student to begin with people who are already invested in their success—family, friends, professors, internship supervisors, and academic advisors. From that group alone, most students are able to generate a list of people who would be rich sources of information on careers in the field. The people on this list form the network and will be contacted for informational interviews. Students should request no more than 30 minutes of someone's time for such an interview.

Contacts can be made in one of two ways. The student can ask someone who knows them to "pave the way" with an introduction. For example, a professor may contact a professional in this way: "One of my students, Julie Smith, is very interested in a career in print journalism, emphasizing copyediting. I'd like to refer her to you for an informational interview, so she can get some advice on her career path." This approach makes it easy for Julie to call the contact and request an informational interview.

Or, the student herself can make the contact directly, asking for an informational interview, as in this example: "Hello, Mr. Jones, my name is Mary Smith. I'm a senior communications major at State University. I got your name from Dr. Martin, who suggested your name as someone working in the newspaper field with responsibility for copyediting. I'd like to meet with you to discuss careers in this area and get your advice."

Even school assignments can lead to informational interview contacts. One of the authors, as an undergraduate, interviewed newspaper editors as part of a project for a journalism class. The contact turned into an informational interview, which led to a summer internship at one of the papers.

Once an informational interview is secured, the student should prepare for it just as if it were a real interview—because it just might be. They should

1. Research the company.
2. Research the field.
3. Wear appropriate attire (See Figure 12.2 for a detailed description.)
4. Plan an agenda of questions to ask the contact person. A sample agenda of questions is offered in Figure 12.3.

FIGURE 12.2   Agenda for an Informational Interview

Overview of the Interview
- Remind the person you're meeting how you got his or her name.
- Emphasize that you are just looking for advice on a career you are considering.

Background of the Interviewee
- Can you tell me about your career path and how you got to the position you hold today?
- Is this a typical career path for a person in this field?

Current Job Description
- Please describe your current position.
- What is a typical day like for you?
- What do you like best about your job?
- What do you like least about your job?

State of the Field
- Some of my research shows that this field is growing. In your experience is this true?
- What are your predictions for the way the field will change in the next 5 to10 years?
- How do you think that will affect the employment picture?

Advice
- What would you recommend for a college student considering a career in this field?
- I have my resume with me. Would you mind looking at it and giving me your reaction? Are there any changes you might suggest?
- If this is a field I want to pursue, is there anyone else you might recommend that I should talk to?

Thank you for your time and information.

During an informational interview, students should never ask for a job—just for information. They may ask their contacts to review their resume for suggestions, and ask who else to speak to in the field. And they should always follow up with a thank-you note within 24 hours of the interview.

With each informational interview, students will find their confidence increases along with the size of their network. They will be more informed about the field and the position, and more likely to impress someone enough to get to the next step in the process: an offer for a job interview.

Interviewing for a Job

When that job interview does come through, a student should be well acquainted with many of the techniques learned from their informational interviewing. This time the candidate is not the interviewer, however, but the interviewee. Changing roles will require some practice and training. Seniors can take advantage

FIGURE 12.3   Job Searches beyond Networking

While networking is proven to be the most successful job search strategy, students should not overlook the traditional sources of jobs in mass communication. These include:

Online sources: The best in the media field include journalismjobs.com, editorandpublisher.com, broadcastingandcable.com, and professional Web sites such as PRSA.org (Public Relations) and AFA.org (advertising).

Classified ads: While many jobs are never advertised, some actually are, so it pays to keep an eye on the classified ads in the local paper or on the newspaper's Web site. You may have to respond to a blind P.O. Box, but it's worth a try. Additionally, if you wish to move to a specific location, targeting the classifieds in that particular city may yield some leads.

Company Web sites: If you've targeted a particular company or a particular industry, check out the postings on the companies' Web sites. For example, at www.ClearChannel.com, you can search by division, location, and position—and find out where their representatives will be at career fairs.

Alma mater: Students often forget to look in their own back yards. When area employers contact local colleges, those jobs go up on the college's career center Web site. When professors hear about jobs, they often refer them directly to a student they know who has an interest in the field. After you graduate, it is to your benefit to stay in touch with your career office, professors, and the alumni office at your college.

of workshops offered by their college career centers and practice mock interviews with career advisors and volunteers (often alumni). In addition to ensuring that the student's resume and appearance are appropriate, these experiences will help the candidate answer questions, which is the key activity in an employment interview.

Some of the common interview questions that students will be asked (which are probably quite familiar to many students already) include:

- Tell me about yourself.
- Where do you want to be in five years?
- Why did you choose to go to your college?
- What are your strengths and weaknesses?

However, more and more employers are using a style of interviewing known as *behavior-based interviewing* or *behavioral event interviews*. This type of interview is predicated on the belief that past performance predicts future performance. So, rather than asking for a canned answer ("what would you do if . . ."), the employer is looking for evidence that students possess a trait that is required for this position. Behavior-based questions generally ask you to "tell me about a time when . . ." followed by a certain situation. It might be something similar to these questions:

- Tell me about a time when you worked successfully with a team to complete a job under pressure.

- What was the most challenging situation you encountered as president of your school's television club last year?
- Tell me about the most successful project you worked on during your internship.

As students prepare for interviews, they should consider significant events from their college years—events related to anything on their resumes (classes, work experiences, extracurricular activities, and co-curricular activities) that they may be asked about during an interview.

As with the informational interviews, preparation for actual job interviews should also include researching the company, preparing the questions to ask about the job and the company, dressing in a professional way, and making sure

FIGURE 12.4   Dressing for Success

The career center Web site of St. John Fisher College recommends the following tips to students to help them successfully dress for an interview:

- Always get the best interview outfit you can afford.
- Wear the outfit at least twice in advance of any interview to increase your comfort level.
- Leave off the perfume and aftershave; many people are sensitive to scents.
- Travel as lightly as possible, so you are not juggling a coat, briefcase, umbrella, purse, scarf, and so on. Leave items in the car or ask the receptionist if there is a coat closet you might use.
- Be sure to arrive early so you have time to double check your appearance in the restroom mirror.

Men's dress should include:

- Two-piece suit for most professional positions or a high-quality sports coat and slacks for less corporate environments
- High-quality dress shirt, plain or with a discrete pattern
- Nice tie, nothing cute or with logos
- Good leather belt to match shoes
- Polished conservative shoes with dark socks
- Undershirt optional (but required if you have tattoos)
- Fresh shave and haircut
- Remove any earrings or other pierced jewelry
- Minimal jewelry
- No hats—ever.

Women's dress should include:

- A skirted suit, which is preferred and has the most authority for corporate and business positions. A conservative pants suit is acceptable for less formal settings.
- Conservative blouse, plain or with a discrete pattern, no sweaters.
- Pantyhose (take an extra pair for emergencies)
- Low-heeled polished traditional pumps
- Conservative jewelry and make-up
- Conservative hairstyle.

to know where to go and how long the interview will take. Asking questions about the workplace is especially important for would-be journalists. One of the main tasks of an entry-level reporter is asking questions, and the person conducting the interview wants to see the interviewee's skill at doing so. A journalism interviewee who responds with a blank stare when a newspaper editor or broadcast news director says, "So, what questions do you have for me?" probably will not get the job. Take along extra resumes in the event it has been misplaced. And students should not forget to write thank-you notes to any key people they spoke with, ideally sent within 24 hours after they leave the interview. They should request business cards of each person they meet, so they are sure to spell their names correctly and have accurate contact information as well.

Considering Graduate School

There are some good reasons to attend graduate school directly after an undergraduate program. A student is already in the classroom/study frame of mind and knows the routine; although, in grad school, the depth of material that classes cover is ratcheted up a notch or two, and the required study skills are intensified.

In addition, the prospect of looking for a job after graduation can be frightening for many students. That first professional position represents the official break from the family stability and school routine that students have known for 16 (or more) years. At this challenging juncture in their lives, many graduating seniors consider attending graduate school instead of entering the work force.

Some graduating seniors are very sure of their career plans, and it may make sense for them to seek an advanced degree in that field in order to have an advantage in their job search. Many graduate programs also have significant internship and networking opportunities that operate at a higher level than those found in an undergraduate program.

At the same time, there are reasons to put off attending graduate study directly after college. Most students will change jobs several times in the early years after graduating, before they settle on the career that suits them best. Without specific career goals, graduate school may be putting specialization in the wrong area. Additionally, there is value in having some work experience to apply to academic work in a graduate program. Finally, in entry-level jobs in the mass media, there is no requirement for a graduate degree. Indeed, a master's degree will not even earn a higher salary level in most mass media jobs. In the AEJMC survey of journalism and mass communication graduates referenced earlier in this chapter, graduate students reported higher levels of job offers than undergraduates (73 percent for graduate degrees, almost 70 percent for undergraduate degrees), and a higher median salary ($33,000 for master's degree, $27,800 for bachelor's degree). But the difference was not significant given the investment of time and money a graduate degree requires. Additionally, the survey noted that graduate employment rates have been in a slump and are recovering at a slower pace than undergraduate employment rates.

As an added factor, finances play a role for many students, who carry heavy loans from their undergraduate years. While there are some assistantships and other forms of financial aid available for graduate school, paying back undergraduate debt assumes a higher priority for many students.

Career Development Activities for Students

1. Ask a professor for two or three contacts from his or her network with whom you could conduct informational interviews. Then do the interviews.

2. Find out whether your college has a database of alumni who are available to critique resumes, do informational interviews, or offer other career-preparation activities for current students. If the school does have such alumni resources, spend some time exploring the database to identify people whom you should try to contact and meet.

3. Visit your college's career center and have your resume critiqued. Find out what other services the center can offer to help you prepare for the job world.

4. If you have not done an internship yet, make an appointment with the internship director at your college or in your academic department, and find out what the guidelines are to complete one. If you have done an internship, or are currently doing one, identify some people you have met through the internship with whom you could conduct informational interviews.

REFERENCES

Becker, L. B., Vlad, T., & McLean, J. D. (2007, November). Job market recovery stalls. *AEJMC News 41*(1), 6–9.

13 Theory Applications for Media Practitioners

"Whereof, what's past is prologue . . ."
—Shakespeare, The Tempest, Act II, Scene 1

This book begins with a discussion of theory, especially its definition, purpose, and goals, and its relationship to knowledge, learning, and discovery. So, in the spirit of many theory-based courses that integrate past learning with the goal of guiding future performance, it returns to where it begins—a discussion of theory. The goal is to build upon ideas presented earlier, now that the general topics of theory and research have been explored more thoroughly and a number of specific theories about the mass media have been described in more detail.

The Relevance of Theory

When many students are first exposed to theory, they fail to see its relevance and balk at the idea of getting closer to it, like a child facing a plate of broccoli as described in the book's introduction. This is not surprising. Many mass communication programs emphasize skills development, built around classes in which students learn to write newspaper stories, magazine articles, news releases, and advertisements and to produce radio broadcasts, television shows, and Web sites. Most students enjoy the classes that teach these skills and feel as if learning them is the reason they are in college studying communication in the first place. They find it easy to see the relevance of such courses, especially if they work in campus media, do an internship, or have a part-time job in a media organization where they can practice what they have learned in the classroom in a real-life situation. On the other hand, courses that dwell on theory do not seem as relevant; they are so, well, theoretical, which many students mistakenly interpret to mean the opposite of practical.

What students who have this attitude fail to take into account is how closely theory relates to real life. It is important to remember that while the theory itself may be an abstraction, the principles to which it relates are anchored in reality.

Recall from Chapter 1 the definition of theory: a statement that seeks to predict or explain how certain phenomena are related to each other. Often, the purpose of theorizing about this relationship is to answer an important question, such as this example from Chapter 1: the big bang and other theories of astronomy seek to answer questions of how the universe began and how it has developed to reach its current state. In the preface, a similar walk-through example applies the theory of global warming/global climate change to real-life situations. The theory may be an abstract idea, but the questions it helps people to answer are real.

The Theory-Driven Life

In a similar fashion, many of the beliefs, or rules-of-thumb, that guide people through life rightly could be called theories. Most people attend college to get a degree that will lead to an interesting and productive career. In a sense, they are hoping to validate a theory that says "a college education is closely related to success that people have with their lives." Is this really a theory? Well, it seeks to *explain* the relationship of education and success in life, *predicting* a greater measure of success for those with more education. In a similar vein, many people believe that a strong work ethic also is related to success in life: academic success, professional success, athletic success.

These two common principles at first glance seem very different from all of the more formal theories that have been examined throughout this text, but they can be evaluated similarly despite the apparent differences. To see how this works, it is important to recall that theories frequently relate two constructs or variables, and propose ways in which they are connected or correlated to each other. In the "theory of success," the variables are willingness to work hard in a given field and the success one achieves in it. The way most people would see the theory, these constructs are related in a basically proportional way, and the theory could be stated like this:

> A stronger work ethic or greater willingness to work hard translates into more-successful performance, while a weaker work ethic means less-successful outcomes.

Evaluating this theory according to the criteria detailed in Chapter 1 (from Littlejohn 1999, pp. 35–37), it is found to be:

■ **Wide in scope**: It could be applied to a large variety of endeavors, including careers in advertising, broadcasting, media production, print journalism, public relations, law, education, medicine, engineering, and so on.

■ **Clearly appropriate**: Any assumptions are logical and consistent. There is nothing *un*reasonable about thinking that work and reward are linked to one another, and in fact there is a lot of logic and common sense behind the assumption that they are related. It also is thoroughly grounded in the "real world." For example, students know that doing internships demonstrates their work ethic to a potential employer, and increases the likelihood of landing a good job in the field after graduation.

- **Very simple** (or parsimonious); Theories do not come much simpler than this one.

- **Moderate in heuristic value:** The ability to generate new ways of thinking about the subject to which the theory pertains. For example, it could be used to develop other, similar theories about the work-reward relationship such as the need for multitasking or the importance of speed and efficiency in the modern workplace.

- **Relatively open:** Adaptable, with the ability to apply to different areas of effort as people become interested in them. For example, the theory could apply to what it takes to become a successful Web programmer—studying the manuals about codes, spending time debugging an installation, and so on, which would be a fairly new application of this old adage because, until about 15 years ago, there were no Web programmers.

- **Validity:** The ability to predict and explain the relationship that it is supposed to predict and explain is the one area in which this theory has some weaknesses or problems. As with many social science theories, operationalizing the constructs is one of the most challenging parts of applying this theory. What, specifically, is "work ethic" and how can it be defined and measured? What is the definition of "success?" That can vary for practically every individual. These constructs would be especially hard to operationalize with numerical values, although it probably could be done qualitatively.

Nevertheless, when evaluated according to Littlejohn's criteria, the "theory of work ethic and success," which predicts how one construct relates to the other, largely meets the test of being a theory, and stands as just one example of how theories can be used for a more complete understanding of the world around us. Many of the principles that U.S. society is based upon—such as representative democracy, a capitalist/mixed economy, and the rule of law—also can be seen as theories about how society is supposed to function. In fact, all three of those ideas are treated as more-or-less formal theories in such social science disciplines as political science and economics.

In short, much of our ability to understand life and the world around us depends on understanding how various things relate to one another. The principles that people rely on to predict and explain how these relationships take place can rightly be called theories. Students who think studying theory is pointless or impractical are dismissing a very important tool that they can use for a better understanding of the world around them.

Formal Theories and Media Genres

Chapters 5 through 8 present details about many of the formal theories used to understand and interpret mass communication and its effects on the society around it. The starting point for this discussion is that communication—and in particular, symbolic communication, or the use of words and images to signify both real-world objects and more abstract ideas—is the essential element of human society. Humans have engaged in symbolic communication for thousands of years, although for most of that time such communication took place between individuals or in small groups in face-to-face interactions. It has only been in the modern era that technologically aided mass communication activities such as printed materials, television broadcasts, or Internet presentations have been a part of the equation. It is only in the past few decades that these types of communication have been formally studied and explored through theories to help answer questions about the way human beings relate to one another in society.

Theory behind the Scenes

These formal theories in particular are considered by many students to be irrelevant and impractical. On one level the complaint is a valid one. No newly graduated student interviewing for a job at a television station is going to be asked to identify George Gerbner or engage in a discussion with the station manager about cultivation theory. One of this book's authors worked for more than 20 years as a newspaper reporter and editor, and never once heard the words "agenda setting" mentioned in the newsroom.

But complaints that media organizations pay no direct or specific attention to these theories miss the point. Journalists might not sit around in their newsrooms saying "we are going to set the agenda on this story." But when they talk about "the public's need to know," isn't that the same thing as setting the agenda? A newspaper or television news show that does an investigative report about a city hall scandal creates the report with the goal of bringing public attention to the situation by *using the media reporting to set the public agenda*. Just because journalists do not overtly talk about agenda setting, that does not mean they are not actively, and often deliberately, engaging in it.

For more than a year the daily newspaper in the city where the authors live has been crusading on its editorial pages against what it the editors call "coarse culture," especially gangsta rap and what the newspaper editorialists see as that music genre's glorification of an angry, criminal mindset and degrading attitude toward women. They have written editorials about this topic, published community essays and letters to the editor about it, and collected write-in coupons that have been forwarded to major record labels urging them to stop the production and sale of recordings with these themes. Clearly the newspaper is trying to set an agenda on this topic, focusing public attention on it in the hopes of creating some change in attitudes toward it.

But at least one other mass communication theory is at work in their efforts as well. Implicit in the entire campaign against gangsta rap and related forms of cultural expression is the idea that when young listeners are exposed to these songs they will get a warped view of what is valuable and important in the lives of young, urban African-Americans and perhaps adopt these anti-social ideas for themselves. Sharp readers may already have recognized what theory appears to underlie the newspaper's concerns. It is, of course, cultivation theory, which says that repeated, long-term exposure to media that do things such as glorify violence (or at least downplay its adverse impacts) can affect how people feel about violent acts and even affect their likelihood of engaging in them. The newspaper's effort is firmly rooted in the same concept.

There are elements of Bandura's social learning theory in the newspaper's project as well, to the degree that editors fear that music glorifying the "gangsta" persona could lead young fans to act like their favorite rap stars who talk tough, carry guns, and get in trouble with the law. It is a safe assumption that the editorial board offices at the newspaper are not decorated with photos of George Gerbner and Albert Bandura, but the ideas and research of these scholars lie behind the paper's entire effort to fight "coarse culture."

Media-Specific Applications of Theory

Every theory described in this book applies to some type of media work, but some of them are more specific to certain media genres than others. Students who enter careers in advertising, for example, might find it more useful to refer to different theories than their friends who become journalists in trying to understand the implications and effects of their particular type of media work.

Applying Theory to Print and Broadcast Journalism. As described above, *agenda setting* clearly is a mass communication theory that can be used for better understanding of the effect that journalists have on the world around them. By extension, it is useful for graduating college students considering careers in journalism to understand agenda setting and its implications.

In the classic formulation expressed by Cohen and used by McCombs and Shaw in their groundbreaking research, the attention brought to various topics by journalistic coverage does not tell people what to think, but does help to define what they *think about* by making some issues more salient (significant to the audience) than others. As described in Chapter 7, this process is more powerful for what are called unobtrusive issues—those that audience members have no direct involvement with—than for obtrusive ones that are a part of their daily lives.

Another influence on journalistic coverage rooted in this theory is what is called inter-media agenda setting. In other words, coverage decisions by some media—especially large, influential national outlets such as CNN, the *New York Times*, and *USA Today*—can affect which stories are covered by other media and how they are covered. This also happens at the local level where many recent journalism graduates will start their careers. Local news often uses feeds from the national news to fill airtime or to bring a breaking story to viewers, and local reporters may put a local spin on a national story, such as interviewing members of the local Muslim community about the war in Iraq. In addition, local television and radio stations often pick up on items from the community's newspaper in figuring out where they will send their news crews. Or if television or radio breaks a story and most people in the community already know about it, the newspaper reporter will handle it differently than if it is a scoop she alone has developed. These are examples of how media help to set the agenda for each other, which in turn affects the setting of the public's agenda.

But agenda setting is not the only mass communication theory that is useful in understanding the work of journalists. Another is *framing*, the process of defining an orientation or way of looking at a particular topic through selection of the facts that are reported about it or the wording used to explain or describe it. Is electronic eavesdropping on conversations within U.S. borders a reasonable and necessary tool for uncovering terrorist plots before they can be put into action? Or is it an abuse of government power and infringement of civil liberties? Is Congressional legislation that sets deadlines for withdrawing soldiers from Iraq "a timetable for bringing the troops home" as Democrat supporters maintained, or is it "setting surrender dates," as the Republican Senate leader called it during debate on the issue in mid-2007? A story on these topics might use either frame, depending on the sources quoted and other aspects of how it was constructed. Individual journalists may get to choose a frame for a story, or a frame may be part of the story given by the assignment editor or news director.

Diffusion is another theory with implications for journalistic work. Recall that diffusion really evolved from the two-step flow theory, which in itself was about how information that people received from the mass media actually was filtered through other people. "Did you hear about . . ." is still an expression many people use, or hear, with regularity. Research into news diffusion has tended to focus on big events, such as presidential assassinations or the September. 11, 2001, terrorist attacks. But it happens as an everyday routine for many news consumers as well, who pass along a copy of the newspaper to a friend or family member saying "take a look at this," or who e-mail story links from their favorite news media Web sites to friends and family members.

Three other theories covered earlier in the book are also somewhat relevant for anyone considering a career in journalism. They are the *knowledge gap hypothesis*, the *spiral of silence*, and Herman and Chomsky's *propaganda model*. All three point out the potential danger for news coverage to exclude certain members of society. The knowledge gap says that people with greater wealth and education not only use media more but benefit more from that use, contributing to widening the gap between these "haves" in a society and its "have-nots." The spiral of silence describes how ideas expressed in major media may seem to be the most popular, indirectly influencing people with different or alternative ideas to keep them under wraps. Chomsky and Herman describe a similar process, with the added element that the promotion of dominant ideas is deliberate and done by powerful interests in society to maintain and enhance that power by promoting a dominant image of the status quo.

Theory behind Entertainment Programming.   Some of the same theories that journalists need to think about as they go about their work apply to those working in entertainment-related industries, especially television, radio, recordings and motion pictures. The *knowledge gap*, after all, was demonstrated through research of how families from different social and economic levels had different reactions to *Sesame Street*.

But when it comes to entertainment media, the theory that most people would say is most relevant is *cultivation*. Gerbner's work and that of many other researchers who use cultivation has concerned entertainment television—which in terms of sheer broadcast volume and time spent by audience members far outpaces news. Cultivation theory proposes that this extensive, long-term exposure to televised images affects the audience members' view of reality—to the point that this television-centric view is thought to be the reality. Some talk radio programs, such as those found on National Public Radio, are reasoned and informative. But many other radio-talk shows consist of hosts and callers arguing with each other or belittling those who disagree with their views. Is that the best way to resolve a situation when parties disagree? Long-term exposure to media that take this approach could lead to a society with that attitude; some social commentators think we may have reached that point already.

On a more individual level, *social learning theory* can be applied to audience exposures to entertainment media as well. Entertainment programming can be a powerful source of stereotypes, including dysfunctional ones such as the so-called thin ideal that leads some young women to have eating disorders because they do not think they fit social standards of what makes a woman attractive as those standards are portrayed in magazines and on television. And, of course, an understanding of *uses and gratifications* will help media practitioners develop programming that meets the needs of their audience. Knowing whether the audience is tuning in to a particular reality show for information, tension release, or social integration with friends is valuable knowledge for advertisers and for network executives designing promotions and developing content for the show

Another set of theories relevant to entertainment media stem from the critical and cultural studies perspective addressing the nature and role of the media in creating cultural goods. Schiller's *commodification of culture theory*, and the earlier theories of the *Frankfurt School* that it builds upon, suggest that mass-produced cultural goods produced for commercial reasons will end up being less diverse and of poorer quality than society deserves. The *British School* of cultural studies focuses on how "marginalized" groups can reclaim their place in the media environment.

Theories at Work in Advertising/Public Relations. Students who choose to work in advertising and public relations will find special relevance in any of the various theories that address *persuasive* communication. The original research into persuasive processes by Carl Hovland more than 60 years ago established principles that are pertinent to this day, especially strategies such as the use of *one-sided* versus *two-sided appeals* and questions of *credibility of sources*. A thorough understanding of the concept of *information diffusion* also can be beneficial for someone engaged in advertising or public relations work. Reinforcement of media messages by personal interaction and Rogers' findings that those most likely to adopt a new idea or a new technology share certain characteristics both help to explain the impact and effectiveness of a new-product introduction or a new image promoted by an organization.

With regard to advertising in particular, the *elaboration likelihood model* offers useful background about how individuals are likely to respond to the messages they receive, especially via the peripheral route, which is frequently used in image-oriented and celebrity-endorsement advertising. Similarly, the concept of *schemas*—that individual backgrounds and experiences flavor how recipients react and respond to information—ties in closely with the common advertising strategy of targeting messages to particular demographics. Demographic and psychographic strategies that modern advertising uses so extensively are really just presumptions that audience members will share similar schemas based on some identifiable characteristic such as their age, gender, or income level. Understanding the schema theory is something that anyone involved in target or niche marketing can put to use in a practical way.

Public relations practitioners should be aware of all of these theories as well, along with *framing* and *agenda setting*. Framing describes how the selection of particular words, images, or ideas elaborates on a theme and creates a particular "picture in someone's head," to paraphrase Walter Lippmann. And creating those pictures is exactly the goal of much PR activity. Picking frames and employing public relations strategies that are deliberately designed to put things on the public's agenda (by making sure they are given prominence in the media) is sometimes called *agenda building*, so understanding how these theories operate is a powerful tool for PR practitioners.

Theories for Any Genre.   Another set of theories are relevant and useful for media workers of any genre in our contemporary, converged, increasingly globalized world. These include *media determinism*, as discussed by Marshall McLuhan, whose central idea was that the primary medium people use to interact with one another contributes to how society ends up being structured. McLuhan described the tribal, print, and electronic eras, and how the transition from each era has changed social structures. Now, it can be argued, McLuhan's third stage has been supplanted by a fourth era of media as the extensions of man—namely, the networked age. As media become more digitized and more interconnected, social structures change accordingly. College students do not have to look any further than their own lives to see evidence of this. Cellular phones, e-mail, instant messaging, Facebook, and MySpace have changed the social interactions of today's students into something their parents barely recognize and never experienced when they were in college a generation ago.

A somewhat older, but related and equally relevant, idea is the *uses and gratifications* perspective. As explained in Chapter 6, this perspective says that there is no universal agreement on the level or degree to which people are deliberate or purposeful in their use of media versus how much is accidental, habitual, or incidental. But it is clear that at least some of the time people are very deliberate and purposeful, and select a particular medium to meet a need they feel must be gratified at that time. It is also clear that technology is giving audience members increased control over which messages they are exposed to as well as how and when they are received, which makes the idea of active audiences more relevant. Finally, the greater corporate concentration in media gives relevance to the branch of critical theory known as *political economy theory*—that media messages are to at least to some degree a function of the economic interests of those that own the media outlets.

Relevance of Research

If there is a fundamental rule about working in communication, it is this: communicators must know their audiences. *Grey's Anatomy* and *Sesame Street* are both television shows, but have little in common. Similarly, an "edgy" drama produced for adult movie-goers differs dramatically from a children's film. Story selection, writing style, and advertising in *Maxim* and *GQ* are different from *Elle* and *Cosmopolitan*, and all of those magazines are different from local newspapers. In a similar vein, the *New York Times, USA Today,* and the *Wall Street Journal* are all national newspapers, yet all are distinctly different because of their different audiences.

How do the writers, producers, and managers of all these different media outlets know who their audiences are and what appeals to them? Research. This critical part of the media world involves using such measurements as:

- Ratings for broadcast, such as those compiled by A. C. Nielsen for television and Arbitron for radio (Everett, 2003).

- Readership and circulation data for newspapers and magazines, which is studied by both the editorial (news/content creation) and advertising departments of a publication (McGrath, 2003).

- Assessment of the internal and external business environments to help improve the image or positioning of an organization (Culbertson, 2003).

- Assessment of markets, product positioning, efficiency, and likely impact of the messages and audience attitudes in advertising (Bowers, 2003).

Granted, this research, which is used to guide professional decision making, is somewhat different from the academic research described in the first four chapters of this book. But it is not as different as some students might think; the research skills described in this book relate directly to the work many students will find as professionals in the field.

A professional research report will start with an introduction and overview of the field from secondary sources, not so different from the introduction and review of the literature detailed in Chapter 4. Some of these reports might even rely on relevant research from an academic publication such as the *Newspaper Research Journal*, although more often they will use trade journals, general publications such as newspapers or news magazines, and previous research reports for this background material.

The actual data collection and analysis of most professional reports includes one or more of the research techniques explained in Chapter 3, especially surveys and focus groups. Sometimes other methods are used as well; one of the most extensive professional research projects ever conducted by the newspaper industry—called The Impact Study—used content analysis to categorize more than 47,000 articles from 100 daily newspapers by coverage topics such as sports, politics, crime/disaster, and entertainment (Nesbitt & Lynch, 2002).

Research is a critical part of helping media organizations know their audiences so they can create the messages sent to those audiences. Research is often the last stage in the media process, as practitioners get feedback from their audiences on the success of their message strategies. Public relations campaigns, in particular, frequently end with research about how well the campaign worked in reaching the target audience, as well as whether the goals of the campaign were reached. For example, the community where the authors live conducted a campaign of television, radio, and print public service announcements for teens called, "Not me, not now" to discourage high school students from being sexually active. The campaign was evaluated not only by noting the statistics of teen pregnancies in the area, but also by taking surveys and holding focus groups to gauge the effect of the messages on attitudes of the teens toward sex.

Summary

According to research by this book's authors, many college programs in mass communication have courses that integrate prior learning with new experiences to create fresh insights through use of theory-based research projects (Rosenberry & Vicker, 2006). The purpose of this book has been the same: to help students tie together aspects of their college education by showing how knowledge of theories and research coupled with a grounding in practical matters (such as ethics, legal, and economic principles of media operations, and ideas for finding jobs) all need to be a part of the toolkit that they carry across the stage on graduation day. It brings to mind Shakespeare's quip used at the beginning of this chapter—that the past is prologue for the future, that integration of material from a student's prior learning must have a future focus. What we think of as "tomorrow" is only a few hours away from becoming "today." The future has a habit of becoming the present, and life is lived in a present that is informed by an understanding of experiences past.

R E F E R E N C E S

Bowers, T. (2003). Advertising research. In G. H. Stempel III, D. H. Weaver, & G. C. Wilhoit. (Eds.). *Mass communication research and theory*. Boston: Allyn and Bacon/Longman.

Culbertson, H. M. (2003). Applied public relations research. In G. H. Stempel III, D. H. Weaver, & G. C. Wilhoit (Eds.), *Mass communication research and theory*. Boston: Allyn and Bacon/Longman.

Everett, S. (2003). Broadcast research. In G. H. Stempel III, D. H. Weaver, & G. C. Wilhoit (Eds.), *Mass communication research and theory*. Boston: Allyn and Bacon/Longman.

Littlejohn, S. (1999). *Theories of human communication*. Belmont, CA: Wadsworth Publishing Co.

McGrath, K. (2003). Newspaper research. In G. H. Stempel III, D. H. Weaver, & G. C. Wilhoit (Eds.), *Mass communication research and theory*. Boston: Allyn and Bacon/Longman.

Nesbitt, M., & Lynch, S. (2002). How to analyze your content and increase your readership. The Poynter Institute. Retrieved August 17, 2006, from: http://www.poynter.org/dg.lts/id.9644/content.content/view.html.

Rosenberry, J., & Vicker, L. (2006, Autumn). Capstone courses in mass communication programs. *Journalism & Mass Communication Educator 61*(3), 267–284.

INDEX

CREDITS

ASNE Statement of Principles on pages 236 to 237 used with permission of the American Society of Newspaper Editors.

RTNDA Code of Ethics and Professional Conduct on pages 238 to 240 used with permission of the Radio-Television News Directors Association.

PRSA ethical statements on pages 240 to 245 reprinted with permission from the Public Relations Society of America, www. prsa. org.

AAF Advertising Ethics and Principles on page 245 used with permission from the American Advertising Federation.